MW01181402

Literary Couplings

Literary Couplings

Writing Couples, Collaborators, and the Construction of Authorship

Edited by

Marjorie Stone

and

Judith Thompson

THE UNIVERSITY OF WISCONSIN PRESS

This book was published with the support of
the Anonymous Fund for the Humanities
of the University of Wisconsin–Madison.

The University of Wisconsin Press
1930 Monroe Street
Madison, Wisconsin 53711

www.wisc.edu/wisconsinpress/

3 Henrietta Street
London WC2E 8LU, England

1   3   5   4   2

Printed in the United States of America

Library of Congress Cataloging-in-Publication Data
Literary couplings: writing couples, collaborators, and the construction
of authorship / edited by Marjorie Stone and Judith Thompson.
p.   cm.
Includes bibliographical references and index.
ISBN-13: 978-0-299-21760-0 (cloth: alk. paper)
1. English literature—History and criticism.
2. Authorship—Collaboration.
I. Stone, Marjorie, 1951– II. Thompson, Judith, 1957–
PR149.C58L58   2006
820.9—dc22   2005033030

Contents

Acknowledgments

While the web of collaboration involved in a book like this is too intricate to be captured in a list, we would above all like to thank our contributors for entering so enthusiastically, creatively, and patiently into the spirit of an evolving project. They generously and energetically responded to all of our requests for further reflection and revision, first in drafting the essays based on their preliminary proposals and then in serially revising these essays to make them speak more fully to one another and to the aims of the collection as these unfolded. We, in turn, were led to modify and reframe many of the assumptions we began with in response to their illuminating scholarly work within a range of different historical fields. We would also like to thank the graduate students in our seminar on literary couples for some of the questions that first inspired this collection; our colleague Andy Wainwright for collaborative suggestions that led to the refining of our title; Patricia Clements, Holly Laird, and Susan Leonardi for insightful and constructive criticism as readers for the University of Wisconsin Press; and Sheilah Wilson and David Anderson for attentive and intelligent research and manuscript assistance. At a time when models of the "solitary researcher" still tend to prevail, even as granting agencies increasingly promote large-scale interdisciplinary collaborations, small-scale collaborative projects like this one tend to fall between the cracks of funding structures — and this one is no exception. However, we would like to thank the Department of English at Dalhousie University and the university's Research Development Fund for timely support for research assistance, as well as the Social Sciences and Humanities Research Council of Canada for its support of some of the research out of which this project grew. Finally, we are grateful to Raphael Kadushin and Sheila Moermond of the Press for their expertise and patience.

Prologue

Signs of the Times: Five Snapshots of Contemporary Authorship

Snapshot 1

"In the modern era it isn't enough to write," comments Tony Kushner, author of the highly successful play *Angels in America.* "[Y]ou must also be a Writer. . . . You become a character in a metadrama into which your own dramatizing has pitched you. The rewards can be fantastic, the punishment dismal; it's a zero-sum game, and its . . . marker is that you pretend you play it solo, preserving the myth that you alone are the wellspring of your creativity. It's a very popular myth."[1] Elsewhere Kushner describes drama as an inherently collaborative form: "It's not like writing a novel; you're not stuck in a room with your brain." Yet he nevertheless emphasizes that a playwright should do his own dramaturgy. "You have absolute responsibility for it. It is your work."[2]

Snapshot 2

"It's a film that Tom Stoppard wrote. It's really amazing," Gwyneth Paltrow said on live satellite TV a year before *Shakespeare in Love* won Best Picture and she won Best Actress at the 1999 Oscars. Citing her comment, movie critic Peter Howell noted that one of the titles considered for the film was *How Should I Love Thee?*— thus revealing the influence of one of history's most famous literary couples. According to

Howell, Shakespeare became the "hottest guy in tights" based on the film's success. But the same could not be said for Marc Norman, one of the coauthors of its screenplay. Norman's American script was turned over to well-known playwright Tom Stoppard to give it a "proper English flavor," but the collaboration led "many to wrongly assume that Stoppard did the lion's share of the work," when he merely "added some secondary characters and dialogue and made the script better," as Norman acknowledged. Among other things, Stoppard suggested adding Marlowe, Shakespeare's rival, as a character.[3] The screenplay for the film implies that to some degree Shakespeare himself owed his titles and subjects to others: *Romeo and Juliet* to Marlowe and *Twelfth Night* to his fictional ladylove Viola, played by Paltrow.

Snapshot 3

WONG: Collaboration is an idea that makes many writers who emphasize individual creativity uneasy. You two work together. Would you describe your collaborative process?

ERDRICH: It's not very mysterious.

DORRIS: We'll start talking about something a long time in advance of it—the germ of a plot, or a story that has occurred to us, or an observation that we've seen. *A Yellow Raft in Blue Water* started out with the title. . . . After we talk, one of us, whoever thought of it probably, will write a draft. It might be a paragraph; it might be ten pages; it might be something in between. We then share that draft with the other person. Shortly thereafter they will sit down with a pencil and make comments about what works and what doesn't work, what needs expanding, and what might be over-written. Then they give that draft with their suggestions back to the person who wrote it, who has the option of taking or leaving them, but almost always taking them. Then that person does a new draft, gives it back to the other, and goes through the same process again. This exchange takes place five or six times."[4]

Snapshot 4

"Literary Ex-Lovers Heading to Court," reads the July 1, 1998, headline describing the legal struggle between Evelyn Lau, author of *Runaway:*

Diary of a Street Kid, based on her experience as a prostitute, and W. P. Kinsella, author of *Shoeless Joe,* the novel upon which the 1989 Kevin Costner film *Field of Dreams* was based.[5] Lau (in her twenties) and Kinsella (in his sixties) had a written agreement allowing either to use their relationship in fiction, but Lau had published not a fictional story but a memoir—her version of the relationship—entitled "W. P. and Me" in a Vancouver magazine in 1997. Kinsella charged that Lau had invaded his privacy by revealing intimate details (such as his sexual performance), although he had also written about their relationship in a story entitled "Lonesome Polecat in Love," which concerned "an old guy in love with a young Asian woman." The trial date in March 1999 coincided with the publisher's release of Lau's seventh book, *Choose Me,* which recounted the story of an "unmistakable skinny figure in a fake suede jacket."[6]

Snapshot 5

It became one of the most controversial cases of cross-cultural collaboration and appropriation of voice in Canada. In 1981 Maria Campbell's best-selling book *Halfbreed,* about her life as a Metis woman, was transformed into the prize-winning play *Jessica* after being collaboratively improvised, or "sybilled," by the actress Linda Griffiths in consultation with Campbell and others at Toronto's Theatre Passe Muraille. Soon thereafter the partnership dissolved into a series of protracted and painfully contentious dialogues like the following, recorded in the collaboratively published *Book of Jessica* (1989), which purports to present an objective documentary record framing "the book" of the play's text with a chronological "history" of the key events:

> CAMPBELL: "Our elders teach us that we don't own, can never own the land, the stories, not in the way that the outside views ownership. . . . [I]n Jessica, who created the story? I didn't create it myself and you didn't either. We have to stop thinking 'you and me.' There were other people in the room, whose energy, yes, even words, went into creating it, and here we are spreading our wings and saying, 'Mine.' That's what people do with the lands when they fight over them."
>
> GRIFFITHS: "But on the white side of the homestead, somebody might live on a piece of land, and not be able to make a go of it

and leave. . . . Somebody else comes in, and somehow, that family clears the land, breaks the rocks, makes enough room for the garden. . . . I've worked on *Jessica* until I thought I'd go crazy. . . . I stand on the land that is *Jessica* because I'm the mother that tilled the soil. That's where I come from too, and I don't think it's entirely reprehensible, although I know it completely wrecked the land for your people."

CAMPBELL: "That's right."[7]

Notes

1. Cited by Iris Smith, "Authors in America," 125.
2. Vorlicky and Jonas, eds., *Tony Kushner in Conversation*, 162.
3. Peter Howell, "The Hottest Guy in Tights," sec. D, p. 16.
4. Chavkin and Chavkin, eds., *Conversations with Louise Erdrich and Michael Dorris*, 35.
5. Bailey, sec. B, p. 8.
6. Thomas, "Searching for Mr. Sugar Daddy," sec. D, p. 15.
7. Griffiths and Campbell, *The Book of Jessica*, 91–92.

Literary Couplings

Contexts and Heterotexts

A Theoretical and Historical Introduction

MARJORIE STONE & JUDITH THOMPSON /
JUDITH THOMPSON & MARJORIE STONE

"Joined at the Nib": The Literary Couplings of Authors and Readers

Readers have long been fascinated by writing couples. The sibling intimacies of Dorothy and William Wordsworth have intrigued both academic scholars and popular biographers. Several films and books have traced the birth of *Frankenstein* in the tempestuously creative lives of Percy and Mary Shelley, which were triangulated with Byron's and entangled in the afterlife of Mary Wollstonecraft's relationship with William Godwin. There has also been perennial interest in the sharp-tongued dialogues of that eighteenth-century odd couple Boswell and Johnson, the romantic courtship of Elizabeth Barrett and Robert Browning, Virginia Woolf's artistically productive relationship with Vita Sackville-West, and the marital and poetical altercations of Sylvia Plath and Ted Hughes. As the "snapshots" in our prologue suggest, interest in such relationships—especially in their more conflicted manifestations—remains strong in a period when literary couples like Louise Erdrich and Michael Dorris (Snapshot 3) or W. P. Kinsella and Evelyn Lau

(Snapshot 4) have been incorporated into celebrity culture. Both inside and outside the academy, however, attention has traditionally been focused on the *lives* of literary couples, not their texts. Typical examples include Phyllis Rose's subtle analysis of Victorian marriages in *Parallel Lives: Five Victorian Marriages* (1984); John Tytell's *Passionate Lives: D. H. Lawrence, F. Scott Fitzgerald, Henry Miller, Dylan Thomas, Sylvia Plath . . . in Love* (1995); and editors Whitney Chadwick and Isabelle de Courtivron's study of visual and verbal artists in *Significant Others: Creativity and Intimate Partnership* (1993). Ruth Perry and Martine Watson Brownley's collection *Mothering the Mind: Twelve Studies of Writers and Their Silent Partners* (1984), gives more attention to writers' works, but even in this instance the focus is primarily on the pyschodynamics of nurturing relationships. A 2001 photo article entitled "Joined at the Nib" in the books section of Toronto's *Globe and Mail* reflects the prevailing emphasis in its focus on the domestic arrangements of the featured writers rather than on connections between the works their "nibs" create (Vasconcelos).

While readers recognize that the lived experience of writing couples can be intricately intertwined, the texts such partners produce are still organized into separate oeuvres, or "solo" performances, in the words of Tony Kushner in our opening snapshot. The "man and his works" approach associated with nineteenth-century hero worship of the solitary genius now finds its complement in the "woman and her works" approach underlying feminist recuperations of women writers' achievements. The separation thus effected, in the case of heterosexual couples, is entrenched by literary genealogies or histories that are segregated by sex, celebrating, in the case of women writers, what Elaine Showalter's classic study termed "a literature of their own." Anthologies of literary couples or collaborators are likewise rare, as are editions like Alice S. Rossi's *John Stuart Mill and Harriet Taylor Mill: Essays on Sex Equality* (1970), which brings together this writing couple's works on a similar subject or in an identical genre. Same-sex couples are less likely to be disjoined, particularly when they publish their works as full-fledged collaborations; this is the case with "Michael Field," the authorial identity adopted by the Victorian authors Katherine Bradley and her niece Edith Cooper. At the same time, as demonstrated by Jeffrey Masten's research on Beaumont and Fletcher in *Textual Intercourse* (1997), collaborative authorship has traditionally been marginalized within literary histories, approached "as a mere subset or aberrant kind of individual authorship," as Masten notes, or even seen as "obscurely repellent, " as Holly Laird suggests in an article on Field.[1]

The present study explores literary *couplings* of diverse kinds from the Renaissance to the present, countering the assumptions about authorship that have led to relative neglect of the textual interactions and collaborations of writers in intimate relationships. Our focus is not only or even primarily on the erotic connections that "coupling" might initially imply. On the contrary, we use this term to subsume many different kinds of coupled and/or collaborative literary relationships (sexual and/or textual, professional, conjugal, companionate, sibling, parent-child), as these relationships are formed not only by writers themselves but also by readers, critics, and literary historians. Our contributors investigate literary coupling as a compositional activity, a publishing strategy and/or interpretive practice, as well as (in many contexts) a sexual or familial connection. Beyond asking who wrote what and why, they consider who is paired with whom and why? The essays gathered together here (several of which draw on previously unpublished archival material) have been written by scholars in Canada, the United States, the United Kingdom, and Australia specifically for this collection. They reflect current research in diverse historical fields, as well as recent transformations in theoretical conceptions of authorship and textuality. Attending to the (admittedly fascinating) lives of writers principally to cast light on the processes of literary production and reception, our contributors question interpretive practices that privilege the biographical over the textual, approach coupled writers' works as discrete products of solitary inspiration, or treat collaboratively written texts as aberrations. Collectively their essays suggest that the construction of literary couples has much to tell us about the construction of authorship.

When the focus is on the processes and conventions of literary coupling, as opposed to the more static concept of "literary couples," old questions resurface with a new urgency and new questions come into view. How and why do writers come together to engage in textual creation, and how do they inscribe or erase their relationships in the texts they produce? In what ways are such literary couplings shaped by familial structures, economic connections, and the traditional repertoire of roles played out in creative relationships, including muse, mentor, apprentice, private audience, literary precursor, or literary successor? Is literary collaboration a manifestation of cultural instability and therefore a feature of avant-garde movements, as some critics have argued? More generally, are coupled and/or collaborative writing relationships more common in certain periods or cultures and not others, or are they simply more likely to be recognized or sanctioned in certain cultural contexts? (In our own age—at least in Western culture—there is a re-surgence of interest in such writing practices; whether there has been an actual increase, in part stimulated by new electronic technologies, is more difficult to determine.)

Another set of questions arises while reflecting on the binary forma-tion of "the couple." Why is it so dominant and how is it complicated through triangulations and group dynamics of various kinds, such as writers' "circles"? Two may be good "company" but is three or more always a crowd when it comes to writing relationships? What, for ex-ample, would have happened if there had been three Brontë children instead of four, who formed into pairs to produce that extraordinary body of juvenilia? While these essays collectively suggest that dyadic partnership remains the human relationship in which intensely dialogic or collaborative modes of writing most often occur, our contributors also question, complicate, or dissolve coupled partnerships, recognizing that these binaries can be as oppressive and obsessive in literary history as in popular culture. In so doing, they lead us to consider how writers resist or benefit from being subsumed under the structure of the couple, whether they actually collaborate or not. Moreover, they raise the ques-tion whether certain kinds of relationships are more conducive to re-ciprocal exchange between writers, while others are more likely to re-produce patterns of dominance. For example, do heterosexual couples differ from same-sex couples in this respect? How do both compare with other kinds of writing partners, such as siblings or parent-child pairs?

As we have indicated, the literary couplings this book considers are also those performed by readers and critics. Why, for example, are the works of Robert Browning more likely to be paired with those of Alfred Tennyson in anthologies, literary histories, and critical scholarship than with the works of Elizabeth Barrett Browning? Were Victorian readers and critics more inclined to recognize and celebrate the companionate partnerships of literary couples than readers in either the Romantic or the modern period? Have textual interactions and collaborative writing practices been more fully "in the closet" in the case of same-sex couples than that of mixed-sex couples? Or have female members of cross-gender couples been those most "closeted" by the invisibility that incor-poration in a couple confers?[2] How do generic conventions and the ex-pectations arising from them influence literary couplings by authors and readers? Do certain genres—for example, travel writing as opposed to lyric poetry—open up more opportunities for coupled writing than others? Finally—and this is a key question—at what point do coupled writing practices cross over into collaborative creativity, and how does one define that vexed term "collaboration"?

These are just some of the myriad questions that have arisen from our exploration with other scholars of literary couples and collaborators in diverse historical contexts. That they are not entirely the same questions we began with is a sign of current transformations in ideas about authorship, textuality, and collaboration. The initial catalyst for this collection was our shared observation (in the mid-1990s) that the texts—as opposed to the lives—of writing couples were seldom studied intensively in conjunction with one another. There were revealing exceptions, of course. Literary histories, anthologies, and studies grouped under the label "literary collaboration" in standard bibliographies did routinely couple male, canonical heterosexual writers such as Willliam Wordsworth and Samuel Coleridge, Ezra Pound and T. S. Eliot, or Joseph Conrad and Ford Madox Ford. But detailed studies of the textual relations and joint writing practices of other types of couples—cross-gender couples, female couples, or writing couples in intimate relationships other than erotic (e.g., parent-child or sibling relationships)—were much less common. The relative absence of studies addressing the complexity of writing configurations and textual interactions that we encountered in our own research first led us to try team-teaching a graduate seminar on literary couples and then to issue a call for essays on "Literary Couples: Intertextual Dialogues," in which we encouraged co-written submissions. Our initial title suggests how much we were implicitly working within a solitary author model, which the project would increasingly lead us to question.

The deconstruction of our embedded assumptions was initially stimulated both by our own experience of co-writing and by the collaborative consultations we encouraged among our contributors. Like Linda K. Hughes and Michael Lund, who describe a similar process of academic collaboration, we found ourselves experiencing the "blurred boundaries of authorship."[3] When we worked in close proximity, with one of us at the keyboard, the conversational process of give-and-take, negotiation, reassessment, and readjustment produced a braided text in which it is impossible to say who produced what. When we worked at a distance, one of us would draft a chunk of text and pass it along to the other for commentary, reshaping, and continuation. While this process of "chunking" offered more scope for individual agency, the drafts we created often incorporated or built upon ideas and phrases initially produced in conversation. Our own changing compositional practices thus reinforced our awareness of the complexity of coupled authorship, as well as the methodological problems inherent in attempts to separate out one person's idea or hand from that of another. Further reflection was prompted by our contributors' collaborations. While many of the essays we received were singly authored, others were "seamlessly" co-written or followed various dialogic formats. The writing practices incorporated in this book thus exemplify some of the modes of coupled authorship it treats.

Whether singly or doubly authored, our contributors' essays led us to reexamine the interface between coupled writing relationships in different historical contexts and the rapidly expanding body of research on the construction of authorship and on collaboration that had accumulated through the 1990s. The second section of this introduction outlines some of the theoretical and scholarly developments that have informed this study, together with the broader cultural transformations these have both mirrored and helped generate. The third section outlines the historical methodology that underlies the structure of this book, the rationale for our focus on mixed forms of literary coupling (as opposed to "collaboration" more strictly defined), and the theory of authors as "heterotexts" that we propose to help advance the deconstruction of the "solitary genius" model of literary creation. The fourth section briefly reviews definitions of collaboration that have functioned to screen out some of the forms of coupled authorship this study treats. The fifth and final section summarizes the contribution of each essay to a more historically informed understanding of writing couples and collaborators across a range of periods.

Constructions of Authorship: Theories and Practices, Transitions and Continuities

As our prefatory "snapshots" suggest, in many different contexts—including literature, theater, film, and popular culture—assumptions about artistic creation seem to be undergoing a metamorphosis, together with the legal, economic, and institutional practices that reflect and perpetuate them. In Tony Kushner's words, the idea that the author is a figure working in solitude is increasingly seen as "a myth"—one that Jack Stillinger, the author of *Multiple Authorship and the Myth of Solitary Genius* (1991), attributes to Romantic ideologies of the inspired creator. One need not look too far to find cause for increasing skepticism concerning the figure of the "solitary genius" in the wake of all of the following: poststructuralist theories of textuality and subjectivity proclaiming the "death of the author"; new paradigms of scholarly editing and textual production; interdisciplinary research on the history of copyright and changing constructions of authorship; feminist, postcolonial, and queer reframings of literary histories; studies of contemporary compositional practices in business, science, and education; and the proliferation of collaborative electronic hypertexts. We map some key transformations in these fields here and survey them in more detail in our concluding essay.

Developments in the fields of textual editing and historical research on authorship have been particularly dramatic. One index of these is Jack Stillinger's influential exploration of the "multiple" figures who often play a part in producing literary works along with the "nominal author," including "a friend, a spouse, a ghost [writer], an agent, an editor, a translator, a publisher, a censor, a transcriber, a printer." Another is Jerome McGann's conceptualization of literary texts as "collaborative events" in *The Textual Condition*.[4] Working at the juncture of literary and legal history in *The Construction of Authorship: Textual Appropriation in Law and Literature* (1994), Martha Woodmansee and Peter Jaszi present the emerging consensus that the "modern regime" of the solitary author is "the result of a quite radical reconceptualization of the creative process that culminated less than 200 years ago in the heroic self-presentation of Romantic poets." Their conclusions are borne out by Masten, who points out in *Textual Intercourse: Collaboration, Authorship, and Sexualities in Renaissance Drama* that even Shakespeare — viewed as the definitive figure of the "individual Author" and solitary genius since the eighteenth century — should properly be recognized as a collaborating playwright within a company that staged corporately produced plays.[5] As our concluding survey indicates, Masten's view is one shared by many Shakespearean critics and editors.

Woodmansee and Jaszi's interdisciplinary collection suggests that we may currently be at the cusp of a paradigm shift in conceptions of authorship, as Romantic conceptions of "egotistically sublime" authority yield before the recognition that literary creation has historically been much more collaborative than models of the solitary genius imply. Alternatively, one might argue that new scholarship on the history of

authorship grows, in part, out of changes in contemporary writing practices, since what we see in the past often depends on the lens of the
present. At the very least, one can say that scholarly interest in various
forms of collaboration has been on the rise, while academics themselves,
stimulated by newer information technologies, are engaged in collaborative writing on a scale unprecedented in the humanities. Witness, for
example, the Orlando Project team, whose members are working to
produce an electronic database and four print volumes on the history of
British women's writing. As team members indicated two years into the
project, their work quickly became far more intensively collaborative
then they initially envisioned.[6]

The late 1980s and 1990s saw a number of important studies of authorship and literary collaboration. In its focus on homoerotic writing
partnerships, Masten's 1997 analysis of the "corporate" authorship of
early modern drama is akin to Wayne Koestenbaum's groundbreaking
Double Talk: The Erotics of Male Literary Collaboration (1989), with its thesis
that the "double signature" of collaboration alters our perception of
authorship. The impact of Koestenbaum's work is acknowledged in
another pioneering study principally in the field of rhetoric and composition theory, where interest in collaboration arose well before it did
in literary criticism. *Singular Texts / Plural Authors: Perspectives on Collaborative Writing* (1990), coauthored by Lisa Ede and Andrea Lunsford (or
"RDLISEDEANDREALUNSFORDLISA A," to use the merged name
on their title page), materially altered our own thinking at an early stage
in this book through its studies of the actual processes of collaborative
writing in business, science, and the classroom. Research of this kind is
also integrated with theories of literary authorship in the 1994 anthology
Author-ity and Textuality: Current Views of Collaborative Writing, which was
team-edited by James S. Leonard, Christine E. Wharton, Robert Murray Davis, and Jeannette Harris.

Feminist criticism has been one of the most fertile sites for research
on collaboration, evident in an overflowing panel on the subject spon-
sored by the Women's Caucus at the 1991 meeting of the Modern Language Association, publications in *Signs* (by, for example, Carey Kaplan
and Ellen Cronan Rose), and a two-part "Forum on Collaborations"
edited by Holly Laird in two successive issues (1994 and 1995) of *Tulsa
Studies in Women's Literature*. The turn of the millennium ushered in a new
phase in this research, with three wide-ranging studies that were both re-
cuperative and revisionary. In *Writing Double: Women's Literary Partnerships*

Bette London warns that in focusing on Sandra Gilbert and Susan Gubar's "madwoman in the attic" as the woman writer's "dark double," critics have marginalized "women's actual collaborations." She then investigates some "motley" female collaborators with "varied and uncertain literary reputations." Laird's own *Women Coauthors* explores the dynamics of "collaborative desire" in "approximate and cosigned collaborations" by British, American, and Canadian women writers from the mid-nineteenth century to the postmodern period. In *Rethinking Women's Collaborative Writing*, Lorraine York (one of our own contributors) is more skeptical of such desire. Her study of contemporary and postcolonial collaborations in poetry, theater, and the novel critiques the "fusion model" prevailing in earlier feminist scholarship. She aptly appropriates as one of her epigraphs a passage from Susan Leonardi and Rebecca Pope's dynamic dialogue in the *Tulsa* "Forum": "After all, when our lips speak together, as often as not they disagree."[7]

Many accounts of changing constructions of authorship and collaboration begin not with the studies we have noted here but with the seminal effects of poststructuralist literary theory predating these, in particular Roland Barthes's "Death of the Author" and Michel Foucault's "What Is an Author?" Ironically, however, the standard historical narratives tracing the deconstruction of authorship back to these roots tend to construct a myth of origins that reinscribes the Author at a metatextual level by casting Foucault or Barthes as the solitary creators of a new theory of textuality. In fact, one might argue that Foucault himself, despite quoting Samuel Beckett's "What matter who's speaking?" indirectly promotes such heroizing practices by proposing the new (and relatively uncritiqued) metacategory of "initiators of discursive practices"—authors of "a theory, for instance, of a tradition, or a discipline"—the category into which he himself falls. Moreover, as Stillinger notes, the very theorists who anatomize the "death of the author" can be "quite ferocious" in defending authorial prerogatives.[8] We have not followed this usual narrative trajectory here because we have found historical and empirical studies that attend to actual writing, editing, publishing, and reading practices to be much more effective than theory alone in challenging us to rethink our own habitual approaches to literary couplings of various kinds.[9]

Despite the theoretical and scholarly developments we have outlined, the idea that the "writer-writes-alone" (to use Linda Brodkey's phrase) remains remarkably persistent in literary criticism, the classroom, mass culture, the marketplace, and the law.[10] The 1999 film *Shakespeare in Love* (see Snapshot 2) may present a genius inspired by Christopher Marlowe and others, but this popular hit predictably also depicts the eponymous Bard at the "moment of creation," scribbling in solitude in a garret. Moreover, the regime of the solitary author has obscured the collaborative partnership involved in the film's screenplay. In the academy as well, our first impulse with any text is still to bring it under the unitary sign of *the* proprietary author; the author classification remains the dominant means of codifying, archiving, teaching, analyzing, and legislating literary works. As scholars and teachers develop course outlines, use or compile anthologies, write literary histories, investigate how an author wrote and revised, or study the relations between authors, many—we would even say most—of us do not routinely stop to examine, in Foucault's words, "how the author was individualized in a culture such as ours, what status we have given the author, for instance, when we began our research into authenticity and attribution; the systems of valorization in which he was included; or the moment when the stories of heroes gave way to an author's biography." Masten points out that even "the most rigorous new historicist evaluations of Shakespeare . . . have largely adhered to an individuated, non-collaborative Shakespeare" based on anachronistic assumptions about authorship not yet established in the early seventeenth century.[11]

In the courts, where—Foucault and Beckett notwithstanding—it usually *does* matter who the law recognizes as "speaking," Romantic conceptions of authorship have remained particularly resistant to the accumulating scholarship on collaboration. One of the historical ironies accompanying the exponential expansion of the World Wide Web is the fact that corporations now routinely invoke Romantic ideologies of individual creation in defending their "intellectual property." Jaszi and other contributors to *The Construction of Authorship* point to legal cases in which authorship conventions are now extended to computer software and data networks, as well as to song lyrics and identifiable attributes of celebrities.[12] The 1999 court decision concerning the songwriting credits of Lilith Fair founder Sarah McLachlan is a case in point. Despite the judge's conclusion that Darryl Neudorf had "made a significant contribution" by contributing the verse vocal melody for some of McLachlan's songs, he concluded that Neudorf did not "qualify as a co-writer" because he had failed to make clear a "mutual intent" to coauthor.[13]

Issues of legal proprietorship (and appropriation) have also been thrown into relief by postcolonial perspectives on authorship as well as contemporary celebrity culture. The conflict between Maria Campbell, the Métis author of *Halfbreed,* and Linda Griffiths, the actor who helped to "sybil" *Halfbreed* into the play *Jessica* (see Snapshot 5), makes visible the ideologies of colonization underlying copyright conventions that are entrenched in a Eurocentric culture of the book—the culture that Griffiths reinscribes by listing herself as the primary author of *The Book of Jessica* (1989). As she resists Griffiths's attempts to control the terms of this collaborative book's copyright, Campbell struggles to articulate a different vision of an oral, communal culture in which the creations of the artist are not owned. Yet throughout the "book" that frames her speech one senses the difficulties created for her by what Adrienne Rich calls "the oppressor's language." For Campbell and Griffiths, who began without any written agreement, the "contract" that Griffiths instigated rapidly became a locus of intense struggle. Other literary couples sometimes prepare in advance for such conflicts—like the now de-coupled Evelyn Lau and W. P. Kinsella (see Snapshot 4)—to little or no effect. Engaged in a legal dispute over their authorial and privacy rights and the terms of the contract that permitted each of them to write about their relationship, Kinsella and Lau attempted both to profit from a media-saturated culture and to control their exposure within it, much as the more prominent celebrities studied by Rosemary Coombe try to regulate the "authorized" use of their images, names, signatures, characteristic phrases, and performance styles.[14]

In an initially happier experience of creative partnership (see Snapshot 3), Louise Erdrich, the "author" of *Love Medicine* (1984), and Michael Dorris, the "author" of *A Yellow Raft in Blue Water* (1987), detail the intensive sharing of ideas and drafts that led to these two novels, followed by their closer collaboration in the co-writing of *The Crown of Columbus* (1991), which was published under both their names. "The basis of the collaboration . . . is talk—weeks of conversation," Dorris says of the composition of *Love Medicine.* In the next beat Erdrich says, "The details of clothes and action are invented and thought about between the two of us." Their collaboration, sustained over a number of years and entering into the writing of several novels, remains remarkable despite the tragic conclusion to the partnership, including the breakup of their marriage, Dorris's subsequent suicide, and the news that he had been "about to be charged with sexual abuse."[15] Yet despite the interviews that attest to the collaborative process they engaged in, *Love Medicine,* the most famous of these three novels, is usually identified and discussed as if it were a solo composition by Erdrich.

As such critical practices suggest, slippages continue to occur as new theories of textuality and authorship slide back into deeply ingrained assumptions about literary composition. The contradictions fore-grounded in our opening snapshot of Tony Kushner—on the one hand rejecting the "myth" that the writer plays "it solo," and on the other im-plicitly endorsing the concept of the proprietary author—are thus rep-resentative of our age. We may indeed be at the cusp of a cultural shift of the kind that Woodmansee and Jaszi describe, marking the end of the "regime" of the solitary author. Yet, as this brief outline of scholarship and cultural transformations indicates, the times are decidedly mixed. Then again, perhaps they have always been so. As our contributors demonstrate, past historical practices of authorship are often more com-plex than they are assumed to be in studies that advance monolithic generalizations about particular eras. Accommodation of this hetero-geneity is fundamental to our theoretical framework—one that has not so much shaped as grown out of the historical methodology underlying this collection of essays. Consequently, we do not privilege the "theoret-ical tidiness" that Koestenbaum and other scholars arrive at by focusing on a group of writers selected by gender, period, or particular type of collaborative relationship.[16]

The Heterogeneity of Coupled Authorship: Toward a History of "Heterotextuality"

Literary Couplings takes an integrated approach to its heterogeneous subject in three principal ways. First, we seek to integrate historically grounded investigation of writing partnerships with interdisciplinary, theoretical work on authorship, textuality, and literary production. Sec-ond, we combine contextualized analysis of coupled writing practices in past historical periods with an exploration of modern or contemporary experiments in collaboration. Third, we include studies of both hetero-sexual and homosexual writing relationships, along with other kinds of partnerships whose importance has been overshadowed by the privileg-ing of the erotic. Including essays by sixteen scholars and spanning four centuries of literary history, our collection calls into question two complementary—though contradictory—assumptions. One commonly held view is that the history of authorship enacts a linear narrative in which the "corporate" writing practices of the early modern period gave way to a Romantic cult of the individual genius, which in turn established a monolithic "regime of the author" reflected in Victorian identifications of authors with their works and the consolidation of copyright laws. Another common assumption is that complex collaborative writing practices are a relatively modern, experimental, or avant-garde phenomenon. By investigating the material, familial, and ideological contexts in which literary texts have been produced, our contributors expose the gap between "Romantic ideologies" of authorship and actual writing practices, demonstrating the persistence of diverse collaborative practices within the very period now designated the "regime of the author." They also show how the coupling together of writers and their texts—by the writers themselves, their publishers, or their readers—is inflected by ideologies of gender and race, generic constraints and opportunities, political concerns ("collaborations" of another kind), and by changing cultural or historical circumstances.

In adopting this integrated approach, we have sought to effect another kind of conceptual coupling, namely, a critical one. By bringing together scholarship across a range of fields, we hope to fill the most significant gaps noted in our concluding survey of scholarship on literary couples and collaboration. These include the absence of a wide historical perspective and the relatively low exchange of ideas among specialists working in different areas. Several studies of literary collaboration (e.g., Koestenbaum, London, Laird, Herd) principally focus on late-nineteenth- or twentieth-century writers. In much of this work there is little acknowledgment of the history of collaborative and "corporate" writing practices uncovered, for example, by Woodmansee and Jaszi, Masten, or Mark Rose, who explore periods in which the very concept of the originary, individual author was not yet established. As a result, one is left with the erroneous impression that the richest interactions between literary couples and certainly the most interesting collaborations are largely a twentieth-century or "avant-garde" phenomenon, anticipated to some degree by such innovative collaborators of the 1880s and 1890s as "Michael Field." In addition, many of these studies overlook the extent to which collaboration was long a feature of the texts produced by African American or indigenous cultures. The view of a journalist for *Newsday*, who found the Erdrich-Dorris collaboration "virtually unprecedented," is an extreme manifestation of these patterns of historical neglect.[17] At the same time, even astute historicists like Masten, who have done so much to rescue early modern authorship from ahistorical modern assumptions about solitary genius, are prone to exaggerate discontinuities between the sixteenth century and our own, as if the corporate models of authorship that they explore simply disappeared under the onslaught of Romanticism. In order to redress such elisions, *Literary Couplings* is organized historically rather than thematically to highlight continuities among differing modes and models of collaborative and coupled authorship from the sixteenth to the late twentieth century.

At the same time, our collection places particular emphasis on the post-Enlightenment period, during which the regime of the solitary author has been presumed to triumph. This approach is designed to question prevailing constructions of Romanticism. While much evidence suggests that the Romantic period *was* a kind of watershed in the history of authorship, leading to the consolidation of ideologies of solitary genius and the legal apparatus of copyright, the work of McGann, Stillinger, and other critics indicates the importance of distinguishing between ideology and practice. Undoubtedly Romantic writers and their inheritors created powerful metaphors of lyric solitude, egotistical sublimity, and heroic individualism. Yet careful analysis of those metaphors in the light of actual writing practices uncovers a surprising variety of collaborative relations and positions. Indeed, as Alison Hickey argued in two important articles published in the late 1990s, collaboration is a prominent feature of the Romantic period despite conventional views of the Romantic writer "musing in solitude"; long before they were labeled "Romantics," writers of this period were identified as working within various poetical fraternities, political alliances, sects, and leagues like the "Lakers" and the "Cockney School." Hickey's essay in this book, along with others on Romantic writers, indicate how analysis of the ideologies, metaphors, material practices, and perceptions of Romanticism can contribute to a more nuanced understanding of this era's impact on the construction of authorship.

Collectively the essays included here underscore the extent to which modes of solitary and coupled authorship undergo an "uneven development," to use Mary Poovey's phrase, "articulated differently by the different institutions, discourses and practices that [they] both constituted and [were] constituted by."[18] One important set of discourses and practices explored here relates to the role of genre in the formation and reception of literary couples and collaborators. A considerable amount of recent scholarship on collaborative textual production concerns the drama. This is not surprising since collaboration has featured prominently in the theater, from the Renaissance collaborators treated by Masten, to Bertolt Brecht's collaborations with Ruth Berlau and others, to the flowering of contemporary feminist theatrical collectives, which provided a context for Griffith's dramatic collaboration with Campbell (see Jennifer Andrews's article in the bibliography). *Literary Couplings* attends, however, to the numerous other genres in which coupled or corporate writing practices have flourished, including literary translation (itself a form of collaboration, as contributor Patricia Demers points out in her essay on the Sidney siblings), travel writing, pornography, novel writing, and editorial work. Several of the essays included here also address the coupled writing practices associated with poetry, a genre that, since the Romantic period, has been identified with the individual lyric voice. The companion poems that James Bednarz sees as a form of collaboration in the Renaissance canon continue to occur in later centuries, as coupled works by the Brownings and by Plath and Hughes suggest. Nevertheless, as our essays on these authors point out, poetry may remain a genre in which coupled authorship encounters more obstacles than in others.

In addition to revealing the uneven effects produced by genre, the essays in this collection underscore the far-reaching effects of gender on writing partnerships and critical practices. As we note earlier, many traditional studies of collaboration tend to privilege male heterosexual couples within writing partnerships that confirm homosocial networks of patriarchal power. More recent studies like Koestenbaum's address homoerotic partnerships, although they do so without necessarily questioning the traditional focus on canonical masculine partners. Like the studies by London and Laird (which appeared after our project was substantially completed), *Literary Couplings* both questions this focus and seeks to extend it. Whereas London and Laird focus exclusively or primarily on women coauthors from the mid-nineteenth century to the present, our collection treats coupled and collaborative relationships among canonical and noncanonical writers of both sexes. Whether they focus on female or male writers, on cross-gender or same-sex relationships, our contributors share an interest in the impact of gender ideologies on literary creativity, textual production, constructions of authorship, and reader response. Collectively they write to uncover these ideologies. In some cases they challenge constructions of cross-gender writing couples that cast one partner as more dominant, innova-tive, or significant than the other (typically the male partner). In other instances they show how parallel gender binaries are often imposed on same-sex couples and collaborators.

In the case of cross-gender couples, the reductive assumptions ex-ploded by many of our contributors are discernible not only in tradi-tional criticism but also in some recent criticism written from a gay or feminist perspective. The traditional view of heterosexual writing rela-tionships is reflected in J. M. Robson's 1968 comment that his recon-struction of John Stuart Mill and Harriet Taylor's writing practices could be "supported by common experience of the way husband and wife collaborate"—a risky assumption to make in the case of such an unconventional couple, not to mention the historical gap between the "common experience" of marital collaboration in 1968 and 1858.[19] One is even more surprised to find similar attitudes expressed by Koesten-baum in 1989. Although he describes his queer theoretical approach to male collaborators writing between 1885 and 1922 as feminist (in some respects it is), Koestenbaum is disturbingly dismissive of the female part-ners in mixed-sex couples of various kinds. He observes that "Sylvia Plath, typing her husband Ted Hughes's poems, resumes an old tradition of wifely subordination," yet he makes no mention of Plath writing her own poems, adding that "I do not discuss this sort of appropriative rela-tion" and explaining that while he analyzes "Wordsworth's collabora-tion with Coleridge," he does not "consider the two men's use of Doro-thy, in whose journal they found material." Thus, Plath is reduced to an amanuensis, Dorothy to her journal and "material" to be quarried. Ar-guing from a feminist position, Kaplan and Cronan Rose articulate a similarly dismissive view of "the heterosexual model" of collaboration they see in Erdrich and Dorris, which appears to them "hierarchical." According to them, Erdrich becomes "a parrot for Dorris's ideas" and a "silent but conspicuously adoring spouse" in joint interviews—a conclu-sion not borne out by *Conversations with Louise Erdrich and Michael Dorris*.[20] Such dismissive references suggest that heterosexual writing couples al-ways work together in the missionary position, so to speak. Koestenbaum applies a similar hierarchical model of the dominant (masculinized) and submissive (feminized) partner to the male couples he treats, thereby re-cuperating a binary heterosexual dynamic that is itself reductive.

In place of such gender binaries and the model of the solitary author that these studies often implicitly reconstitute, we propose a conception of authorship as inherently "heterotextual." Poststructuralist theories have effectively altered conceptions of the unitary text, replacing it with less bounded models of textuality. We propose that the paradigm of the unitary author, which has thus far proven to be more resistant to transformation than the idea of the unitary text, should similarly be replaced by a conception of authors as "heterotexts," woven of varying strands of influence and agency, absorbing or incorporating differing subjectivities, and speaking in multiple voices. The concept of heterotextuality, acknowledges that when we speak of authors, we are speaking of culturally constructed identities inextricably linked to the works that authors produce, as Foucault and others have noted. It thus assimilates the theories of "intertextuality" advanced by Kristeva, Barthes, and others within the concept of the author (or what Foucault terms the "author function"). Moreover, in its reframing of authors as cultural texts, it counters the biographical focus on writers' lives as opposed to their works that seems to occur much more frequently with coupled authors than with individual authors. In its accommodation of heterogeneity, it also grows directly out of our attempt to find a theoretical framework sufficiently flexible to encompass the diversity of literary couplings and collaborations this collection treats. As we soon discovered, these writing relationships could not be stretched in a Procrustean theoretical bed.

In proposing that authorship be viewed as inherently "heterotextual," we explicitly do not mean to endorse a conception of authorship or textuality predicated on a normative heterosexuality. On the contrary, we are writing very much against the grain of prevailing connotations of "hetero." Partly because of the stimulating ways in which queer theory has deconstructed gender ideologies, "hetero" has increasingly come to be associated with monolithic conceptions of "straight" sexuality. Koestenbaum, in fact, even objects to using Mikhail Bakhtin's term "heteroglossia" because "the prefix 'hetero-' suggests this theory's sexual preference."[21] Our use of "heterotextual" is predicated on the value of preserving the older root meanings of "hetero" as "mixed," "heterogeneous," "diverse," as evidenced in compounds such as "heterodox," "heterogynous," "heterotelic," and "heteromorphic." In approaching authors as heterotexts, criticism should not simply segregate various textual strands, tracing them back to authors constructed as solitary subjectivities; nor should it always assume that one subjectivity or voice in a writing relationship is more dominant than another (although attention to structures of power is always called for). Although Chadwick and de Courtivron "started with the assumption that, given our culture's emphasis on solitary creation, one member" of an artistic couple is "always constructed as Significant, and the partner as Other," they concluded with "the realization that although this schema remains powerful, the truths which we are learning to decipher are indeed much more interesting."[22] The contributors to *Literary Couplings* continue the work of deciphering these "much more interesting" truths not by taking the "schema" of Significant and Other as a starting point but rather by exploring its ideological underpinnings, examining the extent to which such a configuration may be retrospectively imposed on writers in earlier periods, or considering how it relies on conceptions of authorship that collaboratively written texts confound.

In emphasizing the heterogeneous patterns of literary coupling and collaboration, we also hope to counteract the privileging of sexual partnerships over other equally important intimate writing relationships. "We make love and we make texts," McGann comments, adding that "love is and has ever been one of the great scenes of textuality"—"love and text are two of our most fundamental social acts." Few would contest such a claim. Yet one of the most widely read books on literary couples— Rose's *Parallel Lives*—focuses on prolific writing partners who "are more unhappy than happy, more unstable than stable . . . more sexless than sexually fulfilled."[23] When love does inform the scene of writing, frequently it is less love itself than conflict in love or the end of love that is one of the great catalysts of textuality. Whether it takes the form of prolonged conflict or passionately affectionate memory, the textual half-life of intimate relationships can be remarkably long, as several essays in the present collection reveal (e.g., Sarah Churchwell on Hughes's *Birthday Letters,* Amber Vogel on Laura Riding and Robert Graves, and Rebecca Carpenter on Mircea Eliade and Maitreyi Devi). But quite apart from love and the passions that survive its end, there are many more quotidian activities, circumstances, and relationships that form the matrix for the coming together of literary couples and their making of texts. For instance, one easily might imagine Dorothy Wordsworth writing, "we make bread and we make texts." In fact, as Anne Wallace suggests in our collection, Dorothy's journals offer an amplification of this conjunction, challenging norms and hierarchical valuations of authorship precisely because their syntax and structure persistently equate domestic and textual, private and public, labor and pleasure. By considering the conjunction of making texts and making children, our contributors also explore the "intricate interweavings of the spheres of biological and textual production and reproduction," which, as Chadwick and de Courtivron suggest, are often manifested in the work of literary couples.[24]

Definitions of Collaboration and Coupled Authorship

Both traditional approaches to literary couples and some recent studies of collaboration have tended to filter out the heterogeneous range of coupled writing practices our collection includes. This consequence is not only linked to assumptions about authors, literary couples, and gender binaries but also hinges on the ways in which literary collaboration has been defined. Dustin Griffin's 1987 taxonomy of "Augustan Collaboration[s]" indicates how traditional definitions of collaborators and collaboration rendered invisible many of the domestic, familial, and sexual conjunctions our collection explores, including wife and husband, daughter and father, aunt and niece, siblings, friends, or lovers and ex-lovers. Griffin identifies six common types of literary collaborators: a professional poet working with an amateur; a "senior established poet" and an apprentice; a pair of friends who work as "equals"; a pair of professionals in a "contractual business arrangement"; a team of professionals supervised by an editor or bookseller; and a group of amateurs in a coterie like the Scriblerus Club. Griffin's categories and the examples he gives (all male writers) do not readily accommodate the less formalized collaborations that occur within intimate relationships, even when writers work together as "a pair of friends," as contributor John Radner's essay on the subtle interactions between Johnson and Boswell suggests. Similar limitations restrict the comprehensiveness of Griffin's attempt to define and classify collaborations according to the "nature of the writing being produced."[25]

Operative definitions of collaboration have ranged from the strict to the very broad, as our concluding survey illustrates in greater detail. In legal contexts definitions tend to be narrow—or precise, depending upon one's view. Jaszi has noted the historical irony of recent decades: as writing has grown increasingly "collective, corporate, and collaborative" with the advent of electronic technologies, there has been "a substantial narrowing of the range of circumstances in which . . . 'collaboration' in the lay sense is recognized as a 'joint work' in the legal one."[26] Within the field of editing and textual criticism, both relatively broad and relatively narrow definitions are evident. Scholars like Stillinger and Paul Eggert differ over whether collaborators should be distinguished from editors, partners, and other "influences" on the textual agency of the author. The broadest definitions of "collaboration" tend to occur in studies of literary influence. For instance, although James P. Bednarz acknowledges the usual "narrow sense" of "collaboration" in speaking of "two or more individuals contributing to the production of a single work," he proposes a definition that includes "theft" from a poetic precursor or contemporary rival. Jewel Spears Brooker similarly argues that collaboration may include what T. S. Eliot terms the writer's "capacity for assimilation" of other artists' works. She also proposes that the relationship between writer and audience involves a form of collaboration, a possibility that Stillinger briefly considers as well.[27]

Although the enlarged definitions of collaboration employed by Bednarz and Brooker may serve important rhetorical ends, they sacrifice important distinctions. In a world where every precursor and every reader is a collaborator, all cats are gray. We thus believe it is useful to retain the more precise understanding of collaboration one finds in Thomas Hines's simple yet comprehensive definition, namely, "work artists do together to produce a joint creation."[28] At the same time, the study of actual writing practices supports a relatively broad definition of this collaborative "work," which might take many forms. In his book *Corporate Authorship: Its Role in Library Cataloguing* (1981) Michael Carpenter addresses the taxonomic challenges posed by collaborative authorship by distinguishing five activities involving "writing down," "writing up," "writing out," "writing in," and "writing over." All these forms of collaborative writing are accommodated by the inclusive definition that Ede and Lunsford adopt, which encompasses "any of the activities that lead to a completed written document," including "written and spoken brainstorming, outlining, note-taking, organizational planning, drafting, revising and editing."[29] However, as their definition makes clear and Hines's implies, collaborative "work" can take the form of speaking as well as writing: speaking before, about, over, between, or beneath *(sotto voce)* another's words.

We have opted for a relatively inclusive—though not infinitely broad—working definition of "collaboration" for the same reasons that we combine literary couples with collaborators in this study: to explore the continuum between coupled writers usually approached as separate authors and writers recognized as fully fledged coauthors; and to uncover the ambiguous zones in which conversation crosses over into shared inspiration, intertextual dialogue, or collaboration. As we have already indicated, unlike several recent studies this collection does not focus solely on "approximate" or full coauthorship.[30] Several of our contributors explore the dialogic exchanges shaping the works of writing couples, some focus on couples who collaborate to a degree, while others treat fully collaborative texts. Herd has noted the need to avoid theorizing collaboration "in terms of an intertextual paradigm of literary production," a point with which we concur. Yet airtight distinctions between collaboration and intertextual dialogue are difficult to sustain in practice, much as Barthes's attempt to distinguish between identifiable "influences" and anonymous networks of "intertextuality" is difficult to sustain.[31] If, as McGann suggests, a literary text is a "field of communicative exchange," at what point does such exchange become collaboration? The question becomes particularly challenging if one surrenders the deeply rooted idea that creativity is contained within the moment of inscription. As Laird rightly notes, "Literary collaboration blurs the boundaries . . . between text and speech; between a text and its contexts."[32] We would argue that this blurring occurs as well in many forms of coupled authorship in which "collaboration" (in its narrower definition) does not occur. In other words, to recall the concept we proposed earlier, coupled authorship opens up the possibility that authors, like the works they produce, are "heterotexts." Moreover, as we have emphasized, one cannot consider the couplings of authors without also considering those performed by readers, critics, and literary historians—who, for example, may decide that one member of a writing couple should be designated an "author" and the other not.

Not surprisingly, in treating varying degrees and kinds of coupled writing partnerships, our contributors express differing views of collaboration. Some, like Robert Gray and Christopher Keep or Lorraine York, underscore the radically innovative features of fully collaborative texts that dissolve authorial boundaries. Others highlight what we have termed the five intractable "A's" of coupled and collaborative authorship: authority, agency, accountability, acknowledgment, and attribution. With the exception of a few contributions, the essays in this collection attend more to the conflicts of coupled authorship than many recent studies of collaboration have done.[33] This is not to deny that coupled and collaborative partnerships can be harmonious. The sibling relationships treated by contributors Anne Wallace and Patricia Demers are examples of productive harmony. One finds a similar kind of harmony in the marital "consociation" between the Victorian Shakespeare critics, the Cowden Clarkes, treated elsewhere by Ann Thompson and Sasha Roberts. Yet writing relationships, like authors, are living entities, and conflicts are often integral to creative growth.

Our contributors also vary significantly in the metaphors they use to conceptualize and understand coupled or collaborative writing practices. We have found that metaphors and analogies often replace or complement definitions in studies of literary couples and collaboration, perhaps because, despite their imprecision, they organically connect writing to a full spectrum of human experience and activity. For example, through metaphors of exchange, bargaining, and games-playing, composition critics and cultural materialists demonstrate how authorship partakes of the same complex strategies of negotiation, mediation, compromise, competition, retaliation, coordination, and obligation that operate in larger institutional structures and economies (e.g., workplace, business, family). As our concluding survey shows, feminist collaborators and theorists have often turned to such domestic metaphors as cooking and quilting to preserve the sense of an interactive creativity that mingles individual and collective energies. Variants of these defining metaphors are evident throughout our collection. Whether the currency of exchange is archaic (e.g., the poetic gifts by which W. B. Yeats and Dorothy Wellesley set themselves in an age-old relation of reciprocal power and obligation) or modern (e.g., the electric energy that Gray and Keep use to illuminate the uninterrupted circulation of text, identity, and desire within fin-de-siècle homosexual networks), our contributors recognize the multiple bonds that link authors and authorship to larger social interactions and structures. They also explore analogies between textual and domestic labor as well as creativity and space. The metaphor of authorship as weaving that Demers, in her essay on the Sidney siblings, borrows from the sixteenth-century Countess of Pembroke anticipates postmodern theories of text as interwoven tissue and also provides a useful supplement to the quilt model of authorship favored by contemporary feminists. In a similar fashion, Wallace reworks the cottage from a metaphor of Romantic solitude into a site of joint domestic industry. An analogous metaphorical reworking of domestic space is undertaken by York, whose essay ranges from the garret to the garden in its exploration of the text as a shared space that is seeded, cultivated, and harvested in common. These differing metaphorical models have influenced the shaping of the present volume. Like York, we have become intensely aware of the strategies of accommodation, coordination, and resistance that are required when two (or more) individuals share a conventionally unitary space of authorship. Like other coauthors, we have also found ourselves turning to metaphors of conversation, singing, interjection, and, on occasion, outcry to express this awareness—all images that reflect the dialogic process of collaboration.

The Essays

To reflect the process of its making while emphasizing its historicist aims, we have constructed this study of coupled authorship in the form of a web consisting of many threads. At the center are thirteen essays focusing chiefly on the two-hundred-year period usually associated with the "regime of the author." These are framed by an introduction and conclusion encouraging further reassessment of this regime from historical and theoretical perspectives. We have arranged the essays in the central section chronologically and retained conventional period labels— though some of our contributors have justifiably questioned them. We have done so in order to highlight both the historically contingent nature of authorship and the extent to which epistemic demarcations are challenged by the heterogeneous authorship practices explored by our contributors. At the same time, while the essays locate themselves and are located by us within specific historical, material, and sociocultural contexts, they also interweave and speak to each other across period boundaries: through their reflections on editing, translation, and "deferred collaboration"; their revisions of theories of genius and the muse; and their investigation of serial, triangular, and group-author formations. In some essays this conversation is overt, most obviously in the epistolary essay on the Brownings, in which Corinne Davies and Marjorie Stone debate whether conjugal union or conflict is more productive poetically. In other "single" essays, whether singly or jointly authored, the traces of heterotextual authorship are hidden within a web of words, reinforcing one of the key issues of this collection, namely, the difficulty of determining where singular authorship ends and collaboration begins.

The historical core of this book opens with two essays comprising the first part, "Early Modern 'Coupled Worke,'" that extend the proliferating scholarship on early modern and eighteenth-century authorship.[34] Patricia Demers's "'Warpe' and 'Webb' in the Sidney Psalms: The 'Coupled Worke' of the Countess of Pembroke and Sir Philip Sidney" reads the Sidneys' work of psalmic paraphrase as a collaborative medium of shared emotion, intellectual play, and devotional service in which the "passionate interchange" between sister and brother mirrors the relationship between source and interpreter, God and humanity. Focusing on a sibling couple joined through the genre of translation rather than on the homoerotic pairings in the drama that Masten and other early modern scholars have emphasized, Demers shows how the Countess of Pembroke authorizes herself *within* a system of patriarchal reproduction by writing through and between the words of her deceased brother. In analogous ways, through the medium of translation both siblings also work through and between the words of the psalmist and the Word of God. Demers uses the phrase "deferred collaboration" to describe the process whereby an individual writer revisits, revises, resists, or reconstructs the words of a deceased writer with whom he or she has been involved in an intimate relationship. In so doing, she introduces an important paradigm of coupled authorship that runs like a connecting thread through several essays in this book, including Gerard Goggin's on Mary Wollstonecraft and William Godwin, Alison Hickey's on the Coleridges, and Sarah Churchwell's on Plath and Hughes.

An understanding of both text and author as not only "coupled worke" but also constructed and contested work underlies the next essay, John Radner's "Constructing an Adventure and Negotiating for Narrative Control: Johnson and Boswell in the Hebrides," which addresses collaborative life-writing at a transitional point in the history of both authorship and subjectivity. Radner extends historical scholarship on eighteenth-century authorship and collaboration by tracing the process of intertextual generation and documentation that created the Life of "Johnson" as text and as author. In this essay Johnson emerges not as a romanticized figure of the heroic "author as personality" but rather as a richly collaborative, deeply conflicted, and much revised heterotext: a composite cultural text whose self-narratives exist "in potential debate with other self-narratives and in real or potential competition with the narratives of others." The most important—though not the only one— of these "others" is James Boswell, with whom Johnson engages in a struggle for narrative control of their joint experience in the Hebrides, and consequently of the public image and final judgment of "Johnson." In analyzing the dynamics of power and competition in the Johnson-Boswell relationship, Radner strikes a chord that resonates in many subsequent essays, most dramatically in Vogel's analysis of Riding and Graves and in Churchwell's analysis of the battle over self-construction in the public sphere engaged in by Plath, Hughes, and their critics. At the same time, Radner's insights into the spiritual dimensions of coupled authorship (as Boswell assumes the role of Johnson's conscience and Johnson worries about his relationship to God, the final Reader) draw attention to an aspect of collaboration seldom discussed in existing criticism but one that is touched upon as well in the essays by Demers and Davies and Stone.

The essays in the second part, "Romantic Joint Labor," continue the investigation of how traditional views of the "great author" are complicated and undercut by the involvement of that author in the formation of the couple. As we have already suggested, Romanticism looms large in all accounts of authorship, the source of potent myths of gender, genre, genius, and subjectivity. Yet, as the essays in this section emphasize, ideologies of authorship were in flux during this period as new modes of circulation, changing gender roles (especially the entry of women writers into the marketplace), new conceptions of family and friendship, and competing political ideologies and factions influenced both the practice and perception of authorship.

Gerard Goggin's essay "Editing Minervas: William Godwin's Liminal Maneuvers in Mary Wollstonecraft's *Wrongs of Woman*" lays bare the politics of gender and editing that have obscured the collaborative energies of Romanticism by examining another case of "deferred collaboration" that also takes the form of a battle for narrative control. What is at stake in William Godwin's rewriting and editing of his dead wife's posthumous novel is the visibility and viability of Wollstonecraft's new mode of authorship: a radical feminist paradigm of reading and writing designed to challenge patriarchal sexual and textual authority. Attempting both to compensate for Wollstonecraft's loss and to exert a libidinous posthumous control over her legacy, Godwin intervenes in the rhetorical strategies and dialogic exchanges of the *Wrongs of Woman*. As editor he suppresses the dialogic and critical orientation of her manuscript and casts himself in the roles of romantic rescuer, Jupiter to her Minerva, and mentor to her apprentice. By using his deferred collaboration to maneuver his dead wife into the very model of authorship she had resisted, Godwin helps to defuse the challenge that her text might have posed.

In the next essay, "Home at Grasmere Again: Revising the Family in Dove Cottage," Anne Wallace engages in a more explicit critique of the way gender politics operate to obscure alternative models of authority and authorship in the Romantic period. In this case, however, the gender politics are those of contemporary criticism. Drawing on the work of Nancy Armstrong, Wallace challenges post-Freudian definitions of family that privilege affective and sexual bonds and blind us to the persistence of corporate models of both kinship and textual production well into the Romantic period. Attempting, like Demers, to get beyond psychobiographical readings of the sibling couple as incestuous, Wallace examines William and Dorothy Wordsworth as joint (and equal) laborers in a domestic economy in which texts were produced as a cooperative enterprise. By relating new materialist histories of the family to changing conceptions of the author, Wallace's model of "cottage industry" textual production provides the missing link in histories of authorship between the corporate modes of the early modern period and the companionate writing relationships of the mid- and late nineteenth century, explored in the third part of this collection.

Alison Hickey offers another complex reinterpretation of Romantic authorship and its relation to domestic, feminine, and material contexts in "'The Body of My Father's Writings': Sara Coleridge's Genial Labor." Like Goggin, Hickey focuses on an instance of posthumous editing as deferred collaboration, but Sara Coleridge, the surviving member of a literary couple with the pen in her hand, is more like the Countess of Pembroke than she is like William Godwin. She resembles Pembroke, too, in the way she works within a patriarchal system, authoring her own individuality in the act of completing another's. Through her monumental task of ordering, annotating, and preparing her father's dismembered works for publication, Sara Coleridge seems to subordinate her own labor (filial, conjugal, maternal, and bodily) to the service of his singular Romantic genius. However, in working jointly with her husband (also a Coleridge) to produce "Coleridge," as father, text, and Author, she also validates her own authorial and filial identity. Here, in effect, the child becomes the mother of the man as Sara Coleridge becomes the site upon which competing claims to Romantic authorial genius are mediated.

By presenting Romantic paternal genius as a product of a Victorian daughter's labor, Hickey's essay unsettles not only Romantic narratives of authorship but also the period divisions that sustain them. For this reason her essay dovetails nicely into the third section of our history of coupled authorship, "Victorian Complementarities and Crosscurrents." The first two essays in this section detect, beneath the belated and anxious Victorian quest for Romantic author/ity, a popular and potentially unsettling tradition of "complementary" or "companionate" textual production, manifested in different ways in the work of the Brownings and the orientalist travel-writing couples explored by Jill Matus. This tradition may testify to the survival or reclamation of earlier traditions, such as the familial writing practices and kinship structures investigated by Wallace or the feminist model of companionate authorship idealized (though not achieved) by Wollstonecraft. At the same time, these Victorian practices of companionate writing both reflect and resist the restrictive norms of gender, class, and sexual identity that shaped ideas about authorship in the nineteenth century. The final essay in this section both underscores the hegemony of these norms and indicates how the binary constructions they rely upon were subverted by a fin-de-siècle homosexual collaboration.

In "'Singing Song for Song': The Brownings 'in the Poetic Relation,'" Corinne Davies and Marjorie Stone debate the extent to which the Brownings attained a harmonious partnership as the two poets read, edited, and revised each other's poems in the courtship period; contemplated a literary collaboration; cast each other as 'siren' muses; and, as a married couple, quarreled over politics and spiritualism. Davies and Stone opt for an epistolary format both to counteract the popular emphasis on the biographical rather than the textual interactions of the Brownings and to call attention to the courtship letters in which the two poets first forged several of their coupled writing practices. This format dramatizes some of the stakes involved in such textual exchanges: Stone and Davies acknowledge the struggle involved in having the first or the "last word," much as the Brownings do. Like the other contributors, they also maintain a double focus, attending not only to the Brownings' textual interactions in their poems and their manuscripts but also to the gendered assumptions underlying the reception and construction of cross-gendered writing couples—assumptions that have by no means disappeared. Indeed, Davies and Stone suggest that the gender ideologies so apparent in Victorian responses to writing couples may be even more insistent in the twentieth century.

Jill Matus expresses a more radical skepticism of Victorian possibilities for companionate authorship in "Collaboration and Collusion:

Two Victorian Couples and Their Orientalist Texts," where she analyzes the trend toward joint production of travel writing in the Victorian
period, showing how it functioned to support the separate-spheres
ideology in which the works of male scholars were "partnered" by more
polite, feminine accounts written by their wives or sisters. Deconstructing the sentimental rhetoric of gendered complementarity surrounding
this arrangement, Matus reveals a web of complicity, communication,
and censorship surrounding parallel representations (textual, sexual,
and cultural) of the East in the work of two orientalist couples, one sibling (Egyptologist Edward Lane and his sister, Sophia Poole) and one
married (Sir Richard Burton and his wife, Lady Isabel Burton). As in
the treatments of more recent cross-cultural collaborations by Carpenter and York, Matus finds these cross-gender and cross-cultural encounters opening a textual space in which binary norms are challenged even
though the challenge is ultimately contained and defused as normative
ideologies of gender, race, and the Orient are reinscribed in the texts
she analyzes.

A greater challenge to Victorian—and Western—binary norms is
posed in Robert Gray and Christopher Keep's essay "'An Uninterrupted Current': Homoeroticism and Collaborative Authorship in
Teleny," which analyzes a fin-de-siècle gay-porn chain-letter novel associated with the circle of Oscar Wilde. In their reading, *Teleny* operates as
a textual and sexual meeting place, as well as a space of oriental fantasy
and desire where authorial and sexual proprieties are tested and ef-
faced. Keep and Gray explore the extent to which transgressive, critical,
deviant, "other" textual (and sexual) practices arise to subvert norms of
authorial and sexual identity at the very moment at which such norms
are being fixed by the discourses of law and psychiatry. The serial authorship of *Teleny* becomes a means to resist normative juridical and
psychophysiological models of homosexual identity and unitary authorship in favor of collective models characterized by fluidity, circulation,
and exchange. As their essay demonstrates, ideologies of authorship are
inescapably implicated in developing nineteenth-century ideologies of
gender, sexuality, and subjectivity.

As the first three sections of our history demonstrate, the "regime of
the author" did not emerge in the "Age of Johnson" and become full-
blown in the "Age of Wordsworth." Rather, it was created in conflict
with other modes of authorship, including remnants of traditional corporate, familial, or companionate practices as well as manifestations of

new radicalisms. Like other formations with which it is implicated (generic traditions, gender ideologies, assumptions of normative sexual identity), authorship develops unevenly, with new forms of individual and coupled authorship coexisting with older forms. Furthermore, as Gray and Keep's analysis of *Teleny* indicates, dominant conceptions of authorship are shaped not only by their time and circumstances but also by the opposing forces they generate. In the twentieth century, heterodox crosscurrents in the history of authorship become even more evident, whether they take the form of a modernist attraction to archaic communalism or a postmodern voice of the margin writing back against master narratives of the age. As modern communication media dissolve some of the boundaries between private and public spheres, coupled or collaborative authors become more self-consciously performative, overtly antagonistic, and public in their struggles for sexual and textual control, which often span entire careers and cross cultural, gender, and period boundaries. Despite the variety of coupled and multiple modernist writing practices, the myth of the solitary author remains strong in the twentieth-century imagination, as reflected both in representations of the scene of writing and in the stereotype of the modernist author as magisterial mythmaker or iconoclast. The tendency of writers in each age to construct their own originality by exaggerating the monolithic quality of their precursors has also contributed to these defining images of literary modernism.

This paradoxical quality of modernist authorship is highlighted in the essay which opens the fourth part of our collection, "Literary Modernity: Mythmakers and Muses." The long, many-phased career and inveterate, innumerable self-revisions of William Butler Yeats reveal, on the one hand, a willingness to relinquish creative authority through experiments in nonrational, nonlinear forms of writing, and, on the other, a magisterial effort to control and (re)present his own creative persona and legacy. Lisa Harper's essay "Courting the Muse: Dorothy Wellesley and W. B. Yeats" focuses on a moment in Yeats's later career when his revulsion with mainstream modernism led him to adopt archaic, communal forms and modes of production. His fascination with these forms is manifested in his relationship with Wellesley, his partner in a complicated system of literary and erotic exchanges that resulted in a chain of ballads and shaped his late poems, plays, and editorial projects. Like the chain-letter novel *Teleny* examined by Keep and Gray, these ballads break down the binary configurations of both authorship and relationship—in this case through tripartite formations where the positions of lover-poet, muse, and intermediary are presented as fluid and interchangeable. Using a framework of gift-exchange theory, Harper traces the complex dynamics of mutual obligation, anxiety, and antagonism operating within reciprocal authorship. She sums up the paradoxical status of the modernist creator by viewing Yeats as a poet whose ability to transform plural vision into singular achievement contributed to the myth of the solitary genius even as he paid homage to the collaborations that enabled such artistry.

A less forgiving view of the modernist mythmaker's collaborative creativity is evident in Amber Vogel's "Not Elizabeth to His Ralegh: Laura Riding, Robert Graves, and the Origins of the White Goddess." Vogel uncovers the collaborative origins of Graves's influential myth of the "White Goddess," which she treats as a paradigm for the way in which (male) modernist writers constitute originality through the appropriation and erasure of their (often female) sources. Drawing on Riding's unpublished letters and reading her neglected essay "The Word Woman" as a forceful attack on the prototypical hierarchical coupling of muse and author, Vogel demystifies one of the great myths of modernism, presenting it as a pliable fiction that "flatters man by disguising from him the mundane and collaborative origins of his ideas." In Riding's own, more caustic terms, Grave's muse-goddess was a "literary machine designed for seizure of the essence of my reality," a tool of "literary plunder" that enabled Graves to transform Riding (his collaborator in many discussions of goddesses and in numerous literary ventures) into a mythic mystification of his own invention. Like Wordsworth erasing the traces of his collaborative domesticity or Godwin retrospectively defusing a feminist challenge to patriarchal authority, Graves is one in a long line of mythmakers who mount a rear-guard action against challenges to the hegemony of the solitary genius. Unlike Wollstonecraft, however, Riding gets the last word in this exchange—at least in Vogel's essay.

In its retrospective revisionary reply to a modernist mythmaker, Vogel's essay heralds the more openly antagonistic forms of "deferred collaboration" that predominate in the late twentieth century, forms discussed in the fifth part of our collection, "Writing Back: Postcolonial and Contemporary Contestation and Retrospection." In Rebecca Carpenter's essay "Competing Versions of a Love Story: Mircea Eliade and Maitreyi Devi," the challenge comes from a postmodern and postcolonial perspective, and the embattled literary couple participates in broader and longer histories of intercultural discourse between occidental and oriental voices. Like a child over whom two parents battle, the "true story" of the love affair between two novelists is claimed by both Mircea Eliade, who penned his version in his 1933 novel *Bengal Nights*, and Maitreyi Devi, whose 1974 novel *It Does Not Die* rewrites and challenges his romanticized and mythologized version of their story. Devi's novel explores and examines the racial, imperialist, and gendered assumptions that shape Eliade's text, arguing that it is permeated by and perpetuates myths of oriental femininity. Deconstructing the cultural and generic binaries (East-West, rational-sensual, romance-realist) that define and confine both the couple and the text, Devi, like Riding, writes to right the authorial balance of power. According to Carpenter, however, Devi seeks not to invert hierarchies but to expose and transcend them. Using the form of the novel to weave her story around his story—alternately correcting and confirming, reinterpreting and reinforcing, rejecting and elaborating—she creates a cross-cultural, cross-period, cross-gender conversation that "never fully ends and is never completely resolved, but certainly 'does not die.'"

In "'Your Sentence was Mine Too': Reading Sylvia Plath in Ted Hughes's *Birthday Letters*," Sarah Churchwell takes on another textual pair that does not die—indeed, the most overdetermined, most famous, and most embattled literary couple of our time. Precisely because it is so visible and public, the relationship of Plath and Hughes offers Churchwell an opportunity to examine the reception and construction of couples and their texts from a self-conscious, postmodern perspective. Churchwell reads Hughes's *Birthday Letters* not merely as a form of deferred, conflicted collaboration with his dead ex-wife but also as an agonistic response to the audience (public or private, individual or cultural, real or imaginary) that has determined their literary reception and reputations. As coupled authors, Plath and Hughes have become inseparably implicated in the gender wars of our era, their texts forever bound together in an ambivalent compact of collusion and resistance with(in) the public sphere, ultimately frustrating any definitive attempt to separate his from hers, I from you, us from them, public from private, author from muse and/or reader.

The concluding essay, Lorraine York's "Crowding the Garret: Women's Collaborative Writing and the Problematics of Space," "writes back" in another sense by engaging in a retrospective and comparative analysis of the history and reception of lesbian collaboration over the last century. In the first (and longer) half of her essay York investigates two pairs of late-Victorian lesbian collaborators who cohabited the space of "genius" in an age when it was deemed only solitary and male. Katharine Bradley and Edith Cooper ("Michael Field") and Edith Somerville and Violet Martin ("Somerville and Ross") developed various compositional strategies (e.g., name games, page sharing) and metaphors of textual production (e.g., gardening or mosaic work) to confront and negotiate the sexual and social prejudices and pitfalls that attended their collaborative endeavors. A century later, although much has changed for female collaborators, York finds that much has remained the same. She considers three contemporary postcolonial and/or cross-cultural pairs of female collaborators: Ayanna Black and Lee Maracle, Gillian Hanscombe and Suniti Namjoshi, and Daphne Marlatt and Betsy Warland. While the partnerships these writers engage in may be more frank and public than those of the earlier couples, the social anxieties about lesbian desire they negotiate are compounded by territorial anxieties that prove to be more intractable. In these postmodern, utopian quests to create new forms of shared textual space, collaboration emerges from the closet of Victorian gender anxiety only to confront postcolonial anxieties of culture and nation. Inevitably, as York shows, authorship involves the sharing and in many cases also the appropriation of cultural space.

Like the other contributors, York does much to bring forms of coupled and collaborative authorship out into the open in literary history. In the end, however, her essay, like the preceding ones, reminds us how far we still have to go in order to grasp both the complex dynamics and the multiple varieties of literary partnership. The lesbian collaborators York considers do succeed in fashioning rooms of their own—rooms that, as Virginia Woolf recognized, inevitably must be "shared."[35] But dominant paradigms of authorship and the scene of writing still make it very difficult for us to conceptualize these spaces and the transformations they generate.

In order to facilitate this necessary reconceptualization, we conclude our collection with "Taking Joint Stock: A Critical Survey of Scholarship on Literary Couples and Collaboration." Designed to complement the present introductory overview, this essay serves as a reference guide, theoretical backdrop, and analytical commentary on the body of ideas out of which this volume grew. Although it is by no means exhaustive, our survey addresses a need in current scholarship to bridge the gap separating studies of writing couples and/or literary collaborators in various specialized fields, including literary biography, feminist and queer criticism, postcolonial studies, composition and pedagogy, editing and textual studies, and the history of authorship and copyright. In bringing together research from such disparate quarters, we hope to provoke new critical dialogues and to stimulate further reflection on the ways in which literary couplings inflect our historical understanding of authorship and textual production. Since this project has from the outset been informed by dialogic exchange—with one another, with our contributors, with existing scholarship, and with various readers—we present this analytical commentary as part of an ongoing critical conversation. Appropriately, the medium for much of this exchange has been electronic. In the age of the World Wide Web, global chat rooms, and instantaneous transmission of voice texts, the line between speech and writing, like that between identities and authors, has been blurred, with the result that the act of coupling in language has become both more critical and more common.

Notes

We have reversed the "normal" alphabetical order of our names to draw attention to the way in which conventions of indexing introduce inequalities and hierarchies even in collaborative authorship.

1. Jeffrey Masten, *Textual Intercourse*, 16; Holly Laird, "Contradictory Legacies," 116.
2. This is tantamount, in some respects, to the legal fiction that subsumed a wife's identity with her husband's under English common law. In the words of Sir William Blackstone, "In law husband and wife are one person, and the husband is that person." Cited by Holcombe, *Wives and Property*, 18.
3. See Hughes and Lund, "Union and Reunion: Collaborative Authorship," 50.
4. Stillinger, *Multiple Authorship and the Myth of the Solitary Genius*, v; McGann, *The Textual Condition*, 60.
5. Jaszi and Woodmansee, introduction to *The Construction of Authorship*, 3; Masten, *Textual Intercourse*, 10.
6. While the print volumes are individually authored, their authors are also drawing on the collaborative hypertext database and annotated chronology they have been creating together with an interdisciplinary team of literary scholars, humanities computing experts, postdoctoral fellows, and graduate students. Although the project has developed electronic protocols that record

every contribution to the database by researchers, team members still wrestle with the question of how to translate such data into information suitable for standard measures of individual professional achievement. Interview with Orlando Project collaborators, June 1998.

7. York, *Rethinking Women's Collaborative Writing*, 21; London, *Writing Double*, 2, 31; Laird, *Women Coauthors*, 3, 6.

8. Foucault, "What Is an Author?," 115, 131; Stillinger, *Multiple Authorship*, 192.

9. London similarly records that her work on collaboration was materially furthered by new "scholarship on the social construction of authorship," related work on "history, copyright law, and literary reception," and collaboration studies in the field of composition (*Writing Double*, 5–7).

10. Brodkey, "Modernism and the Scene(s) of Writing," 398.

11. Foucault, "What Is an Author?," 115; Masten, *Textual Intercourse*, 10. Tellingly, London notes that among the 110 photographs included in Jill Krementz's book *The Writer's Desk* (1996), "none pictures writing as anything but solitary" (*Writing Double*, 3).

12. See Jaszi and Woodmansee, introduction to *The Construction of Authorship*, 12. See also Jaszi, "On the Author Effect," 35; Coombe, "Author/izing the Celebrity," 102.

13. In handing down this decision, the judge rejected the testimony of expert witnesses in the music industry, who argued that "when two people work closely together over a prolonged period of time," collaboration should be assumed "unless an agreement exists to the contrary." On the contrary, the judge assumed that authorship should be understood as solitary and individual in such contexts unless a contract or agreement specified otherwise. Chris Dafoe, a reporter on the case, noted that "there is little case law addressing what constitutes artistic collaboration or joint authorship" ("Singer Surfaces from Trial Victorious," sec. A, p. 2).

14. Coombe, "Author/izing the Celebrity," 10–12.

15. Chavkin and Chavkin, eds., *Conversations with Louise Erdrich and Michael Dorris;* Read, "Interview: Louise Erdrich on Native Ground," sec. D, p. 3.

16. Koestenbaum, *Double Talk*, 29. For this reason we also do not focus solely on explicit collaborations, as other recent studies do. On this point, see our survey of definitions of collaboration later in this introduction.

17. See Chavkin and Chavkin, eds., *Conversations with Louise Erdrich and Michael Dorris*, 84; for the prevalence of cross-cultural collaborations in earlier periods, see the studies by Susan Bernardin, Jean Humez, and Albert Stone in the bibliography.

18. Poovey, *Uneven Developments*, 3.

19. Robson, *The Improvement of Mankind*, 58. Given his partnership with Stillinger in editing Mill's *Autobiography*, one wonders how Robson's views may have been subsequently modified.

20. Koestenbaum, *Double Talk*, 13; Kaplan and Cronan Rose, "Strange Bedfellows," 559.

21. Koestenbaum, *Double Talk*, 8.

22. Chadwick and de Courtivron, *Significant Others*, 10.

23. McGann, *The Textual Condition*, 3–4; Rose, *Parallel Lives*, 16.

24. Chadwick and de Courtivron, *Significant Others*, 11.

25. Griffin, "Augustan Collaboration," 2–3.

26. Jaszi, "On the Author Effect," 38, 51–52.

27. Bednarz, "The Collaborator as Thief, " 279, 281; Brooker, "Common Ground and Collaboration in T. S. Eliot," 231; Stillinger, *Multiple Authorship*, 185.

28. Hines, *Collaborative Form: Studies in the Relations of the Arts*, 4: Hines's primary focus is on artistic forms such as opera, which involves collaboration, not on collaborative authorship.

29. Carpenter quote cited by Ede and Lunsford, *Singular Texts / Plural Authors*, 93; Ede and Lunsford, *Singular Texts / Plural Authors*, 14.

30. Koestenbaum is interested in the "double signature" (*Double Talk*, 2); Laird's study focuses on "approximate . . . but not thoroughgoing coauthorships between authors and their editors" as well as full "cosigned collaborations" (*Women Coauthors*, 6). London treats "instances where the presence of two hands can be unambiguously recognized" (20), concluding that "where collaborations are less all-encompassing" than the ones she focuses on, "we have no way of knowing how many authors pass off collaborative creations as solitary achievement" (*Writing Double*, 18). York also focuses on instances of "overt signature" (*Rethinking Women's Collaborative Writing*, 21).

31. Herd, "Collaboration and the Avant-Garde," 54; Barthes, "Theory of the Text."

32. McGann, *The Textual Condition*, 62; Laird, *Women Coauthors*, 5.

33. Koestenbaum, e.g., celebrates the erotics of the "metaphorical sexual intercourse" that men engage in when they collaborate (*Double Talk*, 3), while Laird emphasizes a "celebratory redescription of coauthorship" to balance her subsequent attention to the "problems" as well as the "pleasures" of collaboration ("Collaborative Desire," introd. to *Women Coauthors*, 13, 21).

34. For a comprehensive overview of this scholarship, which appeared as this study was in its final phases, see Heather Hirschfield's article "Early Modern Collaboration and Theories of Authorship."

35. Cited by Brodkey, "Modernism and the Scene(s) of Writing," 406.

I

Early Modern
"Coupled Worke"

"Warpe" and "Webb" in the Sidney Psalms

The "Coupled Worke" of the Countess of Pembroke and Sir Philip Sidney

PATRICIA DEMERS

Sir Philip Sidney (1554–1586) and his sister, the Countess of Pembroke (1561–1621), constituted one of the most powerful literary alliances in early modern England. Both now have major editions of their complete works, with the Clarendon edition of Lady Mary Sidney Herbert being the more recent addition to this pantheon of canonical status. Though subject to the vagaries of critical taste, their lives, reputations, and accomplishments remain inextricably intertwined.

Poet, courtier, soldier, Sidney died in October 1586 at Arnhem, in the Protestant Netherlands, of infection from a wound inflicted twenty-six days earlier at the battle of Zutphen. His state funeral four months later resulted in an unprecedented outpouring of elegies and laments for "England's Mars and Muse."[1] Sidney published only two anonymous poems during his short life, preferring the more aristocratic medium of extensive manuscript circulation for his work: a pastoral entertainment for the queen entitled *The Lady of May; Certain Sonnets*, a combination of thirty-two translated and original poems; *The Old Arcadia*, a five-act tragicomedy recounting intricate searches for love among royalty and rustics, with pastoral interludes or "eglogues"; *The New Arcadia*, an incomplete revision in an expanded three-book epic format ; 108 sonnets and eleven songs comprising *Astrophil and Stella*, which anatomizes the blend of erotics and ethics in a love affair; *A Defence of Poetry*, a spirited, wide-ranging response to Stephen Gosson's attack against poets; *First Week*, a translation of a portion of du Bartas's *La Semaine ou la Création du Monde*; and a metrical paraphrase of the first forty-three psalms. With his portrait enshrined, as early as the seventeenth century, in the Upper Reading Room of the new Bodleian Library and his reputation as "the greatest of the moderns," Sidney has never lacked scholarly champions, who credit him with having "compiled what might be regarded as a School of English Versification," giving "a sense of God's presence" by showing "the prophetic element in the Psalms," and having "changed the private character of manuscript production."[2]

Although in dedicating the *Arcadia* to his sister Sidney affected a gentlemanly casualness about "this idle work . . . which (like the spider's web) will be thought fitter to be swept away, . . . this child which [he was] loath to father," he reminds her—in the more serious hope that the work may be "perchance made much of"—that it was composed "in [her] presence" by a brother "who doth exceedingly love you."[3] The enduring, generative, and erotically charged bonds of this love and the literary projects and judgments that united them are the major motifs in the Sidney legend, which Pembroke promoted. In fact, the tradition of consigning Mary Sidney Herbert to the periphery as merely the agent for ensuring her late brother's renown—revising his work, circulating some in manuscript and shepherding others through the press—persisted until a few decades ago. The exception was Frances Young's pioneering biography, designating her subject as a genuine "intellectual." Felix Schelling considered it both gallant and charitable to admit that he did not "really know the poetical value of her translation of the *Psalms*." T. S. Eliot's so-called apology, addressing none of her works, halfheartedly attempted to raise the circle "from the ignominy of wealthy well-born amateurs of the arts."[4] Recent reformulators of the early modern canon (e.g., Jonathan Goldberg, Beth Wynne Fisken, Margaret Hannay, and Theodore Steinberg) have explored Mary Sidney Herbert's independent, virtuosic range, from the psychological reality and conversational immediacy of her work to its astutely positioned political commentary and metrical daring.

Pembroke actually established more credentials as a translator than her brother, having published under her own name an English version blending "Senecan manner" and "Plutarchan materials" of Robert Garnier's *Tragedie of Antonie*, which "paved the way for explicitly political history plays . . . including those of Shakespeare and Daniel," as well as a prose version of Philippe de Mornay's *Discours de la Vie et de la Mort*, in which she probed and expanded such dicta as life being "a *Penelopes* web, wherein we are alwayes doing and undoing" and "but continuall dyeng."[5] The work circulated in manuscript comprises the "finest English version" of Petrarch's *Trionfo della Morte;* the completion of the Psalter project, in which she doubled back to revise or regularize some of the metrics in Sir Philip's work and translated Psalms 44 to 150, producing "164 distinct stanzaic patterns, with only one repeated"[6]; two dedicatory poems prefacing the presentation copy to Queen Elizabeth of this collaborative metrical psalmic paraphrase; and the pastoral dialogue "Astrea" in praise of the queen. In addition to her renown as a patron of writers and discerning influence on the devotional poetry of Donne, Lanyer, and Herbert, Pembroke continued the revision, arranged the eclogues, and oversaw the publication of the composite folio, consisting of the new *Arcadia* plus the last three books of the old *Arcadia*, called *The Countess of Pembroke's Arcadia*. The emended text, according to its secretary, Hugh Sanford, was "now by more than one interest *The Countess of Pembroke's Arcadia;* done, as it was, for her; as it is, by her."[7] Pembroke also supervised the publication of the *Defence* and the first complete edition of *Astrophil and Stella*, and commissioned a fair copy of the Psalms prepared by John Davies of Hereford. She offered this beautiful manuscript—with "most of the capitals in gold" and gilded "clubbed stems and looped tails of other letters"—to Queen Elizabeth in the names of both translators since, as Pembroke knowingly observed, "A King should onely to a Queene bee sent."[8] Pembroke was a collaborator aware of her own artistic worth. Her best-known portrait, completed by Simon van de Passe in 1618, showcases her role as a translator holding the open book of the Psalms of David.

In this essay I wish to explore the nature of this extraordinary collaboration in the production of the Sidney Psalms. Deferred collaboration is a more accurate label, since one can only speculate as to whether brother and sister began the Psalter project together or if Sidney worked alone, perhaps in the inspiring, encouraging presence of his gifted, likeminded sister. Speculations about Sidney's continuing influence on Pembroke should not hinder discoveries of her unique daring as the partner who created more than two thirds of this text. In the first section

I propose to combine evidence from the two dedicatory poems with contemporary theory interrogating the stability of authorship and the individuality of authorial property.[9] My aim is not to press the arguments of contingency so far as to erase or subsume identity but rather to inquire into the feasibility of the argument that such an exceptional coupling actually contributed to the development of a distinct and distinctly empowered persona for Pembroke. In the second section I plan to test any claims through a brief comparison of two Penitential psalms. Without pitting brother against sister, venerating stories about an incestuous union, or becoming embroiled in lists of substantive variants among the seventeen extant manuscripts, I will examine the sort(s) of poetry each produced in an effort to discover the nature of the newness fashioned by Sidney and Pembroke. Conscious of the pitfalls of the "atomistic habits of philological analysis,"[10] I am more interested in the various ways in which they dissolved the dichotomies of sacred and secular, prayer and art form.

The Dedicatory Poems

> . . . hee did warpe, I weav'd this webb to end;
> the stuffe not ours, our worke no curious thing,
> Wherein yet well wee thought the Psalmist King
> Now English denizend, though Hebrue borne,
> woold to thy musicke undispleased sing,
> Oft having worse, without repining worne;
>
> And I the Cloth in both our names present,
> A liverie robe to bee bestowed by thee.
>   ("Even now that Care," lines 27–34)

In this first of two dedicatory poems prefacing the 1599 manuscript presentation copy of the metrical psalmic paraphrase, Mary Sidney Herbert imaged their "worke" as woven cloth, with her brother supplying the structural lengthwise threads and Pembroke crossing them with the weft or woof. Without such interweaving there would be no resultant "liverie," a word both translators used—Philip in evoking redeemed souls (Psalm 34.10) and Mary in imploring divine protection (Psalm 106.10). The imagery of weaving is wonderfully apt to help orient late-twentieth-century readers of this late-sixteenth-century collaboration.

In the first instance it suggests the work of translation, as practiced by both Sidneys. Puttenham's *Arte of English Poesie* had nicely adjusted the device of *traductio,* and thereby the work of the translator, to the skill of the "tranlacer," who "turne[s] and tranlace[s] a word into many sundry shapes as the Tailor doth his garment."[11] Mistress of residences at Wilton, Ivychurch, Ramsbury, and Baynards Castle, Pembroke, an aristocrat with all the requisite refinements in needlework and music — and who knew a great deal about the composition, intricacy, and decoration of fabrics — chose her metaphor with precision. On account of her "admirable workes in Arras fram'd," she was acclaimed as a needlewoman of renown, "a Patterne and a Patronesse . . . of vertuous industry, and studious learning," along with Mary Tudor and Elizabeth I, according to John Taylor in *The Needles Excellency,* whose sonnet tributes to "great Ladies, who have bin famous for their rare inuentions, and practise with the Needle"[12] are modeled on the psalmist's portrait of the king's daughter presented "in raiment of needlework" (Psalm 45.14). Thomas Moffet, Pembroke's physician, also praised her in the dedication of his mock-heroic treatise on sericulture, *The Silkewormes,* as a "noble Nurse of Learning" whose "heau'nly-humane eies" and lifegiving breath of "sparke or flame" were sufficient "to aeternize" his verse, which recounted not only the life cycle of silkworms but also the "sport [of] man and maide . . . winding, twisting, and . . . weaving" varieties of silken cloth.[13] As a patron, Pembroke's life-giving breath was often invoked. Thomas Heywood's posthumous tribute to her in *Gynaikeion* commended her learning and accomplishment, positioning her within a literary tradition that weaves together past and future in looking back to Sappho and ahead to her niece, Lady Mary Wroth. Heywood borrowed Horace's evocation of Sappho's influence to characterize Pembroke's "Muse" in the still-breathing, flickering flame that the Aeolian girl sung to her lyre.[14]

   The idea of a woven work also provides a nicely allusive introduction to postmodern concepts of early modern authorship, specifically its constructedness and possible instability. Here is a vivid illustration of the text Roland Barthes referred to as "tissue," not in the sense of a "ready-made veil" but as "the generative idea . . . worked out in a perpetual interweaving." In the theory of such a text, for which Barthes coined the term "hyphology (*hyphos* is the tissue and the spider's web)," the prominence of the spider or single author becomes less emphatic since "the spider dissolves in the constructive secretions of its web."[15]

As was noted earlier, both Sidney and Pembroke used the imagery of the web. Their collaborative English metrical paraphrase of a revered, didactic, and devotional compilation of Hebrew songs—with David, the king and sinner, the model of repentance, as its putative author— crystallizes the Foucauldian principle of a "polysemous" text; instead of the "functional principle" of the single author whose signification the culture can limit and exclude, one faces a "proliferation" of meanings and hands.[16] Conjectures about the ways Sidney and Pembroke worked together—both in life and following his death—contribute to an understanding of the resultant text, or "liverie," as a social yet always mysterious series of experiments in expressivity, acknowledging "language as a process of exchange [and] discourse as intercourse."[17]

The second dedicatory poem, "To the Angell spirit of the most excellent Sir Phillip Sidney," shows Pembroke itemizing an "Audit of [her] woe" (line 44) and conducting an adroit exercise in self-fashioning, possibly modeled on the eleventh exercise of Aphthonius's *Progymnasmata,* "the standard school[boy's] textbook on rhetorical self-presentation."[18] She refers to the Psalms as "this coupled worke" (line 2), a significant change from the description in an earlier shorter version as "joynt worke." To me the change in adjective signals a shift from a sharing in common, a holding in conjunction, to a more binding union, association, or combination, often matrimonial or sexual. Humility and inexpressibility topoi do not really keep Pembroke silent throughout the thirteen stanzas, where grief and self-justification share space and emphasis. The first-person singular voice is audacious: "So dar'd my Muse with thine it selfe combine" (line 5); "I call my thoughts" (45); "Truth I invoke" (50); "theise dearest offrings of my hart . . . / I render here" (78, 81); "Deare Soule I take my leave" (88). In the same stanza where she labels her "presumption" a little excessively "too too bold" (25), she also presents the completed Psalter: "Yet here behold . . . / this finish't now" (22–23). Acording to Michael Brennan, "It is possible to sense her determination."[19] Despite being "striken dumbe," she longs to explain "Howe workes [her] hart, [her] sences" (line 46). Reservations about the adequacy of language to express do not prevent her from concluding with an amazing image of "theise dearest offrings of [her] hart / dissolv'd to Inke, while penns impressions move / the bleeding veines of never dying love" (78–80).[20] The blood of Sidney's fatal thigh wound has become a creative medium for Pembroke; his death has released her writing. Such a transformation of media from blood to ink and such a deliquescence into print, albeit under the controlled circumstances of manuscript circulation, indicate that this sister was much more than the keeper of a votive flame for her brother. Among others, Beth Fisken and Jonathan Goldberg have considered how much more than a votary she was, with Fisken seeing the "baroque comparison" of ink and blood reflecting a "latticework of interlacing allegiances" and Goldberg suggestively concentrating on the linkage of ink, blood, and spirit in the page of "their making"—where they are "literally, materially, translated, reproduced"—and scrutinizing the "passionate interchange between brother and sister."[21] Both Jonathan Crewe and Goldberg rehearse John Aubrey's salacious claims that he had "heard old gentlemen say that they [Philip and Mary] lay together," and that Mary spied on her stallions mounting mares and later imitated their sport, with Crewe arguing that "radical endogamy [incest] is the real story of the aristocracy."[22] Although I recognize the passionate identification between brother and sister in the dedicatory material of the Psalter, the texts of the psalms themselves—particularly the Penitentials—yield no evidence or hints of (or any penance for) incest, sodomy, and bestiality according to my reading, The more compelling argument is the emergence of Pembroke, through the generative channel of blood, as a fully fledged writer, collaborator, and partner, finishing her brother's draft and creating "an entirely new work."[23]

The Penitential Psalms

A Brother and a Sister, made by thee
The Organ, where thou art the Harmony.
. . . .
They show us Ilanders our joy, our King,
They tell us *why* and teach us *how* to sing.[24]

Probing, insightful readers—who were not unaware of the value of patronage—recognized the importance of the Sidney Psalms from the outset. Donne identified Sidney and Pembroke, "this *Moses* and this *Miriam*" (line 46), as instructive lyricists for a nation. Well in advance of the completion of the Psalter[25] Spenser dedicated an entire prefatory sonnet of *The Faerie Queene* to Pembroke and disclosed an encomiastic identification of "Urania, sister unto Astrofell" in *Colin Clouts Come Home*

Again (line 487). However, acknowledging that a woman completed the lion's share of this work was a hard pill for some contemporaries to swallow. Sir John Harington—his lament about the "unpublyshed" state of the manuscript notwithstanding—doubted that the translation could have been Pembroke's since "it was more then a woman's skill to express the sence so right as she hath done in her verse, and more then the English or Latin translation could give her."[26] In certain ways Pembroke's reputation has teetered, with threats of either adulation or faint praise on both sides. Students of Sidney have viewed her as "an inveterate tinkerer" whose "unavoidable makeshift" contrasts with Sidney's "precise architectonic skill."[27] As a devotional poet, she has been found "uneven," failing to "measure up to the level of the truly second- or third-rate poems written in the Nineties," and overly ornamented, thereby losing "control of the larger imaginative infrastructure of her own psalm imitations."[28] I propose to examine Sidney's paraphrase of Psalm 6 and Pembroke's paraphrase of Psalm 51 not as an exercise in one-upmanship but rather to investigate if shared sources, values, and attitudes resulted in similar or inherently different type of poetry.

Beyond minor orthographic changes, Pembroke did not revise Sidney's Penitentials (Psalms 6, 32, 38)[29] and she was the sole versifier at work in the remaining four psalms of this septenary (51, 102, 130, 143). Their shared sources included the following: the *Book of Common Prayer*, containing both the prose Psalter of the *Coverdale Bible* and Sternhold and Hopkins's metrical version; the *Huguenot Psalter;* the *Geneva Bible;* Anthony Gilby's translation of works by Théodore Bèze and Clément Marot; commentaries of Bèze and Calvin; and the quantitative metrics of George Buchanan's renderings of the psalms as Horatian odes.[30] As psalms sung when penitents were "publikely reconciled unto the assembly of the Church,"[31] the Penitentials themselves enjoyed a remarkable vogue in the sixteenth and seventeenth centuries,[32] their consolation and direction making them a form of commonplace book "about the intimate connection between remembering and re-marking a text."[33] For Reformation commentators David was a model who served many causes, from Théodore Bèze's justification of French Huguenot revolt against the Catholic Valois monarchy to reformers' characterization of David as a "slandered courtier" who complained against the tongues "in courtly mouths."[34] In addition to sharing Protestant sympathies, Sidney and Pembroke concurred on the artistic value of the psalms, delineated in the *Defence* as "a divine poem" which was "nothing but songs" imitating "the unconceivable excellencies of God" and making David "as in a glass [to] see his own filthiness."[35]

Both Gilby and Bèze must have struck some sympatheticsense chords for the reform-minded Sidneys. Gilby's "Epistle to the Reader" criticizes the recitation of the "Psalms in English . . . rather for taske as it were, and for fashion sake, then for good devotion and with vnderstanding" and elevates the pithiness of paraphrase over commentary as "giuing the full sence and meaning of the holy ghoste in other words, as briefly as may be" and as "most ancient . . . safe to certifie the conscience . . . and most profitable." However, the translation or paraphrase of the Penitentials was not simply an exercise in succinctness or catechizing. What is remarkable about Sidney's version of Psalm 6 is the use of contrastive structures and arresting, often expanded imagery to promote the suit for grounded, deserved, fatherly chastisement. The speaker—usually assumed to be David, distressed in mind and body and expiating guilt over his adultery—comes to realize the need for punishment, the link between sin and the hostility of men, and the saving allegiance between the penitent and God. Sidney has caught the skillful symmetry of the penitential disciplinary turn from the afflicted self to the confident expectation or experience of divine mercy.

Although there is no direct confession of sin in Psalm 6, Sidney's eight, four-line, alternately rhymed stanzas (consisting of three lines of iambic pentameter closing with trochaic dimeters) convey a pulse of penitential imploration leading to jubilant protection. Neither the Coverdale Bible's depiction of "heuy displeasure" (verse 1), the *Geneva Bible*'s "wrath" (verse 1), Marot's regular sixains, nor Sternhold's sturdy fourteeners prepare the reader for Sidney's totally original opening plea:

> Lord, let not me a worme by thee be shent,
>> While Thou art in the heat of thy displeasure:
>> Ne let thy rage, of my due punishment
>>> Become the measure.

Arthur Golding had used the noun "rage" in translating Calvin's commentary on the petition "reprove mee not in thy rage," as had Sternhold, and George Buchanan had the speaker beg not to be seized as he deserved: "Ne me merentem corripe."[36] However, there was no precedent in the books Sidney most likely had consulted for the abject image of the worm imploring not to be disgraced.

All Sidney's amplifications serve to intensify states of physical weakness and spiritual strength. His speaker's bones are not merely "vexed." Possibly taking a cue from Calvin's explanation of "vehement greef" that does not concern "the flesh, which is a tenderer part: but by the name of bones he meeneth that his cheef strength was made too quake,"[37] Sidney conveys the sense of the weakness of the bones in their tenderest core: "for ev'en my bones their marrow spend / With cruel anguish" (lines 7–8). Distinct from Bèze's image of the penitent's "bedde [that] swimeth euerie night washed with . . . teares" and the *Geneva Bible*'s depiction of the "couche watter[ed] with . . . teares," Sidney stresses both the immensity and involuntariness[38] of the moisture:

> My bed, while I with black night mourn alone,
>   With my tears floweth.
>
>   (lines 19–20)

The most stunning image of physical debility is the moth-eaten[39] visage:

> Woe, lyke a moth, my face's beauty eates
>   And age pull'd on with paines all freshness fretteth:
> The while a swarm of foes with vexing feates
>   My life besetteth.
>
>   (lines 21–24)

In keeping with the nature and psychology of the Penitential, the expressions of spiritual strength are more subtle and restrained. The final two stanzas, collapsing three verses, contrast the exultant vanity of the speaker's tormentors and the single, ultimately heard "sobbing voice" (line 27).

> The lord my suite did heare, and gently heare,
> They shall be sham'd and vext, that breed my crying,
> And turn their backs, and strait on backs appeare
>   Their shamefull flying.
>
>   (lines 29–32)

The physical reversal of the speaker's enemies, signaled by the linguistic repetition and reversal of turned backs that bear the sign of shame, may reflect Sidney's awareness of the Hebrew text, which itself concluded with a wordplay, the involuntary reversal of the foes being mirrored in the reversal of letters and sounds of the two verbs: "may they turn back" and "may they be disgraced."[40]

Although Pembroke's Penitential *Miserere Mei, Deus* is generally
better known than the earlier one translated by her brother, the daring,
independence, and vigor of Pembroke's version, incorporating and
extending suggestions from commentaries, certainly are not.[41] With remarkable control and altering insights, she vivifies the "tensions between speech and silence" and the "move from a context of disorienta-
tion to a new orientation."[42] Because theirs is a deferred collaboration,
it does not seem appropriate to impose any lessons Pembroke may have
learned from Sidney as the primary criterion for assessing her work;
such a criterion places Pembroke in the subaltern's role. While it would
be pointless to deny any influence from Sidney, it seems equally fruitless
for a collaborative analysis to insist on this influence as a controlling
principle. To be sure, they both experimented with an array of amplify-
ing techniques, including stanzaic patterns, wordplay, figurative language, assonance, and internal rhyme. Contracting the "heart-broken
soule" to "build up Salems wall" (Psalm 51, lines 49, 52), her Penitential
is characterized by adroit repetitions, proleptic extensions of biblical
metaphors, and simultaneous breathlessness and assurance.

In sifting through Huguenot commentaries, Pembroke aligns herself
with many of their devotional stances while retaining an independence
of expression and form. Bèze's "Argument" to Psalm 51 posits that the
penitence here demonstrates "how great weaknesse there is euen in the
best and most excellent men." David's "publique confession," which
"though he were a king of great power yet he willingly submitteth him
selfe vnto," distinguishes him "from the dainty men of our age."[43] The
emphatic, rhetorically ornamented force of Pembroke's opening stanza

> O Lord, whose grace no limits comprehend;
>> Sweet Lord, whose mercies stand from measure free;
> To mee that grace, to mee that mercie send,
>> And wipe O Lord, my sinnes from sinfull mee
>> O clense, O wash my foule iniquitie:
> Clense still my spotts, still wash awaie my staynings,
> Till staines and spotts in me leave no remaynings.
>
> (lines 1–7)

extends the deliberateness of Bèze's plea: "[W]ash me therfore O my
God againe and againe and often times, whiles the filth of so great wick-
ednesse be vtterly washed away." Her rhyme royal supplies a veritable
catalogue of rhetorical devices: *antimetavole*, or the counterchange, in

lines 1–3 and 6–7; antistrophe, or the "counter-turne," turning counter "in the middest of euery meetre,"[44] in line 3; *epanalepsis,* or the echo sound, in line 4; and *ecphronesis,* or the outcry, in lines 4 and 5.

Her allusions to the privacy of the penitent's schooling, "And inward truth which hardly els discerned, / My trewand soule in thy hid schoole hath learned" (lines 20–21), may owe some debt to Bèze's declaration: "I confesse that thou hast taught me that thy wisedome, not as thou hast done euery one, but as one of thy houshold priuately and most familiarly." Another possible influence is Calvin's commentary on the sinner who has been "taught by God as one of his household" and "become a froward scholer."[45] Equally possible as a conscious and ironic (or unconscious and embedded) source of the description of the "trewand soule in thy hid schoole" is Sidney's image of taking up his "trewand pen" at the conclusion of the first sonnet of *Astrophil and Stella.*

Pembroke's ecstatic—almost aerobic—imploration "That brused bones maie daunce awaie their sadness" (line 28) differs remarkably from Bèze's more staid conclusion, which is in keeping with the Genevan practice of excising any reference to dancing: "So shalt thou soudenly refresh the bones which thou hast worthily broken."[46] The idea of sudden refreshment may have triggered the demonstrable proof of dancing for a woman as experienced with court culture as Pembroke, whose imagery contrasts tellingly with another contemporary woman's verse meditation on the *Miserere.* Anne Lok's[47] sonnet ("Sinne and despair have so possest my hart") dwells obsessively on the weight of sin, whereas petitions to cancel sins' register impart a more buoyant, hope-filled, propulsive mood to Pembroke's metaphrase. The sharpest difference between Lok's negativity and Pembroke's devotional exuberance surfaces in an apparent similarity. Lok describes the bones, conventionally "broken" (verse 8), as "brosed bones that thou with paine / Hast made to weake my febled corps to beare." These bones, she attests, "shall leape for joy, to shewe myne inward chere." "God has caused the pain and weakness, even as God will bring the joy."[48] Pembroke, as Margaret Hannay observes, never suggests that God caused the "brused bones"; not content with inward cheer, these revivified bones will show their new life by dancing "awaie their sadness" (line 28).

Metaphorical flashes and idiosyncratic coinages notwithstanding, Pembroke's expression of joy and sorrow is always temperate, above the white heat of the Reformational fray. Although she may have discovered some formative models in Calvin, Pembroke borrows from the latter in his logically meditative moods. His commentary on the *Miserere* furnishes atmospheric linkages with Psalm 51, in which she develops his schemes of "a couert matching of contraries" and of interiority, whereby David "feeleth . . . his sinnes within." To explain the covert matching of contraries, Calvin contrasts the actions of David and Nathan: "[A]fter David had [gone in] vnto Bathsheba, the Prophet Nathan is sayd to haue come in vnto him. Now by that uyle going in, he was gone out a great way from God." As sins are figured as "filth and vnclennesses that defile vs, and bestaine," so "remission of them is aptly termed a washing away."[49] Invoking the medicinal, absorptive, spiritually purifying qualities of hyssop so prominent in the Pentateuch (Exod. 12.12, Lev. 14.4–6, 49–52, Num. 19.18), Pembroke's speaker petitions:

> Then as thy self to leapers hast assign'd,
> > With hissop, Lord, thy Hissop, purge me soe:
> And that shall cleanse the leaprie[50] of my mind.
> > > > (lines 22–4)

Interiority—"the fittest remedie" according to Calvin—means entering "into our selues, to gather all our wits vnto God," washing "our consciences inwardly with the blood of Chryst," recognizing that "the temple unbuilded . . . was but as a cotage," and having "not a respect for the outward buylding only, but . . . cheefly vpon Gods spirituall sanctuarie, which cannot be buylded by hand and conning of men." Possessing a similar understanding of providential architecture and engineeering, Pembroke's penitent concludes: Awith thy favour build up Salems wall, / And still in peace, maintaine that peacefull place" (lines 52–53).

While Pembroke likely appropriated from Bèze and Calvin, she stands far apart from Buchanan's metric paraphrase. She usually amplifies Buchanan's calm parallels, extending the recognition of sin that shames and disgusts ("pudet heu pigetque") to the acknowledgement through *epizeuxis* of "My filthie fault, my faultie filthiness" (line 9). Pembroke also goes further than the interior rhymes of Buchanan, as in "Spiritum firmum renova novata" (verse 10) and "spiritum sanctum calida incitatus" (verse 12), to emphasize a subtler theological bond between the reformativity of forgiveness and the creativity of grace. In addition to the *brachiologia* of a staccato string of adjectives—"a pure, cleane, spottless hart" (line 31)—her rendering of verses 10–12 blends pre- and postlapsarian moments, connecting the desire for a divinely created cleanness to "breathing grace":

Create in me a pure, cleane, spottless hart:
   Inspire a sprite where love of right maie raigne.
   Ah! cast me not from thee: take not againe
Thy breathing grace! againe thy comfort send me,
And let the guard of thy free sp'rite attend me.

                        (lines 31–35)

What of Pembroke's own breathing grace, which Moffet praised as an animating "sparke or flame"? Acceptance or rejection of her metrical invention and importance in her own right continues to determine most critical responses. Pembroke's psalms are clearly at the opposite pole to the common meters and ballad stanzas of Sternhold and Hopkins. Surrounded as she no doubt was by contemporary psalmic paraphrases — from the metrical versions of Lok's nephew, Michael Cosworth, to the hexameters of patronized Abraham Fraunce — she stamped the Psalter with a daring, subtle individuality.

Is her accomplishment also recognizably, inherently different from that of her brother/angel spirit/posthumous collaborator? Any attempt to demarcate the strict boundaries or frontiers of individual authorial property in a collaborative project is doomed. Given the nature of this unconventional collaboration, deferred by death, I think readers are justified in recreating an "archaeology of the artifact"[51] that pays special attention to the layered, incremental work of the surviving partner who brought this work to completion. The collaborators' shared devotional probity leads to distinctive verse and speech forms, voicing alienation and profound trust through ragged and pathetic as well as extravagant and hope-filled images. This "coupled" work enacts "co-laboring"[52] in a genuinely metaphorical way, with ligatures of blood, emotion, and artistic and devotional creeds binding two translators separated by years and life experiences. As for the passionate identification between brother and sister, one has the evidence of their poetics and reports of gossip, which together offer a scant concrete basis upon which to build "the preposterous logic of incestuous, cross-gender identification." However, a portrait of Pembroke as merely "pious and desexualized" is as inadequate as Aubrey's malicious whispering.[53] Of the duo, I find Pembroke the more metrically daring and open to contemporary sources — the truly "hypertextual"[54] one whose poetry explores innumerable pathways to devotion and ambition. Yet I must also admit that it is impossible to determine if these features are the result of temperament, aptitude, inclination, or the luxury of time. The answer is probably some combination of these factors. It is too facile and essentializing to resort to gender as an explanation of their differences. Although large issues and a commonality of texts join brother and sister, Sidney and Pembroke remain individual interpreters, with idiosyncratic locutions and cadences, understandings of paraphrase and translation that range from the spare to the baroque, and concepts of license that can be tame or unfettered.

Notes

1. William A. Ringler Jr., ed., *The Poems of Sir Philip Sidney*, i.

2. Ringler, *The Poems*, xv; Hallett Smith, "English Metrical Psalms in the Sixteenth Century," 269; A. C. Hamilton, *Sir Philip Sidney*, 74; H. R. Woudhuysen, *Sir Philip Sidney and the Circulation of Manuscripts 1558–1640*, 8.

3. Victor Skretkowicz, ed., *The Countess of Pembroke's Arcadia (The Old Arcadia)*, 3.

4. Frances Young, *Mary Sidney, Countess of Pembroke*, 203; Felix E. Schelling, "Sidney's Sister, Pembroke's Mother," 118; T. S. Eliot, "Apology for the Countess of Pembroke," 48.

5. Virginia Walcott Beauchamp, "Sidney's Sister as Translator of Garnier," 13; Margaret Hannay, Noel Kinnamon, Michael Brennan, eds., *The Collected Works of Mary Sidney Herbert, Countess of Pembroke*, 1: 39. All quotations from Pembroke are based on this edition.

6. Gary Waller, ed., *The Triumph of Death and Other Unpublished and Uncollected Poems by Mary Sidney*, iii; Gary Waller, *Mary Sidney, Countess of Pembroke: A Critical Study*, 190.

7. Victor Skretkowicz, ed., *The Countess of Pembroke's Arcadia (The New Arcadia)*, lxii.

8. Noel Kinnamon, "The Sidney Psalms: the Penshurst and Tixall Manuscripts," 140; "Even now that care," line 53, *The Collected Works of Mary Sidney Herbert*, 1:103.

9. This theory destabilizes what Roger Chartier has described as the author-function: "an essential weapon in the struggle waged against the spread and distribution of texts which were thought to be heterodox"; see "Figures of the Author," trans. L. G. Cochrane, *Of Authors and Origins*, 19. Re-engaging with the materiality and historical constructedness of texts, Jonathan Goldberg claims that "the value of texts lies in their contingency, not in some security or consolation they might offer" in *Voice Terminal Echo; Postmodernism and English Renaissance Texts*, 7. By rehearsing Dr. Johnson's charges against Macpherson's Ossian poems and his ghost-writing of Chambers's lectures on British law, Martha Woodmansee exposes how secret collaboration—fraudulent or

friendly—constitutes "a mode of writing which puts [the] notion of authorship in question"; see Woodsmansee & Jaszi, eds., "On the Authoring Effect," *The Construction of Authorship*, 21.

10. Robert Alter, "The Psalms," *The Literary Guide to the Bible*, 256.

11. George Puttenham, *The Arte of English Poesie*, 203.

12. John Taylor, *The Needles Excellency; A New Booke wherin are diuers Admirable Workes wrought with the Needle*, B3, B.

13. Thomas Moffet, *The Silkewormes and their Flies, Liuely described in verse (1599)*, 73.

14. Thomas Heywood, *Gynaikeion or Nine Bookes of Various History Concerning Women*, 398. On the issue of Pembroke's influence on her niece, Lady Mary Wroth, Margaret Hannay points out shadow identities for Pembroke in Wroth's *Urania* and a possible reworking of Pembroke's verse in Wroth's sonnet "O that I might but now as senselesse bee"; see *The Collected Works of Mary Sidney Herbert*, 1:31 and Mary Wroth, *The Countesse of Montgomeries URANIA*, 416.

15. Roland Barthes, *The Pleasure of the Text*, 64.

16. Michel Foucault, "What is an Author?" *The Foucault Reader*, 119.

17. Jeffrey Masten, *Textual Intercourse*, 20.

18. Lisa Jardine, *Reading Shakespeare Historically*, 145. However, my reading of the poem as audacious and self-proclamatory differs from Jardine's contentions about Pembroke losing "her selfhood into his" and providing "no clue whatsoever to [her] authentic voice."

19. Michael Brennan, "'A First raisde by thy blest hand, and what is mine / inspired by thee:' "The Sidney Psalter and the Countess of Pembroke's completion of the Sidneian Psalms," 43.

20. I am grateful to Marie Loughlin for the suggestions in her paper, "'Dissolved to ink while pens' impressions move': Bleeding and Authorship in Mary Sidney's 'To the Angel Spirit,'" delivered at the Conference of the Association of Canadian College and University Teachers of English, St. John's, Newfoundland, 2 June 1997.

21. Beth Wynne Fisken, "To the Angell spirit . . . : Mary Sidney's Entry into the World of Words," 269–70. Jonathan Goldberg, "The Countess of Pembroke's literal translation," *Subject and Object in Renaissance Culture*, 329; *Sodometries: Renaissance Texts, Modern Sexualities*, 101. Goldberg's earlier observation and acknowledgment of its source in Daniel Sibony's essay in *Yale French Studies*, that "Hamlet's 'inky cloak' invests him in writing," is also very suggestive for Pembroke's transformation of blood to ink; see "Hamlet's Hand," 313.

22. Goldberg, "Literal translation," 327–28. Jonathan Crewe, *Hidden Designs: The Critical Profession and Renaissance Literature*, 83.

23. Woudhuysen, *Sir Philip Sidney and the Circulation of Manuscripts*, 231.

24. John Donne, "Vpon the translation of the Psalmes by Sir Philip Sydney, and the Countesse of Pembroke his Sister," *Poetical Works*, lines 16–16, 21–2.

25. Spenser's sonnet was published in 1590; Michael Brennan conjectures that Pembroke had completed a "draft" of the whole Psalter by 1594, in "The Date of the Countess of Pembroke's Translation of the Psalms," 435.

26. John Harington, *Nugae Antiquae*, 1, 173. In *Sir Philip Sidney and the Circulation of Manuscripts*, H. R. Woudhuysen quotes Harington's lament about the Psalter's unpublished state and suggests a social link between Harington and the Countess. *Nugae Antiquae* includes eight of Mary Sidney's psalms; Margaret Hannay dismisses Harington's charge about the Countess's inability as "absurd" in *Philip's Phoenix: Mary Sidney, Countess of Pembroke*, 134.

27. Ringler, *The Poems of Sir Philip Sidney*, 502. Richard Lanham, *The Old Arcadia*, 183.

28. Coburn Freer, "The Countess of Pembroke in a World of Words," *Style*, 38. Rivkah Zim, *English Metrical Psalms; Poetry as Praise and Prayer 1535–1601*, 195.

29. The Countess reversed and rephrased two lines in Psalm 32; see Ringler, *The Poems of Sir Philip Sidney*, 315.

30. Ian D. McFarlane lists over 100 editions of Buchanan's psalm paraphrases, apparently first appearing in late 1565 or early 1566; see *Buchanan*, 102, 249, 255, 500–06. References to the *Geneva Bible* are based on *The Geneva Bible. A facsimile of the 1560 Edition*. Intro. L. E. Berry.

31. Théodore de Bèze, *The Psalmes of David, truly opened and explaned by paraphrasis*, 359.

32. To cite only a few, Lady Jane Grey declaimed a dramatic recitation of Psalm 51 on the scaffold, while Milton responded scornfully to Charles I's appropriation of the Psalter for political purposes; see John R. Knott, *Discourses of Martyrdom in English Literature, 1563–1694*, 164, and *Milton's Complete Prose Works*, 3: 381–82.

33. Max W. Thomas, "Reading and Writing the Renaissance Commonplace Book: A Question of Authorship?" *The Construction of Authorship*, 410.

34. John L. King, *Tudor Royal Iconography: Literature and Art in an Age of Religious Crisis*, 80. John Calvin, *The Psalms of Dauid and others. With M. John Caluins Commentaries*, 203. Anne Lake Prescott, "Evil Tongues at the Court of Saul: the Renaissance David as a Slandered Courtier," 167.

35. *A Defence of Poetry*, 22, 25, 42.

36. Golding, trans., *The Psalms of Dauid*, 14; George Buchanan, *Paraphrasis Psalmorum Davidis Poetica, multo quam ante hac castigatior: Auctore Georgio Buchanano*, 37.

37. Psalms 6.2, *Geneva Bible;* Calvin, *The Psalms of Dauid*, 16.

38. Bèze, *The Psalmes of David*, 9. Psalms 6.6, *The Geneva Bible*. David is certainly no stranger to tears; see 2 Samuel 1.12; 3.32; 12.21; 15.30; 19.1.

39. One possible, though highly conjectural, source could be the Hebrew verb describing the weakness of the eyes in verse 7, through a form of the verb meaning "to be moth-eaten." However, the question of the Sidneys' knowledge of Hebrew remains vexed. Theodore Steinberg makes the strongest case

for the Sidneys' access "either to the Hebrew language or to an accomplished 'Hebrician.'" The examples he cites, in addition to Babington, include Ralph Baynes, Thomas Bodley, Hugh Broughton, John Rainolds, William Alabaster and Thomas Gataker. As Steinberg reasons, "consequently, given the history of Christian Hebraica, the importance of Hebrew studies in the Reformation, Philip Sidney's interest in metrics, and Mary's interest in continuing her brother's work, as well as her own intelligence and interests, it would almost be more surprising if they had not known enough Hebrew to help them in their work on the Psalms"; see "The Sidneys and the Psalms," 8, 12.

40. John R. Kohlenberger III, editor. *The NIV Interlinear Hebrew-English Old Testament*, 352.

41. David Greer has transcribed a modern version, "O Lord, whose grace," of a manuscript setting of Pembroke's Psalm 51, based on BL Add MS 15117; see *The English Lute Songs; Songs from Manuscript Sources I*, 12–15.

42. Alter, "The Psalms," *The Literary Guide to the Bible*, 260; Walter Brueggemann, *The Message of the Psalms*, 20.

43. Bèze, *The Psalmes of David*, 126–27.

44. Puttenham, *The Arte of English Poesie*, 198.

45. Calvin, *The Psalms of Dauid and others*, 104.

46. Margaret Hannay notes that Bèze, Calvin, Lok, and the *Geneva Bible* "take out references to dancing even when present in the original Hebrew"; see "'Unlock my lipps': The *Miserere mei Deus* of Anne Vaughan Lok and Mary Sidney Herbert, Countess of Pembroke," *Privileging Gender in Early Modern England*, ed. Jean R. Brink, 31. Bèze, *The Psalmes of David*, 129.

47. Anne Lok, "A Meditation of a Penitent Sinner: Written in Maner of a Paraphrase upon the 51. Psalme of Dauid," *Sermons of John Calvin, upon the Songe that Ezechias made after he had bene sicke and afflicted by the hand of God*. For further background on Lok and her circle, see, for example, Patrick Collinson, "The Role of Women in the English Reformation Illustrated by the Life and Friendships of Anne Locke," *Godly People; Essays on English Protestantism and Puritanism*, 273–87; and Susanne Woods, "The Body Penitent: A 1560 Calvinist Sonnet Sequence," 137–40.

48. Hannay, "'Unlock my lipps,'" 31.

49. Calvin, *The Psalms of David and others*, 201–5.

50. Theodore Steinberg cites Pembroke's "references to cleansing the leprosy of the mind, since the Talmudic commentaries on these verses identified leprosy as the punishment for slander," as reflecting her "familiarity with the Hebrew originals" ("The Sidneys and the Psalms," 7–8).

51. Stephen Orgel, "What is an Editor?" 25.

52. Stacey Schlau and Electa Arenal, "Escrbiendo yo, escribiendo ella, escribiendo nosotras: On Co-Laboring," 49.

53. Goldberg, "Literal Translation," 326.

54. Louise Schleiner, *Tudor & Stuart Women Writers*, 57.

Constructing an Adventure and Negotiating for Narrative Control

Johnson and Boswell in the Hebrides

JOHN B. RADNER

On 18 August 1773 Samuel Johnson and James Boswell finally began the journey to "the Western Isles of Scotland" they had imagined making since shortly after they met in 1763. The trip, like the whole relationship, was richly and variously collaborative. Johnson and Boswell continued to play the roles they had developed as each learned to use the other to establish or confirm aspects of himself; and they played new, often surprising roles, too, in situations that invited or demanded fresh experiences.[1] Beginning the previous spring, they regularly conferred and contended with each other about when to begin, what to take, where to go, how long to stay, and who was really in charge. They also collaborated and competed in narrating the trip. Nowhere more clearly and suggestively than in the texts they wrote about this trip do we get a sense of Johnson and Boswell as two subjectivities continuously interacting: seeking and often achieving intimacy, yet also setting up boundaries and maintaining a sense of separation; sharing memories and fantasies as well as some of the texts they were currently producing, yet also striving to control the trip, the relationship, and the representation of all they experienced.[2]

When Boswell woke up on the second day of the trip, Johnson showed him what he had written about their first day of travel. Soon Boswell began showing Johnson *his* account of what they had done, including his comments on Johnson's notes. (For clarity's sake I will refer to what Johnson called his "book of remarks"[3] as his notebook, in contrast to Boswell's journal.) Then, seven days into the trip, Johnson wrote what Boswell described as "a long letter to Mrs. Thrale" ("I wondered to see him write so much so easily"),[4] the first of eleven travel letters to Thrale that Johnson did *not* share with Boswell. For the next seventy-six days Johnson and Boswell continued to exchange notebook and journal, while Johnson kept his letters private. Every day they observed things together, played their respective roles in public conversations, talked over what they had experienced, and planned what to do next. On most days each spent some time recording in notebook or journal what they had done, and on many days each read some of what the other had written, each process of writing or reading adding another layer of retrospection to each man's experience. (On a number of occasions Johnson also wrote to Hester Thrale and Boswell wrote to his wife.) Day after day each measured and defined himself against what he found in the other's conversation and writing, journeying further into the mind of his friend and traveling companion. In addition to paying special attention to specific objects and events in order to record the experience later, each might also wonder how the other would eventually describe what was just then happening. (Each would regularly come to the blank pages where the other would later recount recent events.) Each reader could respond in conversation or in his own text to what he found in the other's text; like authors of serial publications, each writer might get feedback from his reader before writing the next installment. In addition, since each reader was also a participant in the drama that both would eventually narrate, each could respond to what the other had already written—and perhaps even affect what might be written later—by acting up, acting out, and doing or saying something that would almost surely get recorded.

Following the trip, as Johnson and Boswell imagined publishing their respective accounts, they wrote more privately. In the spring of 1774 Johnson drew on his notebook and letters in writing *A Journey to the Western Islands*. Boswell supplied key materials but had no chance to review the manuscript before publication. Two months after the *Journey* was published, Boswell brought his Hebrides journal to London, hoping to publish a companion volume to Johnson's book. However, when he discovered that Johnson insisted on reviewing such a text, Boswell backed off. He revised the Hebrides journal for publication only after Johnson was no longer alive to see how he had modified what Johnson had read when it was first produced.

Traveling together for eighty-four days would in and of itself have significantly altered the relationship that was already in flux, especially since Boswell had recently made clear his plan to become Johnson's biographer. The changes one can imagine occurring just from their traveling together were intensified and augmented because of the collaborative (and anti-collaborative) production of texts during the trip and the subsequent tussle over publication. In some respects each of their Hebrides texts was unprecedented, as was the sustained cooperation and competition of the journey itself. Johnson had often resolved to keep a journal but had never written a detailed narrative for more than a few days.[5] Boswell had never read someone else's account of what he had seen and done; he had regularly written journals—including journals about his time with Johnson—and had often shown these to others, but aside from what he showed Johnson on 14 July 1763,[6] he had never shown entries to those he was currently writing about. Apart from the specimen of Boswell's journal he saw in 1763, Johnson had never read such a full account of what he had done and said, a text he was encouraged to correct and enrich. Whenever he was away from London, Johnson wrote frequent letters to Hester Thrale, although never such long letters ("longer than I ever wrote before" [2:100]), and never letters narrating events he had already described in his notebook and had mostly read about in Boswell's journal. Until the publication of his *Journey to the Western Islands,* Johnson had never produced a text by substantially revising his own earlier texts; and until 1775 Boswell had never been successfully thwarted in his wish to publish.

A comprehensive study of this trip would necessarily trace back to 1763 the deep and conflicting longings for intimacy and control that each man brought as informing scripts to this long-anticipated journey. It would also have to consider in detail how this period of intense intellectual and physical cooperation and competition—including the sustained struggle to control the private and public narrative of the trip—helped transform the latter half of the Johnson-Boswell relationship. Here I intend to focus primarily on the collaborative nature of the Hebrides texts in order to suggest that collaborative life writing could inevitably produce conflicts involving self-construction, self-understanding, and self-ownership.

Each of the texts describing the Hebrides trip—including the (probably quite different) versions of Boswell's journal that Boswell and Johnson imagined being published in 1775—was in various ways collaboratively produced. At the most basic level they were collaborative because they described the jointly conceived and executed trip that they, in turn, helped (re)shape. Like most written texts, each was also collaborative in the sense of being written with a specific audience in mind: a single initial reader for those written in Scotland (notebook, journal, letters), a more diverse audience for those imagined and written later. They were also collaborative because they responded to texts written by the other. Each extant text (and the missing notebook) was written with the knowledge that there already existed or would be other narratives recounting the same moment and was therefore, to some extent, in dialogue with these other texts. Boswell in his journal and Johnson in his letters were often re-writing what the other had already described, and each was perhaps writing in anticipation of what the other would write later. The texts written or planned after the trip were collaborative revisions of what each had written earlier, revisions affected by each writer's awareness that a rival account of the trip and the relationship was potentially or already in print. With the significant exception of Johnson's letters, each of these texts was also collaborative because Johnson and Boswell gave the other space, tried to understand and accommodate one another's point of view, and invited response and even fuller participation (though Boswell wanted a much larger role in producing the *Journey* than Johnson permitted). Finally—and I think most interestingly— Boswell's journal and Johnson's *Journey* were each, in various ways, privately addressed to the other, complementing their conversation throughout this eighty-four-day trip, saying what could be communicated only through a written text.[7] Boswell used his journal to ask Johnson questions he might have asked directly but seemingly did not, to communicate feelings and attitudes he could best or only express by writing as if to a general audience, to convey a full sense of his rich relationship with Johnson, and to establish Boswell's credentials as Johnson's biographer. When he revised his notebook and letters for a large audience—as well as for Boswell and Thrale—Johnson included material he knew would be especially significant to the man whose journal Johnson had earlier partially resisted, items he knew only Boswell would fully appreciate, statements about himself and Boswell and their relationship that he could express only in this indirect mode.

Instead of attempting complete readings of the texts Johnson and Boswell produced as they traveled and wrote or imagined later, I briefly want to suggest how each text comes most fully to life when viewed as collaboratively constructed. As part of this process, I also wish to explore how collaborative writing about their shared experience heightened concerns about identity and privacy that were always part of an evolving relationship, which began with Boswell asking Johnson to help plan his life and by Easter 1773 had Boswell confirmed as the one who would write Johnson's *Life*.

Because Johnson's "book of remarks" has not survived, one must infer its contents from other texts (see *Hebrides*, 270, 315, 333). In format and tone it probably resembled what Johnson wrote when he traveled through Wales in 1774 and to Paris in 1775, including a fair amount of narrative, much precise description and discriminating analysis, an occasional autobiographical memory, yet few longings or regrets (see *Diaries*, 163–222, 228–56). One can plausibly infer from the lack of comment in Boswell's journal that Johnson wrote nothing in his notebook that antagonized Boswell. But all one knows for certain about the notebook is that Johnson kept it steadily and regularly shared it with Boswell, starting on the morning of 19 August, when Boswell woke and "Found Mr. Johns. up. He shewed me his notes of yesterday's jaunt. Wonderfully minute, and exact except as to not seeing trees and hedges" (*Hebrides*, 38, n.1). Whatever lay behind this seemingly intimate gesture— Johnson may have been pleased that he had so quickly begun to write the sort of journal he had often resolved to keep and shared his first entry to help keep himself on track; or he may have been trying to control the narration of the trip as he had controlled their itinerary the day before (*Hebrides*, 35; *Letters*, 2:54); or Johnson may have shared what *he* wrote in order to encourage Boswell to show Johnson *his* journal— Boswell soon began showing his journal to Johnson, significantly transforming their relationship in the process.

In contrast to Johnson's notebook—a text about which one can only conjecture—Boswell's *Hebrides* journal is abundantly available. Given such good material and the fact that he had Johnson as a steady reader, Boswell wrote more about the first nine weeks of this trip than about any comparable period in his life. Boswell's journals were always collaborative in the sense that he gave considerable space to what others had said

in his presence, and wrote with the knowledge that he might later
share entries with special friends. Yet here the dynamic was different.
The major character in the drama being recorded was the first to read
Boswell's account of what he and Johnson had done and said. Having
helped produce scenes and conversations, Boswell selectively narrated
what had happened, probably recalling how Johnson had already described these events in his notebook, perhaps wondering what Johnson
was writing in his letters to Thrale, and always knowing that Johnson
would later read whatever he had written. Like Johnson's notebook,
Boswell's ongoing account soon became part of this richly collaborative
trip. Though Boswell was known to plan ahead, there is no evidence to
suggest that he anticipated sharing his journal with Johnson before he
read Johnson's notebook on 19 August. Nor do I think either man realized at the start just how satisfying and frustrating this process would be,
or how it would radically alter their friendship by foreshadowing Boswell's role as Johnson's biographer.

Throughout the journal Boswell presented their shared experience
from his perspective, inviting Johnson to clarify or perhaps rewrite what
had already happened in order to help Boswell (re)shape the rest of this
journey—and consequently the balance of their relationship. Most obvious are the blanks Boswell left when he "was not quite sure of what
[Johnson] had said" (*Hebrides*, 294), blanks that functioned as requests
for Johnson to supply the missing word(s). Also fairly clear are the notes
Boswell occasionally wrote to himself about topics he wished to discuss:
"I must set him to inquire if evil has place in Raasay" (153); "I must have
this more amply discussed with him" (188); "This too must be discussed" (193); "I must hear Mr. Johnson upon this subject" (329; see also
60, 165, 219). Ostensibly memos to himself, these notes functioned as
questions to Johnson when he read Boswell's text.

For the most part, however, in the journal Boswell addressed unspecified others who might someday read his text, and the power of
Boswell's appeal to Johnson depended on his bringing these others to
mind as Johnson read the journal. He listed a number of Johnson's
"particularities which it is impossible to explain"—like never wearing a
nightcap, always sleeping with a window open, and often "speaking to
himself" (297–98)—in the hope that Johnson would comment (298, n.1).
He recorded enigmatic statements—"It is true, whether I am in earnest
or no" (226)—in effect asking Johnson to correct or clarify. He described Johnson's puzzling behavior—his laughing "with a glee that

was astonishing" as he imagined what he might do with an island Mac-Leod had offered him, "how he would build a house, how he would fortify it . . . how he would sally out and *take* the Isle of Muck" (211)—in the process requesting some explanation. When he speculated about Johnson's motives—he "suppose[d]" that Johnson was "displeased" that Boswell had told the MacLeods that 18 September was his birthday "from wishing to have nothing particular done on his account" (183)— he was inviting Johnson to confirm or correct this interpretation.

More important, Boswell used the journal to report behavior that frightened and disturbed him, as well as to explain why he had done what seemed most to upset Johnson. For instance, the entry for 1 September described Johnson's unexpected, relationship-threatening anger when Boswell rode off toward Glenelg, explaining at length why he had started to ride ahead until Johnson "called [him] back with a tremendous shout" (though not why he had neglected to tell Johnson that he was leaving): "[M]y intentions were not improper. I wished to be forward to see if Sir A. Macdonald had sent his boat; and if not, how we were to sail, and how we were to lodge, all which I thought I could best settle myself, without his having any trouble. . . . [H]is attention to everything in his way, and his uncommon desire to be always in the right, would make him weigh if he knew of the particulars; and therefore it was right for me to weigh them, and let him have them only in effect" (110–11; see also 251–52). By fully explaining what he was too flustered to express at the time, and by including a complimentary critique of Johnson ("To apply his great mind to minute particulars is wrong"), Boswell tried fully to justify himself to Johnson, and perhaps prompt Johnson to explain the "passion" he had refused to clarify at the time, or later that night, or the next morning (110–13).

Similarly, Boswell used the entry for 16 September to tell how "truly curious" it was to hear Johnson say that he had "*often* thought" of "keeping a seraglio," but mainly to describe how he felt when Johnson first said he would "admit" Boswell into his seraglio only "if he were properly prepared" as "a very good eunuch" ("He'd do his part well"), and then responded to Boswell's aggressive reply ("I take it . . . better than you would do your part") by expatiating "with such fluency" on Boswell's "office as eunuch . . . that it really hurt me." Having shown the scene from his own perspective ("He made me quite contemptible for the moment"), Boswell asked Johnson to confirm that he "imagined him to be more serious in this extraordinary raillery than he really was," or at least to acknowledge that Boswell was "of a firmer metal than Langton and can stand a rub better" (177).

Boswell might easily have asked Johnson directly about the various things he made notes about to discuss sometime, and he might even have asked why Johnson was upset at having his birthday acknowledged. However, the journal makes clear that when Boswell first tried to explain his riding ahead to Glenelg, he "justified [him]self but lamely" (110) in the face of Johnson's anger. When Boswell tried to defend himself later that night, "Johnson was still violent upon that subject" and shocked Boswell by saying that if he had not come back when called, Johnson would "have returned with you to Edinburgh and then parted, and never spoke to you more" (112). The following morning, when an anxious Boswell told Johnson "how uneasy he had made me by what he had said," Johnson admitted that he had spoken "in passion," and would have been "ten times worse" than Boswell had he acted on his threat. But it was only in the journal, narrating the scene for a reader who had not been there, that Boswell could tell Johnson why his riding ahead made perfect sense, ask him to explain his passion, and confirm his promise to give him "fair warning in case of any quarrel" (112–13). It was also only in this shared journal that Boswell dared to express to Johnson—and for the first time could easily express—the discomfort and anger he had often felt at Johnson's harsh teasing.

By sharing his journal with Johnson, putting himself constantly on duty, Boswell invited Johnson to share and endorse Boswell's controlling vision of Boswell, of Johnson, and of their relationship. More consistently, it seems, than in his actual conversations with Johnson as Boswell had recorded these, or in all but a few early letters, Boswell showed Johnson his melancholy (118, 122), his fears and insecurities (37 n.9, 75, 95, 149, 249–50, 289–90), and his worries about excessive drinking (119, 160, 222, 240) partly to ask for help and partly to reaffirm that Johnson loved him despite his weaknesses. At the same time, Boswell presented himself as a mature Johnsonian who valued Johnson's clarification of "the satisfaction of Christ" (63) and shared Johnson's political principles (162–63). He demonstrated his ability to record scenery (141–51), describe the construction of cottages (219–20), and explain customs like "fosterage" (259–60) with the specificity, precision, and clear sense of economy he associated with Johnson's notebook and conversation, and undoubtedly was pleased when Johnson copied into his notebook part of Boswell's journal on Raasay (241–42). He constructed brief and sustained

"Johnsonian" reflections on country life (122), happiness (153), self-deception (224), reading logs (237), and why the "scenes through which a man has gone improve by lying in the memory" (329). In addition, he showed that he still maintained positions Johnson had seemingly refuted, often including arguments Boswell himself had been unable or unwilling to voice earlier (141, 183, 193, 238).

In general, Boswell used the journal to establish his authority to narrate this portion of Johnson's life and his credentials to narrate the rest. He regularly reported in the journal what their hosts and others had told Boswell about Johnson (47, 170, 208, 232, 236, 244). He also repeatedly showed how Johnson appeared in a variety of unusual situations: striding across Inch Keith "like a giant among the luxuriant thistles and nettles" (36), "asleep in his miserable sty [in Glenmoriston] . . . with a coloured handkerchief tied round his head" (106), sitting "high on the stern [of Raasay's boat] like a magnificent Triton" (127), or creeping "wonderfully" into a cave near Ullinish (199). Boswell also carefully described a number of dramatic interchanges, like the comical "double talking" on 5 October when Johnson and Mr. Hector Maclean each simultaneously talked *at* the other while neither really listened (256–57). Besides flattering and amusing Johnson, these passages demonstrated Boswell's access to material about this trip that only he could make available to Johnson.

Boswell also used the journal to demonstrate his ability to appreciate and assess Johnson. Though there were moments when Johnson's behavior puzzled him, Boswell generally wrote with assurance about Johnson's motives and character: "He is really generous, loves influence, and has a way of gaining it" (103). "[T]hough he treats his friends with uncommon freedom, he does not like a return" (177). Early in the journal he told how, when Johnson appeared "to faint in his resolution" for the trip ("If we must *ride* much, we shall not go; and there's an end on't"), Boswell got him to recommit to "our wild Tour" by shrewdly challenging his courage and ability: "Why, sir, you was beginning to despond yesterday. You're a delicate Londoner—you're a macaroni! You can't ride!" (58). Boswell also knew Johnson well enough to "contriv[e] that he shall be easy wherever he goes" (231), and on occasion to cover for him (174, 299).

Throughout the journal Boswell assessed Johnson with seeming impartiality and poise. He praised Johnson's intellectual and moral achievements, including his "minute observation" (293) and amazing "variety of knowledge" (208), courage (322), "firmness of mind" (118, 105), "proper pride" (287), and "delicacy" (288). Moreover, he described Johnson with a detached, critical perspective that his companion might not easily have anticipated from Boswell's conversation. When he quoted Johnson's observations and arguments, Boswell regularly included an endorsement ("Mr. Johnson justly observed" [99]), an objection ("Here, however, I think Mr. Johnson mistaken" [99]), or some other addition ("I could illustrate this by saying . . ." [64]). He spelled out what was in character for Johnson (responding to disappointment with "philosophy," as "the Rambler . . . nobly teaches" [112], or reacting with "good humour" when "a neat, pretty little girl . . . sat down on [his] knee . . . put her hands round his neck and kissed him" [226]) and what was not (imagining Boswell's dish milk was "better than his" and wanting to taste it [107], or acting "as if he [Johnson] had been a *young buck* indeed" and so falling down while dismounting [165]). He analyzed Johnson's "robust sophistry" (341; see also 216, 234, 265), critically described his "copious exaggeration" on the subject of Scotland before the Union (95), his seemingly groundless anger (110–12), his insensitive and even cruel aggression (177), his harsh and seemingly gratuitous insults (293, 294, 322), his playful (107) and petulant (227) opposition, and his occasional resistance to Boswell's efforts to manage the trip collaboratively ("I shall not consult you" [236], 218, 301–2). At one point the journal even expressed exasperation and anger at Johnson's insulting failure to appreciate Boswell's responsibility and general good sense: "Mr. Johnson was displeased at my bustling and walking quickly up and down. He said it did not hasten us a bit. It was getting on horseback in the ship. 'All boys do it,' said he; 'and you are longer a boy than others.' He himself has no alertness, or whatever it may be called; so he may dislike it, as *Oderunt hilarem tristes* ['Gloomy people hate a merry fellow']" (294).

Ideally Johnson would read the journal, answer Boswell's questions, explain what was puzzling or disturbing, and open himself up more fully. He would see Boswell's worth, accept his criticisms, and change his own behavior. He would applaud Boswell's "admirable talent of leading the conversation . . . starting topics and making the company pursue them" (231), and agree that the trip (and the relationship) was a "co-partnery" in which each played a complementary role, and "each was to do all he could to promote its success" (243). He would recognize how intelligently he was appreciated by Boswell and acknowledge this "scrupulously exact" journal as "a very exact picture of his life" (245)—a

full and judicious narrative of this adventurous trip, enriched with stories about Johnson that Boswell had earlier heard from Johnson and
from others, with his own memories of past events, and with the fruits of
his attentive study of Johnson. He would confirm Boswell's ability to
understand and appraise Johnson's character, his right to narrate (and
perhaps even co-produce) the rest of Johnson's life (300).

Johnson's frequent reading of the journal, his provision of extra
paper, and his urging Boswell to beg for more rather than "contract"
the journal (271; see also 293) reflect his delight with this remarkably full
text, which contained "as much of what I say and do, as of all other occurrences together," as he told Hester Thrale midway through the trip
(*Letters*, 2:95). His explicit praise—"It grows better and better" (*Hebrides*,
188); "The more I read of this, I think the more highly of you" (226)—
suggests that the sustained "conversation" Johnson had with Boswell as
he read the journal was one reason he wrote to Thrale near the end of
the trip that Boswell "has better faculties, than I had imagined, more
justness of discernment, and more fecundity of images" (*Letters*, 2:115).
At the same time, Johnson's behavior during the trip suggests that he
was not totally delighted with this seductively full narrative of the trip
that only Boswell had made possible, for he refused to cooperate fully
with this collaborative project. Of course, everything Johnson did or
said provided Boswell with material, even his sleeping (106) or not coming down to breakfast (218). On 22 August and again on 14 October
Johnson "readily" answered questions about "several particulars of his
life from his early years" (300) while Boswell wrote down his responses,
and throughout the trip Johnson shared autobiographical memories
and private fantasies to what seems like an unprecedented extent (see,
e.g., 45, 50, 169, 174, 176, 192, 252), though perhaps Boswell was simply
more assiduous in recording these than in the past. But aside from once
filling in "blanks" and correcting "mistakes" in the journal (293–94),
and once rejecting Boswell's analysis of his "fallacy in logic" (216, 245),
Johnson almost aggressively failed to respond, as Boswell "hoped he
would have done" (298, n.3), to the many hints, queries, and intention-
ally provocative statements, leaving his biographer momentarily unin-
formed. Helping produce Boswell's journal was more fully collaborative
than writing a chapter for Charlotte Lennox's work *The Female Quixote*
(1752) or (starting in 1772) dictating legal briefs to Boswell, and much
more was at stake than in Johnson's sustained collaboration with Sir
Robert Chambers on his Vinerian Lectures (1766–69).[8] Johnson's desire

for intimate, open-ended adventure conflicted both with Boswell's wish
to record and assess and with Johnson's longing for control. Even as he
answered his biographer's explicit questions about his early life and delighted in Boswell's ample account of their journey, Johnson resisted the
power of the journal to pin him down. He retained power by concealing
the real cause of his unexpected anger on 1 September, and by repeatedly withholding full information. He also held a conversation with
Hester Thrale from which Boswell was pointedly excluded, and he subsequently published his own account of the trip.

By turning away from his layered conversation with Boswell to
correspond with Thrale—Johnson wrote her more letters in these three
months than he had sent Boswell in the previous ten years—Johnson
actively resisted the confining power of Boswell's narrative, momentarily escaped Boswell's judgmental scrutiny, and told his own story. Even
when he was not writing *against* Boswell by constructing versions of what
had happened that were at odds with Boswell's "exact picture of his life,"
he was consciously writing apart from Boswell, though always aware of
what had been written in Boswell's journal and his own notebook. These
letters differ strikingly from the journal—and probably from the notebook as well—in their overall account of the journey and the Johnson-
Boswell relationship. Where Boswell showed Johnson being guided—
even manipulated—by a Boswell who boasted of his ability to set
Johnson physically and mentally in motion, Johnson often represented
himself as very much in charge even during moments that Boswell described quite differently (see, e.g., *Letters*, 2:77 vs. *Hebrides*, 112). At times
Johnson simply ignored Boswell, writing whole letters without assigning
any specific role to Boswell (2:81–84) or even mentioning him (2:62–65).
In addition, many references to Boswell are unflattering, especially
those describing the Inn at Glenelg, a passage written just after Johnson
interrupted his narrative to complain that "Boswel, with some of his
troublesome kindness, has informed this family, and reminded me that
the eighteenth of September is my birthday" (2:75). Johnson reported
Boswell's ineffectual anger and impatience ("Boswel blustered, but
nothing could he get" [2:76]), in contrast to his own poise ("Boswel was
very angry, and reproached [Sir Alexander Macdonald] with his improper parsimony. I did not much reflect upon the conduct of a man
with whom I was not likely to converse as long at any other time" [2:77]).
He also described Boswell's timidity at sea (2:100, 107), his fear of ghosts
(2: 92, 105), and recounted with delight how the Countess of Eglington

"called Boswel the boy," who happily was "in a good school" with John-son (2:116).

Instead of emphasizing how much fun he was having with Boswell, Johnson expressed his longing for the Thrales (2:54, 65, 103). A day or two before his birthday and again two weeks later Johnson implied that Boswell lacked the ability to set his mind in motion, claiming that if the Thrales had been there, "we should have produced some reflections among us either poetical or philosophical" (2:73), "we should have ex-cited the attention, and enlarged the observations of each other" (2:94–95). Momentarily free of the pressure of Boswell's company, Johnson could relax while writing these letters, secure in the knowledge that Bos-well would not be a reader. On 15 September he played with the idea of having the Thrales visit the island Macleod offered him (2:71). A few days later Johnson made up for the lack of letters *from* Thrale by musing at length about how she was "possibly imagining that I am withdrawn from the gay and the busy world into regions of peace and pastoral felic-ity, and enjoying the reliques of the golden age" (2:78). In Boswell's com-pany Johnson "could not bear to be treated like an old or infirm man, and was very unwilling to accept of any assistance," so at Iona, "when Sir Allan Maclean and [Boswell] submitted to be carried on men's shoul-ders from the boat to the shore . . . [Johnson] sprang into the sea and waded vigorously out" (*Hebrides*, 363–64). In his letters to Thrale, how-ever, Johnson regularly spoke of his poor health (2:62, 75, 98, 102), re-garding his physical limitations with self-mocking humor ("Scrambling I have not willingly left off, the power of scrambling has left me" [2:114]). On his birthday he expressed at great length some of his fearful, angry thoughts when he looked "back upon threescore and four years, in which little has been done, and little has been enjoyed" (2:75)—thoughts he did not fully share with Boswell. He wrote mini-essays on the use of travel and on the unhappiness of life in these islands, as if to compensate for his limited ability to explore this rugged landscape with Boswell (2:78–79, 88–89). Toward the end of his last long letter from the Hebrides, John-son declared his desire "to instruct myself in the whole system of pastoral life" (2:94), devoting thirteen paragraphs to a discussion of the food, fuel, housing, climate, and livestock on the Hebrides, displaying a thorough-ness and analytical sophistication never approached by Boswell's jour-nal, a poise that anticipated the book Johnson planned to write.

Soon after he returned to London, Johnson drew on the two texts he had produced incrementally throughout the trip to write what he hoped would be not only the first but the only public account of the journey, a book that would justify this extended adventure and establish his control over his own story. While clearly addressing whoever might read a book that analyzed life in the Hebrides and proposed changes in government policy, Johnson also wrote directly and privately to Thrale—and especially to Boswell—whenever he wrote about Boswell and himself. To Thrale, Johnson was knowingly winking, assured she would see how differently Boswell and Johnson appeared in the *Journey* than in his letters. To Boswell, Johnson's communication in the *Journey* was much richer, as he finally responded to Boswell's journal. He publicly affirmed an unqualified respect for Boswell, acknowledged that his criticisms were on target, partially explained the anger that so upset Boswell on 1 September, and edged toward openly assigning him the role of his own conscience.

Johnson replaced the "Boswell" who mainly inhabited his letters with the "Boswell" of the journal. He deleted references to Boswell's "troublesome kindness," his ineffectual anger, and his fear of ghosts. When a strong wind blew their ship to Col, both travelers (and not just Boswell) "were willing to call it a tempest," with Johnson adding, "I was sea-sick and lay down. Mr. Boswell kept the deck."[9] Johnson also assigned Boswell positive qualities he knew would be appreciated, such as "gaiety of conversation and civility of manners," "acuteness of observation [which] would help my inquiry" (3), and "inquisitiveness . . . seconded by great activity" (11; see also 117, 125, 133, 138, 144, 145). Having mainly described Boswell's ineffectual—even inaccurate—voice in his letters, Johnson here credited Boswell with sensible reflections on what they observed (125, 133). He even suggested that his five-page chapter on "The Highlands" (43–47) contained what he and Boswell had discussed on 1 September while riding together "at leisure to extend our speculations, and to investigate the reason of those peculiarities by which such rugged regions as these before us are generally distinguished" (43). Johnson also privileged Boswell's feelings, first reporting his being "much affected" by the ruins of Iona, then adding that their ride the next afternoon "was through a country of such gloomy desolation, that Mr. Boswell thought no part of the Highlands equally terrifick" (153). Johnson's competition with Boswell to see and describe and analyze, as reported throughout Boswell's journal (see, e.g., 107, 266–67), has here been replaced by praise of Boswell's mental powers and sensibility. We last see Boswell "clamber[ing]" with Johnson through the ruined "old castle" at Auchinleck (161), partly fulfilling the fantasy of domestic intimacy Johnson had articulated when he first heard Boswell describe his family estate ("I must be there, and we will live in the Old Castle; and if there is no room remaining, we will build one").[10] Having already imagined a reciprocal process when he wrote Thrale from Auchinleck that "Boswell will praise my resolution and perseverance; and I shall in return celebrate his good humour and perpetual cheerfulness" (2:115), Johnson now described Boswell in ways that would surely please, perhaps hoping his fellow-traveler would endorse the new image of a Johnson who was cautious but still decisive, compassionate but tough-minded, nostalgic but sensible.

Johnson further encouraged Boswell to endorse this revised "Johnson" by acknowledging some of Boswell's explicit criticisms. As if agreeing that he had been excessively pushy, Johnson masked his competitiveness, occasionally even denying having been in charge when both surviving early accounts agreed that Johnson had taken the lead. At the Buller of Buchan, for instance, Johnson wrote that "*we* saw some boats, and rowers, and resolved to explore the Buller" (*Journey*, 20; emphasis added), a significant change from what Boswell (*Hebrides*, 72) and Johnson (*Letters*, 2:62) had written previously. Early in the *Journey* Johnson also mocked his notorious anti-Scottish prejudice by reporting that at the inn at Montrose "we did not find a reception such as we thought proportionate to the commercial opulence of the place; but Mr. Boswell desired me to observe that the innkeeper was an Englishman, and I then defended him as well as I could" (*Journey*, 12; see also *Hebrides*, 48–50).

Johnson even edged toward apologizing for his angry attack on Boswell's "incivility" in riding ahead to Glenelg, and for his shocking declaration afterward that "had you gone on, I was thinking that I should have returned with you to Edinburgh and then parted, and never spoke to you more" (*Hebrides*, 110–12). In describing the climb over Rattikin that preceded his surprising outburst, Johnson added the following key information he had kept from both Boswell and Thrale (2: 76): "Upon one of the precipices, my horse, weary with the steepness of the rise, staggered a little, and I called in haste to the Highlander to hold him. This was the only moment of my journey, in which I thought myself endangered" (48). This is the sort of personal material Johnson usually eliminated in transforming notebook and letters into a public narrative. There seems to be no apparent reason to tell readers about his fear, but this fact could show Boswell why Johnson became so upset when he suddenly rode away. Having come to see this episode from Boswell's point of view—first when they discussed it the next morning and more fully when he saw in the journal how deeply his threat had troubled Boswell—Johnson now helped Boswell view it from his perspective by describing how he had felt when his weary horse "staggered a little."

In a richly suggestive passage midway through the *Journey* Johnson also partially apologized to Boswell for having resisted his necessary planning, complimenting him for his energy and clear sense of purpose: "At Dunvegan, I had tasted lotus, and was in danger of forgetting that I was ever to depart, till Mr Boswell sagely reproached me with my sluggishness and softness. I had no very forcible defence to make, and we agreed to pursue our journey" (71; see also *Hebrides*, 185). Though Johnson's rhetoric is self-mockingly inflated, the point remains crucial. This passage comes close to stating what I think Johnson began to realize as he read Boswell's journal and then more fully grasped as he relived the trip while writing the *Journey:* Boswell was beginning to assume the role of Johnson's conscience. By writing a journal where he "moralised, and found my faults, and laid them up to reproach me" (*Letters*, 2:228)—as Johnson wrote Thrale in June 1775, knowing she had just read Boswell's journal—and by collecting information for a biography that would be written only after Johnson had died, Boswell began to be connected in Johnson's mind with death and judgment. Although Johnson kept to himself the meditations he recorded during Holy Week, in 1773 he shared most of Good Friday with Boswell, and at dinner on Easter Sunday he discussed the biographical project.[11] In September 1777 he confessed some of his birthday fears to Thrale, not Boswell. But in writing to Thrale on his birthday, and again in his private diary six days later, Johnson admitted that he might have forgotten this birthday—and his need on that particular day to review his past and resolve to change—had not Boswell disrupted his holiday detachment by reminding him (*Letters*, 2:75; *Diaries*, 160). Having already used the journal to confirm that Johnson had agreed to "write expressly in support of Christianity" (*Hebrides*, 64), and to give Boswell "fair warning in case of any quarrel" (113), Boswell had unwittingly taken on the role of Johnson's moral conscience, recalling the birthday and, in the process, reminding Johnson to review his life and resolve to change.

Johnson's self-narration as he traveled through Scotland and then described his journey—regularly reading Boswell's journal as he wrote his notebook, letters, and birthday meditation; twice answering Boswell's detailed questions about his early life while probably recalling much that he did not tell Boswell; then creating a public persona for his longest surviving personal narrative—must have heightened his sense of how variously he constructed himself in conversation and writing, depending on the audience and the specific occasion. Each self-narrative was necessarily selective, potentially contradicting other self-narratives, in real or imagined competition with the narratives of others, and reflecting anxious uncertainty concerning God's "reading." The collaborative and competitive process of narrating the Hebrides trip also showed Johnson how difficult it was to assess his own life. If Johnson alone could say with assurance why he had exploded when Boswell rode ahead to Glenelg, or how he felt about his birthday, as Johnson had argued in *Idler* 84,[12] Boswell was clearly the authority on how Johnson's actions affected him. Reading Boswell's journal let Johnson see, on a daily basis, how everything he did had affected his biographer and those who shared their reactions with Boswell. Johnson saw, remembered, and drew on these memories in writing the *Journey*.

While the *Journey* praised Boswell, gave him a voice, and acknowledged his role in Johnson's life, he had no direct role in writing or editing the text Johnson referred to in 1774 as "our travels" (*Letters*, 2:134) and "our 'Journey to the Hebrides'" (155), and in 1777 as "our narrative" (3:31). Johnson realized that Thrale was "tolerably well acquainted with the expedition" once she, too, had read Boswell's account (2:223). However, having printed his own account of their joint experience, Johnson managed to keep Boswell's narrative out of print.

Early in the trip Boswell had probably seen that he wanted to publish his collaboratively constructed journal, which Johnson said "might be printed, were the subject fit for printing" (*Hebrides* 188), thus permitting the world to see how carefully Boswell had produced and recorded this trip, how richly he shared in this part of Johnson's life. Even after Johnson surprised Boswell by mentioning his plan to write about the trip (*Hebrides*, 333, 341), Boswell asked Sir John Pringle about publishing something first.[13] Disappointed that he could not come to London in March 1774, just when Johnson was about to begin writing the *Journey*, in June Boswell vented his anger when he learned that Johnson had sent his manuscript directly to the printer without first showing it to him (*Letters*, 2:144, 145). In March 1775 Boswell brought his Hebrides journal to London, hoping to publish a companion volume to the *Journey*. However, on 27 March, when he mentioned to Johnson his wish to publish a version of this text—which much more appropriately than the *Journey* could be called "our narrative"—Johnson "advised me not to show my journal to anybody, but bid me draw out of it what I thought might be published, and he would look it over."[14] In other words, Johnson now suggested major revision of the text he had read and praised, necessitating a further collaboration over which he might have final control.

Boswell tried but was unable to revise the journal for Johnson to review, mainly because he sensed Johnson's reluctance to have him "*share* reputation with himself." He defiantly showed the journal to Joshua Reynolds immediately after Johnson had advised him not to show it to anyone, and two months later he also showed it to Hester Thrale, knowing this would upset Johnson. At least twice he contemplated defying Johnson even more fully by publishing a version of his journal without clearing it with him,[15] as he had earlier published his book on Corsica despite Johnson's advice that he "mind [his] own affairs and leave the Corsicans to theirs" (*Letters*, 1:273). However, Boswell hesitated, realizing that printing his collaboratively produced account of the trip—a text that combined admiration with occasional disapproval and partially established Boswell's authority by noting Johnson's limitations—would risk aborting the larger biographical project.[16]

Although Johnson retained control of the public narrative of the trip and the relationship, he did so at a cost. The relationship never again achieved the sustained, hopeful intimacy experienced in the Hebrides. Johnson continued to narrate himself to—and through—Boswell, especially in 1776 when they traveled together to Oxford, Birmingham and Lichfield, the landscape of Johnson's early life. Boswell continued to produce, direct, and record Johnson's experience, most notably in the famous dinner (15 May 1776) with John Wilkes. But because Johnson had kept Boswell from publishing a journal that was so full of what Johnson had said and done, so intimately self-revealing, and so open to Johnson's additions and comments, Boswell pulled back. His disappointment and anger at having no part in publicly narrating the trip he had worked so hard to produce helped ensure that he would share only a few more journal entries, despite Johnson's curiosity (*Letters*, 3:79), and also made Boswell reluctant even to talk about plans for another big trip with Johnson (*Letters*, 2:156; 3:57-58, 65-66). Although Boswell published essays on a monthly basis for six years (1777-83), he only shared them with Johnson in 1784,[17] at which time he also showed him the few new entries he had added to the Hebrides journal after 1773 (347-54). In

1785, following Johnson's death the previous year, Boswell completed, revised, and finally published what he had earlier imagined as the first of a series of publications documenting his time spent with Johnson. Boswell added or modified certain passages precisely because Johnson would not now be a reader, but throughout this text—as well as in the *Life of Johnson*, which he began to write in 1786—Boswell continued to interact and converse with the man whose affectionate openness had initially engaged him, but whose anger, personal insults, guardedness, and resistance to full collaboration had so disturbed and puzzled him throughout the Hebrides trip and long thereafter.

Notes

In writing this essay I received astute comments from Elly Greene, Marjorie Stone, and Judith Thompson. I also profited from the suggestions of reviewers at the University of Wisconsin Press.

1. See Bate, *Samuel Johnson*, 462–75; Brady, *James Boswell: The Later Years*, 64–80; Brian Finney, "Boswell's Hebridean Journal and the Ordeal of Dr. Johnson," 319–34; and Radner, "Boswell's and Johnson's Sexual Rivalry," 201–46.

2. The present essay builds on and complements my argument at the start of "'A Very Exact Picture of His Life': Johnson's Role in Writing the *Life of Johnson*," 299–342.

3. Johnson, *The Letters of Samuel Johnson*, 2:95; hereafter *Letters*.

4. Boswell, *Boswell's Journal of a Tour to the Hebrides with Samuel Johnson, LL.D.*, 79; hereafter *Hebrides*.

5. Johnson, *Diaries, Prayers, and Annals*, 71, 82, 110, 147, 155; hereafter *Diaries*.

6. In his letter (Yale MS L528) to Andrew Erskine dated 5–22 July 1763—reprinted in *The General Correspondence of James Boswell, 1757–63* (forthcoming in 2006)—Boswell reported that when Johnson encouraged him "to keep a journal of my life, fair and undisguised," he then "gave him a specimen" to read—probably the entry for 6 July 1763—at which Johnson "laughed placid, and said very well." Material from the Yale Boswell Papers is cited by permission of Yale University.

7. This listing of collaborative modes is indebted to Ede and Lunsford, *Singular Texts/Plural Authors*, as well as to essays by Michael Schrage, James S. Leonard and Christine E. Wharton, Linda K. Hughes and Michael Lund, Jeanette Harris, and Laura Brady collected in *Author-ity and Textuality*, ed. Leonard et al.

8. On Johnson's work with Chambers, see the latter's *Course of Lectures on the English Law*, 1:11–29; see also Woodmansee, "On the Author Effect; Recovering Collectivity," 21–23.

9. Johnson, *A Journey to the Western Islands of Scotland*, 120; hereafter *Journey*.

10. Boswell, *Boswell's London Journal, 1762–1763*, 331.

11. Johnson, *Diaries*, 153, 156–57; Boswell, *Boswell for the Defence, 1769–1774*, 171–75.

12. Johnson, *The Idler and The Adventurer*, 263.

13. On 2 February 1774, responding to a letter not noted in Boswell's registry (Yale MS M253), Pringle advised Boswell to wait until Johnson had published his own account (Yale MS C2308).

14. Boswell, *Boswell: The Ominous Years, 1774–1776*, 102.

15. Crawford, ed., *The Correspondence of James Boswell and William Johnson Temple, 1756–1795*, 1:372, 403.

16. See Radner, "From Paralysis to Power: Boswell with Johnson in 1775–1778," 130–32.

17. Boswell, *Boswell:* The *Applause of the Jury, 1782–1785*, 261.

II

Romantic Joint Labor

Editing Minervas

William Godwin's Liminal Maneuvers in Mary Wollstonecraft's Wrongs of Woman

GERARD GOGGIN

In many works of this species, the hero is allowed to be mortal, and to become wise and virtuous as well as happy, by a train of events and circumstances. The heroines, on the contrary, are to be born immaculate; and to act like goddesses of wisdom, just come forth highly finished Minervas from the head of Jove.

Mary Wollstonecraft, *Wrongs of Woman: or, Maria. A Fragment*

Literary collaboration has been a subject of recent critical fascination. The editors of a collection of essays on mostly twentieth-century literary couples suggest that "although most of the artists and writers concerned have not escaped social stereotypes about masculinity and femininity and their assumed roles with partnership, many have negotiated new relationships to those stereotypes," citing the "richness of the private interactions that operate *within* relationships."[1] In this essay I will examine an earlier period in which stereotypes about masculinity and femininity were being challenged, reshaped, and reinscribed, namely, the early Romantic period of the 1790s. The Romantic writer of the late eighteenth and early nineteenth century has famously been a solitary type. This myth has been challenged by revisionary scholarship on the social nature of Romantic writing, work that provides a context in which to reexamine collaborative literary work and its stakes—the cultural desires involved in reading, writing, annotating, editing, revising, and marketing.[2] The case I discuss here is all the more significant for the sexual politics of collaboration because it involves a celebrated intellectual pair: a

founding figure of modern feminism, Mary Wollstonecraft, and her
lover, William Godwin, internationally famous philosopher of his day
and influential figure in the careers of major Romantic writers such as
Samuel Taylor Coleridge and Percy Bysshe Shelley. The closing decades
of the twentieth century witnessed growing critical and popular fascination with Wollstonecraft, Godwin, their daughter Mary Shelley, and her
lover Percy Bysshe Shelley. Scholarship and speculation on the loves,
lives, works, and biographical and textual interactions among these four
writers has steadily accumulated. Here I wish to reflect upon the erotics
of literary collaboration and the shadows it cast upon futurity by closely
examining William Godwin's editing of Mary Wollstonecraft's novel
Wrongs of Woman. In so doing I hope to provide a fresh perspective on a
very traditional way of fashioning intellectual relationships — pedagogy,
imagined as mentoring.

In his study *Erotic Reckonings* (1994) Thomas Simmons uses mentoring
to theorize the negotiation of tradition and authority among three pairs
of twentieth-century American poets: Ezra Pound and H. D., Yvor
Winters and Janet Lewis, and Louise Bogan and Theodore Roethke.
For Simmons the role of the mentor is inescapably conflicted, "divided
between allegiance to a tradition and allegiance to the personhood of
the apprentice. Implicit in this consideration are principles of seduction,
dominance, and cruelty that potentially threaten the mentor-apprentice
relationship."[3] In all three cases Simmons finds that each poet who
acted as mentor struggles with his or her identity and pedagogic role:
"Without question the artist identified as a mentor takes on the mantle
of power, instruction, and direction, even though he may attempt to
wield it benignly" (3). Of the many texts that treat mentorship, Simmons selects two as archetypal. The first is the relationship in Homer's
Odyssey of Mentor and Athena (or Minerva) to Telemachus, which Simmons considers "seminal, a cultural starting point" (3). The second is
that of Peter Abelard and Heloise in the twelfth century, as contained in
the famous letters: "This text is central because it marks another beginning, the overt equation of mentorship and eroticism in post-classical
culture" (3). Strikingly, these two powerful myths of pedagogy in Western culture that Simmons identifies — Mentor-Minerva and Abelard-
Heloise (with its variant in Jean-Jacques Rousseau's myth of the new
Héloïse) — recur and intertwine in the texts of Godwin and Wollstonecraft, a coincidence I wish to explore in greater detail.

A Scene of Writing

Wollstonecraft's unfinished novel *The Wrongs of Woman: or, Maria. A Fragment* was first published as the first and second volumes of *Posthumous Works of the Author of Vindication of the Rights of Woman*, which were edited by William Godwin and published by Joseph Johnson in January 1798. Godwin's *Memoirs of the Author of a Vindication of the Rights of Woman* appeared in the same month. In the wake of the furor that greeted the *Memoirs*, Godwin altered those passages that proved most offensive for a second "corrected" edition. Notably, the *Posthumous Works* were not reissued.

Wrongs of Woman is the story of Maria, who is drugged, abducted, and imprisoned in an asylum by her vicious husband, George Venables. Maria wakes to find that her baby has been kidnapped. She tries to befriend her jailer, Jemima, in the hope that she will help her to escape. To pass the time, Maria writes a memoir for her daughter and reads books lent to her by a fellow inmate, Henry Darnford. Jemima and Darnford recount their life stories and Maria allows Darnford to read her memoir. Maria and Darnford become lovers, with Jemima acting as their go-between. Accompanied by Jemima, the couple escapes the asylum and sets up house—with Jemima serving as housekeeper. Their happiness is disturbed by Maria's husband, who commences an action against Darnford for adultery and seduction. Maria assumes responsibility for Darnford's defense, penning a critique of marriage that she requests be read aloud in court. Despite her compelling evidence and argument, the judge rejects her defense and counterclaim of false imprisonment. The novel ends inconclusively, with a number of possible endings provided.

Wollstonecraft commenced *Wrongs of Woman* at a time when she was leaving behind memories of her relationship with her lover Gilbert Imlay; enjoying burgeoning friendships with writers such as Mary Hays, Mary Robinson, and Thomas Holcroft; and working for Johnson's *Analytical Review*. Exactly when she commenced the novel is uncertain—although probably in mid 1796—but she was working on it when she and Godwin became lovers. Wollstonecraft's death released her from the difficult composition of her novel, a struggle to which Godwin testifies in the *Memoirs*:

> [T]he principal work, in which she was engaged for more than twelve months before her decease, was a novel, entitled, The Wrongs of

Woman. . . . All her other works were produced with a rapidity, that did
not give her powers time fully to expand. But this was written slowly
and with mature consideration. She began it in several forms, which
she successively rejected, after they were considerably advanced. She
wrote many parts of the work again and again, and, when she had finished what she intended for the first part, she felt herself more urgently
stimulated to revise and improve what she had written, than to proceed, with constancy of application, in the parts that were to follow.[4]

In the "Editor's Preface" to *Wrongs of Woman* Godwin declares: "The
purpose and structure of the following work, had long formed a favourite subject of meditation with its author, and she judged them capable of
producing an important effect. The composition had been in progress
for a period of twelve months. She was anxious to do justice to her conception, and commenced and revised the manuscript several times. So
much of it as is here given to the public, she was far from considering as
finished . . ." (81). Mitzi Myers claims that Wollstonecraft's struggles
with composition stemmed from her anxiety to do justice to an ambitious project and from the "indissolubility of her problems with theme
and form." For Myers this is explained by Wollstonecraft's struggle to
"weave radical ideology into the fictionalized texture of feminine experience."[5] Mary Poovey has also suggested that matters of genre and
gender were responsible for Wollstonecraft's slow progress.[6] Yet it may
be observed that Wollstonecraft's travails in finishing *Wrongs of Woman*
were of a piece with the obstacles she encountered when beginning it, as
reflected in her failure to write the promised second volume of *A Vindication of the Rights of Woman*. In the advertisement to the *Rights of Woman*
Wollstonecraft had announced: "Many subjects, however, which I have
cursorily alluded to, call for particular investigation, especially the laws
relative to women, and the consideration of their peculiar duties. These
will furnish ample matter for a second volume, which in due time will be
published, to elucidate some of the sentiments, and complete many of
the sketches begun in the first."[7] Despite this projection, in the *Memoirs*
Godwin states that "she has scarcely left behind her a single paper, that
can, with any certainty, be assigned to have had this destination" (114).

A number of commentators have puzzled over the dynamics of
Wollstonecraft's relationship with Godwin and its effect on her writing.
Emily Sunstein has suggested that "Godwin's presence and advice may
have drained from the work its drive and spontaneity."[8] Janet Todd has
suggested that Godwin forced Wollstonecraft back into the sentimental

mold and thus is akin to Mr. Francis, the voice of reason and control in Mary Hays's *Emma Courtney* (1796): "[Godwin] is the ultimate controller and editor. His position was strengthened by the sentimental convention that often pretended that a male author like Richardson or Defoe was the editor of a female text which he had himself actually created."[9] However, neither Sunstein's nor Todd's explanations account for the complex dynamics of collaboration between Godwin and Wollstonecraft, a relationship that is intertextual as much as it is intersubjective. Godwin commented on the novel in manuscript, suggested corrections, and ultimately was its editor. These acts are more overdetermined than Sunstein allows, and Todd's dyad of Godwin-Wollstonecraft, or reason-sentiment, obscures the libidinal dynamics of their collaboration.

The point I wish to make here is that *Wrongs of Woman* remained unfinished because the intertextual and intersubjective dynamics of Wollstonecraft's relationship with Godwin are ultimately bound up with a framing scene of instruction and writing. This scene is continuous with the prominent representations of writing, reading, and storytelling in the *Wrongs of Woman*—the textual and narrative transactions occurring among its central characters.[10] These representations suggest a reading that examines how the novel reflects on its own writing—particularly when the circumstances of how the novel was edited and published are taken into account.

The reflexive textuality of *Wrongs of Woman* is the subject of Tilottama Rajan's influential readings of the novels of Godwin and Wollstonecraft.[11] Rajan contends that Wollstonecraft's *Wrongs of Woman* moves in a more radical direction than her early novel *Mary, A Fiction*. The narrative of *Wrongs of Woman* is premised on "greater structural complexity" and contains narratives within a narrative. *Wrongs of Woman* is also an unfinished novel reconstructed by its editor, something that makes its status as a fallen text apparent to its readers. Rajan argues that if *Wrongs of Woman* is characterized by a reflexive meditation on its own textual status, then Godwin's editorial work should be considered an integral part of this. She also highlights the productive collaboration between Godwin and Wollstonecraft in producing the novel. Godwin is his wife's "first explicit reader," "sympathetic and respectful," whose additions "do not direct our interpretation" but instead "place a frame around the text and locate us outside it." In her elaboration and reconsideration of Godwin's editing of Wollstonecraft's oeuvre, Rajan makes the case that Godwin is engaged in a complex reproduction of

Wollstonecraft: "Godwin's choice is rather to 'romantize' Wollstone-craft [in Novalis's 1798 sense]. . . . His editing of Wollstonecraft is his at-tempt to write the revolutionary subject into history so as to initiate the uncertain process of her future reading."[12]

Although Rajan provides a suggestive account of Wollstonecraft and Godwin's collaboration, in what follows I wish to explore a different as-pect of this textuality. I am especially interested in the ways that God-win and Wollstonecraft's textual strategies make sense when we appre-ciate how readers are formed as sexed and gendered subjects. Godwin's editing of Wollstonecraft is very much about the representation of revo-lutionary history, as Rajan suggests. Yet Godwin's textual strategies re-inforce his powerful role as mentor. Godwin's editorial maneuvers are nonetheless at odds with a different possible reading of Wollstonecraft's own political and aesthetic project in *Wrongs of Woman,* namely, that of representing women differently by finding new conventions in which to plot their utter imprisonment in the tyrannical institution of marriage. This implicit conflict can be seen from the triangular sexual dynamics in which his editorial tactics are implicated. Thus, Godwin's role of men-tor involves a different figuring of the Minerva myth than that which Wollstonecraft presages.

A Scene of Instruction

Wollstonecraft's characterization of her work-in-progress in *Wrongs of Woman* conflicts with Godwin's donning of the mantle of literary executor—his pose as her privileged interpreter underwritten by his narrative of their relationship in the *Memoirs.* While in most cases God-win displays a scrupulousness in recording his editorial interventions, his liminal maneuvers in *Wrongs of Woman* nonetheless constitute a sig-nificant creative act of narrative composition. A close reading of these editorial traces will demonstrate how Godwin assimilates the events sur-rounding Wollstonecraft's attempts to begin and complete *Wrongs of Woman* into a story of his own making.

In editing *Wrongs of Woman* Godwin assembled the story and framed it with three substantial sections of prose: an "Editor's Preface," an "Au-thor's Preface," and a "Conclusion By the Editor." As I shall argue, these editorial pieces are significant contributions to the novel in their own right, due to the circumstances of their publication as well as the textual dynamics of the novel.

In the "Editor's Preface" to the novel Godwin states the case for publishing *Wrongs of Woman:* "The public are here presented with the last literary attempt of an author. . . . There is a sentiment, very dear to minds of taste and imagination, that finds a melancholy delight in contemplating these unfinished productions of genius, these sketches of what, if they had been filled up in a manner adequate to the writer's conception, would perhaps have given a new impulse to the manners of a world" (81). Godwin believes that although Wollstonecraft was far from considering the novel finished, the "purpose and structure" of the work "had long formed a favourite subject of meditation with its author, and she judged them capable of producing an important effect" (81). Recording his own method, Godwin explains:

> In revising these sheets for the press, it was necessary for the editor, in some places, to connect the more finished parts with the pages of an older copy, and a line or two in addition sometimes appeared requisite for that purpose. Wherever such a liberty has been taken, the additional phrases will be found inclosed in brackets; it being the editor's most earnest desire, to intrude nothing of himself into the work, but to give to the public the words, as well as ideas, of the real author. . . . What follows in the ensuing pages, is not a preface regularly drawn out by the author, but merely hints for a preface, which, though never filled up in the manner the writer intended, appeared to be worth preserving. (81–82)

Following the "Editor's Preface," the "ensuing "Author's Preface" consists of two separate passages. The first is a fragment Godwin attributes to Wollstonecraft. This contains the author's wish to present her "main object, the desire of exhibiting the misery and oppression, peculiar to women, that arise out of the partial laws and customs of society" (83)—even at the cost of dramatic nicety if necessary. The second passage Godwin identifies as an "extract of a letter from the author to a friend, to whom she communicated her manuscript" (83). There is, however, no evidence for believing that the second half of the "Author's Preface" was viewed by Wollstonecraft as prefatory to the novel. In fact, it derives from an important triangulated critical exchange prefatory to the publishing and reception of the novel. In composing the two prefaces Godwin omits a crucial phrase of Wollstonecraft's that refutes the conceptual foundations of his framing interpretation of *Wrongs of Woman.*

The extract in the second part of the "Author's Preface" derives from Godwin's copy of a letter from Mary Wollstonecraft to George Dyson, roughly dated 15 May 1797.[13] Painter, translator, and political radical, Dyson was an esteemed intimate of Godwin. He was also friendly with Wollstonecraft, who valued his opinion highly enough to seek his opinion of the manuscript of her novel. While Dyson's comments have not survived, Wollstonecraft's response has, and this is partly reproduced by Godwin in his crafting of both prefaces to her last novel. The extract from this letter inserted by Godwin into the "Author's Preface" reads as follows:

> So much of it [the novel] as is here given to the public, she was far from considering as finished, and, in a letter to a friend directly written on this subject, she says, 'I am perfectly aware that some of the incidents ought to be transposed, and heightened by more harmonious shading; and I wished in some degree to avail myself of criticism, before I began to adjust my events into a story, the outline of which I had sketched in my mind.' The only friends to whom the author communicated her manuscript, were Mr Dyson, the translator of the Sorceror, and the present editor; and it was impossible for the most inexperienced author to display a stronger desire of profiting by the censures and sentiments that might be suggested. (81)

In the full version of Wollstonecraft's letter to Dyson one finds the original complete sentence: "I was perfectly aware that some of the incidents ought to be transpossed [sic] and heightened by more harmonious shading; and I wished to avail myself of yours and Mr G's criticism before I began to adjust my events into a story, the outline of which I had sketched in my mind at the commencement; yet I am vexed and surprised at your not thinking the situation of Maria sufficiently important, and can only account for this want of—shall I say it? delicacy of feeling by recollecting that you are a man . . ." (391–92). Another passage appearing in the "Author's Preface" describes "matrimonial despotism of heart and conduct " as the "peculiar Wrongs of Woman" (84). In Wollstonecraft's letter to Dyson, this reads as follows:

> For my part I cannot suppose any situation more distressing than for a woman of sensibility with an improving mind to be bound, to such a man as I have described, for life—obliged to renounce all the humanizing affections, and to avoid cultivating her taste lest her perception of grace, and refinement of sentiment should sharpen to agony the pangs of disappointment. Love, in which the imagination mingles its bewitching

colouring must be fostered by delicacy—I should despise, or rather call her an ordinary woman, who could endure such a husband as I have sketched—yet you do not seem to be disgusted with him!!!

These appear to me (matrimonial despotism of heart & conduct) to be the particular wrongs of woman; because they degrade the mind. What are termed great misfortunes may more forcibly impress the mind of common readers, they have more of what might justly be termed *stage effect* but it is the delineation of finer sensations which, in my opinion, constitutes the merit of our best novels, this is what I have in view; and to shew the wrongs of different classes of women equally oppressive, though from the difference of education, necessarily various. (392)

The extract Godwin prints in the "Author's Preface" to *Wrongs of Woman* omits the words "yet you do not seem to be disgusted with him!!!" This elision gains added significance in the light of Godwin's pruning of another crucial phrase: "[Y]et I am vexed and surprised at your not thinking the situation of Maria sufficiently important, and can only account for this want of—shall I say it? delicacy of feeling by recollecting that you are a man . . ." (391–92).

In his reproduction of the letter, Godwin is full of praise for Wollstonecraft's renown as an author, yet he still regards her as an apprentice eager to benefit from his advice. There is a patronizing tone about all this—especially given Godwin's comparison of Wollstonecraft's alacrity with that of the "most inexperienced author." More important, by only citing part of Wollstonecraft's letter to Dyson Godwin revises her response to his friend's reading of the novel. Instead, he inserts a passage complimentary to himself and Dyson in the "Editor's Preface."

Wollstonecraft's sharp reaction to Dyson in the original letter revolves around a crucial political and aesthetic issue, namely, the importance of the literary representation of the situation of a woman such as Maria. In this sense Wollstonecraft does not fit the role of the appropriately grateful novice portrayed in Godwin's preface—displaying little desire to profit by Dyson's "censures and sentiments" if these conflict with her clear sense of a protofeminist literary project. On the contrary, as Patricia Yaeger suggests in her reading of *Rights of Woman*, Wollstonecraft deploys dialogic devices in her fictional and nonfictional prose that may very well function as an emancipatory strategy: "Wollstonecraft can create the conversations she needs because the act of writing can give her uncanny power over her conversational partners. . . . If

Wollstonecraft's prose can be characterized by the abruptness and energy with which she seizes the role of speaking subject and constructs
fictive dialogues with silent male interlocutors, why isn't this perception
at the centre of Wollstonecraft criticism?"[14] An example of this dialogic
invention may be found in a section of Wollstonecraft's letter to Dyson
that did not find its way into the prefaces to *Wrongs of Woman*. After
Wollstonecraft's first rejoinder to Dyson on the significance of Maria's
situation, she offers to drink tea with him and "converse on the subject "
(392). Here we have the scene of the author engaging in a sustained dialogue with her critics and readers, proleptically inserting herself into
the making of literary history.

Following this offer is a second rejoinder to Dyson on the style of
Jemima's story:

> I am not convinced that your remarks respecting the style of Jemima's
> story is just; but I will reconsider it. You seem to [m]e to confound
> simplicity and vulgarity. Persons who have received a miscellaneous
> education, that is are educated by chance, and the energy of their own
> faculties, commonly display the mixture of refined and common lan-
> guage I have endeavoured to imitate. Besides I do not like *stalking horse*
> sentences
>
> One word more strong Indignation in youth at injustice &c appears
> to me the constant attendant of superiority of understanding . . . (392)

This passage suggests Wollstonecraft's textual strategy, her literary
technique for showing "the wrongs of different classes of women." She
conceives of the political and literary objectives of her work as imbricated, yet this sense is more submerged in the extract in the "Author's
Preface." In the full text of the letter Wollstonecraft argues for a representational practice that allows for a mix of linguistic registers ("refined
and common") on the grounds of greater verisimilitude. She also makes
some counterclaims against more elitist critical and writerly practices,
suggesting honesty ("I do not like *stalking horse* sentences") and overt political response ("strong Indignation in youth at injustice &c") as alternative grounds of intellectual worth. This line of argument appears in
an earlier letter to Godwin, in which Wollstonecraft robustly takes him
to task for the severity of his criticism: "I allude to what you remarked,
relative to my manner of writing—that there was a radical defect in it—
a worm in the bud—. . . for I would wish you to see my heart and mind
just as it appears to myself, without drawing any veil of affected humility over it" (345). According to Mitzi Myers, the tenor of Godwin's

thoughts on Wollstonecraft's manuscript is reflected in his unpublished critique of *Wrongs of Woman:*

> Craving more action, more "distinctness of narrative," he criticized her for neglecting incident, for womanishly indulging in "a feeling about nothing, a building without a foundation." He doubted "whether any human being has the power of expressing feeling more vividly and impressively than you have; but while I admire the appendages of story, I desiderate the substratum." Applying his own orderly novelistic formula, he advised that "each new state of [the heroine's] mind ought perhaps to be introduced by a new and memorable incident; & these incidents might be made beautifully various, surprising & unexpected, though all tending to one point. I do not want a common-place story of a brutal, insensible husband."[15]

Godwin's editorial decisions relating to Wollstonecraft's letter to Dyson have not often been discussed by critics, with the exception of Claudia Johnson and Harriet Jump.[16] While Johnson and Jump both recognize the significance of Godwin's act of selectively quoting from Wollstonecraft's letter, they have not sought to make it integral to a reading of the novel itself. In developing such a reading, I wish to emphasize two important consequences of Godwin's editing. The first is to sunder the aesthetic from the political dimensions of *Wrongs of Woman,* both of which are clearly connected in her letter to Dyson. What emerges from the prefaces is that Godwin as editor felt that Wollstonecraft had a clear topic in mind—the oppression of women—but was in need of literary instruction in order to present this effectively. The second consequence of Godwin's editing is to excise Wollstonecraft's comments on the projected or anticipated critical reception of her work. The evidence of Wollstonecraft's prepublication engagement with the critics of her work is absent from the prefatory texts, which constitute Godwin's founding editorial gestures. In a sense he is in control of the transmission of her text, disclosing yet drawing a veil over his role. This elides Wollstonecraft's vindication of her novel, an apologia in which she suggests that gender and sexuality play an important role in shaping readers and thus in generating different interpretations of her work.

What prompted Godwin's editorial suppression is reflected in his sense of embarrassment in presenting the scene of instruction between Wollstonecraft and Dyson. One could speculate that in his editorial fashioning of *Wrongs of Woman* Godwin is consciously cultivating a pose of editorial and authorial prowess and authority. Although pedagogically and

textually Godwin portrays himself as having the upper hand—or being
on top—in other ways he is unmanned. Instead of admitting Dyson into
a three-way exchange, Godwin is keen to assimilate him to the textual
relays he establishes around *Wrongs of Woman*. In Wollstonecraft's letter
Dyson and Godwin are paired in their hypocritical attempt to police the
rectitude of plot, both narrative and legal, whereby a man has a right to
divorce a woman but not vice versa. Wollstonecraft objects to the ca-
suistry Dyson and Godwin exhibit in finding finer gradations of mercy
based on the degree of victimhood or oppression that Maria is permitted to claim as palliation for her wrongful actions.

   Divorce was a matter that both Wollstonecraft and Godwin were
preoccupied with during this period, as Wollstonecraft proceeded with
her emotional if not legal separation from her former lover Imlay. Wollstonecraft's memories of Imlay and her perceptions of Godwin are entwined and textualized in *Wrongs of Woman*. This is not surprising, for
Wollstonecraft often transposed historical events into fiction and also
revised her personal trail of disasters and her texts. Her letters to Imlay
were significantly rewritten and repositioned before becoming *Letters
Written during a Short Residence in Sweden, Norway, and Denmark* (1796). Wollstonecraft's rewriting in 1796–97 coincides with Godwin's revision of his
own texts, both published and unpublished (he often rewrote personal
letters). One could even suggest that there is a theatrical element here,
with Godwin playing the role of honorable suitor in the act of rescuing
a fallen woman. Godwin's celebrated reading of Wollstonecraft's *A Short
Residence,* an epistolary romance, as "some sort of encoded love story"
between Wollstonecraft and Imlay, as well as his editing of Wollstonecraft's letters to Imlay in *Posthumous Works,* may have cleared the way
for Godwin to move Imlay out of the picture and insert himself into a
love story of his own devising with the author, as his pose of seduced
reader in the *Memoirs* suggests: "If ever there was a book calculated to
make a man [fall] in love with its author, this appears to me to be the
book."[17]

Figuring Literary Parentage

I now wish to examine a revealing trope of Wollstonecraft's that promises to further disrupt her positioning within Godwin's editorial scene of
instruction. In the first fragment in the "Author's Preface" of *Wrongs of*

Woman Wollstonecraft promises a different sort of heroine. Her novel is to be a history of a flesh-and-blood woman rather than an abstract individual. To this end she wishes to represent her heroine as mortal, like her masculine counterpart, rather than "highly finished Minervas from the head of Jove" (83). Minerva, the Roman goddess of wisdom and patroness of the arts and trades, is said to have sprung fully armed from the head of Jupiter (also known as Jove). In the Greek version of the myth as presented in Hesiod's *Theogony*, Zeus swallows his pregnant wife, Metis, and her child, thereby preventing the birth of a son who might succeed and surpass him. Instead Zeus gives birth to the Greek Athena. Wollstonecraft may well have encountered the myth of Minerva in a contemporary text she knew well, namely, the first book of Rousseau's *Émile*. Here Rousseau describes how experience and nature precede and determine instruction:

> Suppose a child born with the size and strength of manhood, entering upon life full grown like Pallas from the brain of Jupiter; such a child-man would be a perfect idiot, an automaton, a statue without motion and almost without feeling; he would see and hear nothing . . . his body would be unaware of contact with neighbouring bodies, he would not even know he had a body, what his hands handled would be in his brain alone; all his sensations would be united in one place, they would exist only in the common "sensorium," he would have only one idea, that of self, to which he would refer all his sensations; and this idea, or rather this feeling, would be the only thing in which he excelled an ordinary child.[18]

Like many other thinkers of the period, Wollstonecraft develops her own ideas through a critique of Rousseau. For instance, Yaeger has suggested that in *Rights of Woman* Wollstonecraft "makes Rousseau her unwilling dialogic partner . . . for when Wollstonecraft reverses a norm and makes Rousseau into a new kind of circulating social message, she makes him into both a speaking partner and a sign. Rousseau—formerly the generator and arbiter of signs—is turned into someone who circulates: a sign whose meaning and value is designated by a woman."[19] Taking this as our cue, if we read Wollstonecraft in light of this passage from Rousseau's text, we may paraphrase her argument along these lines: women need to be educated in life and in novels so that female characters may learn from their experiences just as male protagonists do.

As a powerful account of male paternity that spills over into the literary realm, the myth of Minerva may be used to further elucidate

Godwin's editorial role. In the "Author's Preface" Wollstonecraft expresses the hope that some enlightened readers will "grant that my sketches are not the abortion of a distempered fancy" (*Wrongs*, 83). At the end of *Wrongs of Woman* Godwin adds a final paragraph that adopts this metaphor of textual production as pregnancy. He tries to elaborate how Wollstonecraft has met her narrative contract by metaphorically recuperating the novel's potentially abortive lack of closure, or miscarriage. Godwin argues for the fruitfulness of the possible endings he has collated as the "Conclusion": "[T]hese hints, simple as they are, are pregnant with passion and distress" (184). He compares the promise of Wollstonecraft's fructifying textuality with the desiccated offerings of authors who are unable to conceive: "It is the refuge of barren authors, only, to crowd their fictions with so great a number of events, as to suffer no one of them to sink into the reader's mind. It is the province of true genius to develop events, to discover their capabilities, to ascertain the different passions and sentiments with which they are fraught, and to diversify them with incidents, that give reality to the picture, and take a hold upon the mind of a reader of taste, from which they can never be loosened" (184). As he ushers in this "Conclusion," Godwin strikes the pose of the editor as midwife: a masculine and authoritative figure competent to assist with the birth and pleased to proclaim it to the world. Just as Jupiter gives birth to Minerva, so this trope can become a figure for the male author who metaphorically arrogates the capacity of giving birth.

As Terry J. Castle has pointed out, the comparison between the writer as biological parent and work as offspring "finds first expression, historically, in Plato and returns as a conventional figure referring to literary genesis in classical, medieval, and Renaissance texts."[20] She argues that the topos becomes linked to a programmatic theory of literary creativity in mainstream eighteenth-century neoclassical satire. Here it plays a negative function and is assimilated to the view that the poet is in control of his work. With the emergence of Romantic aesthetics, Castle claims, "childbirth as a image for the making of poems—like the equally archaic trope involving breathing and inspiration—becomes conspicuous and utterly celebrational in import . . . consistently tied, on an intellectual level, to the emergent concepts in English criticism—the synthetic imagination, the spontaneous 'natural' generation of poetry, individual artistic self-expression." Chadwick and de Courtivron have suggested that such figural play may represent a creative approach to literary collaboration: "Reproductive metaphors appear widely in the work of both male and female artists and writers, but they are qualified by Western culture's tendency to associate productivity for women with childbearing, with biological reproduction. . . . [Yet] the lives of Vanessa Bell and Duncan Grant, among others, reveal far more complex and intricate interweavings of the spheres of production and reproduction than those suggested by this stereotype."[21] However, as Godwin takes it up, the trope of literary paternity appears to represent a desire for the appropriation and usurpation of the embodied tropes of maternity. With textual as opposed to living bodies, the boundary between assisting with the birth and wishing to give birth oneself is more porous—an especially potent dream for masculine subjects who dream of bodies that may overcome their biological limitations.

This is evident in a love letter dated 13 July 1796 from Godwin to Wollstonecraft, in which he wryly assumes the mantle of Jupiter: "When I make love, it shall be in a storm, as Jupiter made love to Semele, and turned her at once into a cinder. Do not these menaces terrify you?"[22] Godwin's allusion is to the fate of Semele, whose tryst with Jupiter resulted in the birth of Dionysus. When Hera discovered this, she tricked Jupiter into destroying Semele with thunder and lightning. Rescuing the unborn child Dionysus from the ashes, Jupiter sewed him into his thigh until he was ready to be born. Like the myth of Minerva, this is an encoded fantasy of the father's pregnancy, the old dream of male autogenesis. After swallowing Metis and her baby, Jupiter incorporates the mother's body, stripping it away and giving birth himself from his head, or brain—the organ associated with rationality during the Enlightenment. Ironically, Wollstonecraft's death in childbirth meant that Godwin was left to swallow her textual body in the form of *Wrongs of Woman*, other unpublished works, her letters, and published works. *Posthumous Works* might be said to have emerged from his skull, linked by an editorial umbilical cord to his corpus.

Mentoring and Collaboration

To draw on the childbirth metaphor in this manner in order to trope the literary collaboration between Godwin and Wollstonecraft is to follow only one metonymic thread in this weave. I wish to conclude this essay by tracing another rich connotation, namely, femininity and pedagogy.

In classical mythology Minerva is linked not only with creativity and the arts but also with pedagogy and mentoring. As Thomas Simmons has pointed out, in Homer's *Odyssey* Minerva masquerades as a man, assuming the form of Mentor when aiding Telemachus in his search for his father, Odysseus. Simmons emphasizes that in the *Odyssey* Mentor supports and encourages Telemachus's voyage in search of his father, thereby striving to become the embodiment of a tradition. The twist lies in the way that Athena assumes the guise of Mentor, whose impersonation facilitates the transmission of this patriarchal tradition. Simmons argues that in doing so Athena validates Mentor's role as wise counselor, but that such counsel is not sufficient: "Within the cloak of the mentor must lie the goddess: the self-defined female acquires the identity of the trusted male, using that male mastery of the patriarchal society to achieve a daring and unexpected end." For Simmons Athena acts as a Jungian anima that strengthens the bond to the mother and loosens the ties to the father. In conceptualising the flux of power in the mentoring relationship—especially in relation to sexuality and gender—Simmons assumes that the subject is a unified person, drawing on Jungian concepts such as anima and animus as well as Carol Gilligan's theory of the gendered nature of moral reasoning. Successful mentorship, in Simmons's view, involves a recognition and nurturing of the "erotic process by which mentor and apprentice come to validate each other's independence and power . . . the integration of past and present, reason and instinct, intellectual knowledge and personal knowledge, heterosexuality and homosexuality."[23] Eschewing erotic domination, the apprentice and the mentor may be free. While Simmons articulates a laudable ideal—one prefigured, in key respects, by the radical writings of Wollstonecraft and Godwin—it does not come to grips with the intimate and enduring effects of oppressive social structure that act through processes of subject formation.

Doubtless familiar with the Minerva-Mentor myth from other sources, both Wollstonecraft and Godwin were also acquainted with a pedagogical text that retold the story and was extremely popular in the eighteenth century, namely, *Les Aventures de Télémaque, fils d'Ulysse* (1699), by François de Salignac de la Mothe-Fénelon, archbishop of Cambrai. Fénelon—and his book—was featured in one of the most controversial passages of Godwin's study entitled *An Enquiry Concerning Political Justice* (1792), which Charles Lamb dubbed the "fire cause." Godwin argued

that it was wiser to save Fénelon from a fire than his chambermaid—
even if she were one's own mother—since the author was of greater
moral worth, servants or mothers making unlikely authors. The Mi-
nerva/Mentor–Telemachus myth from Fénelon's *Télémaque* is central to
Godwin's conception of mentoring, as is evident in his 1805 novel *Fleet-
wood; or the New Man of Feeling.*

Wollstonecraft's recital—and re-siting—of the Jupiter-Minerva
myth in *Wrongs of Woman* does not come as a surprise since she had already reworked the Minerva/Mentor–Telemachus myth as a grounding trope for pedagogy. In *Rights of Woman* Wollstonecraft cleared the
way for her theory of education by challenging Rousseau's appropriation of Fénelon's male pedagogical romance. For the Rousseau of *Émile,*
Fénelon's pedagogical principles come in handy to reinforce the specific
and subordinate nature of Sophie's education. Thus, when Sophie reads
Télémaque she is captivated by its amorous overtones, being so impressed
with Telemachus that she desires a man who precisely resembles him.
Rousseau's authorial resolution of this dilemma is to give her Émile in
Telemachus's (imaginary) place: "Let us give Émile his Sophie; let us restore this sweet girl to life and provide her with a less vivid imagination
and a happier fate. I desired to paint an ordinary woman, but by endow-
ing her with a great soul, I have disturbed her reason."[24] Wollstonecraft's
counterploy is to use Fénelon's Telemachus against masculinist schemes
of education—including Rousseau's: "[T]he system of education, which
I earnestly wish to see exploded, seems to pre-suppose what ought never
to be taken for granted, that virtue shields us from the casualties of life;
and that fortune, slipping off her bandage, will smile on a well-educated
female, and bring in her hand an Emilius or a Telemachus. . . . There
have been many women in the world who, instead of being supported by
the reason and virtue of their fathers and brothers, have strengthened
their own minds by struggling with their vices and follies; yet have never
met with a hero, in the shape of a husband . . ." (*Rights*, 162).

In troping mentoring differently from Rousseau, Wollstonecraft
anticipates her remarks in the "Author's Preface" to *Wrongs of Woman.*
In contrast to Rousseau's Sophie, Maria does not rely on fortune to
bring her a Telemachus, nor is she irresistibly attracted or indebted to a
hero-husband, whether Fénelon's protagonist, a Darnford, or George
Venables. Instead, Maria may escape the pressures of such a script and
rework Minerva to permit her to supplant Mentor.

This alternate reading of the trope of mentoring in Wollstonecraft's *Wrongs of Woman* provides a means of understanding the posthumous literary collaboration of the novelist and her editor. As Tilottama Rajan has concluded, although he was generally a scrupulous, sympathetic, and courageous editor, Godwin was nonetheless engaged in framing Wollstonecraft's corpus in ways that were determined by larger social, political, and philosophical contexts. His editing in this instance discloses a gap in interpretation that underscores a tense dialogue between intellectual equals. What appears to be a minor slip has deeper implications, revealing a fault line in textuality as well as sexuality. The scene of collaborative writing, following the death of the author, is one in which power is encoded in questions of instruction. Who teaches, who writes, and who edits whom all matter—even in passionate, companionate, and Romantic marriages.

Notes

1. Chadwick and de Courtivron, eds., *Significant Others*, 8–9.
2. See, e.g., McCalman, "Introduction: A Romantic Age *Companion*," 1–14.
3. Simmons, *Erotic Reckonings: Mastery and Apprenticeship in the Works of Poets and Lovers*, 3. Subsequent references to this source are acknowledged parenthetically in the text.
4. Mary Wollstonecraft, *The Wrongs of Woman: or, Maria. A Fragment*, vol. 1 of *The Works of Mary Wollstonecraft*, 133. Subsequent page references are given parenthetically in the text.
5. Myers, "Unfinished Business: Wollstonecraft's *Maria*," 107, 111.
6. Poovey, *The Proper Lady and the Woman Writer: Ideology as Style in the Works of Mary Wollstonecraft, Mary Shelley, and Jane Austen.*
7. Wollstonecraft, *A Vindication of the Rights of Woman*, vol. 5 of *The Works of Mary Wollstonecraft*, 70. Subsequent page references are given parenthetically in the text.
8. Sunstein, *A Different Face: The Life of Mary Wollstonecraft*, 329.
9. Todd, *The Sign of Angellica: Women, Writing and Fiction, 1660–1800*, 252.
10. I should note here Daniel O'Quinn's thoughtful essay "Trembling: Wollstonecraft, Godwin and the Resistance to Literature," which shares my preoccupation with Godwin's editing of Wollstonecraft's *Wrongs of Woman*. O'Quinn reads the latter as a "performative critique of the ideology of sentimental fiction" (760) and finds that Godwin's interventions weaken this critique: "The struggle between the resistance and the temptation to literature enacted

between Wollstonecraft's halting text and Godwin's editorial practice replicates a struggle that lies at the core of bourgeois auto-formation in the latter years of the eighteenth century" (782). However, O'Quinn overlooks Godwin's acts of exclusion in relation to Wollstonecraft's letter to George Dyson, which is central to my argument.

11. Rajan, "Framing the Corpus: Godwin's Editing of Wollstonecraft in 1798"; Rajan, *The Supplement of Reading: Figures of Understanding in Romantic Theory and Practice*.

12. Rajan, *The Supplement of Reading*, 182; Rajan, "Framing the Corpus," 512.

13. Mary Wollstonecraft, *Collected Letters*, 391–93. Subsequent references to this source are acknowledged parenthetically in the text.

14. Yaeger, *Honey-Mad Women: Emancipatory Strategies in Women's Writing*, 161.

15. Myers, "Unfinished Business," 109–10.

16. Johnson, *Equivocal Beings: Politics, Gender, and Sentimentality in the 1790s. Wollstonecraft, Radcliffe, Burney, Austen;* Jump, *Mary Wollstonecraft: Writer*.

17. See Favret, *Romantic Correspondence: Women, Politics and the Fiction of Letters*, 132; Godwin, *Memoirs of the Author of a Vindication of The Rights of Woman*, vol. 1 of *Collected Novels and Memoirs of William Godwin*, 122.

18. Rousseau, *Émile*, 28.

19. Yaeger, *Honey-Mad Women*, 175–76.

20. Castle, "Lab'ring Bards: Birth *Topoi* and English Poetics, 1660–1820," 194. See also Friedman, "Creativity and the Childbirth Metaphor: Gender Difference in Literary Discourse."

21. Castle, "Lab'ring Bards," 203; Chadwick and de Courtivron, *Significant Others*, 10.

22. Godwin and Wollstonecraft, *Godwin & Mary: Letters of William Godwin and Mary Wollstonecraft*, 8.

23. Simmons, *Erotic Reckonings*, 5, 12.

24. Rousseau, *Émile*, 368.

Home at Grasmere Again

Revising the Family in Dove Cottage

ANNE D. WALLACE

Romantic notions of "author" as isolated genius are remarkably persistent, not only among professional literary critics (as Jack Stillinger demonstrates in *Multiple Authorship and the Myth of Solitary Genius*) but among
our students and presumably also among the less specialized readers
outside the academy whom they represent. Reading William Wordsworth's "I Wandered Lonely as a Cloud" along with Dorothy Wordsworth's journal entry for April 15, 1802 (in which she describes the same
scene) generally disappoints students. William's stock drops and Dorothy's rises, but their inclination is to transfer originary power to Dorothy, not to question their fundamental assumption that true artists work
alone. Granting the coercive force of Romantic ideologies, the persistence of this particular strand suggests broader foundations than those of
"literary" Romanticisms alone.

The supporting role played by domestic ideologies has been mapped
out in a considerable body of criticism, exemplified by the work of
Nancy Armstrong, Mary Poovey, and (for the Americanists) Gillian
Brown. The separation of private domesticity from public productivity,
the fostering of individual consciousness through domestic relations, the

significance of writing as an expression of individual subjectivity—these claims of domestic ideologies ensure a double detachment of the author from both public and private contexts. As an individual deriving motive force from a private domestic space, the author is protected from the supposed moral taint of the marketplace; as a published writer whose work signifies a now mobile individuality, the author is removed from the supposed narrowness of domesticity.

I have avoided gendered pronouns here, but of course the domestic/public separation is gendered, and the critics of domesticity also debate the complex situation of women writers seeking an authorial identity in the masculinized world of paid work. The full impact of these constructions becomes evident when contrasted with earlier configurations of labor and value, in which work of all kinds was less strictly gendered and less closely associated with pay, so that both household and what we now call "public" economies depended on a more diffuse, less monetary productivity. As Kurt Heinzelman has shown, under such conditions it becomes possible to represent authorship as collective, part of an open-ended domestic economy as well as the public monetary economies of industrialized production.

I want to carry on from these perceptions to suggest that fixed definitions of "family"—current academic definitions corresponding to popular notions of the "traditional family"—also play a key role in sustaining the concept of the author as isolated genius. Specifically, I think that our overly stable histories of the family, derived from the intersection of domestic ideologies and modern psychologies, mask the changing significance of the grown sibling in the household. Nancy Armstrong and Leonard Tennenhouse have analyzed the ahistorical "logic of emotions" governing academic studies of the family, which, despite apparent differences, fixate on the conjugal bond in the nuclear family.[1] As Ruth Perry has pointed out, this fixation (her term) operates in literary studies as well, where our readings do not shift to accommodate historical changes in kinship structures and take the affective bond as fundamental. Even where we read sibling relations as having some primary significance, we limit our readings to certain affective/psychosexual meanings that we assume are historically stable.[2] Returning to the oft-considered case of William and Dorothy Wordsworth, I want to recognize the sibling in the house as an unstable economic sign—as a sign, specifically, of the changing valuations of corporate production and domestic labor during the nineteenth century.

Leonore Davidoff and Catherine Hall's 1987 historical survey *Family Fortunes: Men and Women of the English Middle Class, 1780–1850* suggests that during the early stages of industrialization in England, middle-class families and households were defined as much by lateral ties as by conjugal or parent-child bonds.[3] It was in the late eighteenth century, as Davidoff notes in a later article, that "the growth of outwork and by-industries" left middle-class siblings in the home together who would otherwise have gone into service or apprenticeship elsewhere. The resulting material and affective economies depended heavily on horizontal ties among siblings or those derived from sibling ties (e.g., aunt and uncle, niece and nephew, and cousin):

> [B]rothers often went into partnership with the husbands of their sisters or the sister would subsequently marry a brother's partners. . . . [I]n a significant number of cases two brothers from one family would marry two sisters from another, or a brother or sister from one would marry a sister and brother from another [partible inheritance]. . . . Unmarried sisters expected to contribute labour and often capital as well to their family's enterprise, whether run by a father or brother; they also expected to act as housekeeper to adult single brothers, careers of the married siblings' children, and in turn, to be supported by the family enterprise.

In this family model, a model that was idealized and widespread during the late eighteenth and early nineteenth centuries, sibling and spousal relationships are mutually constitutive; households are not self-contained either emotionally or materially, but rather are part of a network of sibling-anchored households; and (an important point not directly addressed in the quotation above) the family's house is the site of labor, both domestic and productive.[4]

Dorothy Wordsworth's *Grasmere Journals* and William Wordsworth's *Home at Grasmere* represent the Dove Cottage household along just these lines. Given the simultaneous composition of these texts (Dorothy's journals date from 1800–1803; the first version of William's poem from 1800–1806), spanning the earliest years of the Wordsworth siblings' residence at Dove Cottage and William's marriage in 1802, one might expect to find certain similarities in their treatment of what one may broadly term "home-making."[5] Both the journals and the poem rhetorically conflate spousal and sibling bonds, constructing the mutually constitutive relationship suggested by Davidoff and Hall. However, as those historians' work also demonstrates, the "corporate household" (my term for the family model I described earlier) of this period was already in flux, shifting gradually and unevenly toward the nuclear configuration.[6] My general formulation implies too smooth a progression, but, essentially, as the sibling in the house changed from a valued source of productive labor to an anomaly in the ideally work-free domestic space, representations of collaborative authorial identities gave way to representations of freestanding authority.

The unevenness of these developments becomes clear in the specific readings that follow. Dorothy's *Grasmere Journals* locate her literary authority in the corporate household, rhetorically equating literary work with housework and valuing grown siblings' collective labor at these linked tasks as a guarantor of a household's material and affective security. The journals' reconstruction of Dove Cottage after William and Mary's marriage as a sibling enterprise cooperative with their spousal union also produces Dorothy's own recommitment to the kind of writing that has (so far) been most productive for her and William, the journal itself. *Home at Grasmere* also develops an extensive argument for the household inclusive of siblings, the narrator's own literary ambitions seeming (for most of the poem) to issue forth from Grasmere Vale's corporate household. Unlike the *Grasmere Journals,* however, *Home at Grasmere* rarely represents indoor domestic labor, disconnecting housework from literary work. As a brief reading against "Michael" shows, this partial separation of the domestic from the public, and of women from men, coincides with the separation of literary authority from the working household. In the final 150 lines of *Home at Grasmere* the narrator abstracts the male poet from the domestic collective, replacing his role as brother in a material household with that of rhapsodist on a figurative marriage of world and mind. In the poem's resolution, then, the brother's detachment from the household constitutes the author's creative isolation.

Dorothy's account of William and Mary's wedding day dramatizes the extent to which spousal and sibling bonds depended on each other in early-nineteenth-century middle-class families. Dorothy's description has drawn much attention, especially since Mary Moorman restored the siblings' exchange of the wedding ring to the text:

> On Monday 4th October 1802, my Brother William was married to Mary Hutchinson. I slept a good deal of the night & rose fresh & well in the morning—at a little after 8 o clock I saw them go down the avenue towards the Church. William had parted from me up stairs. I gave him

the wedding ring—with how deep a blessing! I took it from my forefinger where I had worn it the whole of the night before—he slipped it again onto my finger and blessed me fervently. When they were absent my dear little Sara prepared the breakfast. I kept myself as quiet as I could, but when I saw the two men running up the walk, coming to tell us it was over, I could stand it no longer & threw myself on the bed where I lay in stillness, neither hearing or seeing any thing, till Sara came upstairs to me & said "They are coming." This forced me from the bed where I lay & I moved I knew not how straight forward, faster than my strength could carry me till I met my beloved William & fell upon his bosom. He & John Hutchinson led me to the house & there I stayed to welcome my dear Mary. As soon as we had breakfasted we departed. It rained when we set off. Poor Mary was much agitated when she parted from her Brothers & Sisters & her home.[7]

The context of the restored passage (which runs from "I gave him the wedding ring" to "blessed me fervently") suggests something quite different to me than the current range of readings.[8] Dorothy emphasizes the Hutchinson and Wordsworth siblings even as the marriage takes place: Sara Hutchinson is making breakfast; Mary's brother John accompanies William back to the house; Dorothy meets them and is supported back to the house by William and John. This is not just a question of plot but also of its insistent naming of the siblings and their rotating interactions with each other. Even Mary's departure is figured first as parting from her brothers and sisters and then as a parting from "home."[9]

The wider context of the wedding-day passage—a long retrospective entry beginning on July 27 (when William and Dorothy set out for Calais) and ending on October 8 with the return to Grasmere—reveals even more clearly Dorothy's representation of sibling households supporting the coming marriage. After William and Dorothy return from France, they go to Gallow Hill, a farm purchased in 1800 by Mary Hutchinson's brothers Tom and George and variously inhabited by Tom, George, Mary, Sara, and Joanna Hutchinson, depending on the siblings' housekeeping needs. As Dorothy describes it, Mary arrives first to meet them, "then came Sara, & last of all Joanna. Tom was forking corn standing upon the corn cart" (126). John and George arrive on October 1, and all but Mary ride out together to Hackness on October 2, with "William Jack George & Sara single, I behind Tom" (126). The next day "Mary & Sara were busy packing" (126); the day after this is the wedding. Dorothy's repeated display of mutually supportive material relations among the Hutchinson and Wordsworth siblings within and across their birth families implies that the marriage both depends upon and will further stabilize this configuration.

This implication becomes nearly explicit after the marriage, as Dorothy loads her account of the trip back to Grasmere with similar references. The coherent argument about memory and feeling that structures this part of the entry, anchored in a scheme of shifting sibling and spousal pairs and triplets, constructs the household at which they will arrive in the same mold as those they have left: Dove Cottage before the wedding and Gallow Hill after.[10] Dorothy's repeated comparison of the journeys she and William have already made over this ground (primarily the journey to the marriage) with the journey the three are now making provides the skeleton of her account. Within ten sentences of their departure from Gallow Hill, Dorothy foregrounds this structure, proposing her (and William's) shared memories as the source of an inevitable intrinsic interest now also shared by Mary. After a brief recital of some local topography and history, Dorothy remarks that "Every foot of the Road was, of itself interesting to us, for we had traveled along it on foot Wm & I when we went to fetch our dear Mary, & had sate upon the Turf by the roadside more than once" (127). The potentially shifting meaning of the first-person plural, which at first seems to mean all three and then only the two of them, carries through in "our dear Mary," in which both William and Dorothy seem "paired"—in their obviously different ways—with the bride, and yet the sense of three "siblings" is also strong. This passage also claims—in typically Romantic yet specifically Wordsworthian terms—that Mary can join in William and Dorothy's past feelings by retracing paths and recollecting memories with them, and (implicitly) that a future community of feeling will emerge from these present efforts.

Although Dorothy does not always carry the recollective scheme directly into this construction of communal feeling, she holds to her comparative structure throughout the rest of the entry, maintaining a rotating pairing and rejoining of twos into three. The sheer accumulation of such instances prepares us for the reestablishment of Dove Cottage as a household anchored by sibling feeling and shared domestic labor. The long entry ends with their return to Grasmere: "[F]or my part I cannot describe what I felt, & our dear Mary's feelings would I dare say not be easy to speak of. We went by candle light into the garden & were

astonished at the growth of the Brooms, Portugal Laurels, &c &c &—
The next day, Thursday, we unpacked the Boxes. On Friday 8th we
baked Bread, & Mary & I walked, first upon the Hill side, & then in
John's Grove, then in view of Rydale, the first walk that I had taken with
my Sister" (132). Dorothy's assertion that "our" Mary's feelings must resemble hers in their inexpressibility moves right into a "we" that may be
three, who inspect the garden William and Dorothy have tended. The
"we" that unpacks boxes may be three, the "we" baking bread probably
less so (though it may include their servant, Molly). However these are
numbered, the shared domestic labors of gardening, unpacking, and
baking bread lead to Dorothy and Mary walking (an agent of poetic
composition for the Wordsworths) in the yew grove named by William
for John Wordsworth in a poem, the sequence sketching in brief the en-
compassing of domestic and poetic labors in a single corporate household effort.[11]

One could follow the idealization of the corporate household
into still larger contextual frames, opening into the whole of Dorothy's
journals and still further into the writings of others connected to Dove
Cottage. For instance, Coleridge mourned the death of William and
Dorothy's seafaring brother John as a loss to "*the Concern*," the Grasmere
household to which John had intended to retire with the profits from the
siblings' considerable investment in his last fatal voyage.[12] Mary Hutchinson Wordsworth's unpublished autobiographical memoranda also
document her family's reliance on siblings for material and emotional
support.[13] But even within the relatively limited context of the full journal entry, it seems to me that the power of William and Dorothy's ring
exchange must flow both ways: their enactment of sibling commitment
in marital terms demonstrates a linkage of the sibling and spousal bonds,
validating the approaching marriage as much as the brother's and
sister's continuing importance to each other.

Home at Grasmere, which takes as its subject William and Dorothy's first days at Dove Cottage, also represents these relationships as
comparable and equally—or, perhaps, complementarily—definitive of
"being at home."[14] For instance, the speaker uses two bird images to illustrate his relationship with Emma (Dorothy's alter ego). In the first,
rejoicing in their renewed companionship in the Grasmere household,
the speaker likens himself and Emma to "Birds / Which by the intrud-
ing Fowler had been scared, / Two of a scattered brood that could
not bear / To live in loneliness" (173–76). Once the two have "found

means / To walk abreast . . . / With undivided steps," then their "home was sweet; / Could it be less?" (177–79, 179–80). This image of sibling home-making is supported by a later passage in which the speaker notices the disappearance of "a lonely pair / Of milk-white Swans" that "came, like Emma and myself, to live / Together here in peace and solitude" (322–23, 326–27). The speaker and Emma have watched these swans not only for "their still / And placid way of life and faithful love / Inseparable" (335–37) but because

> their state so much resembled ours
> They also having chosen this abode;
> They strangers, and we strangers; they a pair,
> And we a solitary pair like them.
>
> (338–41)

The speaker enforces the comparison, repeating parallel constructions and simple statements, "like them." But the differences are also striking. Swans mate for life, and this is a mated pair, not "two of a scattered brood." Moreover, the swans are not there, and by the end of the passage the speaker imagines that they may well be dead.[15] Yet the speaker does not explicitly call attention to the mating of the two swans, instead describing them as "Companions, brethren, consecrated friends" and asking, "Shall we behold them yet another year / Surviving, they for us, and we for them, / And neither pair be broken?" (347, 348–50). The solemn intensity of the speaker's question makes the swan pair and the spousal union they represent seem essential to the siblings' sense of home, and vice versa. Together the mated and the sibling pairs of the poem form a "household" in the vale, one that apparently would be at its best if it accommodated both siblings and mates.

Indeed, the controlling metaphor of the poem is that of Grasmere Vale as "One Household . . . One family and one mansion," accommodating everything from birds and dogs to poets (822, 823). And although this household is ordered hierarchically under the "paternal sway" of God (the metaphorical mother is Grasmere Church), it also opens out laterally into a "brood of Cottages" (821, 527). The speaker tells three "cottage stories" purportedly to demonstrate the "old / Substantial virtues" fostered in the vale's household (466–67). In the first a married man seduces a serving girl ("an Inmate of the house")—a family member in the older sense of the term—and dies of remorse (503).[16] The second describes the happy, fruitful home of a shepherd whose six daughters

supply not only the place of their dead mother but also of the sons he
never had. And the third praises a widow who remembers her husband
by means of the grove they planted together. These disparate stories
lead to the speaker's emphatic assertion "No, We are not alone, we do
not stand / My Emma, here misplaced and desolate, / Loving what no
one cares for but ourselves" (646–48). The construction permits no dis-
sonance among these tales of households that seem so variously constituted, nor between the tales of married couples who have been broken
by infidelity or death and the poem's "reality" of a faithful, abiding
sibling pair.

Similarly, despite the many references to the speaker and Emma as
a pair, their own household is "enriched / Already with a Stranger
whom we love / Deeply, a Stranger of our Father's house, / A never-
resting Pilgrim of the Sea" (863–66). "And others whom we love / Will
seek us also," the speaker goes on, "Sisters of our hearts, / And one, like
them, a Brother of our hearts, / Philosopher and Poet" (867–71). The
double metaphor of John Wordsworth, the blood brother, as roving out-
sider and of the Hutchinson sisters and Coleridge as siblings underscores
the fundamental importance of sibling ties in constituting "household"
and "family." Even absent siblings remain a part of the household, while
friends as yet unrelated by marriage may be rhetorically drawn into the
domestic economies of feeling and poetic production by naming them
"sister" and "brother."

The speaker of *Home at Grasmere* concludes the Pilgrims and Brothers
passage by renewing his economic metaphor of enrichment: "Such is
our wealth. . . . we are / And must be, with God's will, a happy band"
(873–74). Kurt Heinzelman has argued that a "radical Wordsworthian
mythos" originally situated the domestic in a shared labor of writing that
William and Dorothy sought to extend into "a larger idea of economy
that included not only their own household but also the households of
their neighbors and friends." In these extended economies William and
Dorothy each resist the increasingly harsh sexual division of labor evident in contemporary economic theories, but with characteristically different turns. Whereas William represents "domestic activity as an infrastructure of support for creativity," Dorothy "articulates and sustains
the idea that the equating of creativity and work is necessary to the success of the household. . . . [T]he coefficient of happiness is the coherent
management of all the labors of a household, including the production
of texts."[17]

Heinzelman's examples of household labor are all out-of-doors—
gardening, orchard tending, enclosing land—examples apt to his argument for these discourses as georgic, but which once again "disappear"
housework. What makes Dorothy's journals so formidable (as my students' reactions always remind me) is their uncategorical juxtaposition
of indoor domestic labor, which much of our culture regards as trivial,
with such obviously "literary" work as reading, writing, and describing
nature. Dorothy portrays herself as cooking, baking, ironing, bleaching
linen, making clothes, preparing medicines, copying poems, writing
letters, walking, and—implicitly and always—writing these journals,
which she has framed as sources of that defining poetic product termed
"pleasure."[18] The journals' run-on grammar, list-like itineraries of
events, and selection and sequencing do not encourage us to sort these
activities into public and private, literary and domestic, outside and inside. Rather, these categories are so mixed as to allow us to read them as
equivalent.

I want to emphasize the difference between the claim I'm making
here and the more generalized descriptions of this revisionary strain in
Dorothy's aesthetics as "particularization" (Susan Levin), "ordinari-
ness" (Pamela Woof), "literalization" (Margaret Homans), or "making
the commonplace aesthetic" (Elizabeth Bohls).[19] Nor do I distinguish
Dorothy's use of these well-known Romantic strategies by means of the
general differences ascribed to gender—her building of community, as
Levin suggests, or her ability (and need) to replicate the mother, as Homans has it. In my view Dorothy's different claim to authority hinges on
a very specific point: the juxtapositional rhetoric of the *Grasmere Journals*
draws indoor domestic labor into the valorized categories of the "everyday" and "commonplace" so that housework appears of a piece with literary authorization.[20]

Consider the following entry dated August 2, 1800: "Wm & Coleridge went to Keswick. John went with them to Wytheburn & staid all
day fishing & brought home 2 small pikes at night. I accompanied them
to Lewthwaite's cottage & on my return papered Wm's room—I afterwards lay down till tea time & after tea worked at my shifts in the orchard. A grey evening—about 8 o'clock it gathered for rain & I had the
scatterings of a shower, but afterwards the lake became of a glassy calm-
ness & all was still. I sate till I could see no longer & then continued my
work in the house" (15). The triple inscription of the journey in ever
smaller circuits connects William and Coleridge's Lakeland wandering,
through brother John's nearer provisioning, and through Dorothy's still

nearer excursion, to Dorothy's wallpapering (itself a suggestive melding of text and house), a simple "&" performing the last conjunction.
Dorothy's sewing, taken outdoors, seems to produce the brief natural
description along with the shifts, and though she only mentions the continued sewing, the writing of the description implicitly occurs inside,
when she "could see no longer" outdoors.[21] Thoroughly mixed and set
out in an ambiguously back-and-forth chronology that permits a back-
and-forth causality, the explicit and implicit works of the entry—poetry,
walking, food gathering, house maintenance, sewing, and journal
writing—appear to be on strikingly egalitarian terms. My difficulty with
such a passage is the specific expectation that shift sewing and written
description have different intrinsic values, and that this expected valuation (not just ours but that of Dorothy's contemporaries) is contradicted
by the journals' rhetoric.

It is, I believe, the sustained equation of literary work and housework in the *Grasmere Journals* that maintains the representational simul-
taneity of the corporate household and Wordsworthian literary authority. One will recall that in her account of the wedding journey Dorothy
sets herself the task of recollecting and refashioning feeling; and the specific feeling she claims to recall/create is that of sibling community, in
which she thoroughly embeds the new spousal union. She has already
figured the couple's espousing as an occasion of her recommitment to
her brother. Now she produces Mary as "my Sister," a relationship le-
gally created by William and Mary's marriage but in this text ratified by
Dorothy's joining Mary first in housework, and then in a walk, and
then, silently, in completing the writing of the journal entry. From the
beginning of the *Grasmere Journals*, when she mixes her own needs with
the desire to give pleasure to her brother William (who has gone off with
their brother John), Dorothy claims literary work as the corporate domestic production of a sibling household. In the journal's penultimate
entry she again vows—in those familiarly mixed terms—to continue
writing: "William has been working beside me, and here ends this imperfect summary. I will take a nice Calais Book and *will* for the future
write regularly and, if I can legibly so much for this my resolution on
Tuesday night, January 11th 1803. Now I am going to take Tapioca for
my supper; and Mary an Egg. William some cold mutton—his poor
chest is tired" (137). As Heinzelman points out, "Dorothy's *Journal* does
not conclude with its overt little gesture toward closure like a public utterance, like a poem." Rather, Dorothy tells us that well-known story
about buying gingerbread, in which, as Heinzelman puts it, "Dorothy

cheerfully gives her two-pence to an enterprising family, which had the good sense to leave a special place for 'the sister' to read to them beside the fire." But for me this story lacks the plaintive quality I think it may have for Heinzelman (he calls it a "good-natured anecdote").[22] Rather, it seems to confirm the still-stable vision in the *Grasmere Journals* of the domestic literary enterprise of the Wordsworth family, in which making gingerbread is as meaningful as making vows—and in which the sister writes as well as reads at home by the fire.

In *Home at Grasmere*, by contrast, indoor domestic labor is suppressed and contained, loosening the potential connection between the domestic and the literary. The most obvious evidence of this is that the narrator never represents himself or Emma doing any kind of indoor labor, this despite a continuing emphasis on domestic economies of other kinds. For instance, the first hundred lines of the poem rely more heavily than any other passage on economic allusions—"fortune," "business," "cost," "dower," "unappropriated," "wealth," "gain"—and these allusions are descriptive of the speaker's "possession" of Grasmere as a home. For "proof" of his possession, his gain, the speaker points to "Yon cottage, where with me my Emma dwells" (97, 98). The siblings come into "a home / Within a home, what was to be, and soon, / Our love within a love," recommending themselves to the personified Vale's domestic affections by their faithfulness throughout the winter and by "the Poet['s] prelusive songs" (261–63, 273). The economic language, the sibling-based home, and the connection of domestic affections and poetry form a familiar cluster of ideas. Notably missing is the direct connection of housework and writing evident in the formulations of the *Grasmere Journals*. The siblings' "homemaking," foregrounded by the title of the poem and by its later claims about the great household of Grasmere Vale, takes place entirely outdoors, in their walking, and in the analogous labors of the dalesmen.

Even in those labors, although there is more of the domestic, the little indoor work is subtly gendered, and literary work seems undomesticated. For instance, in the second "cottage story" six sisters and their father seem to work across gender lines, mixing domestic, pastoral, and artistic (but not literary) labors. Their cottage is distinguished by its appearance as "a studious work / Of many fancies and of many hands" (560–62), metaphorically, at least, a work of art. The narrator attributes most of this artistry to "a hardy Girl, who mounts the rocks . . . [and] fears not the bleak wind," rendering her father "[t]he service of a Boy" as shepherd's apprentice (574–75, 578). This same daughter "also

helped to frame that tiny Plot" farther from the house, a mini-orchard
where gooseberries grow, but completes her out-of-doors cultivation by
decorating the orchard with a metaphorical sign of domesticity, "[a]
mimic Bird's-nest" (583, 588). The speaker then turns back to the domestic space, finding that "most / This Dwelling charms me" at night
when, in the lighted room beyond the window, he sees "the eldest
Daughter at her wheel, / Spinning amain" (598–99). Yet, as Heinzelman points out, this spinning daughter learned her "skill in this or other
household work / . . . from her Father's honored hands" (602–3).

William elaborates domestic containments around the boyish train-
ing of the "hardy Girl" to an extent that makes me question Heinzelman's evenhanded perception in these passages of "men doing so-called
female labor and vice versa."[23] Rather, the sisters do both men's and
women's work under their father's instruction. In sharp contrast to the
variety of housework in the *Grasmere Journals*, only one kind of domestic
labor is represented here (and a questionable one at that, for reasons I'll
explain below). Nor are there any scenes of writing or reading, suggesting that such literary labors are not an integral part of this domesticity.
What we have here is both the more fluid gendering of pre-industrialized
labor and industrialization's increasing restriction of "work" to the out-
of-doors labors of men. To put it another way, William's participation
in the "cult of domesticity," a participation Heinzelman locates in his
later poetry, is already present here, interleaved with a strong critique of
the emergent sexual division of labor. This makes even better sense of
Heinzelman's perception that William differs from Dorothy in valuing
domestic and creative activity: William already separates the two kinds
of work even as he idealizes their simultaneous possibility.

It might be helpful here to turn to "Michael" (1800) in order to observe the very similar interleavings of labor ideologies in the poem's representations of men engaged in childcare and other housework. Most
striking, perhaps, is Michael's mothering of his infant son:

> For oftentimes
> Old Michael, while [Luke] was a babe in arms,
> Had done him female service, not alone
> For dalliance and delight, as is the use
> Of Fathers, but with patient mind enforced
> To acts of tenderness; and he had rocked
> His cradle with a woman's gentle hand.
> (162–68)[24]

Marjorie Levinson has interpreted this as a scene of patriarchal dominance, signaling Michael's "creative appropriation of his son" and their
peculiar relationship as "craftsman to artifact."[25] But Michael's departure from the leisurely "use / Of fathers," "alone / For dalliance and
delight," also engages him in child rearing as labor: "service," "enforced," and "rocked" all underscore the difficulty, laboriousness, and
sheer physical effort of childcare. That Levinson reads this labor as a
traditional craftsman's seems right, as do her concerns about the accompanying objectification of mother and son. But Michael's mothering also reads as domestic labor, and labor of a variety traditionally
thought of (and here labeled) as "female." Similarly, Michael and Luke
take up "such convenient work, as might employ / Their hands by the
fireside" after their outdoors work is done, "card[ing] / Wool for the
House-wife's spindle," and attending equally to "implement[s] of house
or field" (107–9, 111). These passages do not stringently separate indoors
from outdoors, domestic from public, women's from men's labor, suggesting an accompanying valorization of women's work.

That valorization, however, is significantly limited. In his representations of women at work in "Michael," William confines women's visible active labor to spinning and making or mending clothes (84–87,
127–30, 296–97). While he frames the participation of male characters
in indoor work as a celebration of the older integrated domestic economy, which made traditional but nonessential gender distinctions,[26] his
concurrent reduction of other women's work, domestic or otherwise, to
textile manufacture is actually part of the developing code of "separate
spheres" domesticity. As the isolation of the domestic space from the
productive marketplace proceeded, even as fewer homes spun their
own thread or wove their own cloth, textile work (e.g., sewing, knitting,
embroidery, mending) paradoxically became the sole referent of the unmodified word "work" to describe women's exertions. In nineteenth-
century fictional accounts of domesticity, sewing stands in for almost all
other domestic labor. As in the ideal middle-class practice of housekeeping, in which all signs of actual physical labor were to be kept from
view, activities such as cooking, fetching water, cleaning, and washing
are relentlessly elided.[27]

Similar elisions are evident in "Michael." As if by magic, when he
and his son come in from their herding, they find a "cleanly supper-
board" and prepared food, Isabel's implicit labor disappearing into its
products (101). Even the several passages representing her spinning and

sewing include just one phrase in which she is an active subject—"The House-wife plied her own peculiar work" (127)—one couched in language that binds wife to house and marks spinning as her specialty. The image of an active woman is brief indeed: just one line later, her activity is doubly deferred in a metaphor for the wheel's turning, which "[m]ak[es] the cottage thro' the silent hours / Murmur as with the sound of summer flies" (129–30). These are quite different rhetorical constructions than those showing Michael and his son at work in the home:

> both betook themselves
> To such convenient work, as might employ
> Their hands by the fire-side; perhaps to card
> Wool for the House-wife's spindle, or repair
> Some injury done to sickle, flail, or scythe,
> Or other implement of house or field.
>
> (106–11)

The activity of the verbs chosen for the men's actions, the plain display of nouns, and the greater variety and scope of Michael and Luke's specific tasks (which encompass both house and field) contrast sharply with the appearance of Isabel's work in disembodied, metaphorical terms and then only as spinning or sewing.

The resistance of "Michael" to a strict separation of work from housework issues from its representations of men actively performing indoor household labors and contributing to the conventionally female work of childcare. The "catch" is no doubt abundantly clear: if only male characters transgress the boundaries of gendered labor, and if they most actively perform indoor labor, then labor is gender-specialized only—but definitively—for women. One can ameliorate this problem by reading "Michael" (as Heinzelman does) alongside *Home at Grasmere*, in which women also do men's work. However, the problem is re-compounded when one realizes that the latter poem once again restricts indoors domestic labor to the ambiguously significant textile work, suggesting a separation that apparently can be effectively transgressed here, as in "Michael," only by a man's double expertise. The sister who shepherds and cultivates is not the sister who spins, and both are instructed by their father.

These various exclusions and containments of housework coincide, in both poems, with turns away from the corporate household and toward freestanding literary authority. "Michael" again provides a helpful parallel reading since the traditional understanding of the poem's "failed patrimony" plot so heavily inflects critical discussions of the narrator's claims to poetic authority. I do not mean to deny "Michael"'s foregrounding of patriarchal power structures: the land lost to external debts, the son departing to earn the money that will reinvest the family, or the failure of the son to return, thereby ending the fruitful succession of fathers and sons. This strain seems very different from the overtly sibling-oriented plot of its companion poem "The Brothers" or, for that matter, *Home at Grasmere*.

But the failure of Michael and Luke to fulfill their father-son covenant derives from the failure of sibling ties that Michael sought to maintain and that he evidently expected would undergird Luke's inheritance. The "contract of guarantee" by which Michael encumbers his land is "surety for his Brother's Son, a man / Of an industrious life, and ample means," whose forfeiture the narrator describes as the result of "unforseen misfortunes" (221–22, 223). Although the narrator's account conflicts with Michael's suspicious attitude toward his nephew—"An evil Man / That was, and made an evil choice, if he / Were false to us" (246–48)—the rest of the poem adds no confirmation to either explanation, suggesting that the nephew's character does not determine these disastrous events. Instead, the problem seems to be the nephew's literal distance from his uncle's household, from which the nephew claims and receives aid but to which he has become a stranger. That Michael does not know whether his nephew is "an evil Man" locates the breaking point of their mutual obligation in a new mobility that divides corporate, sibling-anchored households into discrete spousal families. When the nephew seeks and the uncle gives surety, they adhere to the older practices of corporate households, in which the fortunes of the nephew are also those of Michael's household, and vice versa. However, the physical and economic distances between the nephew and the uncle permit the intervention of forces the nephew's best efforts cannot avert and the uncle cannot understand. Michael can imagine no *economic* reason for his nephew's failure; his surety and the nephew's labor should have ensured the family's well-being.

Nor can Michael imagine any remedy outside the circles of family obligation. When he recoils from selling "[a] portion of his patrimonial fields" to pay the debt, we may well wonder at his seeming to set a higher value on his lands than his son. The poem leaves little doubt that Michael's attachment to his land is partly a matter of personal feeling,

and to that extent it is Michael's individual ownership that is at stake.
But the origins of Michael's debt in his support of his nephew suggest
that he does not think of his inheritance as a single private accumulation, the value of which belongs to an economically isolated spousal
household. Although Michael owns his land (presumably) as eldest son
and through his labor, his brother (or sister—the term "in-law" was not
yet consistently used) shared the father from whom Michael inherits the
fields.[28] The kind of surety he provided for his nephew depends upon
Michael's holding of the patrimonial lands and upon their mutual expectation of such aid. Thus, to sell his patrimony is not only to dispos-
sess himself and his son (although that is his only directly expressed concern) but is also to alienate his power to assist his siblings and their
children, to lose the ability to stand in surety for them, to fail in his inherited obligations.

Instead, Michael tries to tap into a still more extended familial economy. As he explains to Isabel,

> We have, thou knowest,
> Another Kinsman, he will be our friend
> In this distress. He is a prosperous man,
> Thriving in trade, and Luke to him shall go,
> And with his Kinsman's help and his own thrift,
> He quickly will repair this loss, and then
> May come again to us. If here he stay,
> What can be done? Where every one is poor
> What can be gained?
>
> (257–65)

Michael's error here is not, as Levinson has it, that he "involves his
family in the mechanisms of the market he had thus far avoided"[29] but
rather that he *again* unwittingly does so. Just as he mistook his surety for
his nephew as a household affair within their control and knowledge, so
he mistakes his kinsman's prosperity and his son's labor as sufficient in
this crisis, failing to recognize the literally "unfamiliar" economic forms
that may again intervene in their household and familial economies.
The ambiguous relation "kinsman" emphasizes the fundamental problem of distance, which escalates as Michael reaches beyond his sibling
group. The kinsman's first "good report" and Luke's "loving letters"
(440, 442) suggest their initial efforts to maintain the old forms, the kinsman watching over Luke and Luke dutifully sending words (although
not money, we notice) to his home. But the distances between cottage

and city, between old and new ways, are too great, measured not just by Luke's failure to return but also by his removal to the even greater distances of criminality and an eventual flight to "a hiding-place beyond the seas" (236).

Viewed in this context, Michael's ruin cannot be thought of solely as the ruin of a freeheld patrimony or the closed economy of a spousal household. Michael feels obligated to and expects assistance from a wider family, one that in the not too distant past might have been settled nearby or even within the same household establishment. The poem's plot describes a household both more isolated and less independent than Michael's expectations, one without functioning sibling supports or the comfort of a wider kinship, and yet one opened, not just by their expectations but also by circumstances permanently beyond their control, to outsiders' depredations.

Like the narrator of "Michael," who is led by Michael's story to "think / At random and imperfectly indeed / On man, the heart of man, and human life" (31–33), the speaker of *Home at Grasmere* thinks "On Man, on Nature, and on human Life / . . . in solitude" (959–60). Transiting between his fervent account of the "enriched" household of strangers and brethren and the well-known closing in which he takes up his poetic vocation, the speaker now characterizes this idealized domestic sphere as the "narrow bounds" of some pure enjoyment not adequate to justify his existence:

> That humble Roof enbowered among the trees,
> That calm fireside, it is not even in them,
> Blessed as they are, to furnish a reply
> That satisfies and ends in perfect rest.
> Possessions have I wholly, solely, mine,
> Something within, which yet is shared by none,
> Not even the nearest to me and most dear,
> Something which power and effort may impart.
> I would impart it; I would spread it wide,
> Immortal in the world which is to come.
>
> (893–902)

This something is, of course, poetry, which comes from him alone, from his inner self—now separated from his familial household—and *so* (the causal implication is powerful) immortal. The Eden once associated with the siblings' new home becomes the site of an abstract marriage— not of husband and wife, nor even metaphorically of a "solitary pair" of siblings—of mind and world. The speaker stands outside this married "couple," outside the household of world and mind, and "sing[s] in solitude the spousal verse / Of this great consummation" (1003–4).

These words return us to the beginning of the poem, in which (as in "Tintern Abbey") the speaker at first seems alone in the landscape, claiming sole possession. But the violence of such a return, after nearly nine hundred lines embedding the speaker's authority in a "rich" conglomeration of siblings and spouses, also marks the ideological distance between the corporate household and the solitary genius. *He* cannot fully emerge until he withdraws from his brotherhood, implicitly privatizing the household that now merely measures, in its contrasting corporate pleasures, his more fruitful individuality. In *Home at Grasmere* the grown sibling must leave the house to become the creative poet.

I do not wish to propose a stable, gendered opposition, a simplistically reversed valuation, with Dorothy admirably faithful to the attractive collectivity of her Dove Cottage and William traitorously conspiring to set himself up as the singular genius. Not only do William and Dorothy collaborate in the production of "William Wordsworth" (as Eric C. Walker and Elizabeth A. Fay have variously argued),[30] but William's and Dorothy's constructions of literary authority and domesticity fluctuate within the oeuvre—indeed, within single works—of each author. For instance, in Dorothy's poetry we find lyric narrators claiming the same solitary inspirations she attributes to her brother, wandering through similarly domesticated landscapes but disconnected from the indoor work of a literal household. Certainly at this early date (as Heinzelman and Robert Gordon both argue)[31] William proposed domestic virtue as an essential foundation for everything from national defense to personal achievement.

Rather, the point I wish to make is that rereading these brother-sister relationships—in the context of the Wordsworths' constructions of a corporate household, and in the context of recent histories of the family claiming that such constructions were far from idiosyncratic—articulates complex relationships among family structures, domestic and public economies, and literary authority. Now, the literary figure of the grown sibling in the house can no longer be fully contained by the stable, ahistorical formulations of individual psyches and family affections so monotonously repeated in our critiques of literary sibling relations. Rather, the sibling in the house must also appear as a sign of unevenly developing public economies, and of their fluctuating interactions with similarly unstable domestic economies, both material and affective. Within these contexts the Wordsworths' various formulations of literary production as family business should also lead us to reassess how we constitute literary authority, to historicize the critical tautologies in which text both issues from and reveals a "self" grown in a privatized nuclear household and most fundamentally defined by parent-child and spousal relations. Reading the grown sibling in the house in these ways, one may more fully index the changing valuations of family, domestic labor and paid publication, and literature's originary claims in an industrializing, capitalizing, mobilizing, individualizing culture.

Notes

1. Nancy Armstrong and Leonard Tennenhouse, *The Imaginary Puritan: Literature, Intellectual Labor, and the Origins of Personal Life*, 184. For histories of the family that resist this common scholarly assumption, see: Anderson, *Family Structure in Nineteenth-Century Lancashire;* Berkner, "The Stem Family and the Developmental Cycle of the Peasant Household: An Eighteenth-Century Austrian Example"; Crozier, "Kinship and Occupational Succession"; Davidoff and Hall, *Family Fortunes: Men and Women of the English Middle Class, 1780–1850;* Sabean, "Aspects of Kinship Behaviour and Property in Rural Western Europe before 1800"; Scott and Tilly, "Women's Work and the Family in Nineteenth-Century Europe." Even these scholars, however, rarely leave the well-trodden grounds of marriage patterns, parent-child interactions, and lineal inheritance, remaining dependent on the term "nuclear family" as an unhistoricized descriptor.

2. I develop this claim in a more detailed study upon which this essay is based, starting from Nancy Armstrong's argument that our relentlessly ahistorical, psychological readings of the Brontës' works derive from their own tropes, which "translated all kinds of political information into psychological terms" (*Desire and Domestic Fiction*, 186). According to her, "So powerful is the hermenuetic circle that makes their language of the self into its own basis for meaning that the noblest efforts to evade this trap are ensnared themselves as critics inevitably adopt a modern psychological vocabulary to interpret the Brontës' fiction" (187). Briefly stated, my own argument is that this tautological protocol extends beyond Brontë criticism and is peculiarly persistent in critiques of sibling relations, whether fictional or historical. In the Wordsworths' case, modern psychological models are projected over or through Wordsworthian tropes of the Romantic self. The nature of these projections ranges from traditional

readings of passionate but sexually innocent attachment (e.g., De Selincourt, *Dorothy Wordsworth: A Biography;* Moorman's edition of *The Journals of Dorothy Wordsworth;* Gittings and Manton, *Dorothy Wordsworth;* Woof's introduction to her edition of *The Grasmere Journals*), through explorations of repressed incestuous desire (e.g., Bateson, *Wordsworth: A Reinterpretation;* Reiman, "Poetry of Familiarity: Wordsworth, Dorothy, and Mary Hutchinson"), to more recent turns through Lacanian psychoanalysis and feminism (e.g., Levin, *Dorothy Wordsworth and Romanticism;* Homans, *Bearing the Word: Language and Female Experience in Nineteenth-Century Women's Writing;* Mellor, *Romanticism and Gender*). Nevertheless, all of these critics remain focused on emotion and consciousness as preeminent sites of interpretative significance. However subjectivity is defined, the reader's job remains the recovery—from literary materials—of the "self" represented in the text, plus some explanation of the relation between self and language.

3. Davidoff and Hall do not reach my conclusions. Davidoff's essay "Where the Stranger Begins: The Question of Siblings in Historical Analysis" uses the same evidence to posit a natural sibling community of feeling that may be released or repressed by historical conditions. My own historical argument is based upon the argument made in *Family Fortunes,* especially chapters 4–7 on property, gender, and family.

4. Davidoff, "Where the Stranger Begins," 214. For a thorough discussion of the physical separation of home from business, see Davidoff and Hall, *Family Fortunes,* 364–69.

5. I here follow Beth Darlington's arguments in her Cornell edition of *Home at Grasmere: Part First, Book First of The Recluse,* where she dates the first completed manuscript (MS.B.) to 1806, including long stretches presumed to have been composed in 1800. This sets the composition of the first full version of the poem—my reading text for this essay—in Dove Cottage, with portions of it coinciding with the earliest entries in Dorothy's 1800–1803 journals. The journals and the poem also have comparable publication histories: except for sections of *Home at Grasmere* published as part of *The Excursion* (1814), the texts were reconstructed from manuscripts well after both writers' deaths.

6. "Uneven development" is Mary Poovey's descriptive term for what happens to mid-Victorian gender ideologies, the formation and development of which she characterizes as "uneven both in the sense of being experienced differently by individuals who were positioned differently within the social formation (by sex, class, or race, for example) and in the sense of being articulated differently by the different institutions, discourses, and practices that it both constituted and was constituted by" (*Uneven Developments,* 3). My own usage of "uneven" also refers to a collateral unevenness (perhaps implicit in Poovey) over time, as ideological formations progress, fall back, move laterally, coexist with older forms, and so forth.

7. D. Wordsworth, *The Grasmere Journals*, 126. Subsequent quotations are from Woof's edition and are indicated parenthetically in the text by page number.

8. For traditional readings of the wedding passage, see Woof's note for October 4, 1802, 249–50; see also Gittings and Manton, *Dorothy Wordsworth*, 138–39. For psychoanalytic readings variously inflected with traditionalism and feminism, see: Reiman, "Poetry of Familiarity," 142–49; McCormick, "'I shall be beloved—I want no more': Dorothy Wordsworth's Rhetoric and the Appeal to Feeling in *The Grasmere Journals*," 471–93 (esp. 485–87); and Mellor, *Romanticism and Gender*, 165–66. Although exerting more innovative pressure, Levin (*Dorothy Wordsworth and Romanticism*, 21–30) and Homans (*Bearing the Word*, 65–66) still assume the primacy of spousal and parental affections according to their interpretation of this passage.

9. Woof notes (250) that "parted from her Brothers" and "& Sisters" have both been added by insertion, marking Dorothy's deliberate choice here.

10. In what follows I elaborate on Kurt Heinzelman's perception that "for Dorothy, such pairings tend to go on reproducing themselves as new pairings or as triplings or as any other mathematical combination and permutation that is necessary to keep the household as a unit of work-engendering value intact. . . . These different pairings, different three-somes, emblematically expand the household into a polis of many simultaneously possible households" ("The Cult of Domesticity," 73).

11. For a discussion of how the Wordsworths constructed walking as poetic labor, see the third chapter of my book *Walking, Literature, and English Culture: The Origins and Uses of Peripatetic in the Nineteenth Century*. A detailed discussion of "When first I journeyed hither," the John's Grove poem, can be found on pages 130–33.

12. Coleridge, "Text," in *The Notebooks of Samuel Taylor Coleridge*, 2.2537; emphasis in original.

13. Entries of particular interest in Coleridge's notebooks include: 1.576, 830, 980, 1162, 1163, 1242, 1333, 1415, 1575; 2.2001, 2517, 2527, 2389, 2397, 2427, 2429, 2531, 2623–24, 2628, 2861. I wish to express my thanks to the Wordsworth Library for allowing me to examine (in the summer of 1992) Mary Hutchinson Wordsworth's autobiographical memorandum and its expansion in Dove Cottage MS 167.

14. All quotations from *Home at Grasmere* are from Darlington's Cornell edition, MS.B, and are indicated parenthetically by line number(s) in the text. Darlington attributes most of MS.B (lines 1–457 and 859–74) and, in particular, two passages crucial to my argument (the swan comparison at 322–57 and the "happy band" passage at 859–74) to now-lost manuscripts dating from 1800 (see esp. p.13). The "Prospectus," another crucial passage and the most difficult

portion of the poem to date, she sets at "the period between spring, 1800, and early spring, 1802," with lines 1002–14 (the "spousal verses" passage) added sometime in 1805 or 1806 (22). Although MS.D, which encompasses William's revisions of 1812 and after and is often taken as the authoritative text, reduces the vehemence of the speaker's claims for sibling community somewhat, at crucial points it maintains or reinforces them; see 249–55, 261–62, and 427–29 in Darlington's edition for examples of these different changes.

15. Kenneth Johnston characterizes this passage as "a ridiculous literalism" that ultimately prevents William from developing a publishable version of the poem: "If the swans are gone, just like that, with no explanation or meaning, what does it signify for the fate of another 'solitary pair' coming into the valley?" (*Wordsworth and The Recluse*, 91). For Johnston the elaborated structure of community that follows is a purely defensive reaction to this compositional failure. But I regard the structuring of Grasmere Vale to resemble a great household as a pervading principle of the poem, developed in multiple variations precisely because it is foundational.

16. See Raymond Williams's history of the changing meaning of "family," from its original English sense of servants, visitors, and various relations living under one roof to the early-nineteenth-century "specialization of *family* to the small kin-group in a single house" (*Keywords*, 110).

17. Heinzelman, "The Cult of Domesticity," 53, 52, 55, 56.

18. See the first entry of the *Grasmere Journals* and William's "Preface" to *Lyrical Ballads*, especially the extended defense of pleasure as the one necessary product of poetry (Wordsworth, "Preface," in Wordsworth and Coleridge, *Lyrical Ballads*, 256–60).

19. See the chapter on Dorothy Wordsworth in Bohls's *Women Travel Writers and the Language of Aesthetics, 1716–1818*.

20. I have presented a different version of this argument, one focused on an aesthetics of place, in "'Inhabited Solitudes': Dorothy Wordsworth's Domesticating Walkers," 99–126. Portions of that essay appear in revised form in what follows.

21. I take "shifts" as meaning the woman's garment, in part because of its plural number, in part because of the many sewing references in the journals, and in part because a common referent of the unmodified "worked" and "work" would have been "sewing" (see my discussion of "Michael" later in this essay). However, Marjorie Stone has pointed out to me that "shifts" may here have the sense of turns at work, so that Dorothy may be picking fruit in the orchard or taking her turn at some other outdoor labor. This usage, originally deriving from the coal industry, was in place by the early eighteenth century and would here introduce industrial connotations into a georgic scene.

22. Heinzelman, "Cult of Domesticity," 75; Heinzelman, 76; Heinzelman, 76.

23. Heinzelman, 60.

24. Quotations from "Michael" are from the Cornell edition of *Lyrical Ballads* and are indicated parenthetically in the text by line numbers.

25. Levinson, "Spiritual Economics: A Reading of 'Michael,'" 65.

26. See Heinzelman's summary of the historical situation in "The Cult of Domesticity," 60.

27. For a more extended discussion of this development (though in a different context), see Wallace, "'Nor in Fading Silks Compose': Sewing, Walking, and Poetic Labor in *Aurora Leigh*," 228–33. Differently focused commentaries on housework's "disappearance" in the middle-class home include: F. M. L. Thompson, *The Rise of Respectable Society: A Social History of Victorian Britain, 1830–1900*, 176; Oakley, *Woman's Work: The Housewife, Past and Present;* and Langland, *Nobody's Angels: Middle-Class Women and Domestic Ideology in Victorian Culture*, esp. 41–45 and 71–77.

28. See Trumbach, *The Rise of the Egalitarian Family: Aristocratic Kinship and Domestic Relations in Eighteenth-Century England*, which describes the eighteenth-century usage still followed by the Wordsworths (293–96).

29. Levinson, "Spiritual Economics," 68.

30. Walker, "Dorothy Wordsworth, William Wordsworth, and the Kirkstone Pass," 116–21; Fay, *Becoming Wordsworthian: A Performative Aesthetic*.

31. Heinzelman, "The Cult of Domesticity"; Gordon, "Wordsworth and the Domestic Roots of Power."

"The Body of My Father's Writings"

Sara Coleridge's Genial Labor

ALISON HICKEY

> Of or pertaining to marriage, nuptial; also, pertaining to generation, generative. Of an angel or deity: Presiding over marriage or generation. . . . Cheering, enlivening, inspiriting. . . . Sympathetically cheerful, jovial, kindly. . . . Pertaining to "genius" or natural disposition; natural. . . . Of or pertaining to genius.
>
> *Oxford English Dictionary*, 2nd ed., s.v. "genial"

Apprehensive about the future of Coleridge's unfinished literary projects, Robert Southey wrote in 1803: "I know not when any of his works will appear—& tremble lest an untimely death should leave me the task of putting together the fragments of his materials."[1] This very task fell to Sara Coleridge after her father's death in 1834. In collaboration with her husband (and first cousin), Henry Nelson Coleridge, Sara took on the work of (re)constructing the unity of her father's corpus—or, as she called it, "the body of my father's writings, which I have taken great pains to bring into one."[2] Sara collaborated with Henry on his 1835 edition of *Table Talk;* on two editions of *Aids to Reflection* (1839, 1843); on the *Literary Remains of Samuel Taylor Coleridge* (1836–39); on the third edition of *The Friend* (1837); and on the 1839 single-volume reissue of the *Constitution of the Church and State* and the two *Lay Sermons*. Although Henry alone is listed as the editor of these works, Sara was deeply involved, as her husband's private acknowledgments suggest: "Beloved wife—counsel me. . . . I shall abide ultimately by what you advise. . . . You are conscious of my reverential sense of your fine genius and cultivated mind" (quoted in Griggs, *Coleridge Fille*, 100). Later Sara produced new editions of works that Henry had originally edited, and in 1852 she coedited with her brother Derwent an edition of Coleridge's poems.[3] Her chief contributions to the Coleridgean editorial project, however, were her completion, following Henry's death, of the 1847 edition of the *Biographia Literaria* and her editions of *Notes and Lectures upon Shakespeare* (1849) and *Essays on His Own Times* (1850).

Sara's editorial work constitutes a significant form of collaboration not only with her husband but also with her father. Her labor was essential to producing his texts. Moreover, as I shall argue, her collaboration resulted in both the Coleridgean idea of "individualized" genius and Coleridge as the embodiment of this idea. Bradford Keyes Mudge has rightly called Sara "an unacknowledged collaborator" in the production of Coleridge as a "man of genius." I would add that the notion of genius is itself collaboratively produced—not just by "the cultural marketplace," which is Mudge's chief focus, but by Sara herself in collaboration with her father.[4] Sara's labors on behalf of Coleridgean genius are inseparable from the vexed issue of her relation to her father: as she herself acknowledges, her editing is "a filial phenomenon."[5] It is a particularly complex and overdetermined "filial phenomenon," for Sara is the daughter not only of Coleridge but also, figuratively, of Wordsworth and of her "Uncle Southey," Coleridge's brother-in-law and quondam Pantisocratic "brother." Inheriting the complex dynamic at work among these authors, she is highly conscious of her own position as a site on which rival claims to authorial paternity continue to play themselves out. Negotiating these competing authorial claims both on her as a person and on the texts she edits, Sara makes herself an heir to all three men, eminently qualified to be the consolidator of the fragmentary Coleridge that Southey and Wordsworth failed to unify—and arguably helped to fragment.

Even more than "filial," the term "genial," which Sara frequently uses, suggests the complexity of her relation to her father, his texts, and his genius. Her labors are a "genial phenomenon" in all the senses suggested by my epigraph. Not only is the man father of the child in this relationship: the child is also mother of the man; the child is related to the man by marriage; she "generates" with him; she is inspirited by him; she gives birth to and presides over his genius. This "genial" relationship is complicated by Sara's gender. As Christine Battersby has shown, "the English term 'genius' was as associated with male sexual and generative powers as the Latin *genius,* which originally meant 'the begetting

spirit of the family embodied in the paterfamilias.'" The genius was supposed to ensure the continuance of the property and fertility of the *gens*,
or male clan. Battersby argues that eighteenth- and nineteenth-century
conceptions of genius perpetuate this gendering. According to such conceptions, the genius is a male *author* whose act of creation echoes a male
God's eternal "act of creation in the infinite I AM."[6] He is the sole author of his textual or artistic offspring, which reflects his individuality.
Specifically, he creates without female collaboration. What, exactly,
does it mean for Sara—a "daughter of genius" in more than one
sense—to devote herself to bringing forth her father's genius? What role
can she, a woman, play in the perpetuation of his "begetting spirit"?

Ironically, Sara's efforts to "individualize" her father (who, in a further irony, himself engaged in collaborative forms of authorship and
resisted the idea of individual authorial property) call into question his
supposed status as a singular author and highlight contradictions in the
very notions of genius and the individual author. If individuality is co-
produced, how individual is it? "Genial," which by definition harbors
such conflicts between singularity and multiplicity, becomes a rich term
for characterizing not only Coleridge's writings themselves but also the
complex affiliation of Sara's work to his and, ultimately, the collaborative role of future generations of "genial" readers who will come to his
work through hers and participate in the construction of the author.

As Southey had foreseen, the task of putting together Coleridge's fragments was an arduous one. As Sara wrote of her work on the *Biographia*,
"No one that has not edited a book and such a book as my Father's can
have any *conception* of the trouble and labour—even of the body-trouble
that will never *shew* for the editor, though useful to the book" (quoted in
Griggs, *Coleridge Fille*, 155). Sara inherits not only her father's fragmented
corpus but also his literal body troubles; her life is similarly plagued by
physical illness, "nervous derangement,"[7] and addiction. Her labor of
integration is carried out in the face of these and other threats of disinte-
gration (e.g., her father's death, the early loss of her husband, and her
brother Hartley's dissipation), all of which lend particular urgency to
her project. In her introduction to the *Biographia* Sara connects the quality of her father's writings with his "deranged" health; his mind, she observes, had been "subjected to the influence of bodily disorder," and the
work thus bears the symptoms of this disorder.[8] As Mudge has shown,
Sara's endeavor to bring order to this fragmented corpus is inseparable

from her struggle with her own mental and bodily disorders.[9] One way in which she attempts to redeem the metaphor of bodily fragmentation is by associating her editorial body trouble with the female labor that "shews" not for the laborer but for the body that she brings forth—the body of her father's writings.

Sara's remarks about the strenuousness of her labor are almost invariably coupled with laments about its invisibility. In 1845 she writes of her work on the *Biographia:* "The trouble I take is so ridiculously disproportioned to any effect that can be produced, and we are so apt to measure our importance by the efforts we make, rather than the good we do, that I am obliged to keep reminding myself of this very truth, in order not to become a mighty person in my own eyes, while I remain as small as ever in the eyes of every one else" (*Memoir*, 241–42). In 1848 she writes in a similar vein of her labors on *Notes and Lectures upon Shakespeare:* "No work is so inadequately rewarded either by money or credit as that of editing miscellaneous, fragmentary, immethodical literary remains like those of S. T. C. Such labours cannot be rewarded for they cannot be seen" (quoted. in Griggs, *Coleridge Fille,* 157). Her preoccupation with the discrepancy between what remains invisible and what is "shewn" (in the text or in credit to its producer) reflects her sense of the apparent distance of her editorial toil from the kind of work that makes one a "mighty person"—work she implicitly associates with authoring as opposed to editing. The irony is heightened by the fact that the very texts she is "putting in order"—the *Biographia* and the Shakespeare materials—are those in which Coleridge most memorably advances his ideas on genius. A quality or power both of the creating mind and of the text, genius by definition—especially according to the definition Sara promotes—"shews" in a text; the text, in turn, "shews" the genius to be a mighty person.

Even as she half-creates both this Coleridgean idea of genius and her father as the exemplar of the idea, she appears to resign herself (though not without frustration) to being a small person and occupying an invisible relation to the text. But the dichotomy between visible and invisible, according to her conception of her labor, is not as clear-cut as a cursory reading of her letters might suggest. By performing invisible labors on her father's texts, she makes her father visible as a genius and consequently makes herself visible as his daughter.

Coleridge had been absent at Sara's birth. Upon his return, he was startled to learn that his wife had been "safely brought to bed . . . of a healthy—GIRL! I had never thought of a Girl as a possible event—the word[s] child & man child were perfect Synonimes in my feelings."[10] Nevertheless—and notwithstanding the infrequency of their contact throughout Sara's childhood—a particular bond developed between father and daughter. He came to view her as his intellectual heir, and following his death she devoted herself to the project of restoring his fragmented genius. But the eventual intimacy of father and daughter does not erase the ambivalence that informs Sara's filial project. Her editorial labors on Coleridge's texts are inextricable from the complex process of negotiating a relationship to a father who was largely absent during her childhood and who at times appeared to deny the special significance of their genetic link.

Sara's vexed relationship with her father cannot be understood apart from her filial relations to Wordsworth and Southey. As others have noted, Sara's first name is suggestive of the tensions in her genealogy. The daughter of Sara Fricker Coleridge (Coleridge's wife and Southey's sister-in-law), she also arguably has a namesake in Sara Hutchinson (Wordsworth's sister-in-law and the Sara whom Coleridge saw as the ideal, unattainable alternative to Sara Fricker). Both Earl Leslie Griggs and Carl Woodring connect Sara's birth in December 1802 to the interrelated problems of Coleridge's loss of imagination, his doomed love for Sara Hutchinson, and his sense of exclusion from the Wordsworth-Hutchinson circle, as expressed in "A Letter to [Asra]" (composed in April 1802), representing an early version of the "Dejection" ode.[11] Sara's name evokes the failure of Coleridge's "genial spirits"[12] as codetermined by the interwoven circumstances of his impossible love and his exclusion from Wordsworthian genius, as well as the adoration and devoted ministrations of the women—Dorothy Wordsworth and Mary and Sara Hutchinson—who enabled that genius to thrive. At the same time, the name holds forth the dim possibility of reconciling the antithetical forces that Coleridge saw as tearing his genius apart.

Engaging in the (Wordsworthian) activity of retracing the various influences that went into forming her mind, in her later years Sara repeatedly records her particular debts to each of her father figures. For example, in an 1851 letter to Henry Reed she writes, "I knew—and honor dear Mr Wordsworth perhaps as well as I have ever known any one in the world—more intimately than I knew my Father, and as intimately as I knew my Uncle Southey." She recalls taking long walks with Wordsworth and listening "for hours" to his talk: "[M]y mind and turns of thought were gradually moulded by his conversation and the influences under which I was brought by his means in matters of intellect." By contrast, in matters of "the heart and the moral being," she claims Southey as her most important influence—though in making this avowal she couches it in language recalling Wordsworth's "Tintern Abbey" (*Memoir*, 492–93). In an 1847 letter to Isabella Fenwick Sara articulates her obligations slightly differently: "To my Uncle Southey I owe much—even to his books; to his example, his life and conversation, far more. But to Mr. W. and my father I owe my *thoughts* more than to all other men put together" (315). Thus, she "puts together" and "puts in order" the fragmented genealogy that makes up her being, identifying herself as a single person with a threefold paternity.

The story of Coleridge's *disjecta membra poetae* is intertwined with the story of his relationships with Southey and, especially, with Wordsworth.[13] The three had often negotiated their relationships to their joint productions in terms of paternal metaphors. If the idea of literary parenthood generally assumes a single "Author" embodying the functions of both parents (a Jupiter from whose head Minerva springs full-blown), the involvement of more than one parent disrupts that economy. "Wordsworth's Preface is half a child of my own Brain," Coleridge writes in an 1802 letter, "& so arose out of Conversations, so frequent, that with few exceptions we could scarcely either of us perhaps positively say, which first started any particular Thought" (*CL*, 2:830). The same might be said of many of their writings. The idea of a text sprung from two heads raises the Solomonic specter of "half a child," which—assuming a work is a reflection of its author—in turn implies the fragmentation of the author. As both the daughter of three authors and the daughter of a fragmented "single" author, Sara doubly inherits the effects of multiple authorship. Her endeavor to establish Coleridge publicly as a complete author, worthy of his place in the triumvirate, is simultaneously an endeavor to unify her own fragmented origins. Bringing him "into one" is part of bringing herself into one; she strives to make herself a whole child by making her author a whole author.

That issues of authorial paternity were inextricably interwoven with familial matters is not surprising for these writers, whose domestic arrangements were always interconnected with their textual production. Coleridge was obsessed with Wordsworth's and Southey's "authorship" in both senses of the word; indeed, the two senses often seemed virtually synonymous to him. Both Southey—the paterfamilias and astonishingly regular man of letters for whom Coleridge coined the word "reliability"[14]—and Wordsworth—the embodiment of the creative imagination and the focal point of a circle of loving females committed to bringing forth and fostering his textual and biological offspring—were foils to Coleridge's dereliction.

Coleridge's longing for involvement in Wordsworth's paternity manifests itself particularly in his attachment to the Wordsworth children and his tendency to compare his relationships with them to that with Sara. Especially telling is Coleridge's April 1804 letter to the Wordsworths, in which he equates his love for their son, John (born 18 June 1803), with his love for Sara: "O dear dear Friends! I love you, even to anguish love you: & I know no difference, I feel no difference, between my Love of little Sara, & dear little John. Being equally with me, I could not but love them equally: how could I—the child of the man, for whom I must find another name than Friend, if I call any others but him by the name of Friend" (*CL*, 2:1117–18). In his compulsion to break down barriers between his own child and others, Coleridge erects barriers between himself and her. "My father reproached me," Sara recalled in her *Memoir*, "and contrasted my coldness with the childish caresses of the little Wordsworths" (45). His "knowing no difference" creates difference between kin.

Sara's cultivation of the name and genius of Coleridge, then, is in part an endeavor to repair a genetic and genial link threatened with disruption—to restore the integrity both of the author himself and of her relation to him. Her judicious, cogent, and avowedly sympathetic discussion (in the introduction to the *Biographia*) of the charges of plagiarism leveled against Coleridge by Thomas De Quincey and others (*SCBL*, xi–xlii) is exemplary of this editorial project that balances the impulses of integration and differentiation.[15] Faced with the problem of a man who "knows no difference" between what he has authored and what others have authored, Sara admits the problem and, while making every effort to distinguish and acknowledge sources, emphasizes the incorporation of diverse materials into a Coleridgean whole rather than their improper presence in his text. Just as her discussion of her own intellectual debts to her three fathers is a way of positing her own wholeness, so her discussion of Coleridge's intellectual debts becomes part of her portrait of him as a distinctive individual, the "frame of [whose] intellect . . . was in close connection with his peculiar intellectual strength, his power of abstracting and referring to universal principles" without regard to property (xxxvi).

As Sara adjudicates numerous questions about the sources of Coleridge's ideas, she subordinates the issue of property to what she presents as the larger issue, namely, the nature of his "mode of thought" (cxxxvii). She presents Coleridge's disinclination to recognize boundaries between his own thought and that of others as an identifying feature of his singular intellectual character: "[S]uch was his temper in regard to all *property*, of what kind soever; he did not enough regard or value it whether for himself or his neighbor." To trace his "unusual disregard of . . . property in thought" (xx) through its many moods, as she does in her introduction, is, somewhat paradoxically, to reveal his temperament more fully.

Sara's idea of the author's "peculiar" mode of thought being visible in his work is more fully developed in her introduction to Coleridge's *Essays on His Own Times*, where the issue is that of attributing periodical essays to Coleridge on the basis of internal evidence. Having recast the matter of property as one of "peculiar" intellectual character in the *Biographia*, Sara now has recourse to the idea of "mental idiosyncrasy" in identifying her father's literary property. Here again the proprietary claim is secondary to the emphasis on the "writer's personal identity" as manifested in the texts—the "individualized" quality that distinguishes the man of genius from the man of talent. There is, Sara writes, "a *countenance* in an author's mode of expression . . . [that] render[s] the author clearly recognizable by those well acquainted with his mental idiosyncrasy." From this she concludes: "The more energetic and powerful is any original genius, the more strongly individualized its products must be, and though its creations will be various as well as numerous, all will have a common character among themselves distinguishing them from all others. The great genius does not turn itself into many forms but makes many various modes all represent itself." Thus "Spenser, Shakespeare, Milton, Dante are ever each himself alone," "each adhered to certain forms of composition into which his poetic genius naturally evolved itself." Likewise, Sara asserts, her father's "genius was never hidden in the different forms it assumed or modes in which it was manifested. The identity was more impressive than the diversity in all that proceeded from his mind."[16] Coleridge, like Shakespeare, is "myriad-minded" (*BL*, 2:19) yet always himself. Indeed, as I shall argue, Shakespeare becomes a presiding genius over Sara's work and over her genial relationship to her father. Remarking that her father's "prose was that of a poet" (*EOT*, lxxxvii), she places him in the company of the great poetic geniuses, those whom he himself had celebrated for their "*individualized* and characteristic" diction (*BL,* 2:99).[17] Paradoxically, she is a necessary collaborator in the project of "individualization." (The very word "individualiz*ed,*" which registers the multiplicity out of which the genius is constructed, embodies the paradox.) Even as she seeks to uncover the single, unified character of Coleridge in his diverse texts, her involvement in their production shows the writing of a genius to be "myriad-minded" not just in the idealized way to which Coleridge alludes but also in a more literal way.

"The identity was more impressive than the diversity in all that proceeded from his mind." There is an urgency to this statement, as there usually is to Coleridgean affirmations of oneness in the face of the threat of fragmentation. In "individualizing" Coleridge, Sara singles him out as an author whose genius is reflected in his works. If she, as his child, might be considered one of those works, her project of "individualization" is both symbolic of and integral to the project of identifying herself as the "individualized" work of an "individualized" father. In putting his name to his texts and identifying herself in relation to that name and those texts ("edited by his daughter"), she ascribes herself to him. Collaborating in order to enable her father to shine forth from the page, Sara helps to render visible a countenance that is already genetically reflected in her own; her labor, which makes her a co-producer of his work and of his countenance in that work, reinforces this genetic link that makes *her* her father's work. If Sara inherits Coleridge's genius, she produces the countenance of that genius not directly in her "own" texts but rather in her father's. Her labor may not show, but she can consider the countenance and the name to be partially hers, both because she inherits it and because she collaborates to produce it.

The other Coleridgean collaborator on the project of consolidating Sara's fragmentary author is Henry Nelson Coleridge. The spouses' joint editing of Coleridge's oeuvre constitutes a kind of "genial" labor in which the filial and the conjugal converge. Henry's surname at once doubles, covers, and is covered by Sara's own and her father's, suggesting the ways in which different collaborative relations between individual Coleridges reinforce, challenge, and obscure each other. Sara Coleridge's last name embodies the dilemma of visibility and invisibility at the core of her writerly labor. In marrying her cousin she preserves her "maiden name"—arguably her "own" name except that she has it by virtue of her father and shares it with him. From another perspective, her marrying a Coleridge could be said to efface her "own" name even more effectively than marrying someone of another name would have: upon marrying, she bears the name Coleridge by virtue of law rather than her "own" genealogy. All this points more generally to the limited extent to which one's proper name is actually one's "own": no one person—not even S. T. C. himself—owns the name Coleridge. Nor do the genes associated with that name belong to any single individual.

Intensely aware of the significance of these intersecting systems of names and genetics to her life and work, Sara commits herself to making visible the name Coleridge. The name *Sara* Coleridge remains subordinate: on the title page of the 1847 *Biographia,* below the names of Samuel Taylor Coleridge and Henry Nelson Coleridge, Sara is listed simply as Henry's "widow"; the title page of Coleridge's *Essays on His Own Times* describes the three volumes as "edited by his daughter." But since Sara's name is Coleridge, it gains visibility as well. Sara presents her editorial work as both harmoniously filial and conjugal, although (as Henry's earlier remarks hint) there is also evidence of some genial competition for authority in the project of creating "Coleridge," with each second-generation Coleridge presenting similar intellectual, genetic, and emotional claims in different degrees and proportions.

Whatever differences exist between individuals on a personal or genetic level, for Sara they are subordinated to the Coleridge name. The 1847 *Biographia* enacts the conversation of Coleridgean voices: in the notes and, less visibly, between the lines of the text, "S. C." (as she signs her notes in order to distinguish them from Henry's) converses with her dead father and with her late husband "the Editor," whose work, she explains, "has fallen to me to complete" (*SCBL,* vi). Her completion of one Coleridge's work is inseparable from her completion of the other Coleridge's work. Although she explicates, extends, revises, and occasionally takes issue with each of them, there is always the clear sense that all the voices are contributing to the same Coleridgean project. Rather than putting her doubly Coleridgean name where it would "shew," she enacts its significance by investing her labor in propagating Coleridgean genius.

Thus, the single name "Coleridge" itself embodies the tension between individual authorship and collaborative textual production. The name is, of course, most often assumed to refer to S. T. Coleridge as a single author; ironically, this is so in part because Sara devoted her labors to constructing this author under this name. Having glimpsed her unobtrusive labors, we may acknowledge that the apparently singular name of this "mighty person" encompasses her as well, but the reference, like the editorial work itself, remains inaudible and invisible.

It might seem incongruous that Sara's genial labor should take the form of collecting fragments, editing, correcting—all tasks apparently at odds with the organic ideals of genius expressed in the *Biographia*. For Coleridge,

> What is poetry? is so nearly the same question with, what is a poet? that the answer to the one is involved in the solution of the other. For it is a distinction resulting from the poetic genius itself, which sustains and modifies the images, thoughts, and emotions of the poet's own mind. The poet, described in *ideal* perfection, brings the whole soul of man into activity, with the subordination of its faculties to each other, according to their relative worth and dignity. He diffuses a tone, and spirit of unity, that blends, and (as it were) *fuses*, each into each, by that synthetic and magical power, to which we have exclusively appropriated the name of imagination. (*BL*, 2:15–16)

What this famous definition leaves out is the act of writing, indeed, any concrete reference to text: the unifying appears to occur in the poet's mind and in that of his reader (the "soul of man" may refer to either or both). Presumably this "spirit of unity" is mediated by the text, the conduit for the "poetic genius" that links poet, text, and reader—but the text itself is elided in Coleridge's description of what the poet's mind does in creating it and what the text does in the mind of its reader. In fact, Coleridge often left textual matters to others—as in the case of the *Biographia*, which was committed to paper by John Morgan when Coleridge could not bear to hold a pen. Sara's labors—which, in turn, would not be possible without the prior contributions of Morgan and others—participate in the collective project of restoring the text to its central position. While the emphasis on the body of the text may appear to be simply at odds with the Coleridgean "spirit of unity," the bodily labor is a necessary counterpart to this spirit. Sara helps to give lasting textual form to Coleridge's idealized description of the poet, striving to create, through the medium of the body of work that she has taken such pains to bring into one, the image of a unified Coleridge to realize that Coleridgean ideal.

The problems connected with the act of putting pen to paper make up a recurrent theme in Coleridge, the difficulty often being associated with "body trouble." As Sara writes in the introduction, "Great as was the activity of [Coleridge's] intellect in its own congenial sphere," he faltered when it came time to attend to the "tasks necessary to the completeness and efficiency of what has been produced. . . . He loved to go forward, expanding and ennobling the soul of his teaching, and hated the trouble of turning back to look after its body" (*SCBL*, xxi). Recognizing the tasks that are "necessary to the completeness" of her father's writings, Sara "turns back" to look after the body in the hope that the "trouble" she takes will enable the soul to communicate beyond its "own congenial sphere."

In some ways Sara fulfills a Southeyan role, assuming the responsibility of piecing together her father's fragments, filling in missing links, and fleshing out skeletons. But if she makes herself an heir to her reliable Uncle Southey, this is only a part of the genealogy she claims through her editorial acts. She also learns from Wordsworth, who in his own life and works provides her with a model for creating wholeness out of fragmentation, continuity out of discontinuity. Sara admires Wordsworth's early odes because they "seem to be *organic wholes*"; the "Intimations" ode in particular strikes her as "an image of the individual spirit of which it is an efflux" (*Memoir*, 493).[18] Her editorial remarks attributing individual spirit and organicism to her father sometimes allude to Wordsworth, but even when Wordsworth's influence does not appear in notes or in pointed allusions to specific poems, his "conversation" and mode of thought shape the mind and "turns of thought" of the woman who performs the labor—a mind that works by "turning back" to the past, incorporating fragments, healing breaches, restoring losses, and affirming the wholeness of the life and the work in the face of dissolution. Like Wordsworth, Sara conceives of such work as integral to "going forward."

Sara dedicates her edition of the *Biographia* to Wordsworth. After recalling the friendship of the two men and the early days when they "lived as neighbors, and both together sought the Muse, in the lovely Vale of Stowey," she expresses to Wordsworth her "dearest and proudest wish" that the association of the two men's names "may endure as long as you are both remembered," and that her father "may continue to be spoken of in connection with you, while your writings become more and more fully and widely appreciated" (*SCBL*, vi). If this gesture would seem to make a wide appreciation of Coleridge dependent on Wordsworth, it also implicitly presents Coleridge and the *Biographia* as worthy of such a venerable association. Signing herself "Your Child in heart," Sara affirms that the author she has helped to produce is now complete enough to stand beside the author who has imparted to her so much of what she needed to know to produce him, the father figure who by his example has showed Sara that steady labor can integrate dispersed fragments until they "seem to be *organic wholes*" expressing the author's individual spirit.

The dedication is not, however, an unequivocal gesture of filial piety toward Wordsworth. (How could it be, given the complexity of the association between the two men and of Sara's connection to each of them?) In fact, Wordsworth approved neither of Sara's work on the *Biographia* nor of her editorial labor and bluestockingism in general. Writing to Isabella Fenwick in 1847, he remarked: "Sara Coleridge is about to publish a new Edition of her Father's Literary biography, which she asked permission to dedicate to me; which I could not refuse, though [the] Book contains many things not at all to my taste as far as I am individually concerned."[19] As Stephen Gill has surmised, Wordsworth likely "resented being involuntarily the centrepiece of what professed to be Coleridge's book about himself" and "found both the praise and the censure distasteful—especially the censure."[20] In addition to harboring reservations about the *Biographia* itself and generally disapproving of Sara's intellectual endeavors, Wordsworth considered her unqualified to edit the book since her "opportunities of knowing anything about [her father] were too small for such an Employment, . . . nor could her judgement be free from bias" (*WL*, 813). His discomfort with Sara's labors suggests a proprietary relationship toward Coleridge that can perhaps be viewed partly in terms of an unconscious need to keep Coleridge at the margins of Wordsworthian fame—the very fame that Coleridge, in the *Biographia* above all, had helped to produce.

Sara's notes to the *Biographia* take up the discussion of Wordsworth's poetry, supplementing Coleridge's remarks and adding more of her own. Though she never entertains the slightest doubt that Wordsworth is a great poet, these comments from a daughter figure could certainly have struck the notoriously sensitive poet as presumptuous, and they may even have contributed to his dismissal of her as unqualified to edit the *Biographia*. But "poor dear indefatigable Sara"—to cite Mary Wordsworth's condescending phrase (*WL*, 888–89)—will not be dismissed. Whether she is unaware of the Wordsworths' disapproval (which seems unlikely)[21] or consciously denies it in order to proceed as she feels she must, she works with steadiness and resolve to increase and justify her

father's literary fame—a project that includes writing him back into association with Wordsworth, mending (or at least overwriting) the splits
between them. As Sara explains, she dedicates the book to Wordsworth
because it contains "an account of the Life and Opinions of your friend,
S. T. Coleridge, in which I feel assured that, however you may dissent
from portions of the latter, you take a high and peculiar interest." (When
the *Prelude* was finally published in 1850, Sara was gratified to have this
assurance confirmed: upon reading Wordsworth's tributes to her father,
she avowed that "the history of literature hardly affords a parallel instance of entire union and unreserve between two poets"; not even between Beaumont and Fletcher could there have been "such pure love,
and consonancy of thought & feeling" [*Memoir*, 495].) Perhaps recognizing that her publication goes against the wishes of one of her fathers, she
presents it as a gesture of "deep affection, admiration, and respect" from
his "Child . . . and faithful Friend." She leaves no room for refusal. If
Sara's first allegiance is to authorizing her "own" father, her commitment to his authorship cannot be exclusive, not least because it cannot
be considered absolute. Thus, she insists on her connection to Wordsworth, her father "in heart," even as she dedicates herself to the principal task of appropriating authority to Coleridge—and to herself.

In authorizing herself as the rightful editor of Coleridge's work, Sara
lays claim to both Wordsworth and Coleridge as fathers. Not only her
work on Coleridge's "literary life" but also her understanding of her
own literary life, as well as her own particular genius, is shaped by
Coleridge's and Wordsworth's "lyrical dialogue" and by the language
and structures of particular texts in that lyrical dialogue. "Half a child"
of each of the two men, a child who avowedly "owes [her] *thoughts*" to
them "more than to all other men put together," she authorizes herself
by adopting and modifying their "genial" metaphors in ways that integrate their separate contributions to the dialogue or, rather, confirm
their mutual inseparability.

The intertextual dialogue between "Frost at Midnight" and "Tintern Abbey"—both composed more than four years before her birth—
takes on particular importance in Sara's self-conception as an heir to
her two poetic fathers. In "Frost at Midnight" Coleridge addresses not
Sara but her elder brother Hartley, prophesying that the latter will have
the Wordsworthian childhood he himself never had. For Wordsworth
(as half-created by Coleridge), intimacy with nature dates from the first
dawn of childhood and is carried forward into adulthood; the "filial

bond / Of Nature"[22] affiliates both the child to Nature and the man to
the child. The poet of "Frost at Midnight," acknowledging that he has
been denied such a bond, attempts to affiliate his infant to Nature, substituting a Wordsworthian inheritance for a Coleridgean one:

> But *thou*, my babe! shalt wander like a breeze
> By lakes and sandy shores, beneath the crags
> Of ancient mountain, and beneath the clouds . . .
>   (lines 54–56)

Our sense of the poem's balance and unity depends on our perception of a figurative equivalence between father and son, a continuity
whereby the desire that the father projects onto the babe is fulfilled in
the babe's imagined life of joy, which in turn reflects back on the father,
connecting him vicariously to nature through a filial bond. But the reciprocity between father and son, and between the two phases of the
poem, is accompanied by doubt. The vicariously achieved sense of continuity dramatizes the sense of discontinuity (the speaker's discontinuity
with nature and with his own past) that motivates the father's turn from
himself to his son.

Readers of these lines, including the addressee himself, have seen
Hartley's adult errancy as a painfully ironic literalization of the wander-
ings his father envisions.[23] In ways that are less apparent, the lines are
also a part of Sara's inner landscape as she contemplates her own filial
inheritance. If the address to Hartley affords a problematic model for
Sara, Wordsworth's rewriting of it in "Tintern Abbey" suggests an alternative model (one that is still problematic but nonetheless important).
"Frost at Midnight" provides a particular framework for Sara because
it represents Coleridge bestowing the future on a Coleridgean child.
"Tintern Abbey" offers a different kind of model by making a woman
the future repository of memory for the poet:

>   thy mind
> Shall be a mansion for all lovely forms,
> Thy memory be as a dwelling-place
> For all sweet sounds and harmonies . . .
>   (lines 139–42)[24]

Wordsworth transforms the Coleridgean gesture of giving away the future, of marking its discontinuity with the past, into an act of claiming
the future as a repetition and consolidation of the past. The poem's

concluding turns rewrite those of "Frost at Midnight" in a way that may have helped Sara to see how she might view her own future as a continuation of her father's past—or (to place the emphasis slightly differently) locate the future of her father in herself.

As Griggs has suggested, Hartley's life "retold, in miniature, Coleridge's own story of thwarted ambition, abortive hopes, and unfulfilled promise" (*Coleridge Fille*, 36). Unexpectedly, this first-born, male child perpetuates an inheritance of discontinuity. Sara, the third and last surviving child and only daughter, inserts herself at the point of genealogical disruption, substituting a strong Coleridgean inheritance for a fragmented one. With a clear sense that she is linked, genetically and spiritually, to her father's genius, she creates herself as the inheritor, consolidator, and perpetuator of the Coleridge name. Her marriage to a Coleridge and her bearing of Coleridge children constitute one aspect of this role. (Hartley, conversely, had no children.) The interest of the familial role is doubled by the ways in which it both figures and is figured by Sara's literary work. Through her "body trouble" Sara gives birth to the "body of [her] father's writings"; her female labor proves doubly essential to the continuance of the Coleridgean line whose descent from father to son had gone astray. "Sara," writes Hartley in 1844, "is the inheritrix of [Coleridge's] mind and of his genius. Neither Derwent nor I have much more than the family cleverness, which with hardly an exception accompanies the name of Coleridge."[25]

Coleridge's own sense of the particular nature of Sara's inheritance is symbolized by his wedding gift to her, William Sotheby's hexaglot folio volume of Virgil's *Georgics* (1827). Too ill to travel from Highgate on the day of the wedding, Coleridge inscribed the book as follows:

> After my decease this splendid volume presented to me by William Sotheby . . . is to belong, and I hereby give and appropriate it to my beloved and loveworthy child, Sara Coleridge. And I hope and trust that she will never willingly part with this volume or alienate the same. For if she should marry and should have a Daughter, it is my wish that this volume should descend to *her*, or (if Sara have daughters) to her eldest Daughter, who is to regard it as a Memento provided by her maternal Grandfather, that her dear Mother's accomplishments and her unusual attainments in ancient and modern Languages, were not so much nor so justly the objects of admiration as their co-existence in the same Person with so much piety, simplicity and unaffected meekness—in short, with a mind, character and demeanour so perfectly feminine. (*CL*, 6:692)

Mudge has observed that Coleridge's inscription "defuses [Sara's] attainments by defining them within 'a mind, character and demeanour
so perfectly feminine'" (*Sara Coleridge*, 51). Although this is certainly
worth noting, it captures neither the particularity of the "feminine" role
that Coleridge ascribes to his daughter nor the urgency of his need to
claim her as a second self. Faced with the prospect of his own dissolution, Coleridge proposes a maternal line of intellectual inheritance represented by this symbolic piece of property.

The polyglot *Georgics,* a gathering of dispersed languages around a
common text, embodies a tension between the forces of dissolution and
those of integration. If the book symbolizes the aggregate of Coleridgean "accomplishments and . . . attainments" to be passed in a direct line
from one Coleridge to the next, it also suggests the tendency of Coleridge and the Coleridgean to break down and disperse in fragments.
The *Georgics,* embodying the essentially conservative project of hus-
bandry, evokes genetic metaphors of affiliating the future to the present
and, through the present, to the past. This affiliation, in turn, is achieved
through the farmer's affiliation of his art to the rhythms and processes of
nature and through his channeling of nature's dispersive forces. This
evokes both a Wordsworthian relation to nature and Wordsworthian
acts of integration, such as the poet's grafting of Dorothy onto the end of
"Tintern Abbey." The book itself assembles scattered languages (and
perhaps hints implicitly at their derivation from common roots), but
this polyglotism, which on one level may point to oneness, also suggests
divergence.

Coleridge often associated his study of languages, alongside his
philosophy, with the dissipation of his genius; the languages were associated with the abstruse research that distanced him from Wordsworthian communion with genius and nature.[26] Here, however, he imagines
the consolidation of himself and his accomplishments in the symbolic
book as well as in the person of his daughter. He bestows on Sara not
the language of Nature but—that which more truly links her to him—
the "ancient and modern Languages." In doing so he rewrites "Frost at
Midnight." Rather than attempting to pass on to his son a Wordsworthian inheritance (one it is not in his power to bestow), he passes on to his
daughter a Coleridgean inheritance.[27]

Upon Sara's birth, Coleridge had hardly thought a girl "a possible
event"; "child" was synonymous with "man child." Now, as he be-
queaths this inheritance to his "child, Sara Coleridge," he hardly seems

to think a boy a possible event; "child" has become synonymous with "woman child." The significance of Coleridge's embodying his hopes for continuity in the person of his daughter is illuminated by his comments on Shakespeare's heroines (collected by Henry and Sara in *Literary Remains* and *Notes and Lectures upon Shakespeare*): "In Shakspeare all the elements of womanhood are holy, and there is the sweet, yet dignified feeling of all that *continuates* society, as sense of ancestry and of sex." This feeling "rests not in the analytic processes, but in that same equipoise of the faculties, during which the feelings are representative of all past experience,—not of the individual only, but of all those by whom she has been educated, and their predecessors even up to the first mother that lived." The "blessed beauty of the woman's character" arises from the "exquisite harmony of all the parts of the moral being constituting one living total of head and heart."[28] This commentary resembles Coleridge's praise of Sara not only in its familiar view of women's intellects as softened by feeling but, more specifically, in its suggestion that because their "purity" rests not in the analytic but in the synthetic, women are ideal "continuators."

The passage emerges as an aside to Coleridge's discussion of the scene in *The Tempest* in which Prospero recounts the past to his amazed daughter. Coleridge seems to envision Sara as Miranda to his Prospero—a daughter who becomes the repository of his story (which is also hers), whose "feelings" are "representative . . . of those by whom she has been educated." Her "equipoise of faculties" and "exquisite harmony of parts" will, he hopes, make her the ideal vehicle for restoring his shattered and discontinuous legacy and ensuring its continuance in the future. The daughter whose being comprises "one living total of head and heart" will become the means through which the father is able to conceive of himself as a "living total." Thus, the structural model of Shakespearean romance suggests itself to Coleridge as a possible alternative to that represented by "Frost at Midnight": through the daughter (and especially through her marriage and reproduction) losses are restored, ruptures healed, continuity reestablished. The history of the father's "particular accidents" (*The Tempest*, 5.1.306) can then be told as a story that ends in wholeness.

Coleridge imagines the woman as primarily an embodiment and a vehicle of "continuation" rather than an active producer of it. While his inscription in the *Georgics* makes reference to Sara's "accomplishments and her unusual attainments," he does not refer explicitly to any way in which her scholarly activities might participate directly in "continuat-ing" his legacy. Her contribution, as far as Coleridge seems able to imag-ine it, will be to embody the legacy in her own accomplishments, to pass on the genes/genius, and perhaps to impart her accomplishments to her children; he cannot conceive of the editorial labor she will perform after his death. Whatever the limitations of his conception of her role, he does view her as his intellectual "inheritrix." It thus remains for Sara to complete this role, in the process of which she will transform it.

If "Frost at Midnight," which depicts a (broken) male line of inheri-tance, presents Sara with a flawed paradigm for her own role as "inher-itrix," the Wordsworthian and Coleridgean models of female continua-tion go only partway toward suggesting a viable alternative. Particularly as framed by Coleridge's remarks on daughters as continuators, *The Tempest* must have had a special resonance for Sara as she considered her intertwined roles as daughter and editor. But it is not only the rela-tionship between Prospero and Miranda that captures her attention. The more vital relevance of the play to her situation is intimated in her own buried allusions to it in the *Biographia* and *Essays on His Own Times*. In both works Sara quotes a remark that De Quincey had made about Coleridge's contributions to the daily press. In the *Biographia* it appears as follows:

> Worlds of fine thinking lie buried in that vast abyss, never to be dis-entombed, or restored to human admiration. Like the sea, it has swal-lowed treasures without end, that no diving bell will bring up again. But no where throughout its shoreless magazines of wealth does there lie such a bed of pearls, confounded with the rubbish and 'purgamenta' of ages, as in the political papers of Coleridge. No more appreciable mon-ument could be raised to the memory of Coleridge than a republication of his essays in *The Morning Post*, but still more of those afterwards pub-lished in *The Courier*. (*SCBL*, 727)

Having erected just such a monument in *Essays on His Own Times*, Sara quotes the passage again in the introduction to that work (xv). In addition to proving that she recognizes the value of the advertisement from one of Coleridge's most vigorous challengers, the repetition sug-gests her particular imaginative engagement with the images De Quin-cey conjures up. They are, of course, Shakespeare's images:

> Full fadom five thy father lies,
> Of his bones are coral made:

> Those are pearls that were his eyes:
> Nothing of him that doth fade,
> But doth suffer a sea-change
> Into something rich and strange.
> Sea-nymphs hourly ring his knell:
> *Burthen* [*within*]. Ding-dong.
> Hark now I hear them—ding-dong bell.
> (*The Tempest*, 1.2.397–405)

"The ditty does remember [Sara's] drowned father" (1.2.406), as she confirms by making the allusion explicit in the *Essays*. The reader of the collection, she explains, will need a certain measure of sympathy with the writer's mind" to appreciate the essays as

> *pearls happily won from the deep*, rather than as more fitly to be compared with the submerged remains of some hapless voyager,—relics that, having lost great part of their original lustre, have suffered no glorifying "sea-change." Without any attempt however exactly to estimate their intrinsic value, I bring them forth, confident that they will be prized as dear memorials by a band of genial appraisers; that from those to whom I owe most consideration for their cordial love and reverence for my Father, as an author and as a man,—and the man and the author were in his case especially interfused,—I shall be sure of heartfelt thanks for my unambitious care and labour in the present collection. (*EOT*, xvi)

Without forfeiting the daughterly role of loving and reverent "continuator," Sara silently reshapes that role, connecting herself, in however qualified a manner, with the powers that can transmute submerged relics into something rich and strange. Representing her work as an act of "bringing forth," she calls attention to the essential role of her labor in producing the body of her father's writings. While the submerged childbirth metaphor in "bringing forth" might seem to limit her function to that of a mere vehicle, it significantly focuses attention on the body trouble she invests in the actual texts; she must win them from the deep and invest her "care and labour" to create them as a body that she can "bring forth." The very presence of the childbirth metaphor highlights the fact that her role as continuator consists not only in giving birth to actual children but also in laboring to produce texts; her knowledge of both kinds of labor lends authority to her representation of herself in the latter role. The metaphor is especially striking when one supposes the texts to embody the man ("the man and the author were in his case especially interfused"). The child is mother of the man.

Sara "continuates" her father's engagement with *The Tempest*, connecting the play more closely to herself than he had and winning from it
a richer and stranger image for the labor she actually performs—one far
beyond what he had imagined. At times her confidence in the results of
that labor seems precarious. Even her redundant insistence that she is
"confident that . . . [she will] be sure" suggests that she is not sure. Her
reliance on the kindness of genial readers points to her continuing anxiety over the reception of her father and, by extension, the success of her
labors. Will he really shine forth from these artifacts? What if, despite
her efforts, he remains a miscellaneous collection of fragments? What if,
for all the magnitude of her own labor, she remains a "small person"
who failed to make visible the full value of her father and his works?

This (seemingly genuine) humility becomes part of a strategy by
which Sara attempts to attract sympathetic readers to Coleridge's work.
Rather than claiming that she has succeeded in retrieving pearls
from the deep, she enlists the collaboration of her father's sympathetic
readers—not only those who already know him "as an author and a
man" but also those who have yet to encounter him through his texts.
Readers of Coleridge, she insists, must respond to him with mind and
heart; they must invest labor in the act of reading in order to *make* his remains pearls from the deep. Defending Coleridge against charges of ob-
scurity, in the introduction to the *Biographia* she explains that those who
wish to understand his writings must "attempt to meet him halfway":

> It is the chief use and aim of writings of such a character as his to excite
> the reader to think,—to draw out of his mind a native flame rather than
> to make it bright for a moment by the reflection of alien fires. All literary
> productions indeed demand *some* answering movement on the part of
> readers, but, in common cases, the motion required is so easy, so much
> in known ways and smooth well-beaten tracks, that it seems spontane-
> ous and is more like rest than labor. This is the difficulty with which
> introducers of new thought have to contend; the minds that are to re-
> ceive these accessions must themselves, in order to their reception of
> them, be renewed proportionately, renewed not from without alone,
> but by co-operation from within,—a process full of conflict and struggle,
> like the fermenting of raw juices into generous wines. (*SCBL*, xxi–xxii)

Understanding that she can play an important role in creating the taste
according to which her father is to be enjoyed, in both the *Biographia* and
Essays on His Own Times Sara undertakes the task of teaching her father's
readers how to read. The "generous" mode of reading that she proposes

is patterned after her own: rather than being a mere passive receptacle, the reader must engage in active "co-operation from within," which will not be easy, involving as it does "a process full of conflict and struggle."

Sara thus fulfills her role as "continuator" not only by educating her own children but also a public audience, a group she defines in the *Essays* as "those who now are, or those who hereafter shall be, concerned in my Father's personal history, both his literal descendants and all who are *as children to him* in affectionate reverence for his mind" (*EOT*, xiii). When Sara uses the Coleridgean word "genial" (*EOT*, xvi) to describe these readers, she means something more specific than "sympathetic." The reader she wishes to procure for her father must affiliate himself to Coleridge's genius, as she has. In seeking out such genial readers, Sara embraces Coleridge's own characteristic blurring of the difference between "literal" children and those who are "as" children, but in doing so she revises the significance of the gesture. Her very use of the metaphor of children emphasizes her own special genial relationship to her father, reminding the reader that she is the true daughter of his genius. Yet it also acknowledges that sharing her father is the defining principle of her work. Unless others join her in responding to him with "mind and heart," in "meeting him halfway," in "co-operating" to make him visible in his texts, she will have little to show for her labors.

Notes

1. Quoted in Griggs, "Robert Southey's Estimate of Samuel Taylor Coleridge: A Study in Human Relations," 71.

2. Quoted in Griggs, *Coleridge Fille: A Biography of Sara Coleridge*, 164. Subsequent quotations are cited parenthetically in the text.

3. Sara did almost all of the work for the collection. As Derwent explained in the "Advertisement" (written after Sara's death): "At her earnest request, my name appears with hers on the title-page, but the assistance rendered by me has been, in fact, little more than mechanical" *The Poems of Samuel Taylor Coleridge*, [v].

4. Mudge, *Sara Coleridge, a Victorian Daughter: Her Life and Essays*, 14, 175, 9.

5. S. Coleridge, *Memoir and Letters of Sara Coleridge*, 300. Subsequent quotations are cited parenthetically in the text.

6. Battersby, *Gender and Genius: Towards a Feminist Aesthetics*, 27, 44 (quoting Coleridge's celebrated definition of imagination).

7. S. Coleridge, "Nervousness," quoted in Mudge, *Sara Coleridge*, 201.

8. S. T. Coleridge, *Biographia Literaria*, prepared by H. N. Coleridge and completed by Sara Coleridge, xxii–xxiii. Subsequent quotations are cited parenthetically as *SCBL* in the text.

9. Emphasizing the cultural sources of Sara's illness in terms of societal constraints on women intellectuals, Mudge argues that illness was for Sara "a symbolic reenactment of her own status as marginal intellectual; her (dis)ease both provided the opportunity for intellectual activity and confirmed the deviance that activity represented" (*Sara Coleridge*, 88).

10. S. T. Coleridge, *Collected Letters of Samuel Taylor Coleridge*, 6:902. Subsequent quotations are cited parenthetically as *CL* in the text.

11. Griggs, *Coleridge Fille*, 11; Woodring, "Sara *fille:* Fairy Child."

12. S. T. Coleridge, "Dejection: An Ode," line 39. All references to Coleridge's poetry are to *The Complete Poetical Works of Samuel Taylor Coleridge* and are cited parenthetically in the text.

13. On this literary triangle, see Hickey, "Coleridge, Southey, 'and Co.,'" 305–49. Horace's phrase "disjecta membra poetae" forms the epigraph to Coleridge's 1817 *Sibylline Leaves*.

14. S. T. Coleridge, *Biographia Literaria*, 1:66. Subsequent references to Coleridge's text (as distinguished from Sara's apparatus) are to the Princeton University Press edition, which is cited parenthetically as *BL* in the text.

15. This defense earned her the praise of the very man who had introduced the charges. "Coleridge's admirable daughter" was how De Quincey described her. De Quincey, *The Collected Writings of Thomas De Quincey*, 228.

16. Sara Coleridge, ed., *Essays on His Own Times, Forming a Second Series of The Friend*, by S. T. Coleridge, lxxxv–lxxxvii. Subsequent quotations are cited parenthetically as *EOT* in the text.

17. Coleridge's comments on Shakespeare and Milton form part of an argument attributing such an "*individualized* and characteristic" style to Wordsworth. Sara's assertion of her father's individualized, poetic prose style thus places him not only in the company of Shakespeare and Milton but also side by side with his more immediate compeer.

18. This is an example of Sara's applying what Mudge calls "Coleridgean tenets" to Wordsworth. Yet another irony worth noting is that this apparent efflux of Wordsworth's "individual spirit" owes much to Coleridge.

19. W. and D. Wordsworth, *The Letters of William and Dorothy Wordsworth*, 7: 833–34. Subsequent quotations are cited parenthetically as *WL* in the text.

20. Gill, *William Wordsworth: A Life* (Oxford: Clarendon, 1989), 328.

21. See Mudge, *Sara Coleridge*, 136.

22. Wordsworth, *The Prelude*, lines 263–64.

23. See H. Coleridge, "Dedicatory Sonnet to S. T. Coleridge," in his *New Poems, Including a Selection from His Published Poetry*, 3; and A. Taylor, "'A Father's

Tale': Coleridge Foretells the Life of Hartley." Suffering from alcoholism and never finding a regular occupation, Hartley remained in the Lake District, where he wandered from house to house, relying on the hospitality of his community.

24. W. Wordsworth, *The Poetical Works of William Wordsworth*, 2nd ed., vol. 2.

25. H. Coleridge, *Letters of Hartley Coleridge*, 275. Compare Hartley's similar assertion, made in reference to Sara's "Essay on Rationalism" (1843): "Dear Sara's treatise on Rationalism is a wonder. I say not a wonder of a woman's work—where lives the man that could have written it? None in Great Britain since our Father died. Poor Henry was perfectly right in saying that she inherited more of her father, than either of us; and that not only in the amount but in the quality of her powers." Quoted in *Coleridge Fille*, 131.

26. See *CL*, 1:656. In 1851, while describing Wordsworth's influence on her, Sara remarks that "his discourse as compared with my Father's was as the Latin language to the Greek" (*Memoir*, 492). This would give Wordsworth the central position and Coleridge an eccentric one in the polyglot edition of their lives. Yet in another sense it places Coleridge closer to origins. In the inscription Coleridge's emphasis on his daughter's attainments is also a way of asserting his parental role in contradistinction to that of Sara Fricker Coleridge. As Charles Lamb had commented, "You might pass an age with her [Sara *fille*] without suspecting that she knew any thing but her mother's tongue" (quoted in Griggs, *Coleridge Fille*, 40). Coleridge makes her accomplishments in her father's tongues a matter of familial record.

27. Coleridge's puzzling phrase "if she should marry," combined with his pointed use of Sara's first and last names, implies that even on her wedding day she bears the name "Coleridge" by virtue of her filial rather than her spousal role.

28. S. T. Coleridge, *Notes and Lectures upon Shakespeare, and Some of the Old Poets and Dramatists, with Other Literary Remains of S. T. Coleridge*, 1:99–100.

III

Victorian Complementarities and Crosscurrents

Photograph of Robert Browning's marginalia on a fair copy of Elizabeth Barrett Browning's "The Runaway Slave at Pilgrim's Point," reproduced with the permission of the Armstrong Browning Library, Baylor University, Waco, Texas.

"Singing Song for Song"

The Brownings "in the Poetic Relation"

CORINNE DAVIES & MARJORIE STONE

Dear Cory,

I opened the newspaper recently and encountered once again "How do I love thee?"—this time in an article about a psychotherapist teaching a seminar on "the dying art of love-letter writing." At least this is better than the bathos of a fashion-magazine ad asking "How can I glove you?" or a Canada Postal Service ad inquiring "How shall I mail thee?" On every side we find the romantic story—or the residue of it in those five inescapable words—when what interests us in the Brownings is their poetical and *textual* relations. As usual, the therapist was invoking the Brownings' example without regard for their actual writing; she dispenses advice that they certainly didn't follow! Don't write long letters. Don't use disclaimers. Be accurate in describing your lover's appearance (even to the lover?). Still, I'm grateful for the article because it suggested collaborating through letters, given the geographical obstacles we cannot overcome. We have talked about writing a joint essay on the Brownings so often in hours snatched out of conferences that I suspect it will be difficult to disentangle some of our

ideas. But maybe that reflects what we think needs more investigating
in the case of literary couples like the Brownings

Should we begin with the question of what attracted the Brownings
to each other—in their writing, first, and then in their letters before
they met in person? (That first meeting in May 1845 must have been
a charged moment!) I'm also intrigued by the ways in which they
played the roles of muse, mentor, editor, and audience for each other.
My impression is that they continued to act as muses and audiences
for each other throughout their lives. Following the first flush of
enthusiasm in the courtship and honeymoon period, though, they
seem to have been less inclined to engage in substantive editorial
interventions with each other. Do you agree?

By the way, I propose that we refer to them as EBB and RB. We
certainly don't want to call him "Browning" and her "Elizabeth" or
"Mrs. Browning," as critics traditionally did (much as they spoke of
"Mill" and "Harriet"). And "Barrett Browning" seems an awkward
anachronism. EBB seemed happy with her double-barreled maiden
name Elizabeth Barrett Barrett—there's a name to roll out
resoundingly!—and was pleased when RB pointed out in their
courtship letters that her initials would not change with their
marriage. For a woman who had long signed her manuscripts
"EBB," this continuity must have seemed propitious! (Aurora
Leigh similarly manages to retain her authorial identity by marrying
a cousin with her own last name.)

As we've often remarked, it's surprising the Brownings never
formally collaborated on a poetical work despite RB's hint, early
in their correspondence (May 1845, before they had met), "I should
like to write something in concert with you—how I would try!" (*The
Brownings' Correspondence*, 10:201).[1] Scott Lewis's wonderful edition of
EBB's letters to her sister Arabella includes references to plans, in the
first year of their marriage, to collaborate on a "collection of poems
on Italy," though EBB stresses "with our separate signatures" (see her
letter of March 1847; 1:59). I wonder why she emphasized "separate
signatures"? Were both too invested in the Romantic figure of the
"solitary genius" to contemplate merging their poetic identities?
(EBB's letters in the early 1840s are shot through with references to
her worship of "genius.") The anxieties of authorship and influence
must have taken convoluted forms between two loving partners who
were also ambitious poets. I sense such anxieties at work in the focus

on who has the first word and who has the last in RB's "A Woman's Last Word" and "One Word More" (remember that in manuscript the latter was originally entitled "A Last Word, to E.B.B.").

I know that we both believe the Brownings strongly influenced each other's experiments with genre and poetic technique. Do you think such poetic intimacies encouraged "gender-bending"? In RB's "A Lovers' Quarrel" the male speaker says, "Teach me to flirt a fan / As the Spanish ladies can," and speaks of tinting his lady's "lip / With a burnt stick's tip" to turn her into "such a man!" (Pettigrew & Collins, *Robert Browning: The Poems*, 1:531). Speaking of lovers' quarrels, you know that I'm keenly interested in how these play out through their poetry. How much do you think the Brownings' quarrels (especially over Louis Napoleon or spiritualism) were also the conflicts of their age—like those of Sylvia Plath and Ted Hughes in our own? I suspect you may object to some of these questions. I think I'm more inclined to presuppose hidden conflicts than you are (witness my essay speculating on RB's lines about drowning in bile and why they appear in the middle of a draft of EBB's bitter poem about betrayal in love entitled "My Heart and I"). You, by contrast, have often emphasized the Brownings' shared spiritual and artistic philosophies and the productive harmonies in their writing relationship. Can we address such matters without a struggle for the "last word" ourselves? Since I've had the first, by the way, I agree now to give you the last.

All best wishes,
Marjorie

Dear Marjorie,

I really like your proposal to use their initials for all the reasons you give. Here's collaborative agreement for you early on—if only on a matter of procedure! And it does seem fitting to converse in letter or "textual" form since the Brownings' courtship correspondence originated in their readings of each other's poetry, beginning with those wonderful words of RB to EBB in January 1845: "I love your verses with all my heart, dear Miss Barrett . . . so into me has it gone, and part of me has it become, this great living poetry of yours. . . . I do, as I say, love these books with all my heart—and I love you too." Bold of him to add the "I love you too."

It seems to me that he may have been led to undertake the correspondence in response to his own appearance in the august poetic company of Spenser, Petrarch, and Tennyson in "Lady Geraldine's Courtship" (1844). The fact that she responds to his letter by "daring" to name herself with him "in the poetic relation" bears out Mary Rose Sullivan's suggestion that they "considered themselves engaged in a unique poetic as well as a personal partnership" ("Some 'Interchange of Grace': 'Saul' and *Sonnets from the Portuguese*," 56). In effect, they coauthored the text of their own love story in those courtship letters, written between January 1845 and September 1846, and then acted out that story in their secret marriage and flight to Italy. Do you know Robert Polhemus's *Erotic Faith*? He identifies the case of the Brownings as a paradigm of the dynamic process that fused writing with being in love and the quest for faith in the nineteenth century. He also points out that their textual interactions led to love, marriage, sexual fulfillment, a son (appropriately nicknamed Pen, as literary quizzes remind us!), more poetry, and the Browning myths (25). Ironically, it was the very textuality in the love letters that helped create the myths that now obscure the ways in which their poems speak to each other.

I think the attraction to each other they experienced through their poems is easy to understand. In her book on EBB Dorothy Mermin says that their works were often much alike—"learned, innovative, difficult, marked and marred, almost paradoxically, by both prolixity and extreme compression" (117). As we have discussed, they shared a Dissenting Christian background, Jamaican connections on the paternal side, and antislavery views. They were also drawn to similar themes and subject matter—in particular the quest for "soul-making" and the philosophical belief they shared with Ruskin and others of seeing the infinite in the finite.

All through the love letters, as Sullivan notes, they return quotation for quotation from their poetry and earlier letters, echoing each other in a dialogue of equals. During their courtship they also wrote with each other's works on their desks before them: she had the manuscript for his November 1845 volume *Dramatic Romances and Lyrics* on her desk, and he had the two volumes of her 1844 *Poems* on his. The interactive textuality of the letters shows how well they knew each other's poems. I particularly like one repeated erotic and mysterious intertext concerning the Sirens "singing song for song." It comes from Walter Savage Landor's sonnet "To Robert Browning," representing his response to a presentation copy of Browning's 1845 *Dramatic Romances and Lyrics:*

> But warmer climes
> Bring brighter plumage, stronger wing: the breeze
> Of Alpine heights thou playest with, borne on
> Beyond Sorrento and Amalfi, where
> The Siren waits thee, singing song for song.

In his edition of the love letters Elvan Kintner cites this sonnet (1: 273), saying that Landor's words "came to sound like prophecy" when RB and EBB began to think of marriage and Italy. Quite naturally he writes to her, "You ARE the veritable Siren, and you 'wait me,' and I will sing 'song for song.'" (Kintner 1:352). More surprisingly, many letters later EBB says (in an early example of overt "gender-bending"): "Talk of Sirens,—there must be some masculine ones . . . to justify this voice I hear" (1:540). Each evidently continued to enjoy playing Siren to the other in their erotic and poetic exchange over the next sixteen years. For my "Siren" we might read your "Muse" in the Brownings' poetic relationship.

You're right in saying that despite "singing song for song," the Brownings seem never to have formally produced a collaborative poem. Yet I think their work as editors, copyists, and proofreaders of each other's work amounted to a form of collaboration, especially considering the fifty-six pages of commentary and suggestions for revision (mostly on rhyme and rhythm) that EBB produced in the summer of 1845 in response to RB's manuscripts for *Dramatic Romances and Lyrics* (the commentary published as the fourth appendix in *The Brownings' Correspondence*, vol. 11). As to why they didn't formally collaborate on a single work of poetry, EBB's reply on 5–6 May 1845 to RB's comment about writing something "in concert" is revealing. She carefully but humorously responds that she likes this idea "still better" than he, but that a joint endeavor by the two of them might supply the "critical Board of Trade" with a "grand supply of jests" about "visible darkness, multiplied by two, mounting into palpable obscure" (*The Brownings' Correspondence*, 12:204)—referring to the reputation they both had for producing difficult poetry. She also goes on to describe her attempts at collaboration with Richard Hengist Horne, first in "Psyche Apocalypté" (that rather strange, unfinished allegorical drama), explaining that she "dare not" contemplate another collaboration "just now, if ever," and that she is a "little entangled on the subject of compound works." Apparently she had learned a lesson from this failed venture, and she would not risk another collaboration, not even with RB. (See Sullivan's article

"Elizabeth Barrett Browning and the Art of Collaboration," 47.)
Perhaps she had also drawn certain lessons from her critical
collaboration on *A New Spirit of the Age*, published under Horne's
name in 1844, since she received no credit for her contributions
(which were substantial, as another appendix in the eighth volume
of *The Brownings' Correspondence* makes clear).

Let me return to my main point, namely, that the Brownings *did*
collaborate in significant ways through their roles as editors of each
other's works. I have been very interested in EBB's comments on the
poems that RB was readying for publication in the autumn of 1845.
But if I start on this now, there will never be an end to this letter.

Yours,
Cory

Dear Cory,

As you say, the attraction through their poetry is easy to
understand. Imagine EBB's response upon opening that first letter
and reading such a tribute from a poet she called an indubitable
"genius," one of the "demi-gods," and "king of the mystics" (I'm not
exaggerating—see *The Brownings' Correspondence*, 7:14, 55; 10:20). I
agree with you that the theme of the poet's "soul-making" drew them
together. Despite the differences in form, EBB's 1844 poem "A Vision
of Poets" has many affinities with RB's *Paracelsus*. Both represent
aspiring artists and include a vision of dead poets and peers. RB's
"Childe Roland" (with its dark vision of lost peers) seems to echo, in
turn, the allegorical representation of the world's cruelty and bad
faith through a repulsive landscape in "A Vision of Poets." Remember
that slimy fourth pool on the heath, entangled by nightshade and yew,
where the pilgrim-poet in EBB's poem hears snakes straining against
the soil, and toads and bats seem to brush against his skin? Isn't that
like the grotesque landscape in "Childe Roland"? The difference is
that RB presents the experience of the "world's cruelty" dramatically,
from the inside out, as it were. In "Abt Vogler" too, I hear echoes of
"A Vision of Poets"—particularly EBB's metaphors of mounting
organ chords to convey the transcendence of poetic inspiration.

I think that EBB was most struck by the passionate power of RB's
poetry. I love the passage in which she calls him a "master in clenched
passion,—concentrated passion—burning through the metallic fissures
of language"—and this was written on 14 February 1843, long before

she met him (*The Brownings' Correspondence*,6:325). In December 1842 she similarly praised his "manner of being graphic & passionate," which reminded her of Landor (6:226), whose metaphor of sirens "singing song for song" becomes so resonant in their love letters, as you noted earlier. As Yopie Prins has shown, the Brownings also use allusions to Aeschylus to convey their love for each other. I guess it's not surprising that writers make love through other writers, refracting their desire through texts.

For this reason I take exception to the conventional view that RB initiated the courtship by writing to "Dear Miss Barrett." One could as easily argue that she initiated it by saluting his poetry in "Lady Geraldine's Courtship." She gives his poetry two long lines where she gives Wordsworth's, Mary Howitt's, and Tennyson's only half a line each. And what lines! "Or from Browning some 'Pomegranate' which, if cut down the middle, / Shows a heart within blood-tinctured, of a veined humanity." What a sensuous image! "Tennyson's enchanted reverie" pales by comparison. (Of course, RB's title for his "Bells and Pomegranates" series gave her a lot to work with!) As a "lady" poet, EBB clearly could not sit down and write, "My Dear Mr. Browning. I love your poetry with all my heart. . . . And I love you too." But I'd say that it was her "song" that began the conversation of the love letters. If coupled writers often come together through rituals of gift exchange, her compliment is the first gift.

I've been looking at the criticism on the Brownings in the "poetic relation" and have concluded that it's not surprising that we don't altogether agree. Like you and like Sullivan, some approach their writing relationship as an "interchange of grace." But just as many others underscore their marital, artistic, and political conflicts. In her essay in Ruth Perry's and Martine Watson Brownley's collection *Mothering the Mind,* Mermin has argued eloquently that they nurtured each other's creativity, opened up new poetical territory for each other, and produced their best poetry during their married years. I think we're both inclined to agree with her on this last point. Yet, as you reminded me once, influential Browning critics have argued to the contrary, claiming that EBB was a blight on RB's creativity. And biographers of both writers—Betty Miller or William Irvine and Park Honan on RB and Gardner Taplin on EBB—underscore the couple's poetic and political strife. The emphasis on their political opposition has persisted despite Flavia Alaya's incisive critique of the tendency to exaggerate and mythologize it. I see Alaya's article as essential reading given the tendency to define RB's politics by contrasting them with EBB's, which reflects a frequent pattern in the reception of mixed-sex literary couples. Alaya notes, incidentally, that the Brownings had planned to write paired poems on Louis Napoleon's interventions in Italian politics in 1860 until the Villafranca settlement led RB to believe his poem no longer suited the moment. So their idea for a joint volume of poems on Italy seems to have persisted. Whatever their differences on Louis Napoleon, the letters EBB wrote to Arabella suggest how much they passionately agreed on many issues relating to the Italian Risorgimento. Critics have also defined EBB's poetry by contrasting it with RB's—as in Laura Haigwood's argument that EBB was a Romantic "subjective poet" critiqued by RB, the dramatic "objective poet" in *Men and Women*. Haigwood suggests that RB's critique sprang, in part, from the gender anxiety he experienced in receiving what he termed that "strange, heavy crown, that wreath of Sonnets, put on [him] one morning unawares" (101). The "heavy crown" comment is an oddly ambivalent response to the *Sonnets from the Portuguese*. I think Haigwood rightly discerns a gender anxiety in the Brownings' poetic relations. She notes the oppressiveness of poetic gifts, which seem to demand repayment in kind. Undoubtedly there were also tensions arising from the fact that throughout their married life EBB was the more famous poet. I don't agree, however, with Haigwood's contrast between the subjective EBB and the objective RB. This seems to me too much an unquestioned commonplace in criticism on the Brownings.

It's interesting that in the 1980s male critics like James McNally and George Ridenour found evidence in *The Ring and the Book* of a harmonious partnership between the Brownings continuing after EBB's death, while feminist critics emphasized their persistent poetic strife. In 1984 Nina Auerbach—responding to Phyllis Rose's *Parallel Lives*—argued that *The Ring and the Book* and *Aurora Leigh* embodied "mutually exclusive" visions of life, art, the past, and the present. In fact, she asserted that RB forced EBB "to become the Muse of a tale that she never would have told" as he "resurrect[ed] his sainted wife in order to butcher her in the person of Pompilia" (166–68). Strong stuff! Adrienne Munich has more subtly argued that RB encircled EBB's "rare gold ring of verse" with the "ring" of his own poetry in his closing salute in *The Ring and the Book*, thereby engaging in a "gesture of poetic appropriation" and "colonization" (76). According to Munich, the ring "is a trophy," manifesting his "poetic power." One could also contend, of course, that his gesture reflects poetic anxiety, given his references to the British public's disregard for his works. Perhaps in linking the "ring" of his "book" with EBB's he aspired to enter the golden circle of her international fame.

Like these critics, the Victorians also seemed to have had mixed views of the Brownings' writing relationship, judging by the responses to their marriage cited by Daniel Karlin in his 1997 *SBHC* article on the subject. The American writer Kate Field gushed about the "magnetic fluid of love and poetry that was constantly passing between husband and wife" (Karlin, 47), while the patriarchal Wordsworth, that crusty old codger, was reported to have said, "I hope these two young people understand each other; nobody else will" (Karlin, 38). Karlin also cites Anna Jameson's amazement at the idea of two poets trying to handle the details of daily life, "as if they had never spoken anything but prose in their lives" (38), and Mary Mitford's exclamation: "Married poets! Married *authors* we have had of all ages and of all countries . . . but married poets have been rare indeed" (33). As Karlin notes, the Brownings were often reviewed in tandem, with critics asking whose poetry influenced whom? He says they almost always settled this "in the direction of the wife's poems being influenced by those of the husband's" (41)—although I have seen mid-nineteenth-century reviews that claim the opposite. Whatever the Brownings' views on artistic collaboration, they took advantage of their union by commercially coupling their works, as demonstrated by RB's switch to EBB's publisher, Chapman and Hall, and the advertisements for each other's works in their successive publications. One reviewer cited by Karlin notes that the two poets' 1849 and 1850 volumes were issued in identical green bindings, suggesting "a harmony, a domestic agreement" founded on "melodious principles." However, this identical aspect led to some anxiety about the sex of the texts. "Fortunately," the reviewer comments, "the similarity is confined to name and outsides"; the contents generally show "the sex of the speaker," revealing "those differences absolutely necessary in the conjugal relation" (Karlin, 42). One wonders how this critic would parse the sex of postmodern novels collaboratively written by mixed couples?

I don't think, however, that we should assume nineteenth-century critics were necessarily more anxious than twentieth-century critics about authorial couplings. In fact, it often seems that Victorian readers

more readily accepted literary couples or collaborators—and were less
enamored of "solitary genius" models of authorship—than modernist
readers and our contemporaries. RB specialists tend either to ignore
EBB or to construct her as part of RB's "circle" or as one of his "audiences" (Lee Erikson's term), while feminist critics (as Auerbach said
back in 1984) have treated RB as an "ancillary presence" in setting out
to recover a heroic grandmother. (I plead guilty on this count myself.)
As we have often commented, it's revealing that there have been
so few full-length studies of the Brownings focusing on the "poetic
relation." A. S. Byatt does draw on the Brownings in *Possession* to
represent Ellen and Randolph Ash, but Ellen is not a poet despite
Byatt's use of details of EBB's life to portray her. Byatt turns to
Christina Rossetti and Emily Dickinson as prototypes for her fictitious
woman poet Christabel Lemotte, paired in passionate adultery with
Randolph. "Poor Randolph/Robert!" Byatt seems to be implying.
"He married the wrong woman!" Julia Markus suggests the opposite
in *Dared and Done*, but her focus is primarily biographical too.

I see I have written far too long a letter here, so I will simply add
that I hope we can give equal weight to each poet, not constructing
one as "significant" and the other as "other."

Yours in the critical relation,

Marjorie

Dear Marjorie,

At the outset let me say that some feminist readings of EBB's
poetry, like Auerbach's or Haigwood's, do tend to see only the
conflicts, anxieties, and tensions in their writerly relationship. I
certainly acknowledge these, but I prefer to see the dissonances as
most often issuing in creative resolutions—though I recognize that
these came at a high cost to both. So, by way of debate, let me suggest an
alternative reading to Haigwood's claim that EBB's *Sonnets from the
Portuguese* became an oppressive gift to RB, a "strange, heavy crown."
I believe that this is a key instance not of conflict but of RB "singing
song for song," echoing his wife's sonnets and harking back to his 1835
preface to *Paracelsus*. In this preface RB empowers his readers to don
the poet's "Crown" while their "intelligence," "sympathy," and
"co-operating fancy" involve them in the co-production of the poem.
As he says, "It is certain . . . that a work like mine depends more
immediately on the intelligence and sympathy of the reader for its

success—indeed were my scenes stars it must be his co-operating fancy which, supplying all chasms, shall connect the scattered lights into one constellation—a Lyre or a Crown" (Pettigrew and Collins, *The Poems*, 1:1030).

The idea of a "co-operating fancy" that RB describes here is very interesting, since it breaks down the distinction between poet and reader (and perhaps poet and muse) in complex ways. As a result, it makes the realization of the poetic text a collaborative enterprise—with the "crown" serving as a metaphor for the successful bridging of the perceptual "chasms" between poet and reader—and not (as one might normally expect) a metaphor for the achievement of the "solitary genius." To return to RB's comment on EBB's *Sonnets*, I think he finds this crown "heavy" not because of gender anxiety but because all poetry is demanding. He recognizes his own role in poetic production as both EBB's audience and her collaborative partner. Thus, I read "mysterious and weighty crown" for Haigwood's "strange, heavy" and oppressive one.

The Victorians, as you mentioned, were probably more interested in the Brownings as "coupled writers" than our contemporaries because they could watch the newly married partners' publications unfolding after 1846. Yet both nineteenth- and twentieth-century critics have overlooked the textual interchanges in their earlier works. One I've been exploring lately relates to EBB's "The Romaunt of the Page" and RB's "The Flight of the Duchess" (published five years later, in 1844). These two poems reveal their responses to each other's earlier poetry, their generic experimentation with the ballad-romance genre, the shared political messages on "the woman question" they expressed through the romance form, and their most direct literary collaboration in the form of EBB's lengthy editorial comments on RB's poem.

Why were they both drawn to the ballad-romance in the late 1830s and early 1840s? I think that it provided them with a conventional literary site, ripe for revision, on which to play out their notions of social and sexual politics—which they acted out in their own flight to Italy. The thematic similarities in these two poems are striking. Both deal with the attempt to fashion a proper, gentle, silent wife by her male counterpart, whether medieval knight, duke, or Victorian husband. In both ballads the figure of clothing is used to interrogate socially encoded sexual difference. In "The Romaunt of the Page"

EBB's female protagonist cross-dresses as a page, only to "unman" herself in a tragic moment of defiance and self-recognition before she embraces death. In "The Flight of the Duchess" RB satirically strips the masculine disguise (i.e., "unmans" it) from the Moldavian court to reveal the lifelessness of an outdated pseudochivalric patriarchy. EBB's representation, in her cross-dressing heroine, of the transgressing of social, sexual, and generic archetypes is literal, whereas RB's is metaphorical. Yet in both poems strong women triumph over outmoded systems of chivalry, cut the bonds of femininity, and escape the subservience demanded by the husband.

Writing her "Romaunt" for Mitford's successful gift-book annual *Finden's Tableaux of the Affections* (1839), subtitled *A Series of Picturesque Illustrations of the Womanly Virtues*, EBB ironically undercuts the sentiments and conventions represented throughout the rest of the volume even as she addresses her primarily female audience. After failing to find an audience with his experimental long poems of the 1830s, RB was clearly sensitive to the market potential that the popularity of EBB's *Finden's* ballad-romances proved. In turning to the same form in "The Flight of the Duchess" he similarly undercuts its conventions. The result is a very humorous parody of the fetishizing of history and medievalism in Victorian pseudoballads, combined with a political message on "the woman question":

> She [the new duchess] was to do nothing at all. . . .
> And the Duke's plan admitted a wife, at most . . .
> To sit thus, stand thus, see and be seen,
> At the proper place in the proper minute,
> And die away the life between.
>
> (lines 183–91)

The publication history becomes important here because the final version of "Flight" is a kind of joint production. RB began the poem in 1842; the first nine stanzas (including the lines quoted) appeared in *Hood's Magazine* in April 1845. His continuing revisions of the poem occasioned the lengthiest interchanges in the 1845–46 love letters. Prior to its November 1845 publication in *Dramatic Romances and Lyrics*, EBB worked more extensively on "Flight" than on any of RB's other poems, devoting twelve of her fifty-six pages of editorial commentary to it. Although RB explained to EBB that "nobody ever sees what I do till it is printed" (*The Brownings' Correspondence*, 10:55), he evidently asked her for commentary on these 1845 poems and gave her "The Flight of the Duchess" first.

EBB praised it as a "very singular & striking poem, full of power . . . quite wonderful for the mechanism & and rhyming power of it"— a poem in which "the beauty reveals itself from the grotesqueness" (*The Brownings' Correspondence*, 11:381). But she also attempted to correct the "rhythm," "accents," and "elisions" that resulted in "forced" or unclear lines. Though she worried about her "impertinence," she relentlessly smoothed out rhythm and rhyme, rhetorically asking, "It ought to be musical—ought it not?" At one point she apologetically observes that she has corrected her own previous corrections of RB's lines! (*The Brownings' Correspondence*, 11:18). In the flush of first love, he accepted every one of her suggestions. In fact, Daniel Karlin points out in his book on their courtship that not once in all their years of marriage did RB write a "derogatory word" against her poetry (87).

I don't think RB originally intended "The Flight of the Duchess" as an exhortation to EBB to leave Wimpole Street. But it must have become suggestive for both of them in its promise of escape from England. He astutely avoided including a male rescuer or lover in the second half of the poem, concentrating instead on female strength and language, as well as on a political position emphasizing the liberating potential in collective actions by women. No wonder Deborah Byrd sees an overtly political basis for their marriage. She claims that EBB "married a man who shared her desire to identify and combat the evils of patriarchy" (211). RB, of course, had already attacked patriarchal power over women most violently, explicitly, and luridly in "Porphyria's Lover" and "My Last Duchess," both poems about "the devouring male ego," as U. C. Knoepfelmacher has shown. These poems must have provided an early stimulus to the relationship. In "Flight" the predatory male ego fails, defeated by the combined mystical female wisdom of the gypsy Queen and the courage of the young Duchess. Whereas EBB's page dies alone, this Duchess escapes patriarchal systems to ride off with the gypsy Queen. It's a wonderful story and an amazing poem.

Cory

Dear Cory,

I was intrigued by your description of EBB's collaboration on "The Flight of the Duchess." In fact, this seems to be a striking case of what

Jack Stillinger has described as "multiple authorship" in his book on the myth of the solitary genius—though he doesn't include works by the Brownings in his appendix of examples. I suppose EBB's contributions could be classified as an "influence" (that's how the editorial interventions of domestic or sexual partners often seem to be categorized). The question remains: Where does influence cross over into collaboration when detailed editorial consultation is involved? Either way, you seem to be implying that RB learned from the generic innovation of EBB's ballad-romances (archaic in manner, modern in terms of their gender politics). He also must have enjoyed exchanging ideas with a poet so interested in experiments with irregular rhyme and diction. It's clear from his praise for the rhymes of "The Dead Pan" (which he saw before he met EBB) that he appreciated her innovations on this front.

I think that she, in turn, clearly learned from his "dramatic impersonations," to use one of her own terms (given that "dramatic monologue" was not yet used as a generic category). She left a number of unpublished, unfinished experiments with such "impersonations" (in the "Sonnets" notebook now housed in the Armstrong Browning Library, as well as in a "Poems and Sonnets" notebook at Yale University, both dating from the 1840s). I hear in these the impact of the "clenched passion" she admired in RB's poetry, as well as the colloquial idioms. For example, "Maude Clarence" in the Yale notebook opens abruptly, "God curse him I say! So he trod her in here / Her sweet eyes, her young mouth, her voice still in my ears / With his hard [?] brutal foot in the clay." Like "My Last Duchess" and "The Flight of the Duchess," this fragment opposes a high-spirited young woman (now evidently dead and buried) and a tyrannical, possessive man.

I don't mean to suggest that EBB began experimenting with dramatic-monologue forms *because of* RB's example. Critics and handbooks have tended to represent him as the solitary inventor of the genre. Some acknowledge that Tennyson had also contributed to its evolution between 1830 and 1844, but EBB's independent work at this time on similar kinds of dramatic, single-speaker poems is not generally recognized. I have in mind works such as the 1838 poem "The Virgin Mary to the Child Jesus" (in which Mary speaks sometime after the nativity, when she is alone and struggling to come to terms with being the Mother of God). EBB also transformed "Catarina to Camoens"

from a lyric into a dramatic monologue in successive revisions between
1831–32 and 1844. Then there's the 1844 dramatic ballad "Bertha in
the Lane," with its dying, jealous sister as speaker. RB often praises
both "Bertha" and "Catarina" in the love letters. The "monodrama"
on Aeschylus is another striking example (the work was published
with the attributed title "[Aeschylus' Soliloquy]" in Pettigrew and
Collins's edition of RB's *Poems*, 2:948–51). In their article on the
poem, Margaret Reynolds and Barbara Rosenbaum (Rosenbaum
discovered the Huntington draft manuscript in EBB's hand) nicely
unpack the gender ideologies at work in this misattribution—based
on a fair copy transcription that RB made after her death. In his
handbook on Browning, William DeVane describes the Aeschylus
fragment as "the best of the poems Browning left unpublished," a
work that is "thoroughly mature," in which the "poetry is steadily
excellent" (569–70). As one RB specialist remarked to me, "He never
would have said that if he had thought it was by EBB!"

Her work/His work. How the terms reflect our author-centered
models of classification. My main point is that Brownings mutually
influenced each other's experiments with new dramatic forms—even
if RB went on to become the acknowledged master of the form. Still,
EBB may have played a critical role in prompting his crucial shift away
from stage drama to the dramatic monologue. In the same letter in
which she first mentions the Aeschylus "monodram" (her spelling—
see *The Brownings' Correspondence*, 1:102), she objects to the vulgarity of
stage drama and expresses her preference for a drama that takes "for
a worthier stage the soul itself," to use the terms she later employed
in *Aurora Leigh* (Book 5, l.340). Isn't this the very "stage" that RB
represents in the genre that now bears his signature?

You have been exploring the revisions EBB suggested for "The
Flight of the Duchess." Perhaps, as a return favor, RB seems to
have played a similarly collaborative role in "The Runaway Slave
at Pilgrim's Point." It's interesting that despite their radical
differences, both poems represent the flight of a woman from her
male oppressors. As Julia Markus has concluded in *Dared and Done*,
"The Runaway Slave" is a "peculiar" work for a newlywed woman
to write (92)—although I don't think evidence supports the "mixed
blood" theory Markus advances to explain its explosive mixture of
rape, miscegenation, whipping, and infanticide. I often wonder what
RB thought of this poem as the first work his wife produced following

their marriage (she mailed it to America in late December 1846; see *The Brownings' Correspondence*, 14:86). He evidently read the poem sometime that fall because a fair copy chopped into three pieces by some unscrupulous dealer includes his editorial suggestions.

He did tread carefully in making these, as EBB did with "Flight." Consider his tactful question regarding stanza 21, which describes the slave's graphic recollection of her white-faced baby's struggles as she attempted to smother it, ending with "I twisted it round in my shawl." In the fair copy (where this stanza is number 20), "shawl" is underlined twice in pencil; beside it, sideways in the margin, RB has written: "Does that sound like a slave's article of clothing?" Evidently EBB either thought that a slave might plausibly own a shawl or could not find a better alternative. The line remains unaltered in published texts of the poem. So she didn't accept all of his editorial interventions! But she did incorporate a suggestion he made regarding the second line of stanza 30, describing how the slave hunters formed a circle around the fugitive slave at Pilgrim's Point. In the fair copy this line reads (rather feebly), "Ah ah! they are on me! They enring." The last two words are inserted over an illegible deletion, suggesting that EBB was searching for better wording. Below the line RB has penciled in, "they form a ring" and commented "('enring' suggests to me, 'to shackle,' & c)." This alternate phrasing is used in the first published text of the poem (in the 1848 issue of the antislavery annual *The Liberty Bell*). But in the 1850 edition of her *Poems* it's altered slightly again to read "they hunt in a ring." She accepted as well his suggestion of "exquisite" to modify the "pain" of liberty that the slave dies from in the last stanza. As the fair copy shows (see the photograph on page 150), she had first tried "glorious," then deleted that for an illegible word, then deleted that word again for "wonderful." "Exquisite" is much better.

I find the "ring" metaphor in this interchange particularly fascinating, given the symbolic importance that it later assumes in the last lines of *The Ring and the Book* (where RB encircles EBB's "rare gold of verse" with the "ring" of his own). There's another kind of ring in the manuscript, too, representing RB's most striking addition to this fair copy of "The Runaway Slave." EBB had signed the manuscript with her initials, the ones that remained unaltered after her marriage. RB inserted "my" before "EBB" and enclosed "my EBB" in the "arms" of very thick brackets. It's a charming instance of the fond new husband's terms of endearment is how some might see it. But would others pause at the possessiveness of such a gesture of enclosure—putting her in parentheses, so to speak? Munich's reading of the "enringing" of EBB at the close of *The Ring and the Book* as an act of "appropriation" might come to mind. How would RB or his subsequent readers have responded if EBB had written "my" before the initials "RB" on one his manuscripts shortly after their marriage, then surrounded "my RB" with heavy brackets? Given RB's fascination with possessive men like Porphyria's lover and the Duke of Ferrara, what do you make of this husbandly gesture?

I had better stop before I get to the more conflicted ground of the Brownings' textual relations in the 1850s and '60s—or we'll be on embattled terrain ourselves!

Marjorie

Dear Marjorie:

No need to fear "embattled" terrain as we discuss the Brownings. Let's not forget that they both acknowledged multiple viewpoints in the dramatic form of their work, preferring debate and multiplicity to fixity and narrow-mindedness—or to polite forms of capitulation. However, let me just address a few issues raised in this last letter of yours before I tackle your question on husbandly gestures. I want to underline what you point out early in your last letter, namely, that the dramatic monologue allowed both poets to explore what EBB referred to as the "stage" of the "soul itself." In dedicating his 1863 reprinting of *Sordello* to Joseph Milsand, RB argued that his "stress lay on the incidents in the development of a soul: little else is worth study" (Pettigrew and Collins, *The Poems*, 1:150). Whatever else occurred in the Brownings' poetic relationship, they both remained firmly committed to poetry about the human soul.

Now to the nitty gritty of rings and brackets. RB's use of parentheses and his possessive pronoun in "The Runaway Slave" manuscript tells me what he thought of that poem: he was proud of EBB's strong and powerful work, and of his recent marriage to her. The words from the *Sacrament of Marriage*, "that mystical union," may still have been ringing (pun intended) in his ears: "to have and to hold from this day forward." This kind of having and holding involves a covenant or commitment in love to the other missing in the perverted possessiveness of the Duke and Porphyria's lover. So the bracketing of the initials may be related to something other than entrapment. RB always worked with the double-edged nature of images. In their love for one another in "The Runaway Slave," the slave woman and her slave lover find that their "spirits grew / As free as if unsold." The slave woman "sang his name . . . over and over" after their enforced separation, as RB perhaps sings EBB's name through the bracketing. You are probably not convinced—in which case my second response to the bracketing is to suggest that as far as we know, RB never tried this gesture again!

You say that the ring metaphor from the end of *The Ring and the Book* enters your mind as a result of Munich's interpretation of this image as an act of RB's appropriation. More resonant and closer in time for me is stanza 32 in RB's "Childe Roland to the Dark Tower Came," written in 1852, in which the hills entrap Roland "like giants at a hunting." I think the encircling here suggests to RB the entrapment Roland fears. However, to my mind the ring at the end of *The Ring and the Book* belongs to quite different traditions than the ring of entrapment in "The Runaway Slave" and "Childe Roland." Although Munich's argument sounds convincing within its own context, let me point to other contexts (collaborative in their own implications) that were probably more familiar and shared by both Brownings—I'm referring to alchemical and Neoplatonic ones.

A poet/alchemist ever since his *Paracelsus,* in the central ring metaphor of *The Ring and the Book* RB attempts to turn the dross of his primary factual material into the gold ring of truth about human souls in relation to the mystery of Eternity or of the One. I see RB's alchemical metaphor working on three levels (as described by Anthony Stevens in his *On Jung*): "the material (gold-making), the embryological (life-making) and the psychic (soul-making)" (229). Circles and rings of completion share the same eternal center. Enringing is not, as Munich argues, a "gesture of poetic appropriation" at the end of *The Ring and the Book;* the female figure is more than convenient muse. As Stevens explains, in the alchemical opus the alchemist collaborates with his "soror mystica" (imaginative sister or anima) in a relationship that is transformative. RB's final ring metaphor in *The Ring and the Book* formally acknowledges the symbiotic relationship between EBB's poetry and his in the saving of souls, reserving the last words of his opus for her "rare gold ring of verse."

I'll leave you for now with a question: What was it you wanted to mention about the conflicts you see in the Browning's textual relations in the 1850s and 1860s?

Cory

Dear Cory,

I hadn't thought about the ring metaphors in the contexts of the alchemical traditions you mention; they put quite a different spin on the ending of *The Ring and the Book*. And I like the idea that RB, in bracketing his new wife's initials, is like the slave lover fondly singing her lover's name over and over again. Brackets (and the enclasping ring at the end of *The Ring and the Book*) can be like embracing arms. That underlined *"my"* still looks a little possessive, though—a little like "That's *my* last Duchess painted on the wall" (my emphasis).

As for the Brownings' "textual relations" in the 1850s and 1860s, I think these provide evidence for conflict as well as harmony. I also believe that conflict may sometimes be a greater spur to creativity than conjugal bliss. I won't dwell on the poems portraying lovers' quarrels in *Men and Women*, some of them shaped by the Brownings' quarrels over spiritualism and Louis Napoleon. But it *is* striking, don't you think, that between them the Brownings with their legendary happy marriage produced some of the most powerful poetry about disillusionment in love, erotically charged revenge, and marital breakdown during the Victorian period? For instance, there's EBB's "My Heart and I" and "Bianca Among the Nightingales"—the latter seething with eroticized revenge—and there's RB's bitter version of "modern love" in "James Lee's Wife." Back in 1966 Glenn Sandstrom pointed to the connections between "'James Lee's Wife' and Browning's own wife. A more interesting connection, as I see it, is the textual relationship between RB's representation of marital breakdown in "James Lee's Wife" and EBB's portrayal of their courtship in *Sonnets from the Portuguese*—a connection suggested by the parallel images in the two works.

In short, I think there were inevitably gendered complications and darker dimensions in the Brownings' "singing song for song," as their marriage unfolded—even though it obviously remained a deeply loving marriage in many respects (the letters to Arabella make this clear). Granted, both Landor and the Brownings recast the siren as a figure who is at once inviting muse and fellow singer. This is how

Aurora envisions Romney in *Aurora Leigh*, imagining him as a sensuous "sea-king" (Book 8, l.41) who ultimately joins with her in her artistic mission. Yet old plots die hard. The siren who "waits" to sing "song for song" could, after all, be a kind of anti-muse, a demonic figure luring poet-adventurers to their deaths on a rocky, barren coastline (to use the shipwreck imagery that figures prominently in "James Lee's Wife," where it is associated with the possessively loving wife). The roles of muse and singer, Eurydice and Orpheus, can also be difficult to interchange. Why, after all, is Aurora's siren "sea-king" Romney blinded like Jane Eyre's Rochester before he and Aurora can be married? Could it perhaps be because a too powerful male muse might displace the female singer?

On the subject of sirens, one should remember that there were three of them, not one, singing on that island. Now three, as we all know, can be a crowd—even if, for a while in *Aurora Leigh*, EBB seems to entertain the possibility of an intriguing ménage à trois, consisting of Aurora, Romney, and Marian Erle. Moreover the Brownings did have muses aside from each other. RB manifests an intense desire to possess women not only of the present but also of the past and the future in that very erotic lyric "Women and Roses" in *Men and Women*. There's also that perfect, "infinite" yet transitory moment of coupled intimacy in "By the Fire-side": "We two stood there with never a third . . . Till the trouble grew and stirred" (Pettigrew and Collins, *The Poems*, 1:558).

Now before you begin (quite rightly) to question my habit of finding "trouble" stirring in the Brownings' "poetic relation," allow me a "woman's last word" about "One Word More." What do you make of the salute by RB to his wife and muse at the end of *Men and Women*? I am thinking, in particular, of his addressing her as his "moon of poets," with its echo of Andrea del Sarto's description of his philandering wife, Lucrezia, as "my everybody's moon"? Auerbach notes this echo and reads it as you might expect, given her claims about the Brownings' clashing visions. In "One Word More on Browning's 'One Word More'"—see how the phrase paradoxically breeds repetitions—Mary Ellis Gibson sets out the striking parallels between RB's "last word" and Andrea del Sarto's monologue. She notes that both poems present "an artist addressing his wife; in each the artist considers the significance of his art and ponders his relationship to his audience and to his wife; . . . each artist compares himself with other illustrious artists" (83). Yet Gibson compellingly underscores the crucial differences between RB and Andrea as well, reading "One Word More" as a sincere tribute to EBB.

Sincere it may be, but I'm also inclined to agree with Haigwood's suggestion that RB nevertheless "praises his wife in terms which verge on suggesting that he is the better poet" (109)—the Dante to her Raphael, to use the poem's own terms. He also associates her with images of sinister power. In evoking the hidden, private side of the poet visible only to those intimate with her, he asks if this unknown side may prove to be like a vision of Paradise or "like some portent of an iceberg / Swimming full upon the ship it founders / Hungry with huge teeth of splintered crystals?" (Pettigrew and Collins, *The Poems*, 1: 742). How do you interpret those "hungry" teeth—the dark side of the moon that is the poet-goddess revealed? Didn't Robert Graves insist that women could only be muses, not poets, unless they chose to become the white goddess herself in all her destructive power? It's odd, too, that with all his emphasis on the public versus private sides of his wife in "One Word More," RB does very little to evoke the public poetry that won her fame. Instead, he focuses on the secret, private side of her to which only he has privileged access.

"Those two poets, man and wife, wrote alone; each wrote, but did not bless or quicken one another at their work; *we are closer married*." That's what the Victorian aunt and niece known to the world as "Michael Field" said of the Brownings, according to Holly Laird (see her article on Field, 119). I think Field was wrong about the Brownings. They surely did "quicken" each other at their work—although I don't think they always did so by blessing each other. As Blake says, opposition can be "true friendship." I look forward to your reply. And, please note, you *will* have the last word (for now)!

Yours in the spirit of friendly opposition,

Marjorie

Dear Marjorie:

If you won't dwell on the Brownings' poetry about failed lovers and failed marriages in the later poems, I will at least acknowledge that both of them created many poems of psychological realism that demonstrate what sentimental idealizations of love, selfishness, and possessiveness, and outmoded marital conventions can lead to. The passionate intensity of the embittered or world-weary female speakers in EBB's posthumous *Last Poems* recalls that very similar grotesque energy of RB's monologists from the 1840s and 1850s. And while both Brownings explored with amazingly unsentimental frankness the inner spaces of the woman's mind (in EBB's 1850 *Poems* and RB's 1855 *Men and Women*), the tonalities in *Last Poems* startle me into a final recognition of EBB's brutal honesty when she deals with modern love in modern times, as you have suggested. Bitter grief, sexual frustration, and fury in "Bianca Among the Nightingales" are particularly arresting.

RB edited *Last Poems* for publication with Chapman and Hall after EBB's death in 1861. It thus seems obvious to me that his editorial effort resulted in some transposition of EBB's dominant and disenchanted female voices into his own dramatizations of the pains of modern love in *Dramatis Personae* (1864), most significantly "James Lee's Wife," whose changed title echoes EBB's "Lord Walter's Wife" in *Last Poems*. Whereas the Pettigrew and Collins edition of RB's poetry cites RB's primary debt in "James Lee's Wife," with its representation of a marital breakdown, to George Meredith's *Modern Love,* I find a more obvious source in EBB's monologues in *Last Poems.*

Finding trouble in any marriage is not too difficult, as mid-century Victorian writers of fiction and poetry (including the Brownings) proved. While we might question whether some of EBB's works in *Last Poems* and "James Lee's Wife" provide a final and most troubling focus for our exploration in textual relations, and whether the dynamics of their own marriage—her ever-worsening lung condition (which must have caused stress in the relationship) and disagreements over spiritualism—find expression in the darker monologues of the 1860s, we might also recognize that many other Victorian writers were as focused on these themes as were the Brownings. As I said earlier, I am not trying to cover up tensions in the Brownings' private and poetic relationships. Rather, I am trying to avoid readings with agendas that may be as mythological in their destructive tendencies as the earlier myths were in their sentimentalizing bent.

On to the case in point, then, as we debate RB's "One Word More." I cannot find Haigwood's evidence for identifying EBB with Raphael (although I concede that both wrote sonnets) and RB with Dante. The point is that RB is again "singing song for song" with the siren-poet who is also his muse. The courtship letter of 31 August 1845 reveals EBB's discouraging of his love in words that reverberate in RB's title: "Therefore we must leave this subject—and I must trust you to leave it without one word more" (*The Brownings' Correspondence*, 11:54). After almost ten years of marriage, RB writes his tribute in "One Word More" to the woman who collaborates with him in life and art, and he speaks "this once in my true person."

You are right to point to the threatening image of the iceberg, which is associated with EBB's dark and private side. However, this image gives way to "the paved work of a sapphire / Seen by Moses" in his vision of "the very God" (Pettigrew and Colllins, *The Poems*, 1: 742). There is more than one possibility for "the moonstruck mortal" looking on the other side of the moon. RB's is not a sentimental or chivalrous view of his muse—he does recognize in real awe her opening out to him "for worse or better" (another echo of the marriage ceremony). RB refers quite clearly to the blessing in the relationship at the end of the poem. I can find no diminishment in his admiration for his muse/collaborator, unconscious or otherwise. I find a prophetic engagement with EBB as beloved marriage partner and archetypal figure of Old Testament wisdom to RB. Incidentally, he also signed his name to this poem in subsequent editions, suggesting that he had fulfilled EBB's desire for him to write "RB a poem," that is, a lyric in his own voice.

As my "last word," allow me to observe that in many poems RB and EBB focused on the celebration of love, its creative links to art and Incarnation, and its redemptive qualities for the lovers involved. Throughout their canons voices also sing out mutual love and deliverance for the souls of creator/lovers. Parts of RB's "Saul" and EBB's *Aurora Leigh* view love in conjunction with the belief in art as redemptive. It is, paradoxically, through art that the Brownings embody this truth, so central to the vision of "high art" they both served, which drew them together and in which their voices sang in "that interchange of grace" mentioned in RB's address to his "Lyric Love" Elizabeth after her death (in the invocation closing the first book of *The Ring and the Book*). Moreover, he emphasizes that this muse is herself a poet. In the final lines of the twelfth book he invokes EBB's gold ring of verse, which like his verse will "tell a truth obliquely / Do the thing shall breed thought / and save the soul beside" (859–61).

Recall sections from *Aurora Leigh*, thirteen years earlier, on the high art of poetry in its Incarnational task. In the seventh book Aurora declares that the artist, still intensely human, "holds firmly by the natural to reach the spiritual beyond it" (lines 774–80); in the ninth

book Romney sings out to Aurora, "It is the hour for souls, / That
bodies, leavened by the will and love, / Be lightened to redemption"
(937–40). Singing out Revelation's promise of a new heaven and a
new earth, as David had sung it out before him in RB's "Saul" (and as
Andrea had failed to sing it at the end of "Andrea del Sarto"), Romney
describes the first foundations of the new day. In return, Aurora finally
sings of the precious foundation because she "saw his soul saw." The
shared vision lays foundations in so many ways in this verse-novel—
generically, politically, sexually—including foundations for *The Ring
and the Book*. Soul, art, love, redemption, and truth prevail in the songs
the Brownings sing, growing out of the frustrations, suffering, and loss
inevitable in this finite world.

We have covered a lot of ground, Marjorie, but there's lots more
to go. Perhaps we'll do so elsewhere. As the Brownings knew, there is
always the possibility for "one word more."

Cory

Notes

1. See the bibliography of this volume for complete information on sources
in these letters. EBB's manuscripts are cited in this article with the permission
of the Armstrong Browning Library, Baylor University, Waco, Texas, and
Yale University Library.

Collaboration and Collusion

Two Victorian Writing Couples and Their Orientalist Texts

JILL MATUS

In a lengthy review article on "Lady Travellers" published in the *Quarterly Review* in 1845, Elizabeth Rigby (later Lady Eastlake) made the following bold claim for the distinctiveness of women's travel writing and the special gendered knowledge it could communicate: "Every country . . . to be fairly understood, requires reporters from both sexes. Not that it is precisely recommended that all travellers should hunt the world in couples and give forth their impressions in the double columns of holy wedlock; but that kind of partnership should be tacitly formed between books of travel which, properly understood, we should have imagined to have been the chief aim of matrimony—namely, to supply each other's deficiencies, and correct each other's errors, purely for the good of the public."[1] Redressing each other's deficiencies and correcting each other's errors is a happy vision of complementarity that Rigby wittily applies both to the aims of marriage and the relations of travel book writers. Her slightly bemused approach to the subject is suggested by the characterization of matrimony as a system of checks and balances that exists "purely" to benefit society as a whole. Rigby then applies this inflated rhetoric of separate spheres to travel literature, where books by men and women should be issued in partnership with each other, each redressing the other's shortcomings for the public good. At first glance such tidy complementarity would appear to characterize the cases of the writing couples I examine in this essay. Sophia Poole's *The Englishwoman in Egypt* is a "humble helpmate" to her brother's scholarly, orientalist work *The Manners and Customs of the Modern Egyptians*. Similarly, Isabel Burton's "Household Edition" of her husband's *Book of the Thousand Nights and a Night* offered the Victorian public a version of his translations that could be introduced with propriety into the respectable home and was guaranteed never to bring a blush to a maiden's cheek.[2]

Although the rhetoric of gendered complementarity structures and validates the collaborative projects, such rhetoric often masks a more complex division of labor and mixture of motives than the doctrine of separate spheres admits. In some senses collaboration is also collusion: Sophia Poole writes letters to a friend, but the recipient is imaginary and much of the content of her special woman's perspective derives from her brother's notes. Isabel and Richard Burton collude in the fiction that Isabel has never read the improper material excised from her special women's edition of *The Arabian Nights*. But even in the act of collusion these women writers also assert their individuality and authority. In both writing couples questions of authority over form and content arise, power struggles over representations of the East surface, and surprising contradictions in the attribution of "masculine" and "feminine" knowledge spring up. Though both Sophia Poole and Isabel Burton disclaim a position of dominance in relation to the texts of their male counterparts, their subtle (and sometimes not so subtle) revisions of those prior texts reveal a resistance to simply serving the brother's or husband's greater knowledge and an insistence on their own ways of knowing and truth telling. The texts they produce are sites of struggle and competition even as they pay lip service to the superiority of male "scientific" orientalism and appear to accept the secondary role of impressionistic "female" knowledge shaped by domestic concerns. Sophia Poole is writing for her brother, but also—quietly and implicitly at times—writing back to him. Isabel Burton, conversely, can be said to be "underwriting" her husband in the sense that she writes both to protect his copyright and guarantee his reputation as the finest of orientalists, as well as to censor his translations for a respectable female audience. In this essay I will show how, by means of the collaborative opportunity offered them, writers such as Isabel Burton and Sophia Poole adjudicated the sometimes-competing claims of gendered authorship, personal relationship, feminine propriety, and national superiority.

Lane and Poole in Egypt

On his third trip to Egypt the well-known Egyptologist Edward William Lane was accompanied by his sister and her two young sons, who lived with him in Cairo for a number of years. As Sophia Poole explains in the course of *The Englishwoman in Egypt*, her purpose in traveling to Egypt was to accompany her beloved brother and to confirm what he had already documented in his widely read work *An Account of the Manners and Customs of The Modern Egyptians* (1836):

> My brother's account of the hareem, and all that he has written respecting the manners and customs of the women of this country, I have found to be not only minutely accurate but of the utmost value to me in preparing me for the life which I am now leading. His information on these subjects, being derived only from other men is, of course, imperfect; and he has anxiously desired that I should supply its deficiencies, both by my own personal observation and by learning as much as possible of the state and morals of the women, and the manner in which they are treated, from their own mouths.[3]

Poole's deferential evaluation of her brother's work as "minutely accurate" sets up a tension with her later description of it as "imperfect" and suffering from "deficiencies." As her ensuing observations on the harem show, she is caught between the often-opposing commitments to endorse her brother's work while at the same time speaking the truth about what she has gleaned from her visits to the women's quarters. As far as she is concerned, her role is supplementary, not critical. Where the supplement is contradictory rather than complementary, her writing becomes uneasy, signaling its discomfort as it attempts to mediate the conflict it has raised.

Poole thought she would have opportunities to gain insight into the mode of life of the upper-class ladies in this country. As she wrote, the opportunity of seeing things "highly interesting in themselves, and rendered more so by their being accessible only to a lady, had suggested to him the idea that I might both gratify my own curiosity and collect much information of a novel and interesting nature, which he proposed I should embody in a series of familiar letters to a friend" (preface, 1:v).

Since only women were allowed into the harem when its inhabitants were there, many male orientalists relied on the testimony of female travelers; indeed, Sophia Poole's account of the harem was later quoted in J. A. St. John's *Egypt and Nubia* (1845): "As it was not permitted me to view the harem peopled by its fair inmates, I shall borrow from a female traveller her description of a visit to an establishment similar to that of Ahmed Pasha, though on an inferior and smaller scale."[4]

Though male orientalists appear to depend in a straightforward and acknowledged way on the accounts of their female counterparts, the interdependencies of their accounts are more complicated than they at first appear. When St. John cites Sophia Poole, he rightly imagines that he draws on a firsthand account of a visit to a harem. Yet, as we shall see, Poole's text is intricately shaped and inflected by her brother's orientalist enterprises; both the form and content of *The Englishwoman in Egypt* attest to the involvement of Lane in his sister's text. The preface reveals that the book was orchestrated and controlled by Lane, who supplied his sister with "a large collection of his own unpublished notes, that I might extract from them, and insert in my letters whatever I might think fit." He also promised that he would "select those letters which he should esteem suitable for publication, and mark them to be copied" so that she would not feel restrained by "writing for the press." He thought that "a series of familiar letters to a friend" would be an appropriate feminine form (1:v).[5] At her brother's instigation, then, Sophia Poole produced a series of letters that mimicked a correspondence between friends. The fact that he supplied notes and chose the letters that would make up the personal—and therefore feminine—epistolary publication further underscores the fraternal authority behind this text and accounts for the "with Edward Lane" appended to the title of the publication. The author herself appears only in terms of her relation to him—as "His Sister."

While there is nothing sinister about Lane's manipulation of "feminine form" and sisterly compliance, the ironies of Lane's involvement do highlight the self-conscious ways in which Victorians constructed and gendered genres. More important, the Lane/Poole collaboration illustrates that behind the categorical distinctions between men's and women's areas of expertise and forms of writing, there was a circulation of knowledge that belied the so-called natural separation of literary and other spheres. The prevailing assumptions about the role of the woman travel writer articulated in Poole's preface certainly shape the text of *The Englishwoman in Egypt,* producing an array of tensions and contradictions as Poole attempts to augment her brother's "imperfect" knowledge of Eastern women and to confirm his representations as "minutely accurate." Although she applauds her brother's accounts of Egyptian women, her subsequent discussion of the harem implicitly contradicts his view and defends Egyptian women against charges of licentiousness and indecency. Lane had indeed reinforced long-established equations of Egyptian women and heightened sexuality, even if he absolved them of blame by attributing their "libidinous nature" to the climate and to a "want of proper instruction." Most culpable, in Lane's opinion, is the Egyptian husband's desire to increase his wives' sexual receptivity and encourage their lasciviousness. Although they are secluded, they hear the "immoral songs and tales" of coarse entertainers and see the "voluptuous dances of the ghawazee." The latter are "professed prostitutes" and are actually introduced into the harems of the wealthy to teach the wives their "voluptuous arts." Lane assures the reader that some of the stories of the "intrigues of women in 'The Thousand and One Nights' present faithful pictures of occurrences not infrequent in the modern metropolis of Egypt." As Edward Said has noted, "[E]verything about the Orie — or at least Lane's Orient-in-Egypt — exuded dangerous sex, threatened hygiene and domestic seemliness with an excessive 'freedom of intercourse,' as Lane put it more irrepressibly than usual."[6]

In direct opposition to her brother's published views, Sophia Poole notes that "the ideas entertained by many in Europe of the immorality of the hareem are, I believe, erroneous" (2:74). Poole's simultaneous disagreement with her brother yet endorsement of his views is not, however, an incidental matter attributable to sibling relations. It reflects a larger debate that underlies many Victorian accounts of the harem: the relation between the harem as domestic space and as sexualized space. Billie Melman has argued that Victorian versions of the harem substituted domestication for sexualization: "The Victorians banished the exotic to recreate the harem in the image of the middle-class 'home': domestic, feminine and autonomous."[7] I would qualify this by noting that it is continually in terms of Eastern marriage and sexuality that accounts of domesticity are constructed. I agree with Melman that the exotic, sexualized harem of eighteenth-century travel writing has certainly undergone a change. Nevertheless, deep-seated associations of the harem and sexuality persist, often communicated through an array of images and attributes that would signify prostitution to a Victorian readership.[8] What unsettles Victorian observers is that instead of ignoring sexuality

and marriage practices in the way that the asexual domesticity of the
English doctrine of separate spheres allows, they cannot move beyond
seeing the Eastern domestic space as structured by polygamy and hence
essentially informed and governed by sexuality.

Poole's letters let stand a series of contradictions resulting from the
clash of prevailing stereotypes of Eastern sexuality and her own observations. For example, she says that polygamous and "blindfold" marriages are heinous but owns that the women appear to be happy and
contented. The harem is a virtual prison, but "the middle classes are at
liberty to pay visits, and to go to the bath, when they please." They are
not allowed out to shop, but "female brokers are in the frequent habit of
attending the harems" (2:17–18). On the one hand, she shudders at the
lack of choice and curtailment of personal liberties that Eastern women
appear to suffer in a system of arranged marriage, finding it extraordinary that until they are given away in marriage girls "see only persons
of their own sex" and then "receive as their future lord and master one
with whom no previous acquaintance has been possible!" (1:214). The
system of "marrying blindfold" and without choice is "revolting to the
mind of an Englishwoman" (1:215). On the other hand, her observations
of the contentment, liberty, and powers that Eastern women appear to
enjoy can be set against conventional assumptions about the great evil
of polygamy in harem life. The letters support prevailing assumptions
about the seclusion of the harem but note exceptions that fly in the face
of notions about the uniformity of Eastern domestic life. She finds that
the harem is "a little world of women in which many have passed their
infancy and their childhood; the scene of their joys and sorrows, their
pleasures and their cares, beyond which, they can have no idea of a
wider theatre of action; and from which they anticipate no change but
to the hareem of their husbands" (2:74). Some women, however, are
surprisingly knowledgeable, interested, and informed about political affairs and are able to discuss such topical subjects as religious tolerance.
Though Mrs. Poole notes that "few of the ladies can read and write
even their own language," she also observes that "in one family, the
daughters have been extremely well instructed by their brother, whose
education was completed in Europe. In their library are to be found the
works of the first Italian poets and the best literature of Turkey; and
these they not only read, but understood" (2:31).

Lane and his sister adopted very different approaches to acquiring orientalist knowledge and performing gendered, national identity. This is made clear in their approaches to Eastern dress. During Lane's years in Cairo, he lived in such a way as to blend in as much as possible with Muslim Egyptians. His household there consisted of his wife (a former slave) and sister, both of whom always wore Egyptian attire. As Leila Ahmed has noted, they "never left the house except heavily swathed and veiled."[9] The Sheykh al-Dessouki, a frequent visitor at Lane's house, never saw their faces.[10] However, the title of Poole's text does not foreground national identity for nothing. This is the account of an Englishwoman, who is never anything but staunchly British, an identification she herself repeatedly acknowledges. Confessing that she finds an Egyptian poet's wife particularly beautiful, she admits that this woman resembles an Englishwoman and that her ideas of beauty are probably prejudiced. Amazed by the noise and nudity in the public baths, she notes that "the eyes and ears of an Englishwoman must be closed . . . before she can enjoy the satisfactions it affords" (2:175). The following remarks on her strategic use of English clothing underscore Mrs. Poole's clear understanding of how to use her national identity to best advantage: "In visiting those who are considered the noble of the land, I resume, under my Eastern riding costume, my English dress; thus avoiding the necessity of subjecting myself to any humiliation. In the Turkish in-door costume, the manner of my salutations must have been more submissive than I should have liked; while, as an Englishwoman, I am entertained by the most distinguished, not only as an equal, but generally as a superior" (1:210). Edward Said has written critically of Lane's attempts to live as an Easterner, suggesting that he affects an objectivity in his text, an invisibility, that his assumption of Eastern dress and habits helps him to achieve. Lane performs his identity as orientalist scholar by appearing to blend in with the objects of his study while all the while maintaining a sharp distinction between them and his English self. Unlike Lane, his sister is always overtly present in her letters; the feminine genre of her work calls for impressionistic, personal observation. She dons her English identity for the purposes of her "fieldwork" in the harems; if she is not regarded as an Englishwoman she cannot enter the field effectively. In her brother's case, by contrast, invisibility helps his project. They are both English observers in an Eastern world, the fact of their national identity defining them most powerfully despite their differences in performing gender and manipulating genre.

The Burtons' *Arabian Nights*

From what she would have us know, Lady Isabel Burton was born to
voyage East. For many years after she first met Richard Burton, she fan-
tasized about becoming his wife. When, after his return from the Cri-
mea, they met in the botanical gardens, was it not fate that she was car-
rying Disraeli's *Tancred,* an old friend of her heart and taste? Richard
was her romantic hero, who promised her a "wild, roving, vagabond
life" that she considered she was just the girl to follow, having "no fine
notions and being young and hardy to boot." Against her parents'
wishes she married him, a notorious profligate and virtually penniless
traveler. "I am sure I am not born for a jog-trot life," she confided in her
autobiography. "I am too restless and romantic."[11] Isabel Burton, who
always wished to be known as the wife of Sir Richard, is remembered
today chiefly as the censor of her husband's translation of *The Arabian
Nights* (the "Household Edition")—a "castrated thing," is how Burton
himself darkly referred to it—and as the person responsible for burning
Burton's diaries, letters, journals, and his last work-in-progress, a translation of *The Scented Garden.* She is less well known as the author of
The Inner Life of Syria, Palestine, and the Holy Land, based on her journals,
written during the time she resided in Damascus as wife of the consul.
Although Thomas Wright, Richard Burton's early biographer, refers
slightingly to her as illiterate, Lady Burton's book was quite successful.
By examining her self-representation in this work and her representation of the East, one can better understand Isabel Burton's complicated
and collusive involvement in her husband's orientalist texts.

Isabel Burton's account of life in Damascus offers an array of problematic assumptions about the East. Her book is filled with advice on
how to deal with what she perceives as the primitive aspects of the East
while simultaneously tapping its mystery and spirituality. Disparaging
the experiences of mere tourists, who wend their way on the beaten
track and never commune with the "solemn silent mystery, the romantic halo, of pure Oriental life," she implies that, having lived there, she
is qualified to speak of things oriental.[12] Her strategy is to set herself up
as indisputable authority on the East—a privileged initiate who knows
much but reveals little. The assumption of authority, however, must
be qualified with the usual disclaimer that she writes as a woman and
knows only the sphere appropriate to women. Like the preface to *The
Englishwoman in Egypt,* which disclaims authority, the introduction to *The*

Inner Life of Syria makes clear that its claims are humble and will not encroach on the preserves of male knowledge. Lady Burton promises little history, geography, or politics and no science, ethnography, botany, geology, zoology, mineralogy, or antiquities. She does, however, claim that her work contains things women will want to know. "I have followed my husband everywhere," she begins, "gleaning only women's lore." But, as she insists on telling us, the "women's lore" we hear is selected, trimmed, and carefully screened; on many occasions she stops short, hinting at what she could reveal but has decided not to disclose. Her reasons for censorship extend beyond the protection of her countrywomen by avoiding any offense to innocence and maidenly propriety. She makes it a principle to speak of good where she has seen it and to remain silent where she has not. In addition, there is the principle of noblesse oblige. One can't divulge confidences and expose individuals who have received you "with open arms and in the greatest intimacy" (1:4). Later in her discussion of harems, she opines that there is often no use in talking things over: "What is to be gained by lifting the curtain of the domestic theatre? I am writing for my own sex, and especially for my countrywomen, and yet I leave a thousand things unsaid which would be information, because it would please neither my Eastern friends nor my Western sisters to read a detail of habits so totally different from their own" (1:161). The powerful role of judge in such matters is clearly one that Lady Burton enjoys. Writing, it seems, should present a faithful picture of how you would like things to be and how you would prefer to imagine they had happened.

Isabel Burton visited many harems and was able to "note many things hidden from mankind." However, rather than describe what she sees and understands about harem life, she cannot resist the opportunity to write about how she functioned as an ambassador promulgating the virtues of English home life and marriage. She records the Syrian women's wonder at the fact that her husband has never taken another wife and then provides a disquisition on the merits of monogamy, at the end of which the women are converted: "Ah! how happy you are. You are all like men; you wear men's clothes (riding habit), you bare your faces, you ride by your husband's side, and share all his dangers and councils with him like a brother; and we are kept here like donkeys, and not allowed to see anything or know anything. You are secure of your husband's affections and are alone (only wife), whether you have children or not!" To which Isabel responds. "Some day, perhaps, you will all be like us" (1:154–55). Before she married Richard, Isabel drew up a list of wifely duties. She now reproduces that list for the benefit of Eastern womankind (and English readers), a ploy indicative of the opportunity Burton saw and seized as an author. Indeed, the following summary of her advice shows how it was possible for her to maintain an idealized or even a working version of her own marriage. The wife must: never listen to the bad tales of others about him or allow them to speak disrespectfully of him; never permit anyone to tell you anything of his doings; never make a rude remark or jest; never answer when he finds fault; never be inquisitive when he does not volunteer to tell you; never worry him with trifles; make sure that all his creature comforts are met, and so on. When confronted with such wisdom, she reports, the women of the harem responded: "Mashallah! . . . You speak like a book and how much you know" (1:158).

According to Edward Rice's biography of Sir Richard Burton, Isabel collected much unusual information about harem sexuality—the thousand things left unsaid?—some of which found their way into Burton's massive notebooks and were later worked into his copious annotation of *The Arabian Nights*. "Wealthy harems," Burton wrote, "are hotbeds of Sapphism and Tribadism."[13] The observations, Rice suggests, were based on his wife's researches into lesbian practices.[14] However, Rice does not cite any evidence to support this claim, and it seems unlikely that Burton relied on his wife for such information, given the other examples he adduces based on his wide travels: "Every woman past her first youth has a girl whom she calls my 'myrtyle' (in Damascus). At Aghome, capital of Dahome, I found that a troop of women was kept for the use of the 'Amazons.' Amongst the wild Arabs, who ignore socratic and sapphic perversions, the lover is always more jealous of his beloved's girl-friends than of men rivals. In England we content ourselves with saying that women corrupt women more than men do" (*Supplemental Nights*, 4:234, n.1). Even if not ultimately defensible, Rice's hypothesis draws legitimate attention to the curious web of complicity, intertextuality, and censorship that characterizes the Burtons' textual relations. Their work on *The Book of the Thousand Nights and a Night* (1885–86) illustrates this complexity most clearly. Her husband's champion and defender, Isabel Burton nevertheless had her own ideas about what kinds of knowledge could be communicated to the public and went to great lengths, in the name of decency and propriety, to fashion her public image and that of her husband.

One of the most famous books of the nineteenth century and among the best beloved of many Victorians was *The Arabian Nights*, also known as *The Thousand and One Nights*, or *The Arabian Nights' Entertainments*. In the eighteenth century, English readers knew the work only through anglicized versions and adaptations of Antoine Galland's French translation of 1704.[15] Galland was responsible for toning down the strongly sexual and erotic original, resulting in a classic collection of fairy stories.[16] During the nineteenth century a wave of new translations and versions were produced, due partly to the increasing linguistic skills of Arabists and the West's fascination with the Orient. In 1838 Henry Torrens produced a single volume, followed by Edward William Lane's translation of *The Thousand and One Nights* in monthly installments (1838–40), the second edition of which appeared in 1859, subsequently going into many editions. Stanley Lane-Poole, Lane's grand-nephew, supervised a revised version (1883), and around the same time (1882–84) John Payne's translation *The Book of the Thousand Nights and One Night* received much favorable press despite the fact that only five hundred copies were printed.

Richard Burton's "plain and literal translation of the Arabian Nights' entertainments" was printed solely for subscribers (1885–86), in ten volumes, and limited to one thousand copies. (It raised sixteen thousand guineas; after paying six thousand for expenses, the Burtons were left with a nice profit of ten thousand guineas.) In her account of the venture in *The Life of Captain Sir Richard Francis Burton*, Isabel shows an awareness of the frank, sexual nature of the work. She justifies it by quoting Richard as follows:

> [T]he very point which enables you to understand the action is left out [in most translations] because the translator was afraid of Mrs. Grundy. Arab ideas of morality are different from European, and if we are to understand the Arabs, and if the "Nights" are to be of any value from an anthropological point of view, it can only be written as I have written it. I think it is such a disgrace that our Rulers should rule so many million Easterns, and be as ignorant of them as if they lived in a faraway planet; and it is to give *them* a chance of knowing what they are about, that I leave this legacy to the Government.[17]

Isabel concludes, "[On] his explaining to me his new idea, about its usefulness, its being so good for the Government, I was glad, and I helped him in every way I possibly could" (2:284). Wifely duty dovetails nicely here with service to Empire, permitting Isabel implicitly to rationalize the presence of offensive sexual context. Although she does not directly address the question of sexuality in Richard's notes and translation, she is careful to point out that the edition was privately printed and was intended only for scholars.

According to Isabel, the "translating, writing and correcting devolved upon him; the copying fell to a lady amanuensis;[18] and the financial part devolved upon me" (2:283). Here is how Isabel explains why another edition of *The Arabian Nights* was necessary:

> It was also agreed, in order not to limit to a thousand people what the many should enjoy, that they should not lose this deep well of reading and knowledge, beside which the flood of modern fiction flows thin and shallow, that I should reproduce all my husband's original text, excluding only such words as were not possible to put on the drawing-room table. Mr Justin Huntly [*sic*] McCarthy, jun., helped me a little, so that out of the 3215 original pages, I was able to copyright three thousand pages of my husband's original text, and only exclude two hundred and fifteen. Richard forbade me to read them till he blotted out with ink the worst words and desired me to substitute, not English, but Arab Society words, which I did to his complete satisfaction. (2:284–85)

In her biography of Burton, Isabel reprints a number of reviews of the work from various sources, many of which extol Burton's erudition and frank translation. As the *Morning Advertiser* noted: "In Arabic a spade is usually called a spade, and in the latest English translation it is never designated an agricultural implement" (2:287). Isabel walks a fine line in recognizing the coarseness and impurity in her husband's translation while at the same time defending his motives for producing it with the appended notes, and insisting that she herself has never been exposed to it:

> I have never read, nor do I intend to read, at his own request, and to be true to my promise to him, my husband's "Arabian Nights." . . . I think a man who gives years of study to a great work, purely with the motive that the rulers of his country may thoroughly understand the peoples they are governing by millions, and who gives that knowledge freely and unselfishly, and who while so doing runs the gauntlet of abuse from the vulgar, silly Philistine . . . deserves great commendation. To throw mud at him because the mediaeval Arab lacks the varnish of *our* world of to-day, is as foolish as it would be not to look up because there are a few spots on the sun. (2:290)

"Lady Burton's edition of her Husband's Arabian Nights, translated literally from the Arabic, and prepared for household reading by Justin Huntly [*sic*] McCarthy, M.P." appeared in six volumes, whose covers of virginal white were adorned with the golden lilies of Saint Joseph and "the chaste crescent of the young moon" (*Supplemental Nights*, 6:452). The edition featured the following inscription: "To the women of England, I dedicate this edition of The Arabian Nights, believing that the majority can appreciate fine language, exquisite poetry, and romantic Eastern life, just as well as the thousand students and scholars who secured the original thousand copies."

A comparison of Burton's ten-volume edition with his wife's six-volume "Household Edition" reveals that although the excised 215 pages contain words or stories that are sexual, nevertheless Isabel's pruning and substitutions are by no means consistent. Sometimes she allows "concubine"; at other times she will substitute "slave" or "assistant wife." "Voluptuous grace" becomes "elegance and grace." "High-bosomed virgins" is changed to "high-bosomed maidens," yet "breasts like pomegranates twin" is omitted entirely. Burton explains and distinguishes among a wide range of sexual activities. Isabel deletes specific descriptions and substitutes the more innocuous "embraced" for cohabitation, but she often cuts altogether any mention of the latter. For example, where Burton writes "and he abode with her seven days and their nights" Isabel's text is silent.[19] Tales involving adultery, pederasty, bestiality, and nymphomania are, unsurprisingly, completely excised, so that at times Isabel's version completely omits a few nights; for example, her edition jumps from night 282 to 286. On the face of it Isabel lives up to her promise in the preface of the "Household Edition," namely, that "no mother shall regret her girls' reading this Arabian Nights." But she also inadvertently indicates which nights to remember! By their omission she provides a handy index of those nights that curious and intrepid young ladies might want to look at in the unexpurgated edition. When her "Household Edition" proved unsuccessful, Isabel protested that she was not really its author: "I do not know whether to be amused or provoked because people are prejudiced against 'Lady Burton's edition of the "Arabian Nights"' as a milk-and-water thing. I did not write or translate it; it is *Richard Burton's* 'Arabian Nights' with a coarse word or two cut out here and there . . . and my name was only put upon it to copyright and protect my husband's from piracy" (2:286).

In his appendix to the *Supplemental Nights*, published in six volumes in 1886–88, Burton himself offered an explanation that accorded with Isabel's. He begins by discussing the rumor that his work was about to be pirated:

England and Anglo-America, be it observed, are the only self-styled
civilised countries in the world where an author's brain-work is not held
to be his private property; his book is simply no book unless published
and entered, after a list of seven presentation copies at "Stationers'
Hall"—its only aegis. . . . In my case this act of robbery was proposed
by a German publisher domiciled in London, supported by a French-
man equally industrious, who practices in Paris, and of whose sharp doings in money matters not a few Englishmen have had ample reason
bitterly to complain. . . . Mr. Justin Huntley McCarthy . . . undertook
the task of converting the grand old barbarian into a family man to be
received by "the best circles." His proofs, after due expurgation, were
passed on to my wife, who I may say has never read the original, and
she struck out all that appeared to her over-free. (6:451–52)

Burton continues the saga of the "Household Edition"'s lack of
success—in two years only 457 copies out of the 1,000 printed were
sold—with further indictments of publishers: "But the flattering tale of
Hope again proved to be a snare and a delusion; I had once more dis-
pensed with the services of Mr. Middleman, the publisher, and he naturally refused to aid and abet the dangerous innovation. The hint went
abroad that the book belonged to the category which has borrowed a
name from the ingenious Mr. Bowdler, and vainly half a century of reviewers spoke bravely in its praise" (6: 452). With a measure of satisfaction Burton notes: "The public would have none of it; even innocent
girlhood tossed aside the chaste volumes in utter contempt and would
not condescend to aught but the thing, the whole thing, and nothing but
the thing, unexpurgated and uncastrated. . . . Next time I shall see my
way more clearly to suit the peculiar tastes and prepossessions of the
reading world at home" (6:452).

The Burtons' claim that Isabel never laid eyes on the sexual content of *The Arabian Nights* is belied by a manuscript copy of the original,
which, according to Fawn Brodie, clearly shows that she read every
single offending or obscene word and wrote exasperated comments in
the margin when her sensibilities were too greatly offended. "The truth
was that Isabel slashed her way through the Nights with all the diligence
of a member of the Society for the Suppression of Vice." She also pruned
the anthropological notes considerably, cutting out anything she considered off-color. Burton's "Stet" in response to many of his wife's dele-
tions creates an interesting silent dialogue, a power struggle between
husband and wife within the manuscript. A manuscript in the Quentin

Keynes collection reveals that Burton pieced together "all the material his wife had cut out and threatened to print it privately as 'The Black Book of the Arabian Nights.'"[20] What is striking is Burton's personification of his work—he calls the book "the grand old barbarian"—and his identification with its threatened wholeness and virility at the mercy of the castrating woman. Indeed, he refers to it and other bowdlerized texts as mutilations, castratos. There is, of course, a rich irony in his application of these insistently male metaphors to a text narrated by a woman, herself in fear of the knife and the ultimate mutilation of decapitation. Scheherazade found that one way of keeping her head while others lost theirs was to capitalize on narrative suspense and power. Burton's view of his translation as an extension of his maleness involves a suppression of the gender issues that produced the text in the first place. Just as he projects his own virile identity onto the text, so he rails against censorship and the forces in England that repress sexuality and knowledge—naturally personified as Mrs. Grundy.

Burton is clearly as much concerned with the question of pirating and copyright as he is with censorship and the hypocrisies of the English reading public. It is here that the Burtons' relationship seems to have been far more collusive and united than combative. For if the face of Mrs. Grundy seems at times to be indistinguishable from that of his wife, this is very likely only her public face. Mary Lovell's biography of the couple cites evidence from Isabel's unpublished letters confirming that the Burtons' public statements about Isabel's familiarity with her husband's texts were simply not true. After Burton's death, Isabel admitted that "Richard wished his men friends should think I did not know what he was engaged upon, and had he lived one would have carried that idea out."[21] Not only did Isabel wish to maintain an outward semblance of propriety (a wish that she here attributes to Richard), but she also feared surveillance by the Society for the Suppression of Vice, which was known to interest itself in Burton's activities. Isabel functions as watchdog and copyright protector, a more complicated position than simply that of the stuffy, proper opponent of her husband's libertarian orientalism.

Whether she is editing Burton's *Arabian Nights*, writing her "women's lore," justifying her burning of his work, or producing Burton's biography—which requires over a thousand pages to present him as the man she wished he would have been—Isabel Burton is a mistress of controlled representation, excision, and wishful thinking.[22] As the epigraph to *The Inner Life of Syria, Palestine, and the Holy Land* reveals, she loved the idea of being married to an explorer, a writer, a man of knowledge and learning:

> He travels and expatriates; as the bee
> From flower to flower, so he from land to land,
> The manners, customs, policy of all,
> Pay contributions to the store he gleans;
> He seeks intelligence from every clime,
> And spreads the honey of his deep research
> At his return,—a rich repast for *me*!

Knowing what we do of her tenacious commitment to propriety, the last lines of the apiarian epigraph appear wonderfully ironic. Whatever pleasure the "honey of his deep research" may have yielded her in private, it proved a taxingly rich repast for her when she had to prepare and approve it for public consumption.

Despite the manifold differences between the collaborative relationships, writings, travels, and personal situations of Sophia Poole and Isabel Burton, they share in common a canny resourcefulness in negotiating the conventions of gendered authorship, fulfilling the role of female observer in relation to Eastern others, and juggling the often competing claims of femininity and nationality—woman and Englishwoman. Their writings show how collaborative opportunities with their famous male orientalist counterparts demanded a layered and, at times, self-conscious performance of gender and national identities. That self-consciousness does not emerge in overt reflection or analysis. Rather, it is to be intuited in the practices that these women followed and the way they chose to narrate those practices. In the case of Mrs. Poole, it involves telling us that she dons her English dress under Eastern habit so that she may stand on her dignity among those she visited. In the case of Lady Burton it involves offering an account of the harem that focuses on her own enviable status as an English wife and in adroitly playing the different roles of proper public Victorian and private piracy watchdog. There is a tacit awareness by these women of the constraints, opportunities, and assumptions underlying gendered performance. Notwithstanding the tensions that are inherent in being both a female author who defers publicly to superior male authority and an imperial Englishwoman who judges and (in Burton's case) brings enlightenment to the "benighted" domestic practices of the Eastern other, these two examples suggest that Victorian women did indeed have a sense of the play or flexibility among the various aspects of gendered and national self they were called upon to perform.

Notes

1. Rigby, "Lady Travellers," 99.
2. Although the Burtons' versions of *The Arabian Nights* are not, strictly speaking, travel writing, Rigby's analysis of complementarity and gendered vision is also helpful in structuring discussion of their texts, which are thoroughly dependent on and informed by their experiences in the East.
3. Poole, *The Englishwoman in Egypt: Letters from Cairo, Written During a Residence There in 1842, 3, and 4*, 2:94. Subsequent references appear parenthetically in the text.
4. St. John, *Egypt and Nubia, Their Scenery and Their People: Being Incidents of History and Travel, From the Best and Most Recent Authorities*, 45.
5. On the conventions of women's travel writing in the nineteenth century, see Mills, *Discourses of Difference: An Analysis of Women's Travel Writing and Colonialism*, and Foster, *Across New Worlds: Nineteenth-Century Women Travellers and Their Writings*.
6. Lane, *An Account of the Manners and Customs of the Modern Egyptians*, 305, 304, resp.; Said, *Orientalism*, 167.
7. See Melman, *Women's Orients: English Women and the Middle East, 1718–1918*, 101. While Melman does note that "this is not to say that Victorian travel writers were impervious to the sexual aspect of the harem," I place greater emphasis on the extent to which travel accounts are thoroughly imbricated with the discourse of sexuality.
8. I discuss this further in Matus, "The 'Eastern-Woman Question': Martineau and Nightingale Visit the Harem."
9. See Ahmed, *Edward W. Lane: A Study of his Life and Works and of British Ideas of the Middle East in the Nineteenth Century*, 34. Mrs. Poole's sister-in-law was a former slave of Greek origin her brother had acquired from his friend Hay. Lane lived reclusively; only by calling on his sister or his wife was it possible to see him. On Lane's management of identity as a disguised Westerner, see Said, *Orientalism*, 162–63.
10. Back in England, Lane once again set up a household consisting of his wife, Nefeeseh, his sister, Sophia, and her two sons, Stanley and Reginald Stuart, both of whom distinguished themselves in orientalist studies. In the 1860s

Sophia Poole collaborated with her son Reginald to produce two travel books, for which Francis Frith supplied the photos and she and her son provided descriptions.

11. See Wilkins, *The Romance of Isabel Lady Burton: The Story of Her Life*, 81, 68–69, resp.

12. I. Burton, *The Inner Life of Syria, Palestine, and the Holy Land*, 1:2. Subsequent references appear parenthetically in the text.

13. Quoted in Rice, *Captain Sir Richard Francis Burton*, 405; R. Burton, *Supplemental Nights to The Book of the Thousand and One Nights, with Notes, Anthropological and Explanatory*, 4:234, n.1. Subsequent references appear parenthetically in the text.

14. Lesley Blanch, however, has suggested that he got his information from the "notorious and polyandrous" Lady Jane Digby (*The Wilder Shores of Love*, 180). As for Richard Burton's influence on Isabel's *Inner Life of Syria*, that, too, must not be overstated. Billie Melman has suggested that the work was heavily annotated by him (*Women's Orients*, 280). While it is true that on occasion Isabel cites him in her notes ("my husband informs me . . ."), this does not substantiate the claim of heavy annotation.

15. See the section on Burton in Assad's *Three Victorian Travellers*.

16. For a discussion of Galland's treatment of the work, see McLynn, *Burton: Snow Upon the Desert*.

17. I. Burton, *The Life of Captain Sir Richard Francis Burton*, 2:284. Subsequent references appear parenthetically in the text.

18. Mrs. Victoria Maylor typed both the manuscript of *The Arabian Nights* and *The Scented Garden*. Rice notes that "she was a Catholic, and as such did not seem to be included in the rubric that 'nice' women did not read such works as Burton had been translating" (*Captain Sir Richard Francis Burton*, 473).

19. R. Burton, *The Book of the Thousand Nights and a Night: A Plain and Literal Translation of the Arabian Nights' Entertainments*, 4:292.

20. Brodie, *The Devil Drives: A Life of Sir Richard Burton*, 310, 310–11, 311, resp.

21. Quoted in Lovell, *The Rage to Live: A Biography of Richard and Isabel Burton*, 701.

22. In making his wife his sole literary executor—there is a note to this effect in Isabel's handwriting, with Richard's signature beneath—he effectively gave her carte blanche to deal with his manuscripts, diaries, letters, and unpublished works. She created a furor in her own day by destroying his translations and diaries, which actions continue to be the subject of fervent debate among biographers (e.g., Rice, McLynn, Lovell). In her will she ordered her executors to supervise the publication of Burton's posthumous works, but forbade the printing of a "single immodest word" (Brodie, *The Devil Drives*, 331).

"An Uninterrupted Current"

Homoeroticism and Collaborative Authorship in Teleny

ROBERT GRAY & CHRISTOPHER KEEP

Described by Neil Bartlett as "London's first gay porn novel," *Teleny: Or The Reverse of the Medal: A Physiological Romance of To-Day* first appeared in 1893 in a private edition of two hundred copies. No author's name was given, but its publisher, Leonard Smithers, issued a prospectus in which he described the writer of the new work as "a man of great imagination . . . [whose cultured] style adds an additional piquancy and spice to the narration." Rumors soon circulated that the "man of great imagination" in question could only be Oscar Wilde, whose novel *The Picture of Dorian Gray* had appeared three years earlier amid much clamor concerning its "mephitic odours of moral and spiritual putrefaction."[1] Wilde was indeed well known among the burgeoning gay subculture of the early nineties. Sporting the green carnation that was the distinguishing mark among homosexuals in Paris, the popular playwright, critic, and novelist openly—even recklessly—flouted his homoerotic lifestyle. Among his acquaintances was Charles Hirsch, owner of the Librairie Parisienne, a bookshop that specialized in French literature but also carried on a thriving sideline in erotica. Wilde was a regular customer there and Hirsch had furnished him not only with works by Zola and Maupassant but also with others of a more "Socratic" nature—the popular euphemism for pornography.

Hirsch is the source for the story concerning *Teleny*'s authorship. He claimed that in late 1890 Wilde arrived at his shop with a carefully wrapped package. He arranged to leave it with the bookshop owner, saying that it would be picked up by another man bearing his card. The man Wilde named appeared shortly thereafter and retrieved the package, only to return in a few days' time with the same package and instructions that it would be picked up by yet another man. This procedure was repeated several times over the next few months until, on one occasion, Hirsch's curiosity got the better of him and, taking advantage of a loose ribbon, he opened the package and found a manuscript bearing the single word "Teleny" on the title page. The package that had made its way from man to man by way of his shop was the manuscript of a pornographic novel that had apparently been written in chain-letter fashion, each author contributing a chapter to the text before passing it on to the next. According to Hirsch, the manuscript (which is apparently lost or in some private collection) was an "extraordinary mixture of different handwriting, erasures, interlineations, corrections, and additions obviously made by various hands."[2] It was this manuscript that was published in the edition brought out three years later by Smithers. If Hirsch's account is to be believed, *Teleny*'s anonymity preserved not the unique and consequently vulnerable identity of a specific artist but instead served to acknowledge that the text was, in effect, the work of a community as opposed to an "author" in the proper sense.

Subsequent criticism of *Teleny* has largely revolved around the issue of Wilde's putative involvement in the text, with biographers, editors, and critics lining up on either side of the "he wrote it / he couldn't possibly have written it" divide. Rupert Croft-Cooke, for example, vigorously denounces the attribution, noting that "the style is totally foreign to Wilde's way of thinking or writing. Nothing in the whole novel has, or could have, the slightest suggestion of Wilde's talent in it." Winston Leyland, however, claims that "internal evidence certainly points to Wilde's involvement in the novel as either principal author or chief collaborator/instigator." He imagines a time when the issue will be decided by "advanced computers" that can compare "the syntax, vocabulary, and style" of *Teleny* to "all of Wilde's known prose fiction."[3] Modern editions regularly feature photographs of Wilde on their dust jackets and include introductions by critics supporting Wilde's authorship as a means of off-setting the fact that the text is only "attributed" to him.[4]

Such attempts to return the novel to the monological authority of a single, identifiable personage whose "genius" would somehow legitimize its otherwise marginal status as "literature," or to protect that self-same "genius" from the contaminating influences of the paraliterary, have much the same result. As opposed as they may seem, such approaches foreclose upon the more radical implications of the novel's authorship. Wayne Koestenbaum has argued that all forms of male coauthorship are in some way or other homoerotic. "When two men write together, they indulge in double talk; they rapidly patter to obscure their erotic burden, but the ambiguities of their discourse give the taboo subject some liberty to roam." While effectively drawing out the ways in which the "taboo" of same-sex desire necessarily informs male-male collaboration, Koestenbaum nonetheless leaves intact the priority of the couple, offering an image of collaboration in which the libidinal charge exists only sub rosa as a kind of displacement of the heterosexual dynamic.[5] However, the multiple authorship and overtly pornographic form of *Teleny* allows its authors to engage in something other than "double talk"; the kind of collaboration that occurs among several men need not be produced solely through the often guilt-ridden erotics of disavowal and sublimation. Pornography, in this sense, is a kind of discursive license to address same-sex desire, providing not simply a vocabulary but an imaginative space in which to undertake this collective endeavor.

In what follows our concern is with the irreducible anonymity and multiplicity of what Hirsch recollects as the "extraordinary mixture of different handwriting, erasures, interlineations, corrections, and additions obviously made by various hands." The text is unusually heterogeneous in its style and content, with witty—even Wildean—epigrams and phrases sharing company with the most melodramatic of dialogue, and overtly homosexual scenarios abruptly spliced with long episodes of heterosexual coupling—the latter often betraying a deeply misogynistic and violent streak wholly at odds with the tenderness and jubilation of the scenes concerning its principle characters. *Teleny*'s heteroglossia stands in marked contrast to the individuating tendencies of the "official" discourses concerning both homosexuality and authorship in the late-Victorian period. At the very time that medicine and the law were producing the "homosexual" as a specific object of scrutiny and regulation, the author was being constructed through the extension and formalization of copyright as the sole and unique origin of a text. Although copyright protection had been introduced in England as early as the

1710 Statute of Anne, authors continued to find their works pirated and their rights violated by mercenary publishers well into the 1880s, when the royalty system—under which an author receives a percentage of the published price of every book sold rather than selling the manuscript for an initial sum—became the norm. As Anne Ruggles Gere has pointed out, "The conflation of aesthetic and economic/legal arguments created a context in which copyright laws protecting authors became common-place and the 'man-and-his work' view of texts could emerge."[6] *Teleny* frustrates the "man-and-his-work" paradigm by offering an image of a queer writing practice characterized by fluidity, circulation, and exchange. This valorization of an "uninterrupted circuit" between men offers an alternative not only to models of the author as individual "ge-nius" but to theories of collaborative writing largely modeled on the sex-ual dynamics of the heterosexual couple. At the same time, however, *Teleny* acknowledges the limits of such an alternative. As its pattern of productive misidentifications gives way to the need to provide narrative closure, the text reveals the difficulty of imagining a textuality *and* sexu-ality outside the terms of the heterosexual norm, suggesting that such difficulty is the very condition of queer authorship.

Coined by the Swiss physician Karoly Benkert in 1869, the term "homosexual," like its counterpart "heterosexual," first entered the English language through translations of Richard von Krafft-Ebing's epochal *Psychopathia Sexualis* (1886) in the early 1890s. Indeed, the two terms are reciprocal, each requiring the other in order to secure its dif-ference from the other in the emergent medical discourse of sexology. The result was not simply the description of a particular sexual aberra-tion but the production of a fully developed personality type that might serve as the necessary counterpart to the normative male subject. As Michel Foucault has argued, in the nineteenth century "the homosexual became a personage, a past, a case history, and a childhood, in addition to being a type of life, a life form, and a morphology, with an indiscreet anatomy and possibly a mysterious physiology. . . . The sodomite had been a temporary aberration; the homosexual was now a species."[7] What had previously been simply an act—sodomy—that anyone might conceivably commit now enters into the very marrow of the individual, redefining the subject's sense of selfhood such that it emerges as little more than a metonym of the act. Same-sex desire is read retroactively into the whole history of the individual, lying at the root of his every deviation from the norm and thus condemning him to the abnormal, exiling him to the twilight world of the criminal, the pathological, the diseased, and the insane—and, in so doing, protecting the moral "purity" of the heterosexual as the right and proper subject of the polis.

With its copious "case studies" that recorded the upbringing, education, and sexual proclivities of a series of "representative" subjects, Krafft-Ebing's work helped secure the homosexual within the terms of bourgeois individualism, that discursive construct which presented the subject as a unified, self-intending, self-knowing site of ontological wholeness. The otherwise obscure meanings of the Labouchère Amendment to the Criminal Law Act of 1885, which criminalized "any acts of gross indecency" between two men, whether in private or public, were effectively glossed by this burgeoning discourse on the "antipathetic instinct." With more than one thousand works published on the topic between 1890 and 1908,[8] the formerly vague outlines of the "moral degenerate" were increasingly filled in. It is against the backdrop of this enormous effort to fix the enigma of the sexual invert, this manifest need to force the homosexual to speak the secrets of his "true" sexuality, that one should read the communal authorship of a queer text such as *Teleny*. In its various tracings of "the uninterrupted current" that forms its governing conceit, one hears not so much the articulation of a genuine or authentic "queer voice" as one senses the physical effort on the part of its "various hands" to resist any such violent acts of naming.[9]

Teleny tells the story of Camille Des Grieux and his passionate affair with the Hungarian pianist René Teleny. The "Physiological Romance" is set in London, where the two young men first meet at a charity ball.[10] Sitting in the audience during Teleny's performance, Des Grieux is startled by visions of "Alhambra in all the luxuriant loveliness of its Moorish masonry" and "the sun-lit sands of Egypt," where Adrian bewailed the loss of his servant boy Antinous.[11] He is, in effect, driven out of the West, out of rationality, and out of heterosexuality: "I longed to feel that mighty love which maddens one to crime, to feel the blasting lust of men who live beneath the scorching sun, to drink down deep from the cup of some satyrion philtre" (26). As Edward Said and others have shown, it is conventional within Western writing to imagine the East as an arena for sexual experimentation.[12] However, for queer writers the East is less a place on the map than it is a kind of virtual space in which they can imagine a sexuality beyond that prescribed within the normative confines of the domestic realist novel. It is only in the realm of orientalist fantasy that Des Grieux and Teleny can acquire a language in which they might recognize one another. When the two meet after the performance, Des Grieux discovers that they experienced the same vision; in that instant the two are enjoined in a circuit of mutual desire that effaces the distinction between their separate consciousnesses and exposes each to a fluid exchange of identities. Reflecting on the moment at which their eyes first met, the pianist tells his lover, "[T]here was a current between us, like a spark of electricity running along a wire, was it not?" To which Des Grieux replies, "Yes, an uninterrupted current" (36).

Drawn from the still mysterious and even exotic language of electrification, the "uninterrupted current" becomes a trope by means of which the novel signifies the productive passing of desire from one individual to another in the text, as well as the promiscuity of identifications and liaisons that characterize its narrative development. Des Grieux tells his firsthand account of his relationship with Teleny to an unnamed transcriber/interlocutor whose presence in the text restlessly pushes the act of exchange between men to the fore. "Tell me your story from its very beginning," the narrator instructs Des Grieux. In so doing the narrator constructs a scenario in which the very form of the novel, as a dialogue between men, also serves as a model for its communal or collective authorship (23). In his descriptions of sex with Teleny, Des Grieux uses the transcriber's own body to illustrate his story, re-situating both the narrator and the reader in a more intimate relation with the tale through the familiar pronoun "you": "He was sitting by my side, as close to me as I am now to you; his shoulder was leaning on my shoulder, exactly as yours is. First he passed his hand on mine, but so gently that I could hardly feel it; then slowly his fingers began to lock themselves within mine, just like this; for he seemed to delight in taking possession of me inch by inch" (125–26).

The passage is one of several in which the reader is made aware that the transcriber and Des Grieux are on intimate terms, that this story is but the verbal complement to a physical act of seduction, the one extending the other such that words and limbs become entwined. Near the beginning of the text, for example, Camille is discussing his own penis, "which, as you know," he says to the transcriber, "is a good-sized one" (39). He later says to the transcriber, "[A]s for my penis, or yours, its bulky head—but you blush at the compliment, so we will drop this subject" (65). The use of the second-person pronoun in the passage allows the point of reference to slip from the transcriber to the reader, effectively blurring the distinction between that which is properly "intratextual" and that which is "extratextual:" Des Grieux's story pushes the affective work of sexual desire beyond the bounds of the narrative itself. The community by and for which the text was written is thus inscribed in the text: the body of the male reader becomes another point of relay through which this uninterrupted current runs.

Exploding the boundaries of the "book" as a kind of self-contained artifact, *Teleny* depicts a world in which the circulation of stories is commensurate with that of bodies. This is the world of gossip, in which it is precisely those stories beyond the bounds of "propriety" that become the most important. Through the transcriber's interventions, we know that "like everyone else [he] had heard at this time of the tragic death of [Teleny], who had committed suicide without anyone knowing the real reason, and about which very scandalous gossip was circulating" (21). In the process of telling his tale, Des Grieux informs us that he and Teleny had become so close that there was, through gossip, a public recognition of their love, where "[their] friendship had almost become proverbial, and 'No René without Camille' had become a kind of by-word. . . . [He believes] the ladies now had begun to suspect that [their] excessive friendship was of too loving a nature; and as [he had] heard since, [they] had been nicknamed the angels of Sodom" (147). Such instances could be multiplied, but their significance lies in the fact that gossip is a paraliterary discourse, and that, like the orientalist fantasies that Des Grieux and Teleny share, it occupies a place outside the denotative function of official or rational discourse. As Patricia Meyer Spacks has noted, gossip's allure is intimately related to that of pornography: "[E]ven when it avoids the sexual, [it] bears about it a faint flavour of the erotic. (Of course, sexual activities and emotions supply the most familiar staple of gossip—as of the Western realistic novel.) The atmosphere of erotic titillation suggests gossip's implicit voyeurism."[13] Far from being vilified as a debased mode of knowing, gossip is privileged by *Teleny*. It is not only a "shared secret," a token that establishes one's membership within a community of knowing, but also the specific means by which a community of sexual dissidents can come into being. As Neil Bartlett has written, "[*Teleny*] seems to relate our story, in our language, because it seems that this text—hidden for so long and part of our dark, private world, speaking a pornographic language which seems hardly to have changed at all—this texts speaks of how close to history I am, of how we created our own lives and own desires even then."[14] Shifting between the first-person-singular pronoun and the plural, even as the novel's framing narrative shifts between the first person and the second, Bartlett emphasizes the indeterminacies of the queer subject and its emergence in a language that is "unauthorised." It is not only the uncanny familiarity of the language of homoerotic desire that makes the novel seem recognizably queer but also the very fact that such language is strictly speaking, not of history at all. It is, rather, only dangerously close to history and always living in the shadow of its possible exposure to history.

In *Teleny* gossip, scandal, and innuendo both register the social and legal vulnerability of the queer community of the fin de siècle, and are the linguistic means by which that community comes into being. Des Grieux receives a blackmail letter threatening to expose him as a sodomite if he does not give up Teleny as a lover. The letter is one of the few instances in which the text explicitly acknowledges the legal consequences of homosexuality following the passing of the Labouchère Amendment. Often referred to as the "Blackmailer's Charter,"[15] the amendment had the immediate result of putting any man (as Wilde would soon discover) at risk from any insinuation of having committed sodomy. Language, in the form of the threatening letter, thus acquired a new valency, as that which entailed the possibility not simply of public disgrace but of juridical punishment. The blackmailer's letter in *Teleny*, however, serves quite another purpose. Rather than disabling Des Grieux's emergent sense of himself as a member of the "Priapean creed" (131), it amounts to a veritable ticket of admission to the club of the "blackmailable"; homosexuality, in part, comes to be identified by the very fact of its vulnerability to exposure by the agency of the letter. Teleny discovers that the blackmailer is a mutual friend who is jealous of the ease by which Des Grieux has won the pianist's favors. When they confront the man, Bryancourt, the differences between them dissolve once they recognize their mutual associations and desires—he having written the letter only out of jealousy. "I bear you no grudge," says Bryancourt, "nor do you for that stupid threat of mine, I'm sure" (130). To make amends, he invites the couple to a soirée, where they will meet "a lot of pleasant fellows who'll be delighted to make your acquaintance, and many of whom have long been astonished that you are not one of us" (130). Des Grieux enters into the queer community through the threat of blackmail, which functions as a kind of initiation rite, one of the rewards of which is the spectacle of the grand orgy that marks the culmination of his queer becoming.

The "symposium" to which Bryancourt invites Des Grieux and Teleny recapitulates the orientalism of their initial encounter (130). "[O]n soft Persian and Syrian divans," Des Grieux tells the transcriber, "men, young and good-looking, almost all naked, were lounging there by twos and threes, grouped in attitudes of the most consummate lewdness such as . . . are only seen in the brothels of men in lecherous Spain, or in those of the wanton East" (132). In this notably orientalized space, individuals are recast much as the East is, as depthless surfaces enjoined in the collective task of mutual pleasure. Looking down on the scene for the first time, Des Grieux describes a wild profusion of entwined limbs, orifices, and organs that recalls nothing so much as the heteroglossia of the text itself: "All the couples were cleaving together, kissing each other, rubbing their naked bodies the one against the other, trying what new excess their lechery could devise" (140). "It was," Des Grieux concludes, "like an electric shock amongst us all. 'They enjoy, they enjoy!' was the cry, uttered from every lip" (140). Queer sexuality is thus identified not with the heterosexual couple but with the group, with a kind of excess that ceaselessly spills over the category of the self and spreads out to the many. As Ed Cohen has written, "In affirming the naturalness of Des Grieux's homoerotic experience, this new joyous possibility undermines the monovocalizing strategies the bourgeois heterosexual culture used to ensure the reproduction of its dominance and thus opens the possibility of representing a plurality of male sexualities."[16] Such revelry, in other words, is not simply an affirmation of the burgeoning queer subculture of the nineties. Its emphasis on multiplicity and exchange seeks to subvert the construction of the "homosexual" as singular and identifiable and to replace the certainties of individuation with the pleasures of anonymity and collectivity.

Teleny's emphasis on a mobile and polymorphous sexuality is a function of its fascination with the prospect of a desire based on sameness. For example, in talking with Camille after their introduction, Teleny describes his ideal relationship as that between the artist and a "sympathetic listener," which he defines as "a person with whom a current seems to establish itself; someone who feels, while listening, exactly as [he does] whilst [he is] playing, who sees perhaps the same visions as [he does]" (30). Echoes of the trope can be seen in the novel's fascinations with mirrors, shadows that merge, feelings of amalgamation or melting into one another, and in the recurrent fascination with doubles, as when Teleny speculates that Des Grieux may be his very own doppelgänger and hence one of them must die.[17] The other which is the same, that founding figure in the "uninterrupted current" that imagines Teleny and Des Grieux as both distinct and conjoined, distinguishes it from the forms of desire for the other that characterize the conventional oedipal romance. As Kaja Silverman has argued, "Identity and desire are so complexly imbricated that neither can be explained without recourse to the other."[18] Ontology, in other words, is always caught up in the ways in which the self figures the other to itself.

The relationship of identity and desire is further complicated when, as in this novel, the psychosexual architecture of selfhood is premised on an irreducible ambiguity between the subject's desire for the other and its desire to resemble the other. On the level of subject relations Camille has confusing identifications with those around him. Near the beginning of the text he has a dream in which, "for instance, it seemed to [him] that Teleny was not a man, but a woman; moreover, he was [his] own sister" (37)—this despite the fact that in reality he has no sister. He then proceeds to make love to Teleny, who remains in female form, and he thereby commits incest. On another occasion Teleny takes home the countess and makes love to her while Des Grieux remains on the street and experiences the scene as if he were in the room. He somehow partakes not only of the feelings of the countess as she is penetrated but also those of Teleny as he penetrates her. Later in the text, when the transcriber asks Des Grieux if his mother had "any inkling of [his] love for [his] friend," he once again makes a confusing identification when he replies, "[Y]ou know the husband is always the last to suspect his wife's infidelity," thereby identifying his mother as a husband and himself as the wife who is being inconstant with Teleny (147).

This misidentification of those around him also extends to how Des Grieux describes himself and, in particular, parts of his body as they are constituted within the fluid forms of libidinal identity. For example, during the sequence in which he imagines making love to his imaginary sister, Des Grieux awakens to find an empty bed, exclaiming, "But, where was my sister, or the girl I had enjoyed? Moreover, was this stiff rod I was holding in my hand, mine or Teleny's?" (39). This radical confusion of self, to the point where he cannot even recognize the phallus, that emblem of sexual identity par excellence, as either his own or his male partner's, is compounded by his later confusion of male and female body parts. When Des Grieux describes how he performs fellatio on

Teleny, he says, "I drew [his penis] like a teat" (111). Later he similarly describes the feeling of Teleny's penis penetrating him, claiming that he "felt it wriggling in its sheath like a baby in its mother's womb" (155). Des Grieux thus infantilizes Teleny's penis, after having previously done so to himself, and turns his own rectum into a womb. Sexual identity is thus figured as mobile and arbitrary, drawing upon the available modalities of language to figure that which remains always just on the other side of history.

However, the joyous promiscuity entailed by Camille's capacity for misrecognition ultimately fails before the grounding influence exerted by the oedipal narrative, in which closure is achieved once the characters assume and correctly play out their roles within the normative family unit. The climax of the novel occurs when Des Grieux discovers that his mother and Teleny have been having an affair. Even here, however, Des Grieux at first fails to recognize the significance of the scene. Looking through the keyhole while Teleny makes love to some as yet unidentified woman, he admires the woman's body and almost decides to open the door and join in: "Still the sight of those two naked bodies clasped in such a thrilling embrace . . . overcame for a moment my excruciating jealousy, and I got to be excited to such an ungovernable pitch that I could hardly forbear from rushing into that room" (167). He then comments: "Surely after such overpowering spasms, prolapsus and inflammation of the womb must ensue, but then what rapture she must give" (167). The inflamed womb and the rapture he imagines she gives construct Des Grieux as a subject who speaks what he does not know. He wants to "burst [the door] and have [his] share in the feast, though in a humbler way, and like a beggar go in by the back entrance" (168). In one sense, then, the mother's body is incorporated into the current that runs between the two men; it is, to paraphrase Ezra Pound, the point of resistance that makes the filament glow.

In not recognizing his mother as a "mother" in the oedipal sense, that is to say, in apprehending her as only another body, and thus radically underdetermined with the gender economy of the fin de siècle, Des Grieux is able to actively participate in this scene. He experiences what they experience because they are as yet not individualized. The two people beyond the keyhole are not subjects proper but simply surfaces across which desire runs. But when Des Grieux hears his mother's voice and recognizes it as that of his *mother*, he bursts through the door and confronts the couple as both jilted lover and betrayed son. The scene that, only moments earlier, bore witness to an undifferentiated free play of libidinal energy is suddenly overcoded in the terms of bourgeois domestic drama, complete with all the fixed points of identity that stake out the stability of the oedipal family. Des Grieux becomes a textbook example of the son whose incestuous desires for the mother awaken a murderous rage for the father (or, in this case, his stand-in, the mother's lover) and whose failure to sublimate such attachments (as Freud would argue only a few years later) results in the antipathetic vice of homosexuality. It is not the scheming machinations of Des Grieux's mother or the financial greed of Teleny (who has only agreed to this tryst for monetary reasons) that finally grounds the homoerotic ideal of an uninterrupted current but rather Des Grieux's interpretation of the scene before him. Only when he attributes to these bodies in motion a recognizable subjecthood—thereby placing them within the normative terms of history—is the erotic trajectory of the scene stopped short. Des Grieux's tragic mistake is not to have misread the signs he sees, as was the case for Oedipus, but rather to have read them all too correctly.

The novel's conclusion vacillates between a need to know "the truth" of Teleny's betrayal and the ways in which such "truth" always remains beyond the grasp of the text. Des Grieux flees from the scene between his mother and his lover and, quite literally beside himself with despair, ends up in a hospital.[19] Upon his release three days later, he learns from his business manager that his mother has fled the country. Still concerned for the fate of his erstwhile lover, he confesses that he "could not bear this state of things any longer. Truth, however painful, was preferable to this dreadful suspense" (172). It is the search for this truth that leads him back to Teleny's house, where he finds the door open just as he left it days before. There he discovers something that "freezes the very marrow in [his] bones"—the body of his lover with a knife in its chest (172). Teleny revives for a brief moment, yet his dying words offer Des Grieux the "truth" that he seeks while at the same time complicating its meaning. "I felt racked at not being able to understand a single word of what he wanted to say. After several fruitless attempts I managed to make out—'Forgive!'" (173). The truth Des Grieux uncovers is thus highly ambiguous, as much a plea to be forgiven as a granting of absolution. Though Teleny may wish to be forgiven for having betrayed his lover, Des Grieux must also be absolved for interrupting the current that ran between and beyond their dyadic coupling.

Books," Foucault has written, "were assigned real authors, other than mythical or important religious figures, only when the author became subject to punishment and to the extent to which his discourse was considered transgressive." That is to say, the ability of literature to transgress the ideological norms of a society is closely tied to the juridical means by which the author, in gaining ownership of his or her text, became an individual, a proper name that signs and secures the meanings of the texts that appear under that name. Copyright thus entailed not simply a legal responsibility but the very possibility of interrogating the function of naming as such. "It is as if the author, at the moment he was accepted into the social order of property which governs our culture, was compensating for his new status by . . . restoring the danger of writing which, on another side, had been conferred the benefits of property."[20] In refusing to "name" its author, *Teleny* couples its collaborative authorship with its refusal to name as such. It seeks not a perfect or ideal queer identity, some model of sexuality or authorship to which others might aspire, but rather to question and subvert the very "responsibilities"—whether artistic, legal, or medical—that such an ideal would entail.[21]

The irony of the novel's publication history is that it has enacted the very forms of power over the text that the text itself most insistently calls into question. Marketing the novel as "by" Oscar Wilde or "attributed to" Oscar Wilde is to affix its polyvalence, its many voices and multiple desires, to the name of single "author" and, in so doing, foreclose on its being read as an interrogation of individuation as such. The serial mode of composition, in which the manuscript passes, by way of an intermediary, from one hand to another, is one that acknowledges that any text is, in the words of Derrida, a "differential network, a fabric of traces referring endlessly to something other than itself, to other differential traces."[22] It is, in short, to understand textuality as another form of the sexuality that the novel pursues, the "uninterrupted current" that passes from and through the self, connecting the body of the text, no less than that of the author, to a network of intentions and desires that are not its own but always of the other. To read *Teleny*, as we have attempted, as a kind of gossip—replete with necessary misrecognitions, misalliances, and misreadings—is to see the novel precisely as such a "differential network" that points always to "something other than itself." In the end, even Teleny's death does not halt the ceaseless production and dissemination of the collective story that is queer sexuality. The clergyman who presides over the pianist's funeral foretells that "his remembrance shall perish from the earth, and he shall have no name in the street" (175). But it is precisely "in the street" that Teleny's story is remembered. As Des Grieux notes, "In the meanwhile, [our] story, in veiled words, had appeared in every newspaper. It was too dainty a bit of gossip not to spread about at once like wildfire" (174). The very illegitimacy of gossip, in effect, ensures the survival of that which cannot be recognized from the pulpit.

With its rumored origins and scandalous narrative, *Teleny*, like the story it tells, has survived not so much "in" literary history as on its margins, a visible rem(a)inder of the ways in which queer writers contested the discursive means of naming the "proper" and securing the place of the "author." That it ultimately dramatizes the failure of its "network of traces" does not diminish its attempt to figure homoerotic relations between men in terms other than those of bourgeois individualism. Rather, it should be seen as part of a collective awareness of the difficulty of escaping such terms—both the key to becoming "speaking subjects" with the same rights as any other and the means by which power would extend itself throughout the body politic. To refuse "identity" would simply be to abandon oneself to its dictates. Yet to adopt its rights and privileges, as Foucault says of the author, is also to accept the obligation to transgress them, to find a means by which the multiplicity of voices and desires might yet be represented within the promiscuity of words and bodies.

Notes

1. Bartlett, *Who Was That Man? A Present for Oscar Wilde*, 83; Leyland, introduction to *Teleny* [attrib. Oscar Wilde], 5; quoted in *Oscar Wilde: The Critical Heritage*, ed. Beckson, 72.

2. Quoted in Hyde, *Oscar Wilde: A Biography*, 238.

3. Croft-Cooke, *The Unrecorded Life of Oscar Wilde*, 27; Leyland, "Introduction," 11, 14, resp.

4. The debate over the provenance of *Teleny* was taken up with renewed intensity in the pages of *Forum Homosexualität und Literatur*. See Setz, "Zur Textgestalt des *Teleny*"; Bleibtreu-Ehrenberg, "*Teleny:* Zu einem apokryphen Roman Oscar Wildes."

5. Koestenbaum, *Double Talk: The Erotics of Male Literary Collaboration*, 3; The assumed priority of the heterosexual dyad in Koestenbaum's discussion of male

collaborative writing is implicit not only in his focus on couples but in his belief that the text they produce is the product of such a union, much like a child. He claims that "men who collaborate engage in a metaphorical sexual intercourse, and that the text they balance between them is alternately the child of their sexual union and a shared woman."

6. Gere, "Common Properties of Pleasure: Texts in Nineteenth-Century Women's Clubs," 383. On the introduction of the royalty system and its effect on the relationship between authors and publishers, see Keating, *The Haunted Study: A Social History of the Novel, 1875–1914*, 9–87.

7. Foucault, *The History of Sexuality: Volume One: An Introduction*, 43.

8. On this point see Pearsall, *The Worm in the Bud: The World of Victorian Sexuality*, 448.

9. On the criminalization of homosexuality, see Weeks, *Coming Out: Homosexual Politics in Britain, from the Nineteenth Century to the Present;* Hyde, *The Love that Dared Not Speak its Name;* Cohen, *Talk on the Wilde Side: Toward a Genealogy of a Discourse on Male Sexualities;* and Craft, *Another Kind of Love: Male Homosexual Desire in English Discourse, 1850–1920.*

10. For the edition he published in 1893, Leonard Smithers changed the locale to Paris. Charles Hirsch issued a French edition in 1934 and, based on his knowledge of the original manuscript, changed the setting back to London. The Gay Sunshine Press edition from which we cite retains this latter change.

11. *Teleny,* attributed to Oscar Wilde, 26. Subsequent references appear parenthetically in the text.

12. On orientalism and sexuality, see Said, *Orientalism;* Garber, "Chic of Araby," in *Vested Interests: Cross-Dressing and Cultural Anxiety;* and R. Lewis, *Gendering Orientalism: Race, Femininity and Representation.*

13. Spacks, *Gossip,* 11.

14. Bartlett, *Who Was That Man?*, 83.

15. Showalter, *Sexual Anarchy: Gender and Culture at the Fin de Siècle,* 112.

16. Cohen, "Writing Gone Wilde: Homoerotic Desire in the Closet of Representation," 805.

17. See *Teleny,* 40, 160, 66, 170, 102; 125.

18. Silverman, *Male Subjectivity at the Margins,* 6.

19. In a remarkable scene that extends the doppelgänger motif, while fleeing from Teleny and his mother, Des Grieux runs into someone on the street and encounters "[his] own image. A man exactly like [himself] — [his] Doppelgänger, in fact" (169–70). It is this man, this reflection, who saves Des Grieux when he jumps in the river and then transports him to a hospital. This passage was excised from the 1934 French edition.

20. Foucault, "What Is an Author?," 124, 125.

21. At a time when the concept of the author and the regulation of copyright were being consolidated, *Teleny* frustrated those regulations, for "no copyright

can exist in a work produced as a true collective enterprise rather than by one or more identifiable or anonymous 'authors.'" See Jaszi, "On the Author Effect: Contemporary Copyright and Collective Creativity," 11.

22. Derrida, "Living On: Border Lines," 84.

IV

Literary Modernity

Mythmakers and Muses

Courting the Muse
Dorothy Wellesley and W. B. Yeats

LISA HARPER

The First Gift: Despair and Discovery

> It has sometimes seemed of late years, though not in the poems that I
> have selected for this book, as if the poet could at any moment write a
> poem by recording the fortuitous scene or thought, perhaps it might be
> enough to put into some fashionable rhythm—"I am sitting in a chair,
> there are three dead flies on a corner of the ceiling."
>
> W. B. Yeats, The Oxford Book of Modern Verse

William Butler Yeats discovered Dorothy Wellesley's poetry in 1935
while compiling *The Oxford Book of Modern Verse, 1892–1935*. His "eyes
filled with tears" because a living poet had finally succeeded in restoring
his faith in modern poetry and in his own ability to recognize good verse.[1]
Before finding Wellesley's work, the poetry that Yeats read seemed to
him "clay-cold, clay-heavy" (introd., *Selections*, vii), and in "his worst moments" he believed he could "no longer understand the poetry of other
men" (viii). Yeats read Wellesley's poems "in excitement that was the
more delightful because it showed I had not lost my understanding of

poetry" (vii). Moreover, after reading her poem "Matrix," which Yeats called "perhaps the most moving philosophic poem of our time," he had "a moment's jealousy," believing he was "too old" to spend his last years writing philosophic verse as he had hoped he might (xii).

Wellesley's poems came to Yeats as a kind of serendipitous gift that, like all gifts, was received with pleasure and gratitude combined with anxiety regarding his ability to reciprocate. Paradoxically, her poems restored his confidence in his critical acumen yet provoked doubt about his poetic ability. Not surprisingly, their first meeting in June 1935 was a watershed. Wellesley wrote to Yeats that her creative powers were rejuvenated by her contact with him: "I have been writing ever since you were here."[2] Likewise, Yeats noted that "a ferment has come upon my imagination. If I write more poetry it will be unlike anything I have done" (*Letters*, 6). Their effect on one another was profound.

This first contact initiated a friendship that would be characterized by a complicated system of literary and erotic exchanges. The relationship culminated in 1937 with the publication of their ballads, Yeats's "The Ballad of the Three Bushes" and Wellesley's "The Lady, The Squire, and The Serving-Maid," in the March and September editions of the Cuala Press's *Broadsides*, which they coedited. In both ballads a Lady sends her servant to the unsuspecting Lover to act as her sexual surrogate. The ballad's narrative framework offers a model of poetic inspiration that is complicated by gender identity and erotic desire, mirroring the personal and artistic commerce between Yeats and Wellesley. Like the erotic triangle represented in the ballads, the Yeats-Wellesley friendship was mutually beneficial, yet it also gave rise to significant anxieties for both poets.[3] For Yeats in particular, the relationship raised problematic issues of sexual and artistic identity. Indeed, while Yeats had often been attracted to "collective" forms of authorship (his collaboration with Lady Gregory being only the most famous), his literary liaison with Wellesley may have been intensified by a sense of his own belatedness among literary modernists. Much more was at stake than a simple attraction to the ballad form, a collaborative genre that had intrigued Yeats throughout his life.

Recuperating Wellesley's influence on Yeats raises interesting questions concerning collaboration, appropriation, and authorship that extend beyond the ballads to Yeats's editorship of the *Oxford Book of Modern Verse* and to some of his last great works. Reading their relationship through the framework of gift theory, as articulated by Marcel Mauss, reveals a highly productive yet difficult "scribbling sibling rivalry"[4] characterized by an ongoing competitive reciprocity. Indeed, if the Yeats/Wellesley relationship repeats the dynamic of male appropriation of female wisdom present throughout much of Yeats's work, it also underscores the price paid by the male artist for gaining access to such wisdom through the woman. Characterized by a competitive reciprocity, the Yeats/Wellesley friendship offers a model of collaborative authorship that simultaneously reveals and conceals the multifaceted nature of inspiration and even authorship.

No Free Poems: The Story of the Ballads

Wellesley's ballad "The Lady, The Squire, and The Serving-Maid" tells the story of a Lady who refuses to have sex with her Squire, instead sending her Serving-Maid to take her place:

> O maid go mimic me to-night,
> With him I will not lie.
> 'Tis easy done without the light,
> So, child, make love for me.[5]

The exchange of women's bodies in the ballad establishes an economy consistent with the structure of gift giving, as theorized by Mauss, who postulates that there is no such thing as a free gift. Every gift carries the obligation that the recipient both accept and reciprocate the gift. Thus, the cycle of gifts establishes a "stable system of statuses or an escalating contest for honor." The energy for the gift cycle derives from "individuals who are due to lose."[6] Consequently, if the Squire ceases to love the Lady or lie with the Serving-Maid, he will either lose the Lady or fail to satisfy the Serving-Maid, who is described as "wild in love unwed." If the Lady withholds her love or her Serving-Maid, she will lose the Squire. If the Serving-Maid refuses to lie with and to the Squire, she will be out of a job. Each participant is inextricably connected to the others; the failure of one to properly give and receive with respect to the other two breaks the cycle of exchange.

However, the obligations to give, receive, and reciprocate are more than social laws. Rather, they are inextricably bound up with the nature or spirit of the gift. Specifically, the gift is imbued with the giver's identity; by receiving the gift, the recipient accepts part of the giver's spiritual

essence, or soul, and becomes possessed by it. The recipient must move
the gift along since through it the giver exerts power over the recipient.[7]
In this way the "things exchanged are never completely detached from
those exchanging" and "the alliances established by these continual
transfers are comparatively indissoluble." Mauss concludes that "to retain [the gift] would be dangerous and mortal. . . . [T]hat thing coming
from the person, not only morally, but physically and spiritually, that essence, that food, those goods, whether moveable or immoveable . . . all
exert magical influence over you."[8] Thus, gifts are about power. By giving one attempts to control or gain rank over the recipient. By recipro-
cating one attempts to wrest back control or exert increased influence
over the giver.

Yeats's poem "The Three Bushes" and its accompanying song
sequence retain Wellesley's model of chaste Lady, Chambermaid as
sexual surrogate, and duped Lover. The psychological motivations and
emotional relationships between the three, however, are more fully
elaborated. Unlike Wellesley's ballad, Yeats's poems articulate the dangers and anxieties inherent in gift giving. In his ballad the Lady tells her
Lover she will creep into his bed at midnight because without the
"proper food" of sexual intercourse his love will die.[9] The Lady fears the
loss of his love because without it he cannot "sing those songs of love"
(*Poems*, 296). For Yeats poetic production is at stake.[10] Yeats transforms
Wellesley's Lover into a poet, with the Lady becoming this poet's muse
and inspiration. She admits that she "must drop down dead / If he stop
loving me / Yet what could I but drop down dead / If I lost my chastity?" (*Poems*, 297). Note the use of the imperative: "must drop down
dead." Mirroring Mauss's model of exchange, the Lady-muse and
Lover-poet are bound to each other in obligatory reciprocity. To produce poems the Lover must love his muse and she must return his love.
He gives her his love and his songs; she reciprocates with love and inspiration. Should he fail to "sing those songs of love," she will be "blamed"
(296). Should he fail to love her, she will die. The centrality of blame,
death, and loss of identity reflect Mauss's assertion that the system of exchange is, in fact, a contest involving honor.

However, the cycle of exchange is imperfect because the Lady is
a reluctant muse. She will not give the Lover his "proper food." The
Chambermaid must mediate between the two, thereby completing the
creative triangle. By offering the Lover sexual fulfillment, she enables
the perpetuation of his poetry. Much more than antinomies of mind

and body, the Lady and the Chambermaid are two inseparable and interdependent aspects of the muse that together enable the production of poetry.

Yet this triangular reconfiguration of the muse comes at a high cost for the poet/Lover, who is metonymically reduced to a worm in "The Chambermaid's First Song" and "The Chambermaid's Second Song." When he receives his "proper food" from the Chambermaid, he becomes "weak as a worm," "dull as a worm," "limp as a worm," and "blind as a worm" (301). In his effort to sustain his afflatus, the Lover is physically debilitated, intellectually dulled, sexually impotent, and personally deceived. The cycle of female desire, initiated by the Lady and consummated by the lusty Chambermaid, leads him to accept the gift of female sexuality and turns the virile poet into a worm. This dire consequence suggests the danger of this double-muse. When the poet accepts the women's gifts, he must be possessed by them. In order to create he must be consumed by female desire.[11]

Given this tripartite model of poetic production, the three bushes that deck the graves of Lady, Lover, and Chambermaid must appear as one:

> none living can
> When they have plucked a rose there
> Know where its roots begin.
>
> (*Poems*, 298)

Like the poem, whose origin cannot be located in any single source, the apparent unity of the rose—often a symbol for Yeats of Unity of Being and wholeness[12]—is achieved through a perpetually revolving system of exchange. While Wellesley's poem closes with the image of a single bush uniting three graves, Yeats's three bushes, by virtue of the exchange, are transformed into a single rosebush. Thus, the rose plucked from the one bush that is three is simultaneously a symbol of the gift circulating among the three and the poem created through the efforts of the three. Its precise meaning shifts perpetually, like the cycle of the gift. An elusive signifier, its meaning depends on "where its roots begin." Unity of Being, wholeness, artistic integrity, and self-reliance are, like the one bush that is three, a supreme fiction.

Like the Chambermaid or the puzzling rose, Wellesley occupies a stunningly problematic yet privileged position in Yeats's life. Tim

Armstrong, T. R. Henn, Kathleen Raine, and Edward Partridge all agree that the source for "The Three Bushes" was a ballad that Dorothy Wellesley was working on when Yeats went to stay with her in June 1936. According to Partridge, "While at Penns, [Yeats] must have decided to write his own version of the story, perhaps in a kind of contest with his younger friend." Raine describes Yeats's actions as an appropriation of Wellesley's work, while Armstrong asserts it was an "(amicable) usurpation preceding a gestation." Jon Stallworthy has argued against these claims, claiming that Yeats regarded the story as "at least common property." Catherine Cavanagh tends to agree with him. Elizabeth Butler Cullingford takes a middle ground and calls the episode a "verse-writing competition."[13]

Based on the correspondence between Yeats and Wellesley, it is clear that they were working on their poems simultaneously. Yeats's first reference to his ballad occurs shortly after his June 1936 visit to Penns. He writes, "I add the chorus of my poem about the lady, the poet & the maid" (*Letters*, 64), suggesting that they have discussed the story. By July 2 Yeats has finished his version and writes, "Triumphant; believe I have written a masterpiece. . . . I am longing to read your ballad. I will not send you mine until yours is finished" (69). That same day her poem arrives, and in his postscript Yeats writes: "Here you have a masterpiece. . . . (I have just put in the rhymes, made it a ballad.). . . . This is far better than my laboured livelier verses. This is complete, lovely, lucky, born out of itself, or born out of nothing. My blessing upon you and it" (70–71). Oddly, Yeats did not send his poem to Wellesley but simply revised hers and returned it with his letter. Over the next two weeks Yeats sent Wellesley at least three more versions of her "masterpiece." Finally he sent his own version, writing, "I now like my long Ballad of the Three Bushes again" (73).

Clearly, Yeats initially thought Wellesley's the better poem. It also seems that through his revisions of her poem he reacquired his poetic prowess and gained confidence in his work. Indeed, in the letter accompanying his poem he writes, "I have recovered from the shock of your archaic modernity, which for a moment made me lose faith in myself" (73).

Yeats vacillated wildly in his opinion of Wellesley's ballad. Two weeks after calling her initial version a "masterpiece," he writes, "Yet what you send me is bad" (79). Two months later he reconsiders: "Now I have read your poem patiently and get its whole meaning which I like even better." After enumerating his revisions, he adds, "Do, my dear, let me have it in this form for the Broadsides" (95). Even after this, he sent her two more versions of her poem (in addition to the first three), and when it was published the following September, fifteen months after he received the original ballad, the wrong version appeared. In the final printing, on an errata slip in the October 1937 *Broadside*, Yeats included one final revision of her wording.

Wellesley initially welcomed Yeats's advice but soon systematically refuted his "slanging" and demanded her original poem back, angrily asserting that "there is something false in any case about archaic modernity" (*Letters*, 81). Yeats, on the other hand, reveled in the revisions, offering the strange apology, "Ah my dear how it added to my excitement when I re-made that poem of yours to know it was your poem. I re-made you and myself into a single being. We triumphed over each other and I thought of *The Turtle and the Phoenix*" (82).

The rocky genesis of the two ballads reflects a dynamic remarkably similar to that portrayed within the poems. Yeats received inspiration from Wellesley that was both exciting and troubling. Wellesley received the attention of a major poet and publication of her work, but she was severely criticized by Yeats. Both reaped great benefits from the exchange, yet both suffered great anxiety. Thus, while it is easy to see Wellesley occupying the position of the Lady, the inspiring muse, it is also plausible to see Wellesley as the sexually desirable Chambermaid.

Yeats's association of his sexual desire for Wellesley with his ballad is evinced not just by the "Turtle and Phoenix" letter but in the omnipresence of the ballad's refrain "O my dear" in his letters to her. On June 23, after the meeting where the story of the ballad was probably discussed, he writes: "My dear: I did not write you a letter of thanks, only a short note, there are things beyond thanks & instinct keeps one silent (64). Similarly, in July he writes: "If I cannot come [to you in October] then I will do [my broadcast] from Belfast. But Oh my dear, my dear" (83). In August he writes: "O my dear, let me stay longer than a week" (90), and in October he signs a letter "Your friend, who feels so much more than friend, W. B. Yeats. Over my dressing table is a mirror in a slanting light where every morning I discover how old I am. 'O my dear, O my dear'" (100).

Clearly Yeats recognized the disparity between their ages (he was seventy and she forty-six when they met) and the absurdity of his desire. As Armstrong has noted, the repeated phrase reflects "affection to the woman addressed and a half-mocking admission of weakness, of an

openness to sexual desire." Yeats's attraction is even more explicit in a
letter written to Wellesley while he is working on his poem.[14] Yeats
quotes lines from W. J. Turner's "The Word Made Flesh," which he
says "rend my heart":

> But when a man is old, married & in despair
> Has slept with the bodies of many women;
> Then if he meets a woman whose loveliness
> Is young & yet troubled with power
>
> Terrible is the agony of an old man
> The agony of incommunicable power
> Holding its potency that is like a rocket
> that is full of stars.
>
> (*Letters*, 65)

By analogy, Yeats is the Lover who longs for Wellesley the Chambermaid. And since Yeats yokes their poems with his erotic desire, his
revisions of her work take on an erotic dimension. While Armstrong has
argued that Yeats viewed sexuality as a metaphor for creative activity,[15]
the commerce between Yeats and Wellesley suggests that artistic creativity might also stand in for sexual activity.

Yet the erotic commerce was complicated for Yeats by the fact that
Wellesley was a lesbian and did not reciprocate his desire. Yeats addresses Wellesley's lesbian sexuality and its connection with her work in
three letters. On October 29, 1936, he writes, "O my dear I thank you
for that spectacle of personified sunlight. I can never while I live forget
your movement across the room just before I left, the movement made
to draw attention to the boy in yourself" (*Letters*, 99). A month later he
recalls the same incident, but this time he acknowledges the gender confusion that his attraction creates for him: "My dear, my dear—when
you crossed the room with that boyish movement, it was no man who
looked at you, it was the woman in me. It seems that I can make a
woman express herself as never before. I have looked out of her eyes. I
have shared her desire" (108). Finally, in December Yeats conflates his
problematic sexual desire for Wellesley with her verse: "What makes
your work so good is the masculine element allied to much feminine
charm—your lines have the magnificent swing of your boyish body. I
wish I could be a girl of nineteen for certain hours that I might feel it
even more acutely. But O my dear do force yourself to write, it should
become as natural to you as the movement of your limbs" (113).

Yeats recognizes the challenge that Wellesley's lesbianism creates for him. Confronted by Wellesley, the wild old wicked man longs to be neither old nor a man. In his letters both poets are endowed with a fluid gender identity that conflates sexuality and textuality. Wellesley's loveliness is indeed "troubled with power" since for Yeats she is a both a strong poet and sexually inaccessible.[16] Whether the "it" that Yeats wishes to experience "more acutely" is her verse or her boyish body, both are clearly implied.

If Wellesley's verse is "magnificent" and "natural," like her body, then revising her work permitted Yeats to establish an erotic intimacy with her. Through his revisions he could sustain an erotic dynamic despite the literal impossibility of such a relationship. Yeats's revisions of Wellesley's masterful ballad permitted him to sexually and poetically incarnate himself in her magnificent body of work, thereby recuperating his damaged poetic and sexual ego.[17] Wellesley, as Lady and Chambermaid, provides inspiration that is both exciting and troubling. As Lady she inspires a masterpiece yet causes him to doubt his own greatness. As Chambermaid she elicits a problematic and emasculating sexual desire. Though the sexual dynamic would never again be so clear an issue, their exchange would continue to be fruitful, particularly for Yeats.

In League against Modernism

Indeed, I introduced [Wellesley and Yeats] to each other and little foresaw it would have such bad results.

Lady Ottoline Morrell, letter to D'Arcy Cresswell
dated August 18, 1937

If the story behind "The Three Bushes" is the most stunning example of artistic exchange between Wellesley and Yeats, it is only the most obvious one. While Yeats championed Wellesley's work, her poetry continued to influence his own, and their friendship helped to sustain his aesthetic vision, which he understood as increasingly embattled in his later years.

Yeats's admiration for Wellesley's verse extended well beyond his appreciation of her ballad. It was he, after all, who sought her out, and over the course of their friendship he continued to praise her poems, particularly "Fire," "Matrix," and "Horses." He was so taken by her work that early in 1936 he personally selected and edited a volume of the poems he thought best represented "her talent" (introd., *Selections*, vii). Though the volume was not well received, Wellesley welcomed Yeats's attention, buoyed up by Virginia Woolf's remark that "praise from Yeats is the only solid thing of its kind now existing" (*Letters*, 71).

In his introduction to *Selections from the Poems of Dorothy Wellesley*, Yeats lavishly praises Wellesley's verse for being "as profound in thought as it is swift in movement" (vii); powerful for its "passage after passage [of] a like grandeur, a powerful onrushing masculine rhythm . . . work of accomplished skill" (ix); "precise" (x); and uniting "a modern subject and vocabulary with traditional richness" (x). Yet his praise is not unqualified. The book is "little," the poems are "often beautiful, often obscure, sometimes ill-constructed" (xii). Moreover, in his closing echo of Coleridge— "Where learnt you that heroic measure?" (xv)—Yeats seems mystified by her poetic ability, as if it is unbelievable that a woman and an aristocrat could possess a poetic imagination.

Yeats connects Wellesley's talent to her gender. He writes that "Matrix" "was moving precisely because its wisdom, like that of the Sphinx, was animal below the waist. In its vivid, powerful abrupt lines, passion burst into thought without renouncing its uterine darkness" (xii). The "uterine," or female element, which gives Wellesley's work passion and intensity, troubles Yeats because it is unattainable for him as a male poet. Yet the female element is unconscious and "bursts into thought," unlike "masculine rhythm," which is the work of "skill." Thus, if Yeats is threatened by Wellesley's talent, his anxiety is tempered because the inconsistent and uncontrollable feminine nature of her talent opens the door to his revisions of her work.[18]

If Wellesley was often discouraged by Yeats's attention—at one point she wrote, "Since I have known you I have become impotent of language" (*Letters*, 125)—his praise carried her through many periods of dejection and self-doubt, as in the following letter: "Anyway I felt [Virginia Woolf and Edith Sitwell] were far better at it than I, and went dejected to bed to sleep it off; hugging the thought that you had recognized my poetry before you knew me" (84).

Likewise, Wellesley's influence on Yeats was not limited to the anxiety she provoked, often providing significant inspiration for Yeats's own work. Indeed, their friendships inspired the homage "To Dorothy Wellesley," which Harold Bloom has called "an enduring monument to the relationship" between Yeats and Wellesley," and "a poem of marmoreal beauty." Bloom astutely notes that "implied throughout the poem is her mastery of her art." He posits the belief that Wellesley never achieved such mastery,[19] but this is not what Yeats thought. For Yeats Wellesley is indeed one of the "Proud Furies," "with her torch on high" (*Poems*, 304), and (in Bloom's words) not a "natural but daimonic"[20] creature, a poet capable of formulating the wisdom he admired in "Matrix" and providing the tantalizing story of "The Three Bushes." A formidable figure, she is also fantastically eroticized as he imagines her "Rammed full / of that most sensuous silence of the night" (304). Waiting alone in silence, "No books upon the knee and no one there / But a great dane that cannot bay the moon" (304). Wellesley is marvelously self-sufficient, powerful, even mythic.

Yeats also confessed to Wellesley that he was trying to imitate the style of her "Fire" when he drafted a play—it may well have been *The Herne's Egg*—early in December 1935 (*Letters*, 45). Claiming that he was "tired of my little personal poetry," he confided to her that her "'Matrix' has given me a glimpse of what I want" (9). After he completed "The Lover's Song," he explicitly acknowledged Wellesley's influence: "It is *Matrix* again but air not earth" (102). In April 1938 he thanked her for listening to his poetry: "I altered everything that you questioned I think" (160).

T. R. Henn has argued that it is likely that Yeats had "Matrix" in mind as late as 1938 when he wrote his play *Purgatory*,[21] citing Wellesley's lines "A burnt out house is the mind. / Or a house in building? A room, / Plaster wet on the floor / Generations afoot, ghosts born" (*Selections*, 102–3). But Wellesley's poem "The Deserted House," which Yeats included in *Selections*, resonates just as strongly in the play. In the poem Wellesley recounts a woman's return to her childhood home.

> Knowing the house deserted, amid the darkness of trees
> That seemed to my memories
> Flat as vernal scenery upon a stage,
> Greatly daring I came to the house again;
> Came straight, for I knew its intimacies.
>
> (*Selections*, 78)

The house in Yeats's *Purgatory* is similarly deserted: "The floor is gone, the windows gone, / And where there should be roof there's sky."[22] Arriving at the house, Wellesley's speaker kneels down, "And the ghosts rose up" (79), including the ghost of her father:

> He who gave me life (and his spirit I feared the most)
> walked, silent, for ever alone alongside the lake,
> Whom no living woman had understood.
>
> (79–80)

In Wellesley's poem the speaker's mother also haunts the house and the speaker must relive the abuse her mother visited upon her in the nursery. Yet in coming to the deserted childhood home the speaker finds redemption: "Here is the healing / Here is the answer, the pardon" (81).

Clearly Wellesley's narrative haunted Yeats, for his house is also haunted by the Old Man's parents, and the father is the most hated spirit: "But he killed the house; to kill a house / Where great men grew up, married, died, / I here declare a capital offence" (*Plays*, 539). Though the Old Man's father did not beat him, he abused him by withholding education. Just as Wellesley's speaker finds release and redemption from the past, so the Old Man releases his mother and himself from the cycle of remorse by killing his son. He says his mother's ghost is now in "light because / I finished all that consequence. / I killed that lad because he had grown up. / He would have struck a woman's fancy, / Begot, and passed pollution on" (*Plays*, 540). Although Yeats's play is more fully engaged with issues of patrilineage, engendering, and the consequences of sexual desire, it echoes the concerns with a haunted past, remorse, regret and forgiveness that exist in embryonic form in Wellesley's poem.

Echoes of Wellesley's influence are also present in "Cuchulain Comforted," where the image of Cuchulain sewing his shroud resonates with the singing Serving-Maid in Wellesley's ballad. Yeats was greatly taken by Wellesley's image: "In those first four verses I found something that had never been sung. The maid who had seemed 'wild with love' was able to 'sing aloud' as she hemmed the shroud" (*Letters*, 81). Even more striking is Yeats's association of birds with shrouds, which Wellesley makes in "The Lost Forest," another poem Yeats included in *Selections*. In "Cuchulain Comforted" the character

> strode among the dead;
> Eyes stared out of the branches and were gone.
>
> Then certain Shrouds that muttered head to head
> Came and were gone. He leant upon a tree
> As though to meditate on wounds and blood.
>
> (*Poems*, 332)

The poem continues, "A shroud that seemed to have authority among those bird-like things came," echoing Wellesley's speaker, who knows "that in the darkness the souls abode with the birds (*Selections*, 61–62). The speaker continues:

> Thus do the souls seek company with the birds;
> There rested spirit and feather,
> There in beautiful darkness
> Slept they together.
>
> (63)

Similarly, if Yeats's shrouds become birds—"they had changed their throats and had the throats of birds"—Wellesley's speaker hears a spoken "Word, then behold it was a bird, / that dipping and flying sings" (63).

With respect to Wellesley's poem "The Gyres," it, too, can be reconsidered in this light. If Wellesley is the return of Maud Gonne—beautiful, desirable, but sexually inaccessible—she and Penns in the Rocks also bear striking resemblance to Lady Gregory and Coole. Yeats writes, "I long for your intellect & sanity. Hitherto I have never found these anywhere but at Coole" (*Letters*, 63). Indeed, it must have seemed to Yeats that his friendship with Wellesley was a propitious turning of the Gyres that brought back "Those that Rocky Face holds dear" (*Poems*, 293). Moreover, "the rich dark nothing" from which "workman, noble and saint" are disinterred recalls the "uterine darkness" of "Matrix." In this sense it is fitting that "The Gyres" begins *New Poems*, the volume containing "The Three Bushes" sequence, "To Dorothy Wellesley," "Lapis Lazuli" (a stone that Wellesley collected), and "The Pilgrim," in which the speaker comes to terms with the wisdom of women, the old, and the dead. Yeats said the volume pleased him better than anything he had done and compared it to Wellesley's work: "It is all nonchalant verse—or it seems to me—like the opening of your 'Horses'" (*Letters*, 153).

Wellesley's literary taste continued to influence Yeats's reading and his selections for *The Oxford Book of Modern Verse*. Indeed, she seems to have been able to champion the case of a number of female poets initially overlooked by Yeats. When Wellesley praised Edna St. Vincent Millay, Yeats bought all of Millay's books (*Letters*, 12). One month after she recommended Elinor Wylie's "Hymn to Earth," he included Wylie among those poets who gave him the "most excitement" (19). Similarly, Wellesley's praise of Laura Riding caused Yeats to reread Riding's work. "You are right about Laura Riding," he wrote. "I had rejected her work in some moment of stupidity but when you praised her I re-read her . . . & delighted in her intricate intensity" (58). Even after Yeats apologized to Riding, she still refused to give him permission to include her in his anthology.

Yeats had a similar reaction to Vita Sackville-West's work. He eventually told Wellesley "I take back what I said of your friend Sackville-West," calling "The Greater Cats" "very moving" (*Letters*, 8) and including it in the anthology. Yeats solicited Wellesley's opinion of Edith Sitwell, whom he found "very hard to select from. . . . If you have strong preferences among her poems please tell me" (8).

In addition to Sitwell and Sackville-West, Yeats accepted Wellesley's recommendations and included James Elroy Flecker, Edward Thomas, and Robert Bridges (*Letters*, 28). Yeats explicitly credited her with the selection of the two Kipling poems (115–16). Lady Ottoline Morrell acknowledged Wellesley's influence on the volume and echoed much of the criticism it received: "I was very angry with W B Yeats who edited the New Oxford Anthology & omitted [Ruth Pitter]—& omitted many others, Laurence Whistler who is good; Herbert Palmer; etc. etc. He did it under the influence of Lady Gerald Wellesley, whose Poetry he admires very much."[23]

Though the anthology sold well,[24] it caused a furor. Yeats was roundly criticized for his omission of Wilfred Owen and the "avant-garde political poets" (*Letters*, xi), as well as for his inclusion of Wilfred Blunt, Oliver Gogarty, Turner, Sitwell, and Wellesley herself (xi). Like Lady Ottoline, reviewer Clifford Bax asserted that Yeats did not compile the anthology himself (115).

Yeats was not immune to criticism. In January 1937 he wrote to Wellesley that he had fallen ill from exhaustion due to "overwork and mental strain," noting in particular the "attacks on Anthology (Feeling that I have no nation, that somebody has bitten my apple all round)" (*Letters*, 116). In spite of his deep feelings of alienation, however, Yeats also wrote that, "having looked up every poem unknown to me some critic has complained of my leaving out," he had "nothing to add" (130). What was at stake for Yeats in the reviews of the anthology were his ideas about poetry, ideas he saw reflected in and supported by Wellesley's work.

Though Yeats recognized the greatness of some of the modernist poets, he clearly aligned himself with Wellesley's "archaic modernity," poetry that "looked back" and was "proud of its ancestry, of its traditional high breeding" (*Letters,* 95). Indeed, such retrospection was a primary feature of Yeats's late aesthetic. As spare and unflinchingly modern as his late poetry now seems to contemporary readers, his late style emerged at least in part from a commitment to tradition and to the "archaic" forms that cemented his relationship with Wellesley. In April 1936 he wrote the following to her:

> This difficult work, which is being written everywhere now (a professor from Barcelona tells me they have it there) has the substance of philosophy & is a delight to the poet with his professional pattern; but it is not your road or mine, & ours is the main road, the road of naturalness & swiftness and we have thirty centuries upon our side. We alone can "think like a wise man, yet express our selves like the common people." These new men are goldsmiths working with a glass screwed into one eye, whereas we stride ahead of the crowd, its swordsmen, its jugglers, looking to right & left. "To right and left" by which I mean that we need like Milton, Shakespeare, Shelley, vast sentiments, generalizations supported by tradition. (*Letters,* 58)

On the one hand, Yeats aligned himself with a powerful and ancient literary history. But he also considered Wellesley a kind of comrade in this history. Indeed, Wellesley's perceived talent, the very thing that threatened Yeats's belief in his own work, also enabled Yeats to see her as a colleague and conspirator who supported his poetic vision and achievement. Through a willful reimagining of literary tradition and community, Yeats transformed a rivalry into a community, a threat into an asset and, in so doing, also challenged the notion of the solitary male genius and even, perhaps, of a literary patrilineage.

While Yeats felt antiquated and out of touch with modern poetry, he was supported and defended by Wellesley, who, while young and familiar with contemporary writers, still wrote poetry he understood and appreciated.[25] She was rewarded generously by being granted more pages in the anthology than any other poet except Edith Sitwell, surpassing Eliot, Hopkins, Pound, Lawrence, Wilde, and even Yeats himself. Since friendship hardly justifies aligning Wellesley with the likes of Milton, Shakespeare, and Shelley, her inclusion reflects much more upon Yeats's views of modern poetry, who believed that although the latter was concerned with flux, indecision, and alienation, it should nevertheless be written in a traditional style, diction, and rhythm. While literary history has all but forgotten Wellesley's poetry, it did meet Yeats's criteria. Wellesley gave Yeats the inspiration, close friendship, and connection with the younger generation of poets that rejuvenated his verse, his personal life, and his place in the modern literary community. In return, Wellesley was championed by the national poet of Ireland.

The "scribbling sibling rivalry" between Yeats and Wellesley is thus the story of the series of gifts they exchanged over the last four years of Yeats's life. The economy between them, illustrated most strikingly in the story behind "The Three Bushes," is a direct result of the anxieties created by the enormous burdens of the gifts of friendship, poetry, and inspiration. If Yeats was made more anxious by their commerce and felt his poetic and sexual identity most threatened, it was because, like the Lover, he simultaneously had the most to lose and the most to gain. When all the exchanges are tallied, Yeats clearly benefited more. But it was an exchange that inspired Yeats to sing his passionate "songs of love," as well as his songs of "lust and rage" (*Poems*, 312). Since Wellesley was intimate enough to be with Yeats on his deathbed,[26] he surely would have wanted her story entwined with his own. Indeed, the image of the rosebush is a fitting metaphor for the multifaceted relationship that existed between the two poets and the poetry that emerged from their liaison. It suggests that Yeats's unique genius was, in part, his uncanny ability to generate text from intertext and to transform a plural vision into a single poem, thereby complicating, if not deconstructing, the romantic notion of the individual artist. In so doing, he contributed to the myth of the solitary genius even as he openly paid homage to the collaboration and partnership that enabled such artistry.

Notes

1. Yeats, introduction to Wellesley, *Selections from the Poems of Dorothy Wellesley*, vii. Subsequent references to Yeats's introduction appear parenthetically in the text as "introd., *Selections*."

2. Yeats, *Letters on Poetry from W. B. Yeats to Dorothy Wellesley*, 3; Subsequent references appear parenthetically in the text as *Letters*.

3. Elizabeth Butler Cullingford has analyzed Yeats's use of the ballad as "the vehicle of nationalist [and] sexual politics." See her *Gender and History in Yeats's Love Poetry*, 172.

4. Gilbert and Gubar, *No Man's Land*, 149.

5. Wellesley, "The Lady, The Squire, and The Serving-Maid," in Yeats and Wellesley, eds., *Broadsides: A Collection of New Irish and English Songs*.

6. Mauss, *The Gift: The Form and Reason for Exchange in Archaic Societies*, viii, ix, resp.

7. Ibid., 12.

8. Ibid., 30, 12, resp.

9. Yeats, *The Collected Works of W. B. Yeats.* Vol. I: *The Poems*, 296; Subsequent references appear parenthetically in the text as *Poems*.

10. This fact is revealed even more tellingly in Yeats's early drafts, where the Lover is explicitly identified as a poet. See Partridge, "Yeats's 'The Three Bushes'—Genesis and Structure," 68.

11. Cullingford notes that since the lyric is historically associated with the female or the effeminate, "the lyric writer may exploit the feminine, but he is also contaminated by it" (*Gender and History*, 16). Her reading of the danger of female-gendered verse complements my own understanding of the danger of female sexuality, further supporting the idea that the production of poetry is dangerous for the male poet. While the muse may inspire, she can also pollute.

12. Garab, "Fabulous Artifice: Yeats's 'Three Bushes' Sequence," 238.

13. Partridge, "Yeats's 'The Three Bushes,'" 68; Yeats, *Letters*, xii; T. Armstrong, "Giving Birth to Oneself: Yeats's Late Sexuality," 53; Stallworthy, *Vision and Revision in Yeats's Last Poems*, 81; Cavanagh, *Love and Forgiveness in Yeats's Poetry*, 153n; Cullingford, *Gender and History*, 274.

14. Armstrong, "Giving Birth to Oneself," 51. Partridge, who discusses Yeats's attraction to Wellesley at length, concludes (based on "To Dorothy Wellesley") that Wellesley is neither Lady nor Chambermaid but poet, "a harder, lonelier thing" ("Yeats's 'The Three Bushes,'" 70). He does not go far enough, I think, in considering Wellesley's erotic and artistic influence on Yeats and ultimately reads "The Three Bushes" sequence as a "parable whose aim is to make clear that human love can never be simply spiritual or simply physical" (67). However, he does grant that in the sequence Yeats found "a poetical emotion to dissolve [his] passions" (67).

15. Armstrong, "Giving Birth to Oneself," 55.

16. Cullingford has noted that Yeats "espoused an organic, Keatsian, consciously essentialist 'feminine' poetics in which 'words are as subtle, as complex, as full of mysterious life, as the body of a flower or of a woman'" (*Gender and History*, 13). While I agree with her, such a poetics must have placed Yeats in an anxious position when confronted with a female poet like Wellesley, who seemed to have direct and natural access to such language because of her gender.

17. Cullingford attributes Yeats's eagerness to revise Wellesley's work to the fact that "collective authorship was appropriate for a ballad," yet she also concedes that "literary collaboration was a version of the sexual act" (*Gender and History*, 274). In fact, revision is not the same as collaboration. Yeats never suggested merging his own poem with hers or producing a single poem from the two versions. Thus, it seems clear that Yeats's motivations for the revision,

though perhaps masked by the conventions of the ballad, more clearly reflect his anxiety over her verse and his erotic longing.

18. The dynamic of male appropriation of female wisdom is present in much of Yeats's corpus. See especially "The Herne's Egg" (1938) and "The Gift of Harun Al-Rashid" (1923). Closer to home is the automatic script produced by George Yeats and systematized by W. B. Yeats in *A Vision* (1937). In each case wisdom enters the world through women, but it must be revised, reformulated, and understood by men. This model reflects Armstrong's statement that for Yeats "the feminine stands at a crucial point between the absolute nature of Wisdom and its realization in the world" (44).

19. Bloom, *Yeats*, 440.

20. Ibid., 441.

21. Henn, *The Lonely Tower: Studies in the Poetry of W. B. Yeats*, 316.

22. Yeats, *The Collected Works of W. B. Yeats*. Vol. II: *The Plays*, 538. Subsequent references appear parenthetically in the text as *Plays*.

23. Morrell, *Dear Lady Ginger: An Exchange of Letters Between Lady Ottoline Morrell and D'Arcy Cressswell*, 102.

24. Yeats wrote to Wellesley that fifteen thousand copies were sold in three months (*Letters*, 133), that the book was at the top of the best-seller list in Glasgow and Edinburgh, and that the sale in America was "very great" (130).

25. Yeats's views on modern poetry are articulated in his 1937 BBC broadcast. See Yeats, "On Modern Poetry" in *The Collected Works of W. B. Yeats*. Vol. V: *Later Essays*, 89–102.

26. Virginia Woolf wrote the following to Vita Sackville-West shortly after Yeats's death: "According to Ottoline, he cut a gland, in order to inject virility, woke to see Dotty, and died of the rush of virility injected. But this is malicious. I am sorry he is dead." See Woolf, *Letters of Virginia Woolf*, 6:318. Woolf's comment is emblematic of her own, Sackville-West's, and Lady Ottoline's attitude toward Yeats and Wellesley, supporting my argument that both poets felt somewhat embattled with respect to modernist circles.

Not Elizabeth to His Ralegh

Laura Riding, Robert Graves, and Origins of the White Goddess

AMBER VOGEL

It is almost sixty years since Laura Riding and Robert Graves parted, time enough for a vast store of valuations of these two as people and writers to accumulate, for the comparative worth of their individual contributions to collaborative projects to be sifted and sorted, for the marks made on the literary record as a result of their involvement with one another to be interpreted and reinterpreted in memoirs, essays, biographies, letters, and myriad other texts. The sheer volume makes evident the multiple lenses through which people's relationships with one another may be viewed (whether they should be is another question), the histories unfolding from them, the literary uses to which such histories may be put, and the fascination they continue to hold.

By the time her *Collected Poems* appeared in 1938 (she was then in her late thirties), Laura Riding had to her credit a large body of writing that had already begun to influence the work of others—including the poetry of Robert Graves and W. H. Auden and the methods of the New Critics. Yet within a few years she had publicly renounced poetry writing, as having lost, for her, its effectiveness as a means of truth-telling. Together with her second husband, Schuyler Jackson, she went on to manage a citrus business in Florida, place the name by which she was best known within parentheses, and effectively remove herself from the literary mainstream. Graves, on the other hand, returned to their home in Mallorca after the Second World War, and over a period of decades, saw his fame increase. Books like *The White Goddess,* which popularized his mythic view of poetry writing, and *I, Claudius,* a historical novel that became a successful TV miniseries—not to mention his own complex persona, which readily lent itself to anecdote and literary profiles—attracted a large following.

The opposite trajectories of their respective careers were soon mirrored in the critical and biographical estimations of their work and personalities. I think it is fair to say that Robert Graves's press—which was often generated by his friends, relatives, and acolytes, with whom he usually cooperated—tended to be plentiful and favorable (or at least sympathetic), whereas Laura Riding's side of this significant literary partnership tended to be skirted by timid analysts or interpreted by biased observers or investigators who lacked all the facts. Such a disparity may have resulted, in part, from (Riding) Jackson's refusal to cooperate with—and from her sometimes public criticism of—those she felt were creating an inaccurate record of her experience (and her understanding of that experience) for their own literary or professional purposes. It may have resulted from her reluctance, until the last decades of her life, to enter the biographical and autobiographical fray, to make that kind of defense. But it also seems to have resulted from a curious and steady sort of effacement by Graves and others of her part in a thirteen-year-long collaborative association, despite evidence of her authority and activity within it.

My focus here is not the deletion of Laura Riding's name by Graves and others from their shared bibliography, though this also occurred. Rather, I wish to trace a subtler and more interesting procedure by which an accomplished, influential, and *real* writer was replaced, in biography and literary criticism alike, by a more pliable fiction conjured by her literary partner. Graves's famous White Goddess "is a lovely, slender woman with a hooked nose, deathly pale face, lips red as rowanberries, startlingly blue eyes and long fair hair; she will suddenly transform herself sow, mare, bitch, vixen, she-ass, weasel, serpent, owl, she-wolf, tigress, mermaid or loathsome hag" to whom poets since Homer have owed fealty.[1] "The reason why the hairs stand on end, the eyes water, the throat is constricted, the skin crawls and a shiver runs

down the spine when one writes or reads a true poem is that a true
poem is necessarily an invocation of the White Goddess, or Muse, the
Mother of All Living, the ancient power of fright and lust—the female
spider or the queen-bee whose embrace is death" (12). Graves's dramatic evocation of this figure was further vitalized by its entanglement
and confusion with his life, and his work with Riding, and it came to replace her in the minds of many. As a result, even a reader as astute as
Randall Jarrell was led to say of Riding, "I believe that it is simplest to
think of her as, so to speak, the White Goddess incarnate, the Mother-
Muse in contemporary flesh."[2] After examining the sort of material
(Riding) Jackson consistently and vehemently denounced in her later
letters, I came to realize that this procedure—this effacement of her real
life and work—more easily met the psychological, rhetorical, and aesthetic needs of its various proponents than did the arguments against it.
I gradually began to understand both the persistence of a style of writing
about this woman and the strong terms in which she lodged her protests.

Though not addressed to Graves, some of (Riding) Jackson's later
letters—written forty or fifty years after their parting—constitute yet another distinct type of text growing out of their previous collaborative enterprise. In asides as well as in longer discussions, they present her views
of Graves, of his collaboration with her on numerous literary projects,
and of what she deemed to be his continued mining of her thought and
work for his own profit following the end of their personal association. In
combination with other retrospective writings (e.g., "Some Autobiographical Corrections of Literary History," "About the Fugitives and
Myself," and "Engaging in the Impossible") and the publication of work
written much earlier (most significantly "The Word 'Woman'"), they
represent (Riding) Jackson's effort—undertaken in the last decades of
her life—to restore her name and accomplishments to literary history before Graves's name was indelibly inked in its place. They also constitute
her related effort to correct a popular view of herself as avatar of Graves's
famous White Goddess, which she felt paid no homage to her but instead
represented the connected thefts of her work and her identity.

A closely typed three-page letter on these topics, written to the poet
William Harmon in 1984, is a good example of the style and tone of
(Riding) Jackson's argument. It reads in part:

> Graves invented his musemanship and goddessry literary obscenities
> on his unclean own after his finding himself without the old accustomed

access to the Way of Straight Approaches. There are plenty who
had access to my help and friendship who know that *The White Goddess*
had nothing to do with myself except as mingling thieveries from the
straight broad oath of my thought and twisting together with the steals
a dirty mess of steals from a poetico-mythicological anywhere.—I *never*
meant anything to Graves but as a means of his elevating himself to a
level of public success as a literary figure that his given native endow-
ments could not be made to effect by the mere force of ambition.—He
wrote to Gertrude Stein (having sought her out for friendship with . . .
some ingratiating maligning of me to her) "I was learning from her all
the time."

Here (Riding) Jackson was responding to Martin Seymour-Smith's
recent biography of Graves, about which Harmon was then writing a
review, and to the tenor of the commentaries accreting to it. Like a
spate of other biographical and critical treatments in the 1970s and
1980s, these commentaries typically supported an aggrieved, stoical
Graves against an unstable, unmerciful Riding. They did not investigate
the possibility that the substance and treatment of their work together—
the point of connection between these two personalities—made for
(Riding) Jackson's own injuries and for her less than pleasant attitude
where Graves was concerned. Instead, they offered up dark motives for
her part in the relationship—sinister views of what to her represented
her "help and friendship" and "comradely openness."[3]

Riding's collaboration with Graves—which produced *A Survey of
Modernist Poetry, A Pamphlet Against Anthologies,* a list of publications from
their press, and much other work by the two—was the most varied and
complex. But the range of her collaborative efforts with others was wide
both in chronology and scale: from early attempts to help the Fugitives
(even in tasks as lowly as selling subscriptions for their poetry magazine,
which had awarded her its prize) to the decades-long collaboration with
Schuyler Jackson that produced *Rational Meaning: A New Foundation for the
Definition of Words* (which Harmon eventually edited). The terms in
which (Riding) Jackson tended to describe these connections—or her
initial hopes for them—suggest that she thought of collaboration as a
locus for personal interaction, a way of generating and sustaining relationships, of responding to people and helping them. Years later, in
"Some Autobiographical Corrections of Literary History," (Riding)
Jackson recalled

close working associations I had maintained with a number of writers, to the good of whose own writing, and for the sake of a common human cause of comprehension of the good in language, I had very earnestly and hopefully devoted myself. Of this number, Robert Graves was the closest associate; he for long had the steady confidence of my thought, and to his writing-problems and ambitions my application was intensive, as were my efforts to meet his desire to have as much as he could make his own of my processes of word, mind, moral feeling.[4]

Writing to a young friend, Jay Ansill, following Graves's death (Riding) Jackson repeated her opinion of "this wicked, thieving, lying monster of ambition." Yet she also added the following: "I have no apologies to make to anyone for generosities of hope placed in others, commitments of trust. This has been much and variously betrayed. Without it—this kindness to the possibilities of truth . . .—I should not learn where, in whom, something of human good actually existed."[5]

Rather less generous has been the stream of biographical and critical commentary on Laura Riding's role as collaborator. A great deal of such commentary has consisted of guesswork—and some of it is downright peculiar. In the latter category is a memoir by T. S. Matthews, published in 1973, titled *Jacks or Better*, which (Riding) Jackson called "a slanderous book by a venomous toad of a man," a harsh valuation that nevertheless makes some sense given Matthews's association of Riding with Simon LeGree and Adolf Hitler.[6] In the early 1930s Matthews, an editor at *Time*, had gone to Mallorca to work with Riding and Graves, who received a large number of such visits from writers and artists. He had asked Riding for help with a novel he was writing, which, by his own account, she gave unstintingly. However, he ultimately compared his willingness to accept her help to the sort of "venal mentality . . . that caused 'ordinary' Frenchmen to knuckle under to the German occupation, or even collaborate with it."[7] The title of the chapter in which this occurs ("Muse in Mallorca") and the accompanying description of the author's friendship with Graves begins to suggest how a particular view of Riding—and the language with which to purvey it—came into existence.

Less sinister but still peculiar is the following anecdote by Seymour-Smith: "Gottschalk [historian Louis Gottschalk (Riding) Jackson's first husband] met Graves on a visit to England in 1926 and got the impression that he wrote most of the 'collaborations.'"[8] The date given, the year Laura Riding and Robert Graves met, is rather too early to lend credence either to the quotes that cast suspicion on the word "collaboration" or to any judgment—let alone one so sweeping—on the nature of their work together. And such a tête-à-tête between a woman's ex-husband and her new partner, along with this public pronouncement on what they deemed to be her inadequacies, constitutes a particularly odd—one might even say ungallant—sort of literary critique. But it is, in essence, aligned with more typical analyses, which suggest that (Riding) Jackson was unhelpful, irrelevant, or harmful to her collaborators— all records of their success while Graves was in her sphere notwithstanding. Seymour-Smith also provides this other type of analysis. *A Survey of Modernist Poetry*, an early and influential product of the partnership between Riding and Graves, entwines the American and British strands of their literary backgrounds and their individual poetic practices. They described this as a "word-by-word collaboration," with "Laura Riding" listed before "Robert Graves" on the title page. Seymour-Smith gives Riding some (backhanded) credit for producing the book, but at the same time, he suggests this credit accrues to her only through Graves's indulgence: "Provided that it is understood that she despumated him, reorganized him, relieved his mind of its obsession with psychological theories of poetry—and that he had been asking for exactly this—then their respective contributions to *A Survey of Modernist Poetry* are about equal, although the book is ultimately more his than hers, because he possessed a literary background whereas she did not. They agreed to call it a 'word-by-word' collaboration; and so it was."[9]

(Riding) Jackson noted that "some very queer things have been done to me, and my work" ("Corrections," 9). Indeed, Seymour-Smith and others have had to make wide rhetorical circumlocutions in order to avoid the possibility that Graves was indeed "learning from her all the time"—or *any* of the time—and to support Graves's own version of his creative process. Examples ranging over more than thirty years give the flavor of this ritual and proof of its longevity. In *Swifter Than Reason,* published in 1963, Douglas Day comments: "Whatever the psychological motivations behind this curious relationship, there is little doubt that Laura Riding caused Graves substantially to modify his poetic practice." And he says of Riding: "The effect of such a martial spirit was immediate and drastic on Graves, whose faith in himself and his vocation was straightway renewed." Here, in plain words, are cause and effect: Riding labored with Graves over his work and did him some good by it.

Yet in the rest of Day's commentary this version of a living, active, productive Riding is dismantled. He writes that "we are led . . . to agree with Randall Jarrell's theory that Graves's conception of the White Goddess as the source of poetic inspiration is in large measure a symbolic recreation of his earlier veneration of Laura Riding." He then concludes: "What seems most probable is that Graves, in constructing his concept of the Muse, took the familiar female stereotype he inherited from centuries of romantic literature, and associated it with the antique Goddess who killed and devoured her lovers. He was seeking a name for the abstract concept which he felt lay behind all poetic inspiration, and he found the White Goddess, in all her awesome ferocity. Whether or not Graves believes in her as a true Goddess is irrelevant." Now Day's acknowledgment of Riding's connection with Graves is displaced to an apparition. Riding and her effect become "Graves's conception," his "symbolic recreation," an "abstract concept," and "the familiar female stereotype he inherited." Riding's "martial spirit" is now the White Goddess's "awesome ferocity." And what is "true . . . is irrelevant."[10]

The myth of the White Goddess flatters its believer by hiding the mundane and collaborative origins of his ideas. Such a myth allowed Graves to write, "I suddenly knew (don't ask me how)."[11] Such a myth allowed him to describe—and wonder at—the pouring forth of *The White Goddess*, when "my mind worked at such a furious rate all night, as well as all the next day, that my pen found it difficult to keep pace with the flow of thought."[12] Such a myth also allowed him to say of *The White Goddess*, "It's a crazy book & I didn't mean to write it."[13] But for (Riding) Jackson "Graves's Goddess pornographies," as she labeled them, were hardly so ingenuously arrived at or intended.[14] Instead, she described the White Goddess as "a literary machine designed for seizure of the essence of my reality, out of the literary plunder remaining from the destruction of the personal fact of me."[15] She noted, therefore, "the offensiveness of the characterization of *me* as 'a living incarnation' of Robert Graves's 'The White Goddess'" (211). Recalling his friend Graves for a *New Yorker* article in 1995, Alastair Reid nevertheless wrote: "He discussed endlessly with Laura his growing interest in goddess worship. To it she added the vehemence of her own ideas, and soon she became to Graves not simply critic and mentor and lover and poet but muse. Later, she claimed to have been the source of all Graves's notions of poetry as goddess worship. She was not. She was much more: she was their incarnation." Notable here is the transformation—in the space of

five sentences—of Riding from intellectual to incarnation that defines
the pejorative status of "muse." Just three paragraphs later Reid erases
Riding entirely, with *The White Goddess* becoming "a brilliantly argued
synthesis of all Graves's most fundamental preoccupations: *his* reading
in the classics, *his* conversations with [W. H. R.] Rivers, *his* immersion
in both Celtic and classical myth and history, and *his* own firm sense of
what was required of a dedicated poet" (italics mine).[16]

Seymour-Smith rehearses this procedure when he says of Graves
that "he had, in the context of his own life, already invented Riding. *The
White Goddess* is not, as it has too often been called, simply a 'rationaliza-
tion of Riding.'" Similarly, he contrasts Laura Riding with Graves's second wife, "the unobtrusive figure of Beryl. . . . She eventually exercised a
more profound effect on Graves than Riding. He never 'invented' her as
he invented Riding. His letters to her before they began to live together
are unlike any of his other letters, to anyone. They are not addressed to
a capricious and unpredictable Muse, but to a woman wholly trusted."[17]
According to this scheme—and contrary to all logic—an "unobtrusive
figure" is claimed to have the most profound effect on Graves, while
Riding—all capriciousness, unpredictability, and untrustworthiness to
the contrary—springs whole and ineffectual from Graves's head.

In *On Poetry* Graves had asked: "For some three thousand years, the
inspiration that accompanies poetic trances has been ascribed to a character called the Muse; and although the meaning of 'Muse' has long
been blurred by dishonest or facetious usage, what other word can replace it?" (323). (Riding) Jackson's essay on the word "woman" provides
an answer that Graves may already have known. She mentions to Harmon "notes of mine . . . I left behind . . . at emergency war departure."[18]
This was the unfinished manuscript of "The Word 'Woman,'" left in
Mallorca at the beginning of the Spanish Civil War and restored to
(Riding) Jackson by Beryl Graves decades later. It formed part of the material that (Riding) Jackson felt—and that she had been told through
rumor—had fed Graves's own work, particularly *The White Goddess*,
which likewise seeks to define the relative positions men and women
take in intellectual connection. In "The Word 'Woman'" (Riding) Jackson delineates a pattern of woman's disappearance from man's narrative
of achievement that came to fit her own association with Graves: "Independence from woman has been the object of all the so-called 'creative'
activity of man: the very notion of 'creation' implies the disappearance
of the separate phenomenon 'woman' in male activity."[19] According to

(Riding) Jackson, "Woman disappears from his consciousness in his momentary sensations of victory, and still more effectively, therefore, in his vision of final transfiguration: not merely the immediate fact, but the very word 'woman' disappears" (50).

(Riding) Jackson begins her recovery of the word "woman" by defining it, reaching back to its Anglo-Saxon roots in the word "queen." Inherent in this word is the nexus of gender and authority that Graves's mythology undermines by describing woman's activity and power as conjured out of the man's subconscious and by positing her passivity and silence as conditions for his fealty. In "The Word 'Woman'" (Riding) Jackson describes the mechanism of such a scheme, in which man seems to succeed "by the yielding rather than the active consent of woman," and where "the very notion of 'creation' implies the disappearance of the separate phenomenon 'woman' in male activity" (50, 57). In *The White Goddess*, for example, the political power and success of Elizabeth I (who is also mentioned in "The Word 'Woman'") are explained away as the results of cultishness, as arising—figments of racial memory—out of "an unconscious hankering in Britain after goddesses" (452). According to Graves, "[O]ne of the results of Henry VIII's breach with Rome was that when his daughter Queen Elizabeth became head of the Anglican Church she was popularly regarded as a sort of deity: poets not only made her their Muse but gave her titles—Phoebe, Virginia, Gloriana—which identified her with the Moon-goddess, and the extraordinary hold that she gained on the affections of her subjects was largely due to this cult" (452–53).

Persisting, even against the history of Elizabeth's achievements, Graves returns to this figure in *On Poetry:*

> Strangely enough, the woman who came nearest to an authentic personal Muse in Tudor times was Queen Elizabeth herself, as celebrated by Sir Walter Raleigh. Though he has been accused of flattery, self-seeking and other ignoble traits in his relations with Elizabeth (who was almost twenty years older than he) and though his earlier poems of prosperity in love have disappeared, leaving only complaints of her subsequent unkindness, it is difficult after reading *The Eleventh and Last Book of the Ocean to Cynthia* to challenge the reality of the power she exercised over his heart. (340–41)

In praising Ralegh, Graves sets the minor arts—the formulaic love poem, the courtier's gesture—above the real work, the heavy lifting, of a culture. In stressing "the power she exercised over his heart" despite her "unkindness" and her age, Graves misrepresents the sway Elizabeth managed to hold not only over Ralegh but over a nation in dangerous times—and the remarkably long period during which she was able to do so. All her accomplishments must either be forgotten or misidentified in order to support Graves's mythology, in which "woman . . . is either a Muse or she is nothing" (*The White Goddess*, 500).

Embedded in a letter to Harmon is (Riding) Jackson's recollection of one of Graves's many biographers, James McKinley, who sought her cooperation: "He wanted me to be, he said, the Queen Elizabeth to Graves's Ralegh!"[20] It is easy to understand why any attempt to find in Laura Riding and Robert Graves some reflection of this prototypical male-female relationship—some mimicry of famous gestures in the chivalric tradition—would seem ludicrous to (Riding) Jackson, who must have come to feel that she had kept Graves out of the mud while he had pushed her into it. It is easy to understand why she might prefer not to collaborate in the writing of that particular romance.

Notes

Portions of Laura Riding's previously unpublished correspondence are printed here with the permission of the Board of Literary Management of the late Laura (Riding) Jackson.

1. Graves, *The White Goddess*, 12. Subsequent references appear parenthetically in the text.

2. Jarrell, "Graves and the White Goddess," 26.

3. Riding, letter to William Harmon, 7 May 1984.

4. (Riding) Jackson, "Some Autobiographical Corrrections of Literary History," 1–2. Subsequent references appear parenthetically in the text.

5. Riding, letter to Jay Ansill, 29 December 1985.

6. Riding, letter to Jay Ansill, 29 June 1985.

7. Matthews, *Jacks or Better: A Narrative*, 286.

8. Seymour-Smith, *Robert Graves: His Life and Work*, 138.

9. Ibid., 144.

10. Day, *Swifter than Reason: The Poetry and Criticism of Robert Graves*, 106, 131, 144–45n, 166.

11. Graves, *5 Pens in Hand*, 54.

12. Graves, *On Poetry: Collected Talks and Essays*, 227–28. Subsequent references appear parenthetically in the text.

13. Letter dated 1955, quoted in Seymour-Smith, *Robert Graves*, 405.
14. Riding, letter to William Harmon dated 27 April 1985.
15. Riding, "Robert Graves's *The White Goddess*," 209. Subsequent references appear parenthetically in the text.
16. Reid, "Remembering Robert Graves," 73.
17. Seymour-Smith, *Robert Graves*, 94, 354.
18. Riding, letter to William Harmon dated 7 May 1984.
19. Riding, "The Word 'Woman,'" 57. Subsequent references appear parenthetically in the text.
20. Riding, letter to William Harmon dated 7 May 1984.

V

Writing Back

*Postcolonial and Contemporary Contestation
and Retrospection*

Competing Versions of a Love Story

Mircea Eliade and Maitreyi Devi

REBECCA CARPENTER

At first glance Mircea Eliade and Maitreyi Devi seem less like a literary couple than literary combatants. In 1933 the renowned scholar Mircea Eliade wrote what he claimed to be a semiautobiographical novel about his romance with a young Bengali poet, which he originally entitled *Maitreyi* but later retitled *Bengal Nights*.[1] This novel, as the rather suggestive title implies, is a story of young love and steamy, passionate nights, as well as of cultural conflict. Devi's 1974 novel *It Does Not Die* is her response to Eliade. Reading it in the light of *Bengal Nights*, the reader is forced to examine the racial and colonial assumptions that shape Eliade's text. Taken together, these two works compete for the right to name, to narrate, to determine what the "truth" is—and to invent. Reading these literary creations intertextually illuminates the racial, colonial, and sexual power dynamics underlying both narratives.

In the introduction to his *Double Talk: The Erotics of Male Literary Collaboration*, Wayne Koestenbaum argues that male-male literary collaboration is inherently erotic. He posits the theory that male-male literary collaborators "express homoeroticism and they strive to conceal it," terming the kind of writing that ensues "double talk": "When two men write together . . . they rapidly patter to obscure their erotic burden." In his view, "collaboration is always a sublimation of erotic entanglement."[2] This theory seems debatable even with regard to collaborative writing considered in its strictest sense. Clearly another theoretical model is needed to describe the relationship between writers like Eliade and Devi, where the two are not equal collaborators but rather sensationalistic first writer and reluctant respondent, and where the erotic component of their relationship is not sublimated but the explicit subject of Eliade's writing. Given the high value placed on chastity within Bengali culture, Eliade's novel would be more accurately described as a metaphorical act of violence and violation than an act of "metaphorical sexual intercourse," as Koestenbaum claims.

Interestingly, however, Devi does not respond to Eliade's act of inscriptive violence with an act of equally violent revenge. Instead, she rewrites his story on her own terms, firmly repudiating his inscription of her as the exotic, erotic oriental Other yet preserving his representation of their relationship as something more significant than such a brief, youthful alliance would normally be. Precisely what the relationship signifies becomes the subject of contestation. Rather than merely refuting Eliade's version of events, Devi combines strategies of contradiction and correction with strategies of integration, fusion, and complementarity. She weaves her story around his, alternately correcting and confirming, reinterpreting and reinforcing, rejecting and elaborating. In so doing, Devi asserts her right to equal authorial power.

Race, Gender, and Power

Eliade's text is a novel of Western conquest. His work invites the European reader to participate in his sensual experience of seducing and being seduced by an exotic Other and by the mysterious culture of Bengal. Eliade is not entirely unaware of the nature of his subject position and is self-aware enough to mock some of his initial assumptions, as well as the more overt racism of his compatriots. Nonetheless, his text reproduces many of the standard tropes common to Western representations of the East. Eliade exoticizes and eroticizes the teenage Maitreyi, simultaneously emphasizing her innocence and instinctive sexual talents, her mysteriousness, and her difference. Although Maitreyi is described as passionate and eager to give her body to Eliade, she is also frequently described as "primitive," "enigmatic," "unfathomable," "a savage," and "a barbarian." Eliade's impressions of Maitreyi are clearly shaped by a preexisting colonial discourse that defines the mysterious, sensual East as the opposite of the rational, sensible West. *Bengal Nights* demonstrates the power of prevailing orientalist mythologies and provides an excellent opportunity to interrogate and question representations of the sexuality of Eastern women in texts by European writers.

Maitreyi Devi's *It Does Not Die* presents a compelling voice leading this interrogation. Reversing the usual power dynamic of colonialism, it is Devi, the Bengali woman, who gets the last word in this debate, and thus is in the position of correcting, of presenting the authoritative version of these distant events. She also calls the reader's attention to the fictionality inherent even in Eliade's supposedly autobiographical account by wickedly reversing one of Eliade's most tactless authorial decisions. In *Bengal Nights* Eliade changes his own name to Alain and chooses as his profession that of engineer, yet he only places the thinnest of veils over Maitreyi Devi's identity by referring to her as Maitreyi Sen and describing her as a disciple of the poet Tagore, a fact that accords with the history of the real-life Maitreyi Devi. In *It Does Not Die* Devi mockingly reverses Eliade, leaving his first name and profession unchanged, while her identity is more fully disguised as "Amrita Sen." She refers to Eliade as "Mircea Euclid," mocking Western culture's assumption of rationality by giving him the name of the Greek mathematician and logician. Devi is here implicitly contending that Eliade's way of representing her was not logical. Although he relies on his position of Western authority and preexisting orientalist assumptions to give his writing credence, his theories cannot be proven. More important, by reversing Eliade's act of naming and concealing, Devi calls attention to the fact that in every autobiographical account the author chooses what to conceal and what to reveal. The self revealed in such a text is always a construct, a fictionalized version of oneself; the events narrated are at best a version of the truth and often pure invention. In so doing, Devi seriously challenges Eliade's right to claim "author"-ity over the shared events of their lives. Devi even includes a scene in which Mircea "Euclid" admits that he incorporated many fantastical elements in his novel, thus strongly implying that hers is the more reliable version, the one the reader should trust.

Of course, Devi's power is somewhat illusory. Eliade's version of the story, which was not refuted for over forty years, was first published in

Romanian (1933) and was subsequently translated into Italian (1945), German (1948), French (1950), and Spanish (1952).[3] Devi's book was published in Bengali in 1974 and in English in 1976. Some myopic critics have dismissed the novel either as Devi's pathetic attempt to repair her reputation—Eliade's cliché-ridden purple prose apparently never caused them to question the veracity of his claims—or as an angry assault on a man who told his version of the truth about their relationship.[4] This is, of course, patently false. Both of these novels are clearly fictions. Eliade's is inscribed with many of the orientalist assumptions that have informed many Western fictions about the romance of the East and the sexuality of oriental women, while Devi's is poetic, modern, and experimental. There is no more reason to assume that Amrita "is" Maitreyi Devi than to assume that Stephen Dedalus in *Ulysses* "is" James Joyce in any facile sense. Both works are self-portraits of the artist—with all the artistic shaping that artistry implies—not mirrors of their lives.

Nevertheless, the mistake is understandable. Devi makes it clear throughout her text that she is writing in response to Eliade's text, to counter the truth that he has put before the public. In essence, she suggests that by presenting a thinly veiled version of her (in both senses of the term) in his text, he left her no choice but to write her story. In other words, he has willed her text into existence.[5] Her text, however, goes far beyond a tit-for-tat response to Eliade's salacious novel. Critics who dismiss her work as vindictive fail to realize that Devi's counternarrative does far more than merely deny the truth claims advanced by Eliade in *Bengal Nights*. Though Devi's narrative begins in an angry tone, it ultimately rewrites Eliade's novel in a far more interesting way than merely labeling his claims scurrilous, denying his authority as a narrator, and offering an alternative set of claims to counter his. Devi recasts his narrative, taking the focus off of the erotic issue and placing it instead on the question of what the relationship meant to each of them and why it continued to resonate in their imaginations decades after its conclusion. This ultimately generous recasting of Eliade's novel places this pair of literary texts far beyond the realm of "he said/she said" typical of literary combatants and creates a far more interesting and complex relationship between the two texts. Devi's gesture of artistic conciliation is in keeping with her obvious determination not merely to counter a scandalous narrative but to preserve a romantic story and an intercultural dialogue that truly (as her title promises) "does not die."

Still, it is important not to downplay the anger inherent in Devi's text, nor to abrogate the crucial challenge she poses to Eliade's authority as narrator. Drawing upon his position as an established white, male, Western scholar whose area of expertise is the East, he presumptuously chose to represent his account of their relationship as authoritative. He presents himself as both an irresistibly seductive white man and as a tragic Romeo-like figure thwarted by a tyrannical, freedom-denying Bengali culture. Maitreyi is portrayed as a desperate, irrational, sexually voracious young woman who gave herself to the fruit seller to thwart her parents' will. Devi does not concede on any point where she feels Eliade has represented her unfairly; she challenges and contests him every step of the way. The reader is the ultimate arbiter of the truth, called upon to judge, to sift, and to negotiate between these two contradictory texts. In the end the question of "what really happened" is perhaps less interesting than the strategies each author adopts to represent their love affair. Nevertheless the determination of the truth cannot simply be dismissed with a few blithe deconstructive statements about the "overdetermined" nature of their relationship. To refuse to grapple with the truth is to side with the colonial arrogance that led Eliade to write a semiautobiographical novel about a young woman without sufficiently disguising her identity. When comparing and contrasting these two texts, one cannot help but notice that Eliade's account is decidedly influenced by Western narrative conventions for representing sexual experiences with Eastern women.

Orientalist Discourse and Constructions of Eastern Womanhood

Eliade's text participates in an orientalist discourse that shaped his perceptions of the East and of Eastern women well before his first trip to the Indian subcontinent. As Edward Said has observed, European representations of the Orient often have less to do with the actual Orient than with the European need to define the East as its opposite, its Other.[6] It is therefore not surprising that many European tropes about the Orient are extremely contradictory. The Orient is simultaneously perceived as a place where women are exceptionally modest, reserved, and womanly (unlike the West, where their brazen counterparts flaunt their sexuality

and make unreasonable demands for equal rights), as well as exceptionally seductive, available, sexually knowledgeable, and lascivious (unlike
the West, where their counterparts apparently deny men certain forms
of satisfaction).

Leila Ahmed's research on Western representations of the Muslim
world and Inderpal Grewal's analysis of Western representations of
India further illuminate this subject. Ahmed notes that the West simultaneously positions Muslim women as peculiarly and oppressively contained and as shockingly libidinous and sexually free. There are two
competing and oddly complementary traditions of Western representation of the East. There is, on the one hand, a long tradition of moral
outrage and shock at the "barbaric," "backward" practices of Muslim
cultures. Westerners have long condemned the harem, the veil, and the
practice of polygamy, labeling such traditions "oppressive" and "de-
grading," and have pitied the subservient, ignorant female victims of
this patriarchal backwardness.[7] On the other hand, the West has simultaneously held that there is sexual freedom within the harem, that all
kinds of licentious and immoral acts take place inside, and that harem
women are particularly wanton, lust-driven, immodest, and seductive.[8]
Grewal has argued that Western representations of Indian women followed a similar pattern. Writers such as Harriet Martineau and Rud-
yard Kipling condemned the oppression of Eastern women and their
imprisonment within the harem while simultaneously worrying that
there might be too much freedom and licentious behavior among
women within the harem.[9]

Why the West represented Eastern women's sexuality in this way is
a complex topic. During the past two decades there has been a wealth of
scholarship on Western representations of Eastern women and the cultural imperatives behind these representations. Scholars have argued
that these needs include: the political (it is necessary to position Eastern
people as immoral relative to their Western counterparts in order to
give imperialism a moral imperative);[10] the symbolic (the East is aligned
with the feminine, the West with the masculine; the East is represented
as being receptive to—perhaps even eagerly awaiting—Western pene-
tration and conquest);[11] and the psychological (the West needs to displace those sexual desires inconsistent with its conception of itself onto
an Eastern Other, thus providing a liberatory alternative to the rational,
regulated West).[12] For my present purposes, however, the genesis of and
motives behind Western representations of the libidinous East are less

important than the pervasiveness of these mythologies, which so permeate the mind and prose of Eliade that it is seemingly impossible for him to write a story of cross-cultural love without drawing on these tropes.

Eliade not only draws on but also structures his story around this prevailing mythology. This is clear from the novel's title, suggesting as it does nights of lovemaking in a steamy, exotic climate. A title like *Bengal Nights* draws on a wealth of Western representations of the libidinous East, the land of submissive yet seductive harem women who live to pleasure men in ways that their supposedly more worldly Western counterparts cannot even begin to imagine. Eliade not only participates in this mythology but also thoroughly naturalizes it, representing the Eastern woman as instinctively endowed with a talent for lovemaking. Maitreyi is simultaneously represented as utterly innocent, virginal, untutored, untouched—pure in a way that Western girls, with their all too worldly upbringing, could never be—yet also as a natural seductress, endowed with instinctive erotic talents and a deep craving for sexual fulfillment. Her utter innocence and virginity make Eliade's eventual conquest all the more satisfying.

At the beginning of the novel Maitreyi is represented as having existed in virtual purdah up until this moment. When, after obtaining her father's permission, Alain's friend Lucien touches the fabric of her "costume," she trembles all over and cannot make eye contact (*BN*, 7). Despite this extreme innocence, however, she apparently possesses an instinctive knowledge of what it takes to seduce a man. According to Eliade, only a few weeks later she deliberately paraded around the house in outfits selected to entice and provoke: "Later in the evening she came back, dressed only in that lovely crimson shawl which leaves her practically naked. . . . I knew she had put on that obscene and delicious costume for my benefit. The engineer had gone out; she would not have dared wear it in his presence. She comes to my room continually, without pretext, and is always provocative or malicious. She is magnificent in her passion. Her body is indescribably seductive" (*BN*, 62).

Read in terms of realism, this development borders on the absurd. How could the same young woman who trembled just to have a man touch the hem of her clothing weeks earlier suddenly have the audacity to select and wear an "obscene and delicious costume"? Where did this woman, who was previously afraid to make eye contact with men her own age, learn to be "magnificent in her passion," and when did she become comfortable visiting such men in their bedchambers? The conventions that shape this novel are clearly those of orientalist fantasy and soft porn.

Eliade's accounts of Alain's sexual contact with Maitreyi are always infused with racial overtones. Maitreyi responds to Alain not simply because he is a sexy, seductive, and highly skilled lover—though Eliade clearly gives Alain ample credit on this score—but because she, as a Bengali woman, perceives her white lover as a godlike being: "Maitreyi was desire incarnate, her face immobile, her eyes fixed on me as though I were the embodiment of some god" (*BN*, 96). It is clear that Alain/Eliade feels a sense of pride in having made "first contact" with this alien being. She has loved before, but he is the first to conquer her body.

In keeping with Western mythologies about Eastern women, Eliade constructs Maitreyi as both the conquered/seduced/colonized body and the beguiling/sexually voracious/pleasure-seeking seductress. However, the extent to which Eliade's writing is informed by orientalist assumptions and the clichés of soft porn truly becomes clear in his description of Alain's initial night of lovemaking with Maitreyi. This scene is comical in its excessive appropriation of contradictory Western mythologies about the East. Maitreyi, of course, initiates the sexual encounter, silently entering Alain's chamber and stripping as a way of indicating that she wants him to ravish her:

> She did not reply but undid the edge of her sari, baring herself to the waist: her eyes were closed, her lips tensed. With great effort, she held back her sighs. The sight of her naked flesh, bathed in the soft light that filled my room, seemed to me an unsurpassed miracle. I had often pictured our first night of love, I had conjured in my imagination the bed, transfigured by desire, where I would know her, but I could never have dreamed that Maitreyi, of her own free will, would reveal her young body to me, in my own room, at night. I had wanted our union to be breath-taking, to take place in extra-ordinary circumstances, but this spontaneous gesture exceeded my every hope. I was struck by the simplicity, the naturalness of the initiative taken by a young virgin in coming alone at night into the bedroom of her fiancé because nothing more stood in the way of their union. (*BN*, 111)

The clichés accumulate quickly, as do the conventions of soft porn: Maitreyi is performing simply and naturally; she is both innocent and erotically utterly available. She is a virgin—this needs to be emphasized in accordance with the conventions of the genre—who can barely hold back her sighs as she makes her "naked flesh" visible to Alain in the "soft light." Reading this passage and others that follow, one can only be thankful that Eliade recognized the limitations of his writing enough to make Maitreyi virtually silent during this scene. (She "breathlessly" repeats his name a few times, but other than that she remains silent until just before her departure.) While silencing Maitreyi is, in a sense, a strategy that further reduces her to a libidinous body, one dreads to think what words Eliade might have put in Maitreyi's mouth.[13]

Alain at first fears he will frighten her. He need not have such fears, for Maitreyi is no timid, frigid Western virgin. From this point on Maitreyi represents the embodiment of orientalist tropes celebrating the unencumbered sexuality of the libidinous Eastern woman and her natural talent for pleasing men:

> She discovered herself in our love-making. We had taken to our games again, and she played them whole-heartedly, giving herself without restriction or fear. This young girl, who know [*sic*] nothing of love, had no fear of it; no caress tired her, no male gesture offended her. She knew every audacity, every tenderness. She had almost nothing of prudery, finding a total sensuality in each posture, feeling neither disgust nor fatigue. If she had not been afraid of being heard, she would have shouted with pain and pleasure at the moment of our union, she would have sung afterwards, she would have danced across the room with the light and delicate movements of a little goddess.
>
> She discovered lover's gestures that astounded me. I had believed that my experience granted me some superiority in the art of loving, but in the invention and execution of caresses she was the expert. I found the confidence of her kisses, the perfection of her embraces, the changing, intoxicating rhythms of her body—which were at every moment more daring, more original, more spontaneous—disconcerting, almost humiliating. She understood the tiniest hint, followed every initiative to its conclusion. I was envious of her instinct. She divined my physical desires with a precision that at first embarrassed me. (*BN*, 113)

Maitreyi's sexual "instinct," her sensual inventiveness and artistry, her intuitive understanding of his every male desire, her responsiveness, her utter lack of prudery, her newly lost virginity, the fact that she "discovered herself" through making love to this Western man—Eliade seems determined to satisfy every fantasy that orientalist discourse has conditioned Western audiences to expect in the Eastern bedroom. When offered up to a mid-twentieth-century Western audience, this script of clichés would enjoy a presupposition of plausibility precisely because it draws on broadly accepted tropes about the sexuality of Eastern women. (Did anyone ever make love in just this way, fulfilling each and every hackneyed pornographic formula?) Needless to say, Maitreyi's exotic, erotic oriental body finds complete satisfaction in Alain's strong, unflagging white masculinity; he notes in passing—with typical immodesty—that she departed "several hours later" (*BN*, 112).

This version of the story was considered authoritative not only because it remained unrefuted for decades, nor solely because it was penned by a well-respected white male scholar who was an authority on India. It was authoritative because *this story already existed before Eliade wrote it.* This is the story that Western visitors to the Orient have always told about Eastern women. In this sense, Eliade and Devi are part of a much longer genealogy of "occidental" and "oriental" voices viewing and representing each other, forming part of a much older history of intercultural discourse.

Beyond Binary Logic

It is not at all surprising that Devi's initial reaction to Eliade's text is one of unadulterated anger and a desire to re-present the story, to set her version of the facts before her audience, to subject Eliade to ridicule as a perjuring, perverse, sensationalistic fantasizer whose ignominious, caddish falsehoods are beneath contempt. The novel she ultimately writes, however, rejects such a vindictive—and probably ineffectual—strategy. Rather than countering Eliade's text (and the orientalist discourse that shaped it) by accusing him of lying, Devi's lyrical novel deconstructs the simple binaries upon which Eliade's text is based, which imprison her within the role of the exotic, erotic, sensual, observed Easterner and present him as the sensible, rational, observing Westerner who is capable of greater detachment and accuracy. Instead of making the locus of her text one of factual correction and outraged reprimand, Devi chooses to reveal the inadequacies of Eliade's representational strategies, while at the same time generously salvaging the core of the romantic story he wove, paying tribute to their youthful desire to rise above the cultural differences and misunderstandings that divide them.

Eliade repeatedly frames the differences and the difficulties existing between himself and Devi in terms of racially loaded binaries: he is the logical, rational West, she the illogical, mystical East; he is the moderate West, she the sensual, pleasure-loving, self-indulgent East; he enjoys the freedom of the West, while she is oppressed by the tyranny of the East. To give Eliade his due, he occasionally recognizes that he is engaging in racial typography and seeks both to report and correct his initial false impressions. These moments, however, are few and far between, primarily serving to reinforce the reliability of the rest of what he says. Eliade attempts to establish himself as the kind of narrator who is so reliable that he is willing to correct his own mistakes. Ultimately, however, Eliade seems unable to see Maitreyi except through the prism of his racial assumptions, which, as Said has pointed out, relentlessly construct the East as the diametrical opposite of the West, its Other. When Eliade attempts to re-create Maitreyi Devi in prose, he is unable to wipe away the inscriptions of other European representations of Eastern women and winds up replicating the mythology of the erotic, exotic, unknowable, seductive Eastern woman.

A perfect example of the difference between these two strategies of representation may be found in Eliade's and Devi's dissimilar ways of representing intellectual misunderstandings. When Eliade feels that Maitreyi does not understand him, he resorts to one of three possible explanatory strategies: (1) he describes her mind as "primitive," "superstitious," "mystical," distinctly other than and inferior to his own mind; (2) he decides that he cannot figure out what she is thinking because she is so "unknowable," so "unfathomable"; or (3) he decides that she is ignorant, that she could not have understood him because of her naiveté, her sheltered upbringing as an Eastern woman.

Devi does not disagree with Eliade's assessment that the two of them are often unable to understand each other, but she is far less likely to diagnose the problem as resulting either from her alleged Eastern "mysteriousness" (she, of course, does not see herself as mysterious, nor does she view her own epistemology as any less rational than Eliade's) or from Eliade's Westernness, as though his failure to understand her were somehow an inherent and insurmountable weakness in Western culture, based on some kind of ultimate untranslatability between cultures. Instead, Devi tends to suggest that the main problems between her and Eliade stem from one of the following causes: (1) Eliade's somewhat arrogant tendency to assume that he has gained sufficient knowledge about her culture to be able to comprehend the motives of her family; (2) Eliade's lack of poetic sensibility (Devi is well aware of her own tendency, as a young literary talent, to exercise her poetic talents in everyday conversation); or (3) Eliade's unsubtle sense of humor. While Eliade's tendency to make assumptions about Bengali culture may indeed be indicative of Western attitudes toward the East, Devi does not generalize her criticisms, focusing instead on Eliade's specific failure to understand the motives and the rules that guide her father, her family, and her culture at large.

Eliade's marriage proposal strikes Devi as a particularly noteworthy example of a failure of cross-cultural communication, not to mention the psychosexual dynamics of his position within the Devi household. Eliade was her father's student, as well as a guest living in his house. By viewing himself as Devi's lover and potential husband, Eliade is essentially scripting an incestuous role for himself by engaging in sexual congress with the biological daughter of his mentor/symbolic father.

Further complicating the dynamic between Eliade and Devi is the presence of Rabindranath Tagore, the great poet and Devi's literary mentor. According to both authors' accounts, Devi's relationship with Tagore sometimes elicited the anger and jealousy of Alain/Mircea, who viewed Tagore as a rival for Maitreyi's love and devotion even though the poet was an old man and Devi a teenager. The intensity of the relationship infuriates Alain/Mircea, who perceives an erotic bond existing between mentor and mentored.[14] He fears that the creative and spiritual bonds between Tagore and Devi will displace him, leave him with no meaningful role in Devi's life. The interfering presence of Tagore also disrupts Eliade's attempt to script his love affair with Maitreyi Devi along the lines of an "East meets West" love story, with Eliade playing the role of the romantically adventurous Westerner and Devi playing the role of the erotic Other. There is no place in this script for the legendary Bengali poet, who has the respect of his whole nation and who honors Devi by celebrating her talent as a poet while she is still a teenager. Eliade struggles to reconcile Tagore's presence with the story he wishes to tell. Both Alain/Mircea's relationship with Devi's father and Maitreyi/Amrita's relationship with Tagore further complicate a scene already powerfully charged by conflicting racial, cultural, and gendered assumptions.

In *Bengal Nights* Alain suspects that Devi's father would not only accept his marriage proposal but, in fact, had been hoping that he would propose. These suspicions reach their climax when Eliade sees Maitreyi's mother "smiling benevolently" at the two of them when they have been flirting: "The idea that they were actually encouraging our sentimental games made me feel quite ill. It was as though a plot were being hatched against me: I was meant to fall in love with Maitreyi. That was why we were always left alone together, why the engineer was always retiring to his room to read a detective story, why none of the women who lived on that floor ever came to spy on us. I felt an intense desire to leave, then and there. Nothing revolts me so much as such machinations" (*BN*, 46). Indeed, *Bengal Nights* and *It Does Not Die* both confirm that Eliade had banked on the desirability of his whiteness and his Westernness. In *Bengal Nights* we even learn that he has seriously considered whether Devi's father is laying a trap and actively trying to snare him as a son-in-law. In *It Does Not Die* Devi conveys Mircea's shock when he is informed that her parents would never consent to such a marriage. When Mircea points out that her father has allowed the two of them to work together, Amrita responds that there is a big difference between two people working together and marrying. Eliade's assumptions about the East lead him to misperceive what Maitreyi's father is thinking. He believes that Eastern women are routinely cloistered, shielded from the eyes of men, kept in purdah. He takes the fact that he and Maitreyi have been allowed to converse as evidence that she has been offered to him. He therefore finds it almost impossible to accept Devi's claim that her father would object and accuses her of loving another—perhaps Tagore, whose handwriting she is imitating. Again Devi presents Eliade as illogical, unable to understand her love for Tagore on any level other than a romantic/sexual one.

Interestingly, in *It Does Not Die* this scene does not end with conclusions about the impossibility of cross-cultural communication but rather with the hope that she will be able to teach Eliade to understand her position. When he asks her to forget Tagore, she does not express anger, instead looking forward to the day when he will be able to understand the special nature of her love for Tagore and what the latter means to the Bengali people (*IDND*, 84–85). In so doing, she suggests that cross-cultural communication is possible.

Taken as a whole, the text of *It Does Not Die* is a remarkable gesture of reconciliation and forgiveness. Rather than transforming Eliade into an object of ridicule for his vanity or his limited understanding, Devi struggles to find a position that elucidates her motives and preserves her dignity and individuality without making a mockery of Eliade's claim that theirs was a passionate—and rare—kind of love and spiritual

understanding. Her narrative strategy is ultimately generous: she elects
to stay true to the spirit of Eliade's tale of joyously discovering a soul
mate even while she debunks the orientalist excesses of his representations and presents her competing viewpoint. While Devi is most certainly challenging the authority of Eliade's text, she combines strategies
of contradiction and correction with those of integration, fusion, and
complementarity.

Perhaps the most compelling instance of integration is the conclusion
to this narrative. Devi could easily have struck a devastating blow here,
as Eliade did in his conclusion. Hers includes a confrontation scene concerning the salacious falsehoods in his novel. This scene gave her a
golden opportunity to make Eliade seem like a pervert, a willful liar, a
profiteering Westerner capable of writing anything to make money—in
short, a totally unattractive character. While Devi exercises her prerog-
ative to have the last word in this debate and has Eliade acknowledge
that his version of the story was untrue, she does not present him as contemptible, instead resuscitating Eliade the man while scolding Eliade the
author of *Bengal Nights*. This is more than Eliade did for Maitreyi Devi.
In the concluding chapters of his novel, he represents himself as initially
despondent and near suicidal when he is kicked out of the "Sen" household, only later coming to terms somewhat with his situation. He later
learns that Maitreyi has "given herself to the fruit seller" (*BN*, 175), apparently in an attempt to force her parents to let her go to Alain/Eliade,
and is now having a baby out of wedlock. Though he ends the novel by
speculating as to what he could have done differently—including the
classic tragic lover's line: "I would like to be able to look Maitreyi in the
eyes" (*BN*, 176)—this ending is decidedly unflattering to Devi, suggesting
that she is obsessive, irrational, and sexually loose.

Devi's narrative is far more generous to Eliade. Encountering him
again in his office at the university more than forty years after their last
meeting, she is at first disappointed by him and his inability even to look
her in the eyes (*IDND*, 253). He is totally unable to imagine what good it
could do for the two of them to be reunited since they have each married other people. It is at this point that Amrita/Devi grows angry with
him, arguing that it is absurd to see love as an object, or as an exclusive
property that is given by one person to another. She instead suggests
that when people love, the love illuminates the whole world (*IDND*,
253–54). Though Devi does allow herself to aim one piercing barb at the
great scholar Eliade when she accuses him of having read much without

acquiring wisdom, her rhetoric is neither vengeful nor contemptuous, but rather conciliatory, persuasive, and philosophical. Amrita/Devi is less interested in reprimanding Mircea for having ruined her reputation than in reasoning with him and sharing her insights about what their love meant and still means. Eliade admires her for her bravery and her ability to tell the truth. She credits Gandhi and his *Experiment with Truth* with giving her the strength to be honest about her life. This is Devi's way of attempting to match and counter the plausibility that Eliade's narrative seeks when it draws on preestablished orientalist tropes. By invoking the name of Gandhi and establishing him as a model of truth-telling, Devi gives her narrative a powerful countermanding claim to the truth.

Only after clarifying her position concerning their love relationship does Amrita/Devi confront Mircea about the way he represented her in his book. He defends himself by claiming that he wished to portray her like a Hindu goddess, like Kali (*IDND*, 255). Saying that he wanted to transform her into "a mysterious being, a goddess," Mircea admits that he is participating in orientalist discourse. Amrita/Devi forces Mircea to confront the fact that his love for her and his depiction of her have been grossly distorted as a result of his love affair with this mythology about Eastern womanhood.

Despite her anger over the "nightmare" he has created through his text, Amrita/Devi pities Mircea. Devi portrays Eliade as a suffering soul unable to come to terms with the truth. He appears to be a broken man who has killed off a part of himself—the sensitive side that played music and experienced passionate love—in order to continue to survive in his post-Maitreyi life. He has sublimated his passion for her and channeled it into scholarship for so long that he is now unable to cope with the real, feeling comfortable only in the world of scholarly mythologies. In a beautiful conciliatory passage Maitreyi attempts to reawaken him, to teach him that what has passed since their time together does not matter, that all that matters is an honest recognition of what the two of them shared and continue to share. Rather than ending her story on a note of anger or vengeance, including a defense of her honor or a final attack upon Eliade and his arrogant and egotistical misrepresentation of their love, Devi elects what is in essence a romance-story ending. *It Does Not Die* basically presents us with a more pragmatic *Romeo and Juliet:* instead of committing suicide when life's circumstances dictate that they cannot remain together, they live out reasonably satisfying lives with other

REBECCA CARPENTER

mates, still relishing a love that will not die and looking forward to being reunited after death.

Some postcolonial readers might prefer to see Devi's text end with more ire and less forgiveness, more contempt for and castigation of Eliade for his blind reproduction of orientalist mythologies and less of an effort to resuscitate and preserve the core elements of his romance story. However, Devi's rhetorical and narrative strategies permit her to explore and examine the racial, imperialist, and gendered assumptions that shape Eliade's text—to reveal how thoroughly it is permeated by orientalist mythologies—without requiring her to reject the possibility of intercultural dialogue. While refuting Eliade's arrogant assertion of authority and his translation of their shared history with Maitreyi into a stereotypical oriental tale of mystery and seduction, Devi makes it clear that she does not regret the love they share, that she wields her pen and reveals her heart without fear. By courageously and magnanimously choosing to represent her version of events without destroying the spirit behind Eliade's version, Devi makes of this pair of texts something that neither story could have been independently. She creates a conversation that never completely ends and is never fully resolved yet certainly "does not die."

Notes

1. See Kamani, "A Terrible Hurt: The Untold Story Behind the Publishing of Maitreyi Devi."

2. Koestenbaum, *Double Talk: The Erotics of Male Literary Collaboration*, 3, 4.

3. This pertinent background information is supplied by Kamani. Strangely, the University of Chicago Press's edition of Eliade's *Bengal Nights* only refers to an earlier French translation and a 1987 film version. Subsequent references appear parenthetically in the text as *BN*.

4. Kamani. For an overview of these critical responses, see Kamani, para. 19.

5. Kamani offers a different point of view, arguing that although the University of Chicago Press has slickly decided to market the two books together, *It Does Not Die* was meant to stand on its own—indeed, stood on its own in India for many years, becoming an instant best-seller in a country where at best only a handful of copies of Eliade's text would have been available. While I agree with Kamani that the press should have said more in the biographical sketch

about the success of Devi's romance, it is obvious that while Devi's text can stand on its own, it was written very much in response to Eliade's text. In the opening pages of her narrative, Devi vents her anger when the Westerner Sergui claims that he knows all about her and her romance with Mircea from his book. The latter, and the "nightmare" that Amrita claims it created for her, are a constant theme in *It Does Not Die*. Subsequent references appear parenthetically in the text as *IDND*.

6. Said, *Orientalism*, 1–2.

7. Lata Mani has noted a similar kind of moral outrage surrounding the issue of *sati* in India, arguing that it was used to advance and solidify Western imperialism; see "Contentious Traditions: The Debate on *Sati* in Colonial India."

8. Ahmed, "Western Ethnocentrism and Perceptions of the Harem," 523–25.

9. Grewal, *Home and Harem: Nation, Gender, Empire, and the Cultures of Travel*, 50.

10. Mani's work on Western representations of *sati* and Jenny Sharpe's argument about how rape and the threat to white womanhood were employed to justify repressive measures during moments of crisis under imperial rule further support this premise. See Sharpe, *Allegories of Empire: The Figure of Woman in the Colonial Text*.

11. See, e.g., McClintock, *Imperial Leather: Race, Gender and Sexuality in the Colonial Contest*, 24–25.

12. Cheng, *Joyce, Race, and Empire*, 77–79.

13. For more on the silencing of female characters in colonial fictions and its implications, see Busia, "Silencing Sycorax: On African Colonial Discourse and the Unvoiced Female."

14. For more on the relationships between parenthood, mentorship, eros, and sexual desire, see Simmons, *Erotic Reckonings: Mastery and Apprenticeship in the Work of Poets and Lovers*, 2.

"Your Sentence Was Mine Too"

Reading *Sylvia Plath* in *Ted Hughes's* Birthday Letters

SARAH CHURCHWELL

> A secret! A secret!
> How superior.
> You are blue and huge, a traffic policeman,
> Holding up one palm—. . .
>
> You stumble out,
>
> Dwarf baby,
> The knife in your back.
> "I feel weak."
> The secret is out
>
> Sylvia Plath, "A Secret" (1962)

The sudden publication of Ted Hughes's *Birthday Letters* in February 1998 made headlines on both sides of the Atlantic. This fact was no sooner noted than it was assimilated by the media back into the reception of the poems. Most considerations of *Birthday Letters* opened just as I began mine, namely, by registering the singularity of a collection of poems ever becoming front-page news in the first place. The media thus helped make the collection famous, remarked upon its fame with surprise, and reincorporated that surprising fame into its coverage. In this essay I want to argue that this feedback loop of writing, reading, and reception is the same one that produced *Birthday Letters* itself. Although it has consistently been represented in the popular press as a collection of "secret" poems that "directly" reveal Hughes's "private" memories of his life with Sylvia Plath—to whom he was married and from whom he was estranged when she killed herself in February 1963—*Birthday Letters* can also be read as a public response to disputes over the politics of publication, representation, and literary authority.[1] Ghosts of many other texts haunt *Birthday Letters*, which is not simply a "direct, private, inner" presentation of Hughes's memories of Plath but also a response to the problems of publication.

Birthday Letters was sold as Hughes's "unknown side" of a thirty-five-year battle of the sexes.[2] While it is certainly Hughes's only published chronicle of his marriage to Plath, *Birthday Letters* is also a citational, intertextual account that is ambivalent about its own status as a text. Kaleidoscopically reassembling particularly fraught moments in a long public controversy, *Birthday Letters* responds to many audiences: to Plath and to a shifting public that fought battles in and over her name for more than thirty-five years. Equivocal moves between revelation and concealment characterize this best-selling volume of poetry, which was always flanked by the words "secret," "private," and "direct" in a media that tirelessly mediated between it and its audience. *Birthday Letters*, too, can be read as a mediation, a collection that couples the poetic voices of Sylvia Plath and Ted Hughes. Less biography than biographical criticism, *Birthday Letters* entangles the woman and her work so that reading Plath is inextricably bound up with remembering her in *Birthday Letters*. Hughes plays on the idea of *revision* throughout the collection in order to read, remember, and correct Sylvia Plath.

In this essay I will sketch some of Hughes's "re-visionary" strategies in melding his words with Plath's, focusing in particular on the intricacies of his representation of her poem "Daddy." These necessarily brief readings are not meant to be conclusive but rather suggestive of a method of interpretation. Ultimately I want to propose that *Birthday Letters* is best understood as an "open secret," a volume hesitating uneasily between disclosure and encryption, unsettled by its inability to fix the boundaries between life and art.

Publishing Sylvia Plath

To begin with, it is necessary to recall some of the more familiar aspects of the controversies surrounding Plath and Hughes. In doing so, I do not wish to reconstitute what has been reductively misrepresented as a two-sided argument but rather to reconsider its stakes. Though admittedly selective, these examples culled from an immense history of dispute provide *Birthday Letters* not only with its themes but also with its very language; they are the conversation from which *Birthday Letters* is, so to speak, sampling. The more a given incident was rehearsed in competing accounts, the more it accrued sufficient citational intensity to warrant public response from Hughes.[3] Thus if readers familiar with Plath's reception encounter here some familiar, even stock, examples, that is precisely the point.

I opened this essay with an epigraph from Plath's poem "A Secret"[4] because it suggests, in condensed form, much of the strife, both public and private, to which *Birthday Letters* responds. Like most of the poems Plath intended for the collection she would entitle *Ariel*, "A Secret" was written in the fall of 1962, when she and Ted Hughes were separating as a result of his affair with Assia Gutman Wevill. It was composed the day after Plath finished "Wintering," the poem with which she would decide to close *Ariel*, and the day before Hughes moved out of Court Green, their home in Devon. That same day Sylvia Plath wrote "The Applicant," a biting satire of marriage, and the following day produced what would become probably her most famous poem, "Daddy."

"Wintering," "The Applicant," and "Daddy" were all published relatively quickly after Plath's death, and all have received substantial critical attention. But "A Secret," aptly enough, would be one of the last of Plath's poems to be published, despite her intention to include it in *Ariel*. "A Secret" was, so to speak, kept secret by Hughes, who became Plath's literary heir and executor when she died intestate. It would not be published by a mainstream press until *The Collected Poems* appeared in 1981, nearly twenty years after it was composed, although in 1973 Hughes included it in *Pursuit*, an expensive limited edition (the limited edition itself could be seen as a kind of open secret, poised on the brink between public and private, silence and circulation). Furthermore, the poem is almost never discussed in detail in Plath criticism.[5] "A Secret," which is about the politics of betrayal, mocks the imaginary power with which some people imbue secrecy ("A secret! A secret! / How superior"), which is the Damoclean sword of potential exposure; the poem almost certainly derives directly from Hughes's affair with Wevill. Even within such a biographical context, however, "A Secret" remains one of Plath's more cryptic poems, finding its own "superiority" in the virtuosity of its rapid shifts among metaphors (one of Plath's most characteristic techniques). "A Secret" is implicitly about revealing secrets, about publishing them: the eponymous secret, by its very nature, seeks disclosure ("'But it wants to get out! / Look, look!' . . . My god, there goes the stopper!"). Although the secret is troped as treachery ("the knife in the back"), the poem is unclear about whether it is betrayer or betrayed. Such labile boundaries between assailant and victim, strength and weakness, suppression and exposure characterize not only much of Plath's late poetry but also the disputes surrounding Plath and Hughes, which converge on the theme of betrayal but differ over who betrayed whom.

The story of Sylvia Plath and Ted Hughes is unique in polarizing readers across both sexual and textual lines.[6] From the beginning, many Plath critics were suspicious of the way details of her private life seemed to affect considerations of her art. Hugh Kenner, an admirer of Plath's early poetry, saw in the late poems only a vulgar spectacle affording "Guignol fascination, like executions." He admonished that "such spectacles gather crowds and win plaudits for 'honesty' from critics who should know better. . . . The death poems—say a third of *Ariel*—are bad for anyone's soul. They give a look of literary respectability to voyeurist passions." Paul West went further, asking, "Had Sylvia Plath been ugly, and not died in so deliberate a manner, I wonder if she would have the standing she has."[7] The question for many readers is whether Plath's poetic authority is merited, or derived illegitimately on the basis of details from her personal life. Plath's authority—both authorship and power—hovers precariously between public and private, with many public accounts seeking to undermine her cultural status by locating it in the private, personal, feminine, and trivialized realms of her suicide, her looks, and her domestic drama.

But it is not only Plath's relationship to the private sphere that is vexed; the relationship of her writing to the public arena is even more complicated (as "A Secret" exemplifies). The conventional gendering of "publication" as a masculinized, active statement antipathetic to the feminized silence of the "private" sphere falters under the complexity of Plath's publications. Nor can biographical criticism of Plath be summarily dismissed as fallacious. The publication of Plath's poetry is intimately—and messily—bound up with the details of her private life, for the man who was at the very least the occasion for (if not reducible to the subject of) much of her writing was the man who also edited and published it after her death. The only volume published in Plath's name during her life was *The Colossus*, her first collection of poetry. *Winter Trees* and *Crossing the Water* were both posthumous collections, "arbitrarily" selected by Hughes and misleadingly described.[8] Plath published *The Bell Jar* pseudonymously in Britain to protect the feelings of her family. However, Hughes published it in the United States in 1971 under Plath's real name.[9] In 1975 Plath's *Letters Home: Correspondence, 1950–1963* appeared, officially edited by Aurelia Plath, Sylvia Plath's mother, but in actual fact edited at least three times since material was excised by Mrs. Plath, by Hughes, and by Harper & Row, the book's publisher. In 1977 Hughes published *Johnny Panic and the Bible of Dreams and Other Prose Writings* by Sylvia Plath, another arbitrary collection of published and unpublished stories, essays, and "excerpts" from her working notes.[10] In 1981 Hughes published the long-delayed *Collected Poems of Sylvia Plath*, but as Jacqueline Rose and others have argued, the editing of this collection also remains problematic, for it dismisses everything written before Plath met Hughes as "Juvenilia" and its concordances to "Plath's" earlier publications are confusing and misleading; it also surreptitiously eliminates some of her early poems. The following year Hughes published the heavily edited *The Journals of Sylvia Plath* in the United States.[11] In the original foreword (as well as in a revised version published as a separate article in *Grand Street*) Hughes made the (to many incredible) revelation that he had destroyed Plath's last volume of journals, that she had kept until her death, and that the next to last volume "had been lost."[12] Finally, one should note that all of these collected editions—letters, prose pieces, journals, and poems—were framed by introductions, all of which, with the exception of *Letters Home*, were written by Hughes. Thus, even lesser-known Plath texts were always already mediated, in their public form, by Ted Hughes.

The best-known Plath text, *Ariel*, is the one with the most complicated history, and it is often the controversies surrounding this collection that, unsurprisingly, reappear in *Birthday Letters*. When Plath died in 1963, she left behind the manuscript of a poetry collection entitled *Ariel*, which she had carefully arranged so that the first word of the collection was "love" and the last "spring." The latest poem Plath included was "Death & Co.," composed on November 11, 1962. Although she continued composing poems and seeking publication for most of them, she excluded these later poems from *Ariel*. In 1965 Hughes published a collection called *Ariel*, by Sylvia Plath, but as Marjorie Perloff has argued, he made several major changes to the collection. Hughes included fourteen (mostly later) poems Plath had excluded, cut out twelve poems she had included, and reorganized the whole.[13] The effect was twofold. First, it changed the volume's emphasis from rebirth and regeneration (Plath's ends with the rising of the bees at the close of "Wintering," who "taste the spring") to suicide (Hughes's ends with "Edge" and "Words").

Second, it also excluded many of the poems that Hughes later claimed were "aimed too nakedly," which is to say biographically.[14] Thus, as Perloff has argued, there are two *Ariels*—Plath's and Hughes's—and it is Hughes's that was published and continues to circulate.

Hughes was subsequently charged with "silencing Plath" (although he was also the person who published her writing), an accusation that is closely linked to other concomitant charges of censorship. Not only were some of Plath's poems withheld from publication, but critics and biographers found that what they were permitted to say was also controlled by the agent of the Plath estate, who for many years was Olwyn Hughes, Ted's sister. Unfortunately, Olwyn made little secret of her personal dislike of Plath.[15] Frequently permission to quote from Plath's poetry was withheld when "the Estate" did not agree with the point of view being expressed. This included not just biographers but journalists, critics, and scholars, who argued that copyright control was being abused as a tool of censorship.[16]

Hughes's reordering, editing, and control of virtually all of Plath's published writing renders questionable any claims that her poetry, journals, or letters tell her "version" of their story as she saw it or chose to make it public. When *Birthday Letters* is publicized as Hughes's long-withheld, answering "version" of their story, the implication that he had until then been the passive victim of Plath's prior "version" is equally dubious.[17] None of Plath's writing, with the exception of the "lost" and unfinished novel manuscript *Double Exposure,* proclaims itself as her "story" of her life with Hughes, and even *Double Exposure* was, she said, only semiautobiographical. In her poems Plath writes of isolated, fragmentary instances that are recognizably drawn from incidents in her life with Hughes, but that can easily be read figuratively in ways that transcend the personal (indeed, in the absence of biographical information they can *only* be read figuratively). Nowhere does she write what she declares a narrative of autobiographical poetry in the way Hughes does in *Birthday Letters.* Whereas *Birthday Letters* relies on a strong teleological narrative that emphasizes chronology, temporality, and memory—in other words, seeking temporal priority and closure—Plath did not choose to constitute such a chronicle in her late poems.

Thus, if Plath's position in the public sphere cannot be separated from sexual politics, neither can it be disentangled from what one might call the politics of publication. Many readers have interpreted Plath's "publication" of her "private" rage as an embryonic feminism, an active

repudiation of the private-as-domestic ("writing like mad . . . as if domesticity had choked me," as she famously wrote in a letter).[18] However, as we have seen, Hughes helped put her writings in the public
sphere, and her place there remains vexed for readers who see it as resulting from her "private" suicide rather than from the force of her published words. Nor are Plath's publications in any simple or easy sense
triumphant evidence that her "voice" has been heard. Hughes is everywhere implicated in the history of her poems, at once their (apparent)
subject, editor, publisher, and interpreter.

The boundary between Plath and Hughes continues to be erased in
their public, published texts, as well as in the public disputes about those
texts, which themselves blur the distinctions among author, text, and
reader. For example, in 1971 Hughes wrote an essay entitled "Publishing Sylvia Plath," whose title does not distinguish the woman from the
work. However, the article itself distinguishes among various audiences
while sweepingly condemning their supposedly equivalent demands for
an "anatomy of the birth of the poetry; and . . . her blood, hair, touch,
smell, and a front seat in the kitchen where she died." Hughes declares
that "the scholars may well inherit what they want, some day, and there
are journalists supplying the other audience right now. But neither audience makes me feel she owes them anything" (*WP*, 164). Hughes's
words, ostensibly uttered in defense of Plath, here camouflage a defense
of himself. Plath's audience—always posthumous—from whom Hughes
is defending "her," were not claiming that she owed them something
but rather that he did. Furthermore, they were arguing that Hughes
owed them—Plath's audience—because he owed her. Whereas some
argued that he owed her because of his public (textual) relationship to
her, others attributed the debt to his private (sexual) relationship. Many
in Plath's audience did collapse the difference between the two, and
then further collapsed the difference between themselves and Plath, as if
a debt were owed them as Plath's proxy. Metaphors of obligation—
both moral and economic—permeate the history, as implicit contracts
between reader and writer, husband and wife, executor and deceased
can be interchanged in a long chain of displacement. Hughes elides his
own role in admitting the public into the story; he also implicitly denies
the ways in which he, too, is a member of Plath's "public," insofar as he
is part of her audience.

Instead, he consistently figured himself as fact checker, arbiter of
truth, and coauthor. Janet Malcolm quotes Hughes as complaining in a

letter that what biographers failed to realize was "that the most interesting & dramatic part of S.P.'s life is only 1/2 S.P.—the other 1/2 is *me*.
They can caricature & remake S.P. in the image of their foolish fantasies, & get away with it—and assume, in their brainless way, that it's
perfectly O.K. to give me the same treatment. Apparently forgetting
that I'm still here, to check." And in another letter, also quoted by Malcolm, he attacked both the accuracy and the motives of A. Alvarez's
memoir of Plath on the grounds that Alvarez hadn't collaborated on it
with Hughes: "If your intentions had been documentary style, if your
respect had been for what really happened, and the way things really
went, you would have asked me to be co-author."[19] What Hughes objected to, more often than not, were interpretations, warning biographers "to avoid interpreting my feelings and actions for me, and to be-
ware how they interpreted Sylvia's."[20] Biographers were, of course, not
interpreting his feelings and actions for Hughes but for the public—
accounts that Hughes then read, since he was, after all, also part of the
public. He objected, in other words, to becoming an unwilling audience
to his "own story"—to becoming reader rather than author.

Hughes maintained that his right to a monopoly over the "truth"
about Plath's life was based on his having married her. This equation
of marriage with consummate knowledge is, to say the least, arguable.
(Plath, for one, wrote letters around the time of the breakup of her
marriage in which she pointed to the difference between who she had
thought Hughes was and who she felt he turned out to be.) In his foreword to the 1982 edited *Journals*, Hughes uses his marriage to the woman
metonymically to cement his authoritative interpretation of the poetry,
declaring that Plath found her "voice" when the "real poet" became the
same as the woman he married: "Her real self had showed itself in her
writing, just for a moment, three years earlier, and when I heard it—the
self I had married, after all, and lived with and knew well—in that brief
moment, three lines recited as she went out through a doorway, I knew
that what I had always felt must happen had now begun to happen, that
her real self, being the real poet, would now speak for itself."[21] The real
self, the real poet, and the woman he married are all the same. Having
been unfairly accused of neglecting Plath's headstone, in 1989 Hughes
complained in an oft-quoted letter to *The Guardian* that he had been "accused of trying to suppress Free Speech" every time he attempted to
"correct some fantasy" about Plath.[22] He further objected to the fact
that where his "correction" was "accepted, it rarely displaced a fantasy.

More often, it was added to the repertoire, as a variant hypothesis. . . . The truth simply tends to produce more lies."[23] In trying to partition public accounts neatly into "truth" and "lies," Hughes is objecting to the fact that there *is* a repertoire, that there are other versions, indeed, that the story keeps reproducing itself, so that (his) "truth" can produce (others') "lies."

Even if one were to translate these divisive (and reductive) terms and argue that what Hughes really objected to was the way his account of his private experience could produce alternative public accounts, he was still protesting against the process of reception itself, against the feedback loop in which he was participating. In another oft-quoted letter cited by Malcolm, he wrote of his "simple wish to recapture for myself, if I can, the privacy of my own feelings and conclusions about Sylvia, and to remove the contamination of everyone else's." Representation becomes a virus: readers and stories are "contaminated" by what is implicitly promiscuous intertextuality, a "contagious," messy disorder. The existence of uncontrollable other versions infects an implicitly prelapsarian private experience before the fall into publicity occasioned by Plath's original sin of misrepresentation. But where Olwyn Hughes would blame Plath as the authorial source of what she calls a "contagion" of literary scurrilousness,[24] Ted Hughes would blame academics as readers, who have "indoctrinated" students with "tainted"—because fallacious—ideas about Plath.[25] The problem was that Hughes wanted his private experience to be acknowledged and authorized by readers without being "infected" by their mistaken interpretations. However, as soon as private experience is admitted into the public sphere, it is subject to the forces of reception and interpretation.

Over the years this complex of issues about gender and power, authority and reception, privacy and publication, writing and reading has been reduced and fixed by the popular press into a battle between Ted Hughes and "the feminists." *Birthday Letters* emerged as always already flanked by caricatures of this contest and is only fully intelligible when contextualized within a larger battle over the sovereignty of the literary patriarch. The "calumny," "vilification," "reviling," and "abuse" offered by feminists appeared in nearly all of the popular press's reportage concerning *Birthday Letters,* an aggressive "calumny" opposed to the myth of Hughes's noble "silence."[26] However, it needs to be remembered that the distinguished career Hughes mounted while supposedly maintaining his silence was precisely that of a public voice. The argument has been inverted. Feminists' earlier accusations that Hughes silenced Plath have undergone a complete transformation—thanks to Malcolm's reading of Plath as the "silent woman" whose deathly silence is her ultimate weapon—into a reading of all feminists as aggressive, masculinized speakers who attack the nobly silent Hughes. More remarkable than the low repute in which the popular press holds feminism is the way in which an intensely public (and published) male poet—the poet laureate of Great Britain—is mythologized as victimized and "silent" in a powerfully politicized version of the reciprocal charges in Plath's and Hughes's poetry. Silence becomes a triumphal strategy in a battle over publication. Feminists are written (off) as hysterically screaming, a transposition of earlier accusations about Plath's "shrill" hysteria, the background noise against which Hughes, ironically, can be (not) heard as the heroically feminized suffering, silent man.[27] Hughes's "silence" paved the way for the suddenly vocal *Birthday Letters*, which the *New York Times* declared a "definitive and authoritative statement."[28] The popular press does not seem to find the authority of this definitive "statement" at odds with the prior authority of Hughes's definitive "silence." Indeed, that silence was also interpreted as a definitive and authoritative statement. That is, silence functions on a sliding scale in this story, its weight depending upon an acknowledgment by its audience that effectively renders it not silent but heard.

(Re-)Reading Sylvia Plath

While its reception reconstituted the "privacy" of this collection in order to sell it as a volume that broke secrets, only a few reviewers noted that although the existence of the book itself might have been a "revelation," its narrative told us little we didn't already know.[29] In fact, not much about *Birthday Letters* is private. These are voluntarily published poems by a poet laureate (*the* public poet of Great Britain) reacting as much to the storm of publicity surrounding Plath as to Plath herself. If what Hughes wanted was to "remove the contamination of everyone else's" ideas about Plath, *Birthday Letters* demonstrates the impossibility of "removing" the infection of intertextuality that was caught through reading and publication.

Hughes's liminal position between author and reader, mediating text and interpretation, standing between Plath and her audience (like her "blue and huge . . . traffic policeman / Holding up one palm"), remains at issue throughout *Birthday Letters*, which continually stages scenes of reading that show the way her "book [was] becoming a map" for his interpretations.[30] Plath's death risks rendering Hughes as just another reader of her story, for *Birthday Letters* locates Plath's personal truths not in Hughes's memories but in the "secrets" and "truths" he later discovered in her journals (and, less frequently, in *The Bell Jar*). For the British Hughes "revision" means studying as well as editing: to revise Plath means simultaneously to reread her and to re-write her. In *Birthday Letters* Hughes revises his own prior experiences, "re-visioning" it all again through the prism of later information. "Now, I see, I saw, sitting, the lonely / Girl who was going to die" (*BL*, 68). Most of this revisionary information is gleaned from her journals. For example, in "Your Paris" Hughes implicitly uses his later reading of Plath's journals to locate her "actual" experience and viewpoint, by means of which he can correct his own memories:

> Your practised lips
> Translated the spasms to what you excused
> As your gushy burblings—which I decoded
> Into a language, utterly new to me
> With conjectural, hopelessly wrong meanings—
> You gave me no hint how, at every corner,
> My fingers linked in yours, you expected
> The final face-to-face revelation
> To grab your whole body.
>
> (*BL*, 37–38)

Having read her journals, Hughes no longer "decodes" her words into "hopelessly wrong meanings"—implicitly the journals have offered the truth of what Plath was thinking. In *Birthday Letters* Hughes now rereads his own experience in light of Plath's texts; he also revises her poems in light of her (implicitly "truer") prose.

The "re-vision" that Hughes undertakes of Plath's words and his memories means that he tropes memory in visual terms as snapshots, photographs, pictures, seeing, and re-seeing ("now, I see, I saw"). But these "pictures" also undermine truth and accuracy with doubts about representation, interpretation, and mediation. Thus, "Fulbright Scholars," the very first poem of *Birthday Letters*, was often described in reviews as a memory of "the day Hughes first caught sight of Plath's picture," or, slightly less inaccurately, as "the first time he became aware of Plath in a photograph he saw."[31] But the poem actually depicts the speaker remembering himself, at twenty-five, seeing a photograph in a newspaper in which, he now knows, Plath's face *might* have appeared. Like most of the memories in *Birthday Letters*, it is a memory laden with doubts, retrospectively undermined by questions later knowledge would prompt; in other words, it is not a direct recollection. "Were you among them?" he asks. He remembers the photograph and what he thought but not whether she was there: "I remember that thought. Not / Your face," adding, "Maybe I noticed you." From its opening page, that is, *Birthday Letters* responds not to a first memory of Plath but to a retroactively imagined, publicly mediated, possible viewing of her picture: it is a memory of perhaps forgetting a published representation. "Then I forgot," he says. "Yet I remember / The picture" (*BL*, 3). This confusion of memory over the difference between representation and reality will characterize many of the poems in the collection, which move uneasily between remembering and forgetting, seeking a direct access they cannot recreate. Thus, Hughes's actual first memory of Plath is also likened to a photograph: "First sight. First snapshot isolated / Unalterable, stilled in the camera's glare" (*BL*, 15). Memory is troped as a "snapshot" throughout the poems, a trite association complicated by Hughes's further association of these pictures with stillness, snares, and death: "Remembering it, I see it all in a bubble," Hughes writes. "A rainy wedding picture / On a foreign grave" (*BL*, 123).

Birthday Letters represents the "truth" about Sylvia Plath in terms of direct speech and first readings. (The difference between speech and writing may be the real Derridean ghost of *Birthday Letters*.) In Hughes's rendering, Plath's words sometimes intervene between him and "direct, private, inner" access to her, whereas at other times they provide precisely that direct, private, inner truth. In several poems Hughes remembers reading Plath's journals following her death. In "18 Rugby Street" he discovers from the journal the "real" narrative she was constructing, a story he now knows is "the story of [her] torture" (*BL*, 21–22). Similarly, in "Visit" Hughes describes what it was like to "meet on a page" for the first time her reactions to him when they first met: "Suddenly I read all this— / Your actual words" (*BL*, 8). The image suggests direct access to Plath, rediscovering her "actual words," and yet he is reading them in her journals, like the rest of Plath's audience, having been rendered only another reader (albeit a privileged, "original" reader). Reading is imagined as an act of introduction: he "meets" Plath's words on the page. Hughes opposes looking forward—under the illusion that he might "meet your voice / With all its urgent future"—to the need to "look back / At the book of printed words" to rediscover the past (*BL*, 9). The inadequacy of both memory and writing is clear: the "book of printed words" not only alters memory but seems proleptically to substitute the published ("printed") journals for Plath's handwritten journals, which are what Hughes remembers himself reading. This moment of direct access to "actual words" is a fantasy, as the poem acknowledges. He is discovering her through printed words, but as the poem ends she is "ten years dead. It is only a story. / Your story. My story."

Although some readers objected to this line's equation of their two stories, his story *is* the same as her story, according to his interpretation. Reviewers focused a great deal of attention on the narrative of *Birthday Letters*, which repetitively insists that Plath died in order to "rejoin" her father, who died as a result of untreated diabetes when she was eight. Readers argued over the ethics of this narrative (was it an evasion of responsibility?) and over its plausibility (was this really the reason she died?).[32] But no one asked what seems a begged question: If *Birthday Letters* is Hughes's long-delayed "version," the counter to Plath's previous version, why does "Hughes's" story retell Sylvia Plath's most famous poem? In *Birthday Letters* Hughes lifts the plot of Plath's poem "Daddy" and offers it as the "true story" of her death. Critics like James Fenton argued for the virtue of what I call the "'Daddy' plot," for *Birthday Letters* as family romance, because, they said, it was Plath's own view, and thus Hughes was doing her the honor of taking "her view of herself" seriously.[33] Fenton's explanation authorizes Hughes's poetic claim on the basis of Plath's prior interpretation, which, he argues, Hughes is simply ratifying. But Plath offered many other poetic versions of suicide; among dozens of Plath's poems that imagine self-destruction, only five are also elegies for her father ("Full Fathom Five," "Electra on Azalea Path," "The Colossus," "Little Fugue," and "Daddy"), and of those only "Daddy" and "Full Fathom Five" explicitly suggest that a suicide would reunite the speaker with her dead father. Furthermore, after Plath wrote "Daddy" on October 12, 1962, her father never figured in another poem.[34] The vast majority of Plath's supposedly "suicidal poems" imagine the death of the speaker without reference to any father at all.[35] Furthermore, as Fenton acknowledges, these kinds of "autobiographical" (literal) readings have been "the source of Hughes's misfortunes." If that is so, then Hughes also performs the kinds of readings that are the source of his own misfortunes. All of these arguments take the "Daddy" plot extremely literally, but when Plath worked out this construction in her journals, even she asked herself: "Is this a plausible interpretation?"[36] *Birthday Letters*, purportedly "Hughes's version," his side of the story, repeats her side of the story in order to revise it.[37]

"Daddy" is a poem in which the speaker identifies her husband with her father and angrily rejects both for betraying and abandoning her: "I knew what to do," the speaker tells "Daddy." "I made a model of you / A man in black with a meinkampf look // And a love of the rack and the screw. / And I said, I do, I do" (*CP*, 224). For almost forty years that "man in black" has been read reductively and literally as Ted Hughes. If the poet's husband and the speaker's husband are one and the same, then Hughes is the real-life villain in the tale, implicated in Plath's death. Whether "Daddy" really led Plath to kill herself, whether either Plath or Hughes—or both—really believed in the "Daddy" plot is, finally, a moot point. Given that *Birthday Letters* consistently responds to Plath's writing, and given its own overwhelmingly symbolic structure, one might well read Hughes's invocation of "Daddy" more figuratively.

The overwhelming presence of "Daddy" in *Birthday Letters* can also be read metatextually as Hughes's response to Plath's poem. In Hughes's poems "Daddy" functions as *both* (Plath's image of) Otto Plath and as her poem. The "Daddy" plot gives Hughes his own "model" for an erotics—and politics—of identification. Revealing a persistent anxiety over questions of originality and influence, *Birthday Letters* returns final consequence to the symbolic patriarch, upon whom Hughes blames Plath's suicide. In "accepting" what he writes as Plath's phantasmic identification of himself with her father, Hughes can identify, in a mediated way, with the symbolic authority of the father, but he can also distance himself from that father in order to displace blame onto him. Simultaneously, Hughes denies the *poem* final consequence, insisting upon its "erroneous" interpretations.

In Hughes's version of the "Daddy" plot, Plath ceases to be its author—one even willing to question the plausibility of the plot itself—instead becoming its subject and passive victim. In "The Shot" Hughes imagines Plath as "a high-velocity bullet" that killed "the elect / More or less . . . on impact." "You were undeflected," he writes. "You were gold-jacketed, solid silver / Nickel-tipped. Trajectory perfect," and then describes himself standing hapless in front of her "real target," "Your

Daddy, / The god with the smoking gun" (*BL*, 17). Returning to the secret cause of the dead father reveals a crisis in authority, a fight for the position of author of the dead female body and of the story it symbolizes. A particularly bitter irony seems to linger in the fact that even her suicide, that most solitary of acts, is not Plath's (to) own in Hughes's representation of her in *Birthday Letters*. I emphatically do not want to imply (idiotically) that Plath's suicide was or ought to be read as a triumphant feminist gesture. But Hughes transforms Plath from vengeful, triumphant author of a story—in which she knows "If I've killed one man / I've killed two"—into the mere bullet in her father's gun. If she is murderous, it is not her fault: Hughes leaves it to patriarchs to pull the trigger.

Given Plath's vilification of the "man in black" in "Daddy," and given Hughes's subsequent opposition to the poem's publication—he admitted that he "would have cut 'Daddy' [from *Ariel*] if I'd been in time (there are quite a few things more important than giving the world great poems" (*WP*, 167)—it seems even more noteworthy that *Birthday Letters* relies on "Daddy"'s plot. Hughes's interpretation accepts the poem's apparent association of himself with the man in black. Certainly any claim to maintain an absolute separation between the husband in the poem and the poet's husband must be considered a dubious one, as difficult for Hughes to maintain as for his audience. But, at the same time, when Hughes renders himself in *Birthday Letters* as the "he" in Plath's poetry, he traps himself in a double bind that makes him predominant in her story yet also the subject of her vilification. (This is the double logic of defamation, which says that one recognizably is and isn't the person being represented.)[38] In this collection Hughes seeks to revise his own public identity, which was erroneously defined in Plath's earlier representation of (what he interprets as) him. However, he must accept the terms set by her writing in order to do so.[39] Thus, in *Birthday Letters* Hughes must continually reconstitute the characterization of "himself" that he would dispute, mis-recognizing himself, so to speak, in Plath's representations.

In "Black Coat" Hughes negates Plath's identification of him with her father as an "error" that results from her pathology, error-as-disease, which is specifically an error in the gaze.[40] Hughes responds in "Black Coat" to Plath's poem "Man in Black," in which she writes to a "you" she watches emerging from the sea. Hughes masters this representation by reinscribing himself as author, not audience, writing a poem in which he watches Plath watching him. Hughes imagines that while watching him Plath was creating a "double image / [Her] eye's inbuilt double exposure / . . . the projection of [her] two-way heart's diplopic error" (*BL,* 103). Diplopia means double vision, a "disorder of the sight." Hughes imagines himself, being watched, standing like a "decoy" and a "target" beside the sea "[f]rom which [her] dead father had just crawled." At that moment, Hughes imagines, "I did not feel" when "[h]e slid into me." Hughes remembers and imagines what (he thinks) she must have seen at the time but he did not feel at the time.

Hughes literalizes her poem, remembering being there and then reinterpreting the scene according to the knowledge later afforded him by reading not her poem (which itself makes not a single mention of the "Daddy" figure) but rather her journal—and only selectively. In the journal Plath first describes the poem's occasion—the walk on the beach she and Hughes took together—without mentioning the poem. She describes their walk immediately after recounting a visit to her father's grave, yet she interprets neither scene. Five pages later she alludes to the poem she has since composed, calling it the "only 'love' poem in my book." She then writes, "must do justice to my father's grave," before musingly adding (following two paragraphs about her literary ambitions and anxieties), "the 'dead black' in my poem may be a transference from the visit to my father's grave."[41] This passing interpretation is one Hughes has elected to accept and reinforce (choosing not to interpret the poem alternatively as "the only 'love' poem" in *The Colossus*). He then blames Plath for what he construes as *her* erroneous vision, comparing her eye to a "paparazzo sniper" and proleptically imagining the fatal effect her famous "picture" of Hughes will have in the media. Thus, his memory of the scene is filtered through his interpretation of her poem's representation of him via his selective reading of her journal. Her double vision would seem the obverse of his re-vision.

By the end of "Black Coat," Hughes has declared Plath's viewpoint to be an "error," one of "double exposure." *Double Exposure* was the title of Plath's unfinished last novel, which Hughes said he lost. In an unpublished letter Plath described her last novel (at that time titled *Doubletake*) as a story structured around the idea that a "double take," a second look, is necessary to see a hidden truth. She said it was semiautobiographical, about a woman betrayed by a husband whom she had once idealized but who would turn out to be a cheat who abandoned her.[42] Plath had always been interested in the metaphor of the double: she wrote her undergraduate honor's thesis at Smith on the role of the double in

Dostoyevsky; *The Bell Jar* is constructed around a running pun on doubles and double standards; and *Double Exposure* was clearly arranged around a similar play on words about duplicity. What Plath imagined as a woman's critical reinterpretation of her life Hughes rewrites as a medicalized disorder of Plath's "double vision," her mistakenly blurred viewpoint. Hughes corrects Plath's description of "him" in *Double Exposure* as an adulterer and traitor to make that novel's portrait, by intertextual association, part of Plath's "two-way heart's diplopic error." Her error is excused as part of her "disorder," her "double vision," but the "view" (of Hughes) she presented in her poetry and in her last, lost novel is nonetheless erroneous.[43]

Hughes's "A Picture of Otto" begins with a rewritten line from "Daddy." Plath wrote: "You stand at the blackboard, Daddy, / In the picture I have of you." Hughes opens his poem by adding only the idea of failure to Plath's line: "You stand there at the blackboard: Lutheran / Minister *manqué*" (*BL*, 193). Whereas on the one hand Hughes's representation here literalizes Plath's, on the other hand it is a poem very much about the force of representation itself. Hughes repeatedly emphasizes that he is "inseparable" from Plath's depiction of both of them in "Daddy": "Your ghost inseparable from my shadow / As long as your daughter's words can stir a candle. / She could hardly tell us apart in the end." He moves from her "words" to her "self" without a pause: her poem, read in conjunction with her journals, is taken as evidence of what she really believed. Hughes writes that Plath's lingering words are what render him inseparable from her father, but ironically Hughes's words here do the same: "Inseparable here we must remain // Everything forgiven and in common." The fatalism of this statement mystifies Hughes's own agency in agreeing that they must both remain "here," inseparable on *his* page. But Hughes knows that what he is inseparable from is a "picture of Otto," a representation that appeared in another poem. Like "Daddy," the phrase "Picture of Otto" both refers to the poem itself and to the representation within the poem. Hughes's poem is a picture of a poem about a picture of a person; that is, Hughes's "Picture of Otto" interprets Plath's portrait in "Daddy" of a photograph of her father.

Representations themselves become culpable third parties, mediating between the "truth" of Hughes's and Plath's direct relationship. Indeed, triangles provide *Birthday Letters* with its geometry, for Hughes will consistently triangulate his relationship with Plath over a variously identified third party. The reiterated pivotal, figurative triangle of Hughes, Plath, and Daddy would seem to supplant the more literal and tragic erotic triangle of Hughes, Plath, and Wevill, which appears explicitly only in the poem "Dreamers." But there is another key triangle as well consisting of Hughes, Plath, and other readers that emerges in poems like "Caryatids (2)," "God Help the Wolf After Whom the Dogs Do Not Bark," "The Literary Life," and "The Dogs Are Eating Your Mother," to name just a few. Finally—and most ambivalently—there is a triangle composed of Hughes, Plath, and Plath's writing that recurs throughout the collection. The triangles in *Birthday Letters* suggest the "error" of introducing any mediating figure into their relationship, since that mediation will inevitably destroy them all. These mistaken triangles are all associated with Plath and her writing (bringing Daddy or the public into their lives) rather than with Hughes's more obvious—and more obviously destructive—triangle with Wevill.

Many of Hughes's poems use Plath's titles to revisit texts—not all of which are poems—in which she has been interpreted by other readers as having criticized "him." ("The 59th Bear," for example, is a Plath short story about a wife willing the death of her husband; this story is frequently interpreted as revealing Plath's repressed hostility toward Hughes.) In revising these texts, Hughes can simultaneously correct Plath and "her critics," many of whom criticized him. Plath's poem "The Rabbit Catcher" is an obvious example: Hughes fought a very public battle with Jacqueline Rose and other Plath critics over the poem's interpretation, and the "snares" from Plath's "Rabbit Catcher" recur throughout the poems in *Birthday Letters*, suggesting the traps her representations would set for Hughes.[44] However, some of the most interesting re-visions in *Birthday Letters* of Hughes's role in Plath's writing are more oblique, not overtly advertising themselves as responses to Plath but sampling and correcting her words nonetheless.[45] For example, if read biographically, Plath's poem "The Jailer" is, like "Daddy," one of the most vituperative of Plath's attacks against Hughes, accusing "him" of imprisoning, torturing, raping, murdering, and (unkindest cut of all) "forgetting" her. *Birthday Letters* replies to "The Jailer" by adopting and then transposing all of these images in different poems. In "The Blackbird" Hughes retaliates against Plath's accusations by writing himself back into "The Jailer" not as Plath's torturer but as her victim, similarly imprisoned and unable to imagine being free. Yet he also represents their relationship while commenting metatextually on the imprisonment of that very representation: "You were the jailer of your murderer— / Which imprisoned you. / And since I was your nurse and your protector / Your sentence was mine too" (*BL*, 162). The revising and revisioning that Hughes undertakes here depends upon misrecognizing himself in Plath's poem "The Jailer," just as he misrecognized himself as the "man in black." Revising Plath means that she is both right and wrong ("a pen already writing / Wrong is right, right wrong"). Thus, he inverts her judgment: he was both her prisoner and her "nurse" and "protector," roles that, like Hughes's ambiguous "silence," combine the feminine with the masculine to create a new locus of power and victimization. This ambiguous position is finally that of "coauthor": he may share her punishment, but he also writes her "sentences." By arguing within inverted terms throughout the poem, Hughes suggests that the inescapability of representation may be the real "prison" here, for he never gets out of the "sentence" of publication, of being part of her sentence.

Coda: Open Secrets

Birthday Letters won the Forward Poetry Prize in October 1998, just a few weeks before Ted Hughes would die of cancer. Because of his illness, Hughes could not attend the ceremony, but he wrote a letter to the judges thanking them for the prize, a letter widely quoted in the press. *Birthday Letters*, Hughes explained, "is a gathering of the occasions— written with no plan over about 25 years—in which I tried to open a direct, private, inner contact with my first wife . . . thinking mainly to evoke her presence to myself, and to feel her there listening. Except for a handful, I never thought of publishing these pieces until last year, when quite suddenly I realized I had to publish them, no matter what the consequences."[46] Hughes's description of his decision to publish these poems strikingly resembles what D. A. Miller has characterized as the logic of the "open secret." Hughes describes the poems as "direct, private, inner," implying that they are by definition never to be published—never, that is, until an unspecified moment when he "suddenly realized he had to" make them public. In retrospect the motive seems obvious: Hughes's knowledge that he was dying is the "secret" cause of his decision to publish and, implicitly, to vindicate or at least justify himself. However, the formulation of his letter is worth commenting on because it is the grammar of the volume itself: the grammar of the open secret.

For Miller the open secret inheres in the ambivalent relationship of the subject to the social (what in Hughes's case I have been calling the "public"). The open secret is expressed in "odd compromises between expression and repression," gestures toward secrets that will not be fully revealed. Miller describes the logic as follows: "I have had to intimate my secret, if only *not to tell it;* and conversely, in theatrically continuing to keep my secret, I have already rather given it away. But if I don't tell my secret, why can't I keep it better? And if I can't keep it better, why don't I just tell it?"[47] The open secret characterizes the fundamental mechanism of *Birthday Letters,* making moves between what (again following Miller) one can call allusion and elision. Hughes's description of his decision to publish negotiates between public and private in exactly this way, gesturing toward the centrality of his "sudden realization" that he "had" to publish, a motive to which he alludes and then elides.

One might also note the highly mediated nature of this explanation for Hughes's publication of *Birthday Letters.* It appeared as a letter that presumably would be quoted in the press. This letter was necessitated by Hughes's illness, but it is not the only time Hughes used a letter to discuss his attitudes toward writing about Plath. There has been some speculation as to why Hughes chose to entitle the book *Birthday Letters.* (Some assumed the poems were composed on Plath's birthdays over the years, but only "Freedom of Speech" marks its occasion as Plath's birthday.) It seems appropriate that they are letters, however, since letters were always Hughes's preferred mode for negotiating his ambivalent relationship with the public while objecting to others' writings about Plath's life. Hughes not only consistently "corrected" errors in letters to the British press but also allowed Janet Malcolm to quote from several of his letters in *The Silent Woman,* although he refused to be interviewed directly. Through the indirect mediation of Malcolm's book *about* biographers, Hughes maintained his right not to be "pricked and goaded into vomiting up details" of his life *to* biographers.[48] That Hughes consistently discussed the privacy of his feelings for Plath in letters seems apt since letters themselves ambivalently bridge the public and the private. Indeed, letters might be said to literalize the move from the private to the public, as they move from the sender "out" into the world. But they are also a "private" form, which may or may not be intended for publication. Finally, the poems in *Birthday Letters* seem to be "dead letters": letters that have not arrived and are left unread by their intended recipient.

In poems like "Freedom of Speech" and "Costly Speech" falling toward the end of *Birthday Letters* Hughes brings the mechanism of the open secret into the open, so to speak, by opposing speech to writing. "Costly Speech" repeatedly refers to a mysterious "it" that has been forbidden by Plath's words and by Hughes's "own airier words":

> . . . your own words
> Irrevocably given to your brother,
> Hostage guarantors,
> And my own airier words, conscripted, reporting for duty,
> Forbade it and forbade it.
>
> (*BL,* 170)

The poem will not say what crime "it" is, but "it" has something to do with "US Copyright Law," which her "dead fingers so deftly unpicked." Thus, the crime involves publication and presumably alludes to the defamation trial in which the film version of *The Bell Jar* embroiled Hughes. Not only will the crime go unnamed, but so will the crucial spoken "words / Irrevocably given" to her brother. They will be "costly" but never, ironically, published in the poem that will maintain their definitional status as speech, that which is not written.

Likewise, in "Brasilia," one of the poems that shares a title with a Plath poem, Hughes describes being "dragged into court," which he calls Plath's "arena," where she

> delivered
> The three sentences. Not a whisper
> In the hush.
> Your great love had spoken.
>
> (*BL,* 178)

These "three sentences" have the same consequences as "the most horrible crime," but what they expressed is also never revealed. Given the "court" setting, this would clearly seem to be another pun on prison "sentences," but this statement may also allude to and doubly encrypt the already oblique reference in Hughes's introduction to Plath's edited *Journals,* in which Hughes describes the emergence of Plath's "real" voice. Hughes, it will be remembered, proffers as "evidence" of the emergence of Plath's real self "three lines recited as she walked through the door," but he never relates what that real self said that was so revealing, so essential, merely gesturing toward the importance of a revelation whose content will be concealed. The tropes remained consistent: speech versus silence; real versus false; memory bleeding into inaccurate representation: "Your portraits, tearlessly, / Weep in the books" as "Brasilia" closes. But whether Plath is speaker or spoken still remains ambiguous. Are these tearlessly weeping textual portraits the ones she drew or portraits of her?

Direct speech and direct representation recede farther away as the volume draws to a close. The climactic moment of Plath's death is the most open secret of all: *Birthday Letters* never names it. Instead, the moment of Plath's suicide stretches across two poems, which become so cryptic as to be unintelligible to anyone unfamiliar with the facts of her life or with Plath's poetry. The first, "Night-Ride on Ariel," ends with allusions to Plath's last two poems, the famous "Edge" and the never discussed "Balloons," both of which were composed on February 5, 1963. (Since "Balloons" is about a baby boy popping a balloon and being left with a "red shred" in his "fist," and "Edge" is about a dead woman, it is always assumed that "Edge" was Plath's last poem, but this is an unverifiable—and problematic—assumption.) As "Night-Ride on Ariel" comes to a close, Hughes lifts Plath's phrase "crackling and dragging their blacks" from "Edge." He then ends the poem with an allusion to "Balloons," describing Plath left with a "shred of the exploded dawn / In your fist // That Monday." The reader can only infer Plath's death from extratextual (biographical) or intertextual knowledge that these allusions point to her last two poems. The next poem, "Telos," evades direct discussion of Plath's death by attributing it to her notorious ambition. It imagines Plath attempting to hide from "The Furies of Alpha" (the British equivalent of the American grade "A") by "hurdl[ing] every letter in the Alphabet / And hurling [her]self beyond Omega" only to fall "Into a glittering Universe of Alpha" (*BL*, 176–77). The poem here mimics the movement of the larger narrative, hurling itself beyond the telos of Plath's death and leaping right to the academic response to Plath's death in a "Universe of Alpha." Both poems are in a code keyed to extratextual knowledge. Hughes is assuming that the reader knows the open secret of their story.

Birthday Letters jumps over the "climax" of Plath's death to its denouement, keeping Plath's death private, just as Hughes had always insisted it should be. The poems that, from their place in the sequence, might be expected to reveal Hughes's reaction to Plath's death instead become reactions to the public carnival—to the "peanut-crunching crowd" Plath named in "Lady Lazarus" and Hughes sneers at more than once in *Birthday Letters*, coupling his hostility toward real audiences with her notional crowd. The penultimate poem in *Birthday Letters*, "The Dogs Are Eating Your Mother," attacks Plath's audience—and, by extension, Hughes's own—for "tearing" at what Hughes tells his children, in classic negation, is "not your mother but her body." At the end of his collection Hughes leaves scholars to "[j]erk their tail-stumps, bristle and vomit / Over their symposia" (*BL,* 196). The tables have turned: now it is not scholars "goading" Hughes to "vomit" out details of his life but rather the scholars (like me) who will "vomit" out their interpretations of his book.

Not publishing was not an option: the rest could not be silence. Hughes felt he had to publish these poems "no matter what the consequences," perhaps because, as he explained in a 1995 interview, he felt he shared with Plath a view of poetry as definitionally "a secret confession," the obliquity of which—its metaphorical, coded nature—was precisely a consequence of the dual need to reveal and to conceal this "secret." "The real mystery," Hughes mused, "is this strange need. Why can't we just hide it and shut up?"[49] Ultimately Hughes could not leave readers out of it all together because reading is the heart of *Birthday Letters*.

Notes

A longer version of the present essay entitled "Secrets and Lies: Plath, Privacy, Publication and Ted Hughes's *Birthday Letters*" has appeared in *Contemporary Literature* (winter 2001). Both essays have benefited enormously from the careful suggestions of readers (some anonymous) and even more from discussions with Paul Kelleher, who makes everything smarter.

1. Elizabeth Lund offers a characteristic example: "The man often accused of stifling Plath and pushing her toward suicide is breaking his self-imposed silence. In his new book, 'Birthday Letters'—which made front-page news on both sides of the Atlantic and was an immediate bestseller in Britain and the U.S.—Hughes offers a collection of 88 poems written secretly over 25 years. In it, he speaks as if directly to Plath." "Breaking the Long Silence: Ted Hughes

on Sylvia Plath," 14. See also the following: Alvarez, "Your Story, My Story"; Gray, "Poet's License"; Kakutani, "A Portrait of Plath in Poetry for Its Own Sake"; Kroll, "Answering Ariel"; Lyall, "In Poetry, Ted Hughes Breaks His Silence on Sylvia Plath"; Moseley, "Sylvia Plath's Former Husband Ends 35 Years of Silence"; Motion, "A Thunderbolt from the Blue"; Stothard, "Revealed: The Most Tragic Literary Love Story of Our Time."

2. Erica Wagner has written that these poems "set out the unknown side of the 20th century's most tragic literary love story." "Poet Laureate Breaks Decades of Silence," 18. Katha Pollitt has written that "the storm of publicity surrounding 'Birthday Letters' has turned into a kind of marital spin contest, an episode in the larger war between the sexes. Feminists have long been blamed for demonizing Hughes." "Peering into the Bell Jar," 7.

3. Let me say a word about intentions (mine and Hughes's). At no point am I claiming the ability to distinguish clearly Hughes's conscious from his unconscious intentions. I can surmise, but then so can the reader. My intention here is to try, as much as possible, to read the effects of the texts backward to their publicly known sources, which will necessarily blur neat critical boundaries between text and biography. Several effects—or intentions—can be found in *Birthday Letters:* some self-serving; some critical of Plath and what she did to him; others expressions of real grief or anger whose justifiability changed according to circumstances. (For example, his anger at poets who accuse him of having "real blood on real hands" seems justifiable to me, but not his anger at readers who love Plath's writings for reasons that may differ from his.) The expressions of grief should be self-evident. It is the complexity of Hughes's conversations with Plath and the critics that concerns me here, being the most encrypted and most misrepresented aspect of the collection. With the exception of one unpublished letter by Plath, which I have paraphrased (see n.42), I have also refrained from introducing archival material in an effort to keep the conversation focused on "public" controversies.

4. Plath, *The Collected Poems*, 219–20. Subsequent references appear parenthetically as *CP* in the text.

5. This has gradually begun to change. See Britzolakis, *Sylvia Plath and the Theatre of Mourning*, and Brain, *The Other Sylvia Plath*.

6. It is something of a cliché, in writing about Plath and Hughes, that entering the fray inevitably makes one a target for floating accusations. Certainly the polarization of opinion continues: an earlier version of this essay received simultaneous and contradictory anonymous readers' reports: the first complained that I "bent over backward to avoid mentioning" Hughes's "self-serving" relationship to Plath's writing, while the second disliked the fact that the "tone of the piece" was "often very hostile toward Hughes" because I felt that he always wanted "the last word" and sought to make this "nefarious intention absolutely clear."

7. Kenner, "Sincerity Kills," 43; West, "Crossing the Water," 157.

8. The term appears in Hughes's prefatory note to Plath's *Winter Trees:* "The poems in this volume are all out of the batch from which the *Ariel* poems were more or less arbitrarily chosen." For a good discussion of the problems with the editing of *Winter Trees* and *Crossing the Water,* see Perloff, "On the Road to *Ariel:* The 'Transitional' Poetry of Sylvia Plath."

9. For a discussion of the complicated political aspects surrounding the publication of *The Bell Jar,* see Malcolm, *The Silent Woman: Sylvia Plath and Ted Hughes,* 39–41, 210–13.

10. Hughes also divided these writings (some said officiously) into "the more successful short stories and prose pieces" and "other stories." See J. Rose, *The Haunting of Sylvia Plath,* 73.

11. Hughes authorized the publication of Plath's unabridged journals just before he died; they were published in 2000, two years after *Birthday Letters* appeared.

12. See Malcolm, *The Silent Woman: Sylvia Plath and Ted Hughes,* 3–7; see also Rose, *The Haunting of Sylvia Plath,* 65–113.

13. Perloff, "The Two Ariels: The (Re)making of the Sylvia Plath Canon." In 1971 Hughes defended these decisions in an essay offering several explanations for the *Ariel* that appeared and concluding: "But I no longer remember why I did many things—why the U.S. edition is different from the English, for example. But again, I think most of it was concern for certain people." *Winter Pollen: Occasional Prose,* 166–67.

14. Hughes, *Winter Pollen: Occasional Prose,* 167. Subsequent references appear parenthetically as *WP* in the text.

15. For example, in 1986 she wrote the following to one of Plath's friends: "You liked her. I think she was pretty straight poison." Quoted in Thomson, "Under the Bell Jar," 21. Here is how Olwyn countered complaints about her role as "agent" for the Plath estate: "The myth of the Plath estate is fast becoming as unpleasant and artificial as the Plath myth itself." Letter dated June 17–23, 1988, 677.

16. This practice apparently continued after Hughes's death, as Lynda Bundtzen explains in her preface to *The Other Ariel.* Faber & Faber denied Bundtzen permission to quote both Plath and Hughes on the grounds that "if we agreed to the quotations being published then we would be seen as giving our seal of approval to the comments you make." Bundtzen wryly observes: "I did not know that I needed to 'reflect' anyone else's views in order to express my own in print." Bundtzen, *The Other Ariel,* ix–x.

17. For example, Alvarez has written that the poems in *Birthday Letters* are "scenes from a marriage; Hughes's take on the life they shared. Plath had written her own version." Alvarez, "Your Story," 59.

18. Plath, *Letters Home: Correspondence, 1950–1963*, 466.
19. Quoted in Malcolm, *The Silent Woman: Sylvia Plath and Ted Hughes*, 201, 129.
20. Hughes, "Where Research Becomes Intrusion," 47.
21. Hughes, foreword to *The Journals of Sylvia Plath*, xiv.
22. Hughes, "Sylvia Plath: The Facts of Her Life and the Desecration of Her Grave."
23. Hughes, "The Place Where Sylvia Plath Should Rest in Peace," 22.
24. Quoted in Malcolm, *The Silent Woman: Sylvia Plath and Ted Hughes*, 141. According to Olwyn Hughes, "[Because Sylvia's] work seems to take cruel and poetically licensed aim at those nearest to her, journalists feel free to do the same. Whether such writings are the result of this kind of contagion . . . I do not know." Letter dated September 30, 1976, 43.
25. Hughes, "Where Research Becomes Intrusion," 47.
26. Hughes's "silence" was omnipresent in the book's reception (see n.1). Here is a representative example of the way Hughes's battle with feminism was figured: "Hughes's brief privileged marriage to Sylvia Plath, her suicide and his subsequent silence, turned him into a horned creature at whose character and reputation the feminist dogs have been baying and biting during the thirty-five years since her death." McClatchy, "Old Myths in New Versions," 159.
27. Stephen Spender saw Sylvia Plath as a "priestess cultivating her hysteria," saved from "shrillness" by her "form," arguing that "with Sylvia Plath, her femininity is that her hysteria comes completely out of herself, and yet seems about all of us. And she has turned our horrors and our achievements into the same witches' brew. . . . As with all visionary poetry, one can sup here on horror even with enjoyment." "Warnings from the Grave," 202–3. Richard Dyson has commented on the "depth of derangement" in Plath's "personal experience." "On Sylvia Plath," 209. George Steiner accused Plath of a "brokenness" that is "sharply feminine." "Dying Is an Art," *Sylvia Plath: A Symposium*, 215.
28. Lyall, "A Divided Response to Hughes Poems," E1.
29. Two reviewers who did note the familiarity of the story Hughes was telling were Pollitt ("Peering into the Bell Jar") and Logan ("Soiled Desire").
30. Hughes, *Birthday Letters*, 59. Subsequent references appear parenthetically as *BL* in the text.
31. Davison, "Dear Sylvia," G1; Pastan, "Scenes from a Marriage," 5.
32. Cf. Elaine Showalter: "I'm seeing how much [Hughes] mythologized the relationship and how much he takes a very determinist view of her, that it [the suicide] was because of her father, and that she was doomed to die and there was nothing he could do to stop her. I don't believe in this kind of determinism. I don't believe she was doomed to die. I don't believe that for a minute." Quoted in Lyall, "A Divided Response to Hughes Poems," E1.

33. Cf. Fenton: "Hughes's view of Plath is not far from Plath's of herself." "A Family Romance," 79. Davison has written: "Hughes does Plath the honor of respecting her demons as profoundly as she did herself." "Dear Sylvia," G1.

34. I am indebted to Susan R. Van Dyne for this observation.

35. Among the best known, see "A Birthday Present," "The Detective," "The Bee Meeting," "Fever 103°," "Ariel," "Lady Lazarus," "Getting There," "Death & Co.," and "Edge."

36. In a long passage in the unabridged journals Plath discusses the "psychodrama" that she is exploring. Her tone is cool and analytical, self-conscious about the story as an interpretation. The passage is full of qualifications, insisting that the identification is neither literal nor absolute. Plath is determined to "manipulate" the idea sufficiently to employ it in her writing: "How fascinating all this is. Why can't I master it and manipulate it . . .?" *The Unabridged Journals of Sylvia Plath*, 447.

37. Only a few reviewers noted the triteness of the explanation. One who did was Logan, who was also the only reviewer I have come across who relates the "secrets" in this volume to the unintelligibility of the final poems. See the concluding section of this essay.

38. This logic mirrors Rose's reading of the defamation trial over *The Bell Jar*. See *The Haunting of Sylvia Plath*, 105–11.

39. Diane Wood Middlebrook noted in her review that in Hughes's "response to the challenge laid down most powerfully in his consort's greatest work," he no longer "resist[s] the role written for him by her work." "Poetic Justice for Sylvia Plath," A19.

40. A poem about Plath called "Error" mirrors a poem not included in the volume called "The Error," the biographical details of which clearly suggest it is addressed to Assia Wevill (or her avatar). It appeared in Hughes's *New Selected Poems* in 1995.

41. Plath, *Unabridged Journals*, 477–78.

42. This unpublished letter is in the Plath archive at Smith College. It has accrued its own intertextual existence in Plath criticism and has been paraphrased by many biographers and critics who were denied the right to publish archival material. Its contents are thus something of an "open secret." See the concluding section of this essay.

43. When my essay had been accepted for publication, Lynda Bundtzen was making a similar observation in her book *The Other Ariel*. However, she certifies Hughes's interpretation of "Man in Black" via his reading of Plath's journals, quoting Plath's one sentence suggesting transference and adding an even more explicitly literalizing interpretation by claiming that "what Plath does here is to dress Hughes in her father's coat" (94). What Plath actually does is visit her father's grave, watch her husband at the beach, write a poem about a figure in black at the beach that neither names Hughes nor alludes to her

father, and subsequently muse on the possibility of its having been a moment of transference.

44. The other poems in *Birthday Letters* that borrow a Plath title include: "The Owl," "Ouija," "Wuthering Heights," "Apprehensions," "Totem," and "Brasilia." In addition, one might include the obvious rewritings of Hughes's "Earthenware Head" for Plath's "The Lady and the Earthenware Head"; Hughes's "Black Coat" for Plath's "Man in Black"; "Fever" for "Fever 103°"; "A Picture of Otto" for "Daddy"; and perhaps his poem "A Dream" for Plath's early poem "The Dream" (though it is such a common title as to be unremarkable). Furthermore, not all of these shared titles share incidents. "Fever" and "Fever 103°," for example, take their source from Plath's various illnesses; she suffered throughout her life from sinusitis.

45. For a discussion of some of the other oblique revisions in *Birthday Letters*, see Churchwell, "Secrets and Lies: Plath, Privacy, Publication and Ted Hughes's *Birthday Letters*."

46. Quoted in Gentleman, "Accolade for Hughes's Poems of Love and Loss, 4.

47. Miller, D. A. "Secret Subjects, Open Secrets," 194.

48. Malcolm, *The Silent Woman*, 141–42.

49. Hughes, "The Art of Poetry," 54–94.

Crowding the Garret

*Women's Collaborative Writing and
the Problematics of Space*

LORRAINE YORK

There is a photograph of the late-nineteenth-century Anglo-Irish collaborators "Somerville and Ross" that I find both quietly powerful and suggestive of the very condition of women writing together. Seated together in a garret (that stereotypically favored haunt of the Romantic, inspired [male] artist), Edith Somerville and her cousin Violet Martin (pseud. Martin Ross), surrounded by beloved pets, are gazing deeply into the books on their laps. Or, rather, Edith is gazing at the book on her lap while Violet—who was also her friend, lover, and collaborator—peers not at the book resting on her own lap but over Edith's shoulder at *her* book. This is precisely what I find so emblematic of women's writing relationships, variously formed as they are by their own historical moment, class, sexual choice, culture, and ethnicity: the occupation by two authorial presences of a conventionally unitary authorial space. Two women's eyes inhabit the reading space of that page, just as two women's bodies inhabit the literary "garret" that conventional critics of the day—and of ours—might deem too constricting for more than one author. But here—comfortable, spread out, and not the least bit constrained—we see two women in a position of authorship or, as two of their twentieth-century inheritors, Daphne Marlatt and Betsy War-land, would phrase it, "two women in a birth." In the present essay I will examine this supposed overcrowding of Western individuated author-ship in literary collaborations between women writing in English since the last century. Increasingly, of course, those collaborations have be-come public and overt rather than anxiously closeted. However, as I maintain here, the problematics of space do not come to an end in twentieth-century collaborations. Rather, they often take the form of an uneasy negotiation of shared textual space as utopian frontier—a negoti-ation attended, to be sure, by a whole range of postcolonial complexities.

Although the collaborations I analyze move progressively from the textual closet to the overt acknowledgment of collaboration, it does not follow that I read the history of women's (or men's) collaborations as a progressive enlightenment, ranging from dark secrecy to the broad light of disclosure, or from normative single authorship to greater collabora-tive experimentation in recent decades. Rather, I agree with a number of theorists of collective writing that the Western Romantic individu-ated artist—or, say, the individualist cult of Shakespeare—were closer to aberrations in the history of writing practices than transhistorical norms. As Sean Burke has written in the introduction to his collection of essays on authorship theory, "What distinguishes premodern concep-tions of authorship is their assumption that discourse is primarily an af-fair of public rather than private consciousness."[1] Martha Woodmansee and Peter Jaszi, who have written cogently on authorship issues in rela-tion to copyright law, go further. Not only do they claim that research suggests that "the author in this modern sense" (viz. "an individual who is the sole creator of unique 'works'") "is a relatively recent invention, but that it does not closely reflect contemporary writing practices. In-deed, on inspection, it is not clear that this notion ever coincided closely with the practice of writing."[2]

Although authorship has always been already public, as Wood-mansee and others (such as collaborative critics Lisa Ede and Andrea Lunsford) have argued, at certain historical moments this dominant practice, this "primary" public Western discourse, yielded to a more visible or, at least, more popular image of private authorship. Donald E. Pease has suggested that the increasingly individuated premodern author should be understood in the context of the so-called new men, cultural agents (significantly masculinized by Renaissance historians) who leashed and distributed the cultural power created by explorers' observations of the "New" World. For Pease this distribution caused a crisis in representation and culture since "new" phenomena and experiences ruptured the idea of authorship as a chainlike reliance on the authority of previous authors' texts; those authoritative texts of the past could not hope to offer "precedent" for representing the New World. Pease maintains that, indeed, these new authors "exploited the discontinuity between the things in the new World and the words in the ancient books to claim for their words an unprecedented cultural power." In this respect they were not unlike others "who exploited this dissociation between worlds: explorers, merchants, colonists. . . ."[3] While there are aspects of Pease's theory that I would question—such as its reliance on a conceptualization of "new" experience, unrepresentable by recourse to precedent, and a consequent overdramatization of the New World's power to break open Old World modes of representation—it is valuable for suggesting that authorship itself is always culturally and historically in play as a means of production. For instance, it may be that the ascendance of the Romantic, individuated author in nineteenth-century Europe was similarly caught up in these nation-states' accumulation of a string of colonies, though this was only one of many cultural forces at work. Still, as Burke reminds us, "authorship involves the appropriation of cultural space,"[4] and that appropriation may, in turn, be bound up with historical appropriations of more earthy territories. What this essay will investigate, then, will be the negotiations of cultural space that occur, first, when women collaborators must operate in a century in which "genius," for whatever sociohistorical reasons, was deemed not only male but singular. The second, shorter, part of this essay will focus on twentieth-century collaborators who, in the light of challenges to literary canons, enter the discourse of authorship as explicit, self-conscious collaborators. Even so, they must negotiate certain spatial and territorial issues that do not melt away with this increased public acknowledgment of collaboration. In this sense, this essay will take very seriously Michel Foucault's celebrated spatial metaphor for authorship as, paradoxically, "the empty space left by the author's disappearance"—a space that is, in true Foucauldian style, "reapportion[ed]" rather than emptied of its cultural currency.[5] The negotiation of cultural space has no more dissipated than has the much-vaunted imperialism of the 1900s. So what happens when twentieth-century collaborators, looking to justify their shared entrances on the page, are drawn to images of claiming territory?

The Late Nineteenth Century: Michael Field and the Textual Closet

A particularly claustrophobic nineteenth-century collaboration was that of Katherine Bradley and Edith Cooper, an aunt and niece who signed themselves "Michael Field" on the twenty-six plays and eight collections of poems they wrote from the 1880s until their deaths (just a few months apart) in 1913. Their first joint work, *Bellerophon* (1881), was published under the androgynous pseudonyms Arran and Isla Leigh, and two years later they published *Callirrhoe and Fair Rosamund* under the decidedly masculine name "Michael Field." As T. and D. C. Sturge Moore, the editors of the slim selection from their voluminous journals, observed in 1933, "They were prolific in nicknames, for themselves and others; but as the years went by Katherine became Michael, and Edith, Field or Henry; this last by Michael, either drawn out to Hennery or shortened to Henny."[6] Although they delighted in private naming, Katherine and Edith wished to keep that game private. In the Michael Field correspondence housed in the British Library, there are repeated promises by correspondents in those early years not to reveal the secret of the names. Alexander Laing wrote in solemn tones in 1887, "P.P.S. The secret of authorship which you have confided to me I hold perfectly sacred." Edmund Stedman, editor of *The Victorian Poets*, wrote to assure the poets, "As you wished, I respected your incognita in 'The Victorian Poets,' and I do so now," though he seemed to be under the impression that Michael Field was one singular reticent author rather than two. (His letter, dated August 12, 1888, bears the following salutation: "To Michael Field = Dear Madam.")[7]

Predictably, this name game led to considerable pronominal anxiety on the part of early correspondents. While reading through that correspondence, I was amused to see the variations concocted by uneasy letter writers, some of whom knew more of the secret than others. J. M. Gray, a close friend and confidante, relayed to Katherine and Edith their supporter Robert Browning's greetings: "He knew at once whom I meant, & said very pleasant things of Michael's work—*very*—& told me to take to him 'to both of him,' he said, his best wishes and kindest messages" (letter dated 31 January 1888). Gray, in an unconsciously revealing stroke, inserted Browning's jest, "to both of him" in a marginal addendum—a veritable sign of the quiet marginality of this pronominally "irregular" relationship. In another letter (7 October 1890) Gray inscribes a heraldic shield "For Michael Field her very own selves." Even Katherine was not immune to pronoun difficulties in her attempts to represent "Michael Field." To Gray she writes, "He—I—or we—send the 3 other poems we shd. like printed" (13 October 1886). Although the pronoun game gave the participants some hidden, playful pleasure, I also read it as a sign of cultural anxiety, a joke that at least partly relies on a sense of two women collaboratively writing as an authorial circus trick.[8]

Another telling sign of the depth of the textual closet in which "Michael Field" felt themselves and the spatial complexities it engendered was the intense concern with what I call "parsing" the collaboration, separating out the strands of individual authorship and ownership of a work. Even in a relationship as relatively private as this one (the collaboration was not widely known until the disastrous appearance of *A Question of Memory* on the London stage in 1893), inquiring minds wanted to force the collaboration into a single-author model. Edith Cooper sent *Callirrhoe and Fair Rosamund* to the elderly Robert Browning, soon thereafter making him the first major literary figure to become privy to the secret, and although he would come to treat the collaboration with remarkable respect, he replied to this first missive with the inevitable question of ownership: "Dear Miss Cooper, I should be glad to know—since it is *you* whom I address and must thank—how much of the book that is 'partly yours' is indeed your own part." As more literati were let into the secret, the question was repeated ad nauseam. Katherine rather wearily recounts to Edith a meeting with George Meredith: "He asks which one of us 'does the Males? . . . Who did Bothwell?' comes next." George Moore inquired, with comic (perhaps dark) understatement, "Who does the love scenes?—they are so good. You get such words in them" (*WD*, 2, 82, 201). Eventually, of course, Michael Field became impatient with this desire to parse the collaboration. Writing to Havelock Ellis, who had made the well-worn inquiry, "Michael" reprimanded him: "As to our work, let no man think he can put asunder what god has joined"—heady words for the writer who had pronounced so roundly on earthly unions.[9]

I raise the issue of the readerly parsing of collaboration because it is a major part of the spatial dynamic of women's collaborative work from Michael Field's day to the present. Even in a 1993 study of "creativity and intimate partnership," editors Whitney Chadwick and Isabelle de Courtivron ironically held to this singular model of artistic production in their highlighting of the parsing process: "Investigating notions of collaboration . . . offers one way that we can move toward untangling the . . . singular achievement from the collaborative process."[10] Authorship itself is not significantly re-theorized or rethought in this view of collaboration. Once again the shared collaborative space must be territorialized so that the single, individuated authors can remain intact. This view, of course, is replicated in and reproduced by legal sanctions governing authorship. As Peter Jaszi has noted, copyright law does not adequately come to terms with artistic collaborations of various sorts; he denounces the "law's insistence on formally disaggregating collaborative productions, rather than characterizing them as 'joint works.'"[11] As literary critics, we have more often than not done the same, even though many collaborators would heartily agree with contemporary collaborative critics Carey Kaplan and Ellen Cronan Rose that "at the end of several hours we are scrolling through something neither of us would or could have written alone and honestly cannot say which word 'came from' Carey, which idea 'came from' Ellen."[12]

As Kaplan's and Rose's comment suggests, the sharing of the collaborative page is a complex dynamic of collective and individual praxis. When "Michael Field" sought to describe that dynamic, they frequently did so by recourse to spatial and visual metaphors. As Katherine, signing herself "Michael," wrote to J. M. Gray, "I weed Edith's garden she mine; then examining each other's withering heaps we exclaim—'Well, you might have spared that'—or, 'that weak twining thing had yet a grace'—but the presiding horticulturalist is ruthless, & it is borne away to the barrow" (9 June 1889).[13] Each poet is here envisioned as occupying territory, but that very territory is reworked—cultivated—and thereby shared with the other. Power is by no means denied; there is a "presiding horticulturalist" who presumably wins the debate of the moment, whatever it may be, but Michael Field tellingly emphasize the function rather than the personal occupant of that function (to draw on a Foucauldian distinction about authorship). Still, the pressure of the demand to "disentangle" the collaboration was intense, and at times "Michael Field were invariably touched by its discourse. When Edith did reply to Browning's early question about artistic ownership, she did so with a mixture of communitarian and individualistic discourses: "Some of the scenes of our play are like mosaic-work—the mingled, various product of our two brains. [She then goes on to acknowledge "ownership" of various scenes.] I think that if our contributions were disentangled and one subtracted from the other, the amount would be

almost even. This happy union of two in work and aspiration is sheltered and expressed by 'Michael Field.' Please regard him as the author" (*WD*, 3). "Michael Field" could and would speak the mathematical, territorial discourse of authorship if they needed to. Still, I read
much more of the social will to please and justify in Edith's mathematical rationale to Browning and more of the heartfelt in her invocation of
the "mingled" and "various" mosaic work—a metaphor that both inscribes and deconstructs personal artistic territory (the tessera cannot
conceptually exist independent of the concept of "mosaic"). Indeed, the
manuscript examples of their journals reveal the justice of Edith's metaphor; there is usually a main author of entries, but then the other poet
enters comments or emendations on the facing page. One long poem
that appears in their journal shows both hands at work on separate stanzas (though this may be Michael Field's preferred method of fair copying), and on one page they each try a version of the same stanza.[14] Edith
describes their inspiration for the closing lines of *Otho* (1891) in a phrase
that significantly mutualizes the Promethean discourse of artistic inspiration: "Our brains struck fire each from each."[15]

Just as "Michael Field," in a touching move, carefully tipped the
predominantly vicious reviews of *A Question of Memory* into their journal,
I think they internalized some of the underlying assumptions about Promethean genius and the solitary poet circulating in Victorian culture.
For instance, in the journals they tend to speak of inspiration as individual and revision as collective and interactive. But I think they also
chafed under these assumptions, just as generations of English poets before and after them chafed under the long, solitary shadow of Shakespeare. Thus, in what is probably their best-known poem, "Prologue,"
Shakespeare figures both as reference and as pressure point:

> It was deep April, and the morn
> Shakespeare was born;
> The world was on us, pressing sore;
> My Love and I took hands and swore,
> Against the world, to be
> Poets and lovers evermore.
>
>   (18)

As Jeffrey A. Masten has remarked in an essay on Beaumont and
Fletcher, "In a scholarly field dominated by the singular figure of Shake-
speare, it is easily forgotten that collaboration was the Renaissance
English theatre's dominant mode of textual production."[16] How

fitting that these two poets, one of whom described their work to Robert Browning as working "together in the manner of Beaumont and Fletcher" (*WD*, 4), should have felt similarly overshadowed by this avatar of singular genius.

Only when Edith and Katherine were secret collaborators could they be together on the page in the sort of "fellowship" (to quote Katherine's last poem, written in Edith's memory) sheltered from dominant constructions of genius. Predictably, then, their letters to associates such as J. M. Gray and Robert Browning, laying upon them injunctions of silence, are solemn, lecturing, and even pleading at times. When this collaborative relationship came up against public utterance in the form of a performance of *A Question of Memory*, the two poets felt most solitary—bereft of their collaborative space. This performance, plagued by many negotiations, second thoughts, and worries on the part of both poets, was an anxious traversal of the private and public spaces of their collaboration. They felt that only when they remained secret—and therefore publicly presentable as a single poet—could they gain access to honest criticism. When they feared that Robert Browning was letting the secret of their dual authorship slip out, they upbraided him with this very rationale: "[Y]ou are robbing us of real criticism, such as man gives man" (*WD*, 7). Indeed, if the critic writing in the 11 November 1893 issue of *Winters Weekly Magazine* is to be believed, that is exactly what happened when the secret was revealed to the world at the premiere: the mixture of hisses and applause died away to pure applause when "two graceful young ladies" stood up, revealing themselves as Michael Field (though this critic typically uses this narrative to demonstrate the courtesy of English manhood at its best!).[17] As Edith recorded her response to this painful evening of disclosure and disgrace, "I felt suddenly as if I stood in a clearing where there was no humanity—where I was a mortal alone" (*WD*, 82). The secret space of collaboration, where creative "fellowship" can thrive, became a publicly devastated paradise lost.

The Anglo-Irish collaborators Edith Oenone Somerville and Violet Martin (pseud. Martin Ross) operated in a much more public space than did Michael Field. In 1889 they published their first novel, *An Irish Cousin* (subsequently affectionately christened "the shocker" by its authors because of some sensationalist elements). Buoyed up by some positive reviews, they went on to assemble light-hearted travel writings— *Through Connemara in a Governess Cart* (1892) and *In the Vine Country*

(1893)—before achieving a measure of success with *The Real Charlotte* (1894) and, to a greater degree, *Some Experiences of an Irish R.M.* (1899). The farcical fox-hunting stories of the latter created a public demand for more of this material, and Somerville and Ross obliged, until Martin's death in 1915 and beyond, according to Somerville, who claimed to have continued this close collaboration with her cousin's spirit beyond the grave through séances. By comparison with the contemporaneous Michael Field, this collaboration inhabited a most public-seeming space. (Edith Somerville was even awarded a doctor of letters degree by Dublin University in 1922, though her attempts to have the university authorities confer the honorary degree on the deceased Violet Martin received a rather chilly bureaucratic response.) One would have thought that the anxieties of public and private space would not have been as pressing, and certainly the pressure to (re)present the collaboration as a single writing "genius" would have been negligible, but such was not the case. Given the public venues in which this collaboration thrived, however, the pressure to represent singular authorship came mainly from Somerville and Ross's critics. The anxiety of collaborative space was transferred to the public sphere. One of the pair's most fervent expressions of faith in the collaborative process, namely, Martin's avowal to Somerville that to "write with you doubles the triumph and enjoyment, having first halved the trouble and anxiety,"[18] is itself a response to the criticism leveled by one reader that "though I think the book [*The Irish Cousin*] a success, and cannot pick out the fastenings of the two hands, I yet think the next novel ought to be by *one* of them." [19]

In the matter of the very names they chose to publish under, I discern both an increased openness to publicity and a persistent secrecy. Of course, Edith Somerville used her own surname even though both of the cousins' families were opposed to the idea primarily because they felt it was beneath the families' dignity to have their names associated with trade.[20] As a result of that pressure, their first novel was published under the masculine pseudonyms "Geilles Herring and Martin Ross," but such a bowing to family pressures irked Edith, who remarked to Violet in an early letter, "I can't send it [an early story] off until you say what signature you want. Is it our names—or what? You once said you wanted Martin Somerville—*I* think our good names" (*Letters*, 129). Though Edith got her own way the next time and thereafter, signing her own "good name" Somerville, Violet Martin continued to prefer the semisecrecy of "Martin Ross," with rumors continuing to circulate for a while as to their gender. As with so many other issues of space in this collaboration, the apparent greater openness and publicity belies the persistence of anxieties about public and private space that Michael Field knew so well.

Indeed, space is a major issue in the collaboration of Somerville and Ross—in several senses. On the most material level, Edith and Violet had to fight their families most determinedly for working space, even though, as Gifford Lewis has argued, it was the family's tradition of working collectively on creative productions such as plays and masques that arguably fostered the cousins' projects.[21] As their nephew, Chaucer scholar Neville Coghill, recalled, "[T]hey would sit in a studio, or in a Railway carriage or wherever it might be" (*Letters*, 145). "It might be" almost anywhere, for, as Edith recollected, they "were hunted from place to place like the Vaudois, seeking in vain a cave wherein we could hold our services unmolested."[22] The families, as Anglo-Irish "old" families, had certain expectations of the young women's participation in visiting and entertaining, and writing together in the collaborative "cave" certainly did not count for many service points. To quote Edith's account once again, "When not actually reviled, we were treated with much the same disapproving sufferance that is shown to an outside dog that sneaks into the house on a wet day."[23]

When they weren't being curbed by their families, they were physically separated by some miles, Edith at "Drishane," in West Cork, and Martin at "Ross," near Galway, until 1900, when Martin moved to Drishane. This is a condition shared by many contemporary collaborators. Lunsford and Ede conclude their critical survey with a contemporary transoceanic scene of collaboration: "Lisa is on a consulting trip in the east and Andrea is in her office, feet up, gathering notes for one more marathon telephone conversation."[24] "Like other long-distance collaborators," write Kaplan and Rose, "we usually work physically separated from each other, exchanging and editing each other's drafts by mail or modem."[25] However, in a time bereft of telephone, fax, or computer, the mail had to suffice for Somerville and Ross, as Gifford Lewis, the editor of their selected letters, observes, "[M]anuscripts oscillated between Drishane and Ross for six months or so before clean-copying and the journey eastwards to their publishers in London" (*Letters*, xxii). As Edith plaintively wrote to Martin, "I wish you were here, or I was there—it would save much time and trouble" (*Letters*, 103).

Though Edith and Violet had difficulties with the geographical frustrations of writing between "here" and "there," they developed creative strategies for sharing the space of the page that bounced back and forth across counties. Like Michael Field, they would write on one (in this case the right-hand) side of an exercise book, with revisions entered either above the original words or on the left-hand page.[26] More so than Michael Field, they evolved a shared writing strategy that openly acknowledged the role of conflict in their deliberations. For instance, one of Edith's favored terms of criticism was "puke," and in their letters they almost seem to relish the prospect of a good editorial battle. As Edith bellicosely commented, "I know you must loathe my sticking in these putrid things [love scenes] and then fighting for them. . . . Please goodness we will have many a tooth and naily fight next month—but don't let us combat by post; it is too wearing" (*Letters*, 65, 63). Although it certainly was tiring to negotiate the spaces of the page across the spaces of geography, the letters reveal a remarkable ability to share detailed criticism of passages, right down to the adjectives and possessives. I was particularly impressed by these women's ability to be frank with each other. As Edith writes to Martin on one occasion, "What struck me when I read it first, was a certain tightness and want of the ideas being expanded. It read too strong. Like over-strong tea" (*Letters*, 101)—to fall back upon that most stereotypical of Irish images. Recorded accounts of their working relationship, however, suggest that this frank exchange was part of a larger process of consensus-building. As their nephew Neville Coghill explained, "[T]hey talked their stories and their characters and their every sentence into being. As soon as anything was agreed it was written down and not a word was written down without agreement" (*Letters*, 145). In her later memoir entitled *Irish Memories*, his aunt Edith corroborated this account: "Our work was done conversationally. One or other—not infrequently both simultaneously—would state a proposition. This would be argued, combated perhaps, approved or modified; it would then be written down by the (wholly fortuitous) holder of the pen, would be scratched out, scribbled in."[27]

Edith's parenthetical claim "wholly fortuitous" is a reaction to the public pressures bearing down on the collaborative textual space shared conversationally by Somerville and Ross—what she would call, time and time again, the old question of "who holds the pen." Because of the heightened publicity surrounding this collaboration, there was a similarly heightened desire on the part of the public to "parse" or disentangle the collaboration, to force these two unruly collaborators into the conceptual mold of individual creativity and "genius." It was, of course, a desire familiar to the contemporary writing pair Michael Field, and it seems to have particularly irked Edith. As she reported to Violet, editors "attacked me to know which of us wrote which parts—by chapters or how—the usual old thing." On another occasion she was similarly "attacked" by a reader after the publication of *The Real Charlotte:* "'And is it you that do the story & Miss Martin the' &c &c for some time" (*Letters*, 243, 207). After enduring several years of this kind of dissection, with critics vying with each other to discern separate authorship of particular passages in their novels and stories, Edith finally vented her anger: "Already various journalists have been tearing at me to write, to give them data for articles, anything, to try and make money out of what to me is a sacred thing . . . how abhorrent is to me all the senseless curiosity as to 'which held the pen.'"[28]

Senseless curiosity seems to have had a rather long shelf life since, until fairly recently, virtually all of the authors of extended criticism of Somerville and Ross have exhibited its effects. In more recent books on women's collaborations, Holly Laird and Bette London read these shared texts, in Laird's words, "as the realization of relationships [instead] of dissecting the relationships behind the writing."[29] But before London's book appeared in 1999, the published criticism was full of repeated attempts to parse the collaboration and, in effect, to reformat it in terms of individuated authorship. Gifford Lewis, for instance, confidently asserted that "we can track the two personalities in their manuscripts," and, soon thereafter she made the claim for Edith as "the major partner in their writing," as though she first needed to parse the collaboration in order to resuscitate the "major," singular author from its shards.[30] Novelist-critic Molly Keane, introducing both Lewis's edition of the selected letters and the Hogarth Press's reissue of *The Real Charlotte*, strives to articulate a division of labor. Martin "held the rapier pen," while Edith "had the stronger force of invention."[31] Edith was "the more emotional writer of the two," whereas Martin was "the remorseless censor" (*Letters*, xviii). Maurice Collis devotes a disproportionate amount of his dual biography of Somerville and Ross to the same sort of disentangling exercise, attempting to deduce the (single) authorship of passages and chapters on the basis of such evidence as the stylistic markers of their individual letters. Such an obsession with decollaborating Somerville and Ross ultimately leads him to adopt an oddly mathematical understanding of collaboration, asking of Edith's writing life after Violet's death, "Could the survivor carry on? There was only half as much talent available."[32] John Cronin, in his 1972 volume on *Somerville and Ross*, plays the same "find the suture" game, even though he reminds readers that "any successful literary collaboration is by its very nature greater than the sum of its parts." Still, he proceeds to do sums, and it becomes clear that the two women's collaboration poses a particularly difficult short-division problem for him as an evaluative critic: How does one apportion praise or criticism when one is dealing with "a closely knit partnership, one member of which outlived the other by a whole generation"?[33] Hilary Robinson marvels at the "lack of fastenings" in the collaborative prose yet then proceeds to worry the seams she does perceive.[34] Even Violet Powell, who, near the beginning of *The Irish Cousins*, likens Somerville and Ross's collaboration to the woven "shot-silk, where the color changes but the texture remains constant," partway through that study calls *Some Irish Yesteryears* "a valuable book for disentangling the threads of Somerville and Ross."[35] Most critics of this collaborative team, it seems, can only apprehend the woven authorship by picking at its threads, trained as they are to associate their own critical enterprise with the oeuvre of an individual writer. Far better is the response recorded by Edith Somerville at a séance, when she asked the "spirit" of Violet Martin about the possibilities of collaboration beyond the grave: "I shouldn't know which were my own thoughts and which yours," to which the disembodied Violet replied, with a prescient touch of the Foucauldian, "That would not matter."[36] ("What matter who's speaking" is how Foucault concludes his "What Is an Author?")[37]

This anxiety on the part of critics and readers to determine "who's speaking" is—as with Michael Field—caught up in their cultural constructions of "genius." However, I think it is just as entangled with social anxiety about lesbian desire. In homophobic passage after passage, critics of Somerville and Ross "defend" Somerville and Ross against claims expressed in Collis's biography that the two women were lovers. Powell, for instance, informs us that Edith was not a lesbian because she "was not ill at ease with men"![38] And Robinson hastily assures us that though their love for each other was paramount, "it never transgressed the bounds set by Christianity."[39] But the homophobia prize definitely goes to Lewis, who never seems content to let the matter rest. In a bizarre turn of logic, she maintains that Somerville and Ross couldn't be lesbians because their observations of men and of the relations between men and women are "chillingly accurate." Subsequently she quotes a number of

Edith's and Violet's teasing retorts to each other, mystifyingly conclud-ing, "This is not the language of a Sapphic sexual love."[40] When Edith and the departed Violet decide not to care "which were my thoughts and which yours," they intellectually enact an aspect of mutuality that is fully eroticized in many contemporary women's collaborations. Com-pare, for instance, this concluding erotic passage from Suniti Namjoshi and Gillian Hanscombe's 1986 collection *Flesh and Paper:* ". . . and some-times there was the wondering about who was who. . . ."[41] In terms of nineteenth-century English authorship, critics then and now have wished to disentangle the legs and arms of these collaborations, for the spectacle of two women "holding the pen" may have suggested all too easily the notion that they might hold each other too.

Twentieth-Century Collaborative Spaces

Although many twentieth-century collaborators like Namjoshi and Hanscombe or Daphne Marlatt and Betsy Warland have jettisoned the pseudonym and its hothouse trappings, the issue of traversing public and private spaces that preoccupied Michael Field and Somerville and Ross has not evaporated. In *Two Women in a Birth*, Marlatt and War-land's collected collaborative poetry, the poets confront each other in that most stereotypically private of domestic spaces, the bathroom, to express their anxiety about the public reception of their joint effort:

> at the bathroom sink
> "so, do you think the collaboration is working?"
> "yes, do you?"
> "yes . . . i don't know what the others will think of it—"[42]

The very idea of this poetic discussion being set in a prototypical room of solitude indicates that even the "private" space is—perhaps like writing—always already public. In Namjoshi and Hanscombe's *Flesh and Paper* the two poet-speakers develop an entire idiom for talking about their anxieties concerning appearing in public: "side by side" instead of "face to face" (in their private, erotic meetings). Whether this anxiety manifests itself in a public space, as it did for Michael Field in the thea-ter after the premiere of *A Question of Memory*, or in the dubiously private confines of a shared bathroom, the fact remains that traversing public and private spaces retains an aura of risk and anxiety.

What mainly distinguishes these late-twentieth-century collaborations by women from their predecessors of a century ago is the contemporary collaborators' explicit representations of the process of creating
collaborative art through negotiation. For instance, in her shared *renga*
(a traditional Japanese shared poem) with Lee Maracle, Ayanna Black
moves into Jamaican nation language. At the end of their cycle, they
work with the format's rigid-seeming placement of their names in the
margins by making those names part of the poem:

> Dawn soft glow
> Playfully casting light
>   on the ceremony of dance,
> a song of blessed peace   Maracle
> Black   We link hands
>   round the rising sun.[43]

By incorporating their names—their markers of identity and
community—and bringing the verses identified as "theirs" closer together than is the case with the other sets of *renga* in the collection, the
poets have spatially performed the very dance of cross-cultural communication that they explore in their set entitled "A Celebration."

Sometimes this spatial performance seems less celebratory. In "Subject to Change" Marlatt and Warland bring a discussion of collaboration into their piece involving a frank representation of disagreement (a
representation, if you will, of the discuss-and-argue technique that Somerville and Ross felt they had to pass through in order to *get* to the collaborative product). As Laird describes Marlatt and Warland's poem,
"Rather than a single, fixed structure or comprehensive system for collaboration, they offer instead their active interaction: their enacted
movements and shiftings of fear, fight, love, and flight."[44] At one particularly painful point the two poets break off onto their own pages (as indicated by different typefaces). "You left," one poet mourns. They do
rejoin each other on the shared page, and when they do, it's to analyze
why the capitalist question, *"where's mine?"* has acted as an *"axe split in the
poem"* (*Two Women*, 158, 159): *"up till now when we've collaborated we've had individual control of our individual pieces so we could shape them according to our own
sense of form . . . we've had to give up individual control"* (*Two Women*, 160). The
insistent ringing of the word "individual" is a clue to what has ruptured
the shared textuality: it's the same force that has led readers to "disentangle" the collaborations of Michael Field and Somerville and Ross.

Although contemporary collaborators do, on the whole, feel much more freedom to place these spatial negotiations on the page, spatial anxiety itself by no means dissipates as a result of this greater frankness. Rather, it flows into other channels. Prime among them I would count the temptation to recreate the shared textual space as utopian frontier. Sometimes merely the temptation to forge a utopia is evident, whereas at other times it is attended by a countervailing awareness of the temptation. In Namjoshi and Hanscombe's *Flesh and Paper*, for instance, the poets repeatedly dream of a beach where two women can enjoy each other without interruption or oppression (8, 10, 12, 23, 54, 63). It's a tempting vision for collaborators who feel public scrutiny bearing down upon them. I am reminded of a somewhat mysterious passage from Michael Field's journals, a passage that I believe encodes and protects Katherine and Edith's love—that most deeply guarded secret of all: "No, Henry, I don't think I can soon forget that half-hour we spent on the beach together—as little children entering the kingdom of Bacchus."[45] And yet by the end of the collection, through a process of philosophical debate, Namjoshi and Hanscombe conclude that, to quote the title of their final poem, "there is no undiscovered country"— no protected, private beaches, no utopias. They sense, to quote London's observations about women's literary collaborations, that the "utopian features that collaborators regularly articulate in their unions can thus be considered both informative and suspect."[46] In spite of their knowledge of the "suspect" nature of utopias, their desire for what Adrienne Rich termed "the dream of a common language" pries open their philosophical resolve in the very last lines of the collection and lets the utopian vision of a new territory reshape itself tentatively, interrogatively:

> But in spite of a hurtful history
> shall we still speak of a peopled place
> where women may walk freely
> in the still, breathable air?
> *(Flesh and Paper, 64)*

As the poets recognize, the notion of territory in its material forms may be problematic, but its visionary counterpart remains an ever-receding, steadfast horizon, like these closing lines. As Homi K. Bhabha has observed, "Nations . . . lose their origins in the myths of time and only fully realize their horizons in the mind's eye."[47]

For these poets this question of the mind-forged utopian horizon is deeply implicated in discourses of geography and that most anxious or, as Bhabha would say, "ambivalent" discourse: nation. Crossing oceans, borders, going to another land, "this foreign beach," as Namjoshi and Hanscombe render it—these are all gestures in this anxious traversal of cultural space. *Flesh and Paper* opens by invoking Australia (the birthplace of Hanscombe), and, near the end, narrates the poets' journey to India (the birthplace of Namjoshi). Is the desired beach a form of middle meeting ground between these two individual locations, a dream of a new, shared home? If so, it, too, must be illusory, for, as one of the poets somberly recognizes, "it's our bodies, not our passports, / fit so uncommonly well" (*Flesh and Paper*, 63). Once again anxiety, displacement, and imbalance mark this text, which seeks a space that cannot and yet somehow needs to be imagined as a new nation.

In Marlatt's and Warland's poetry utopia is just as powerful—and as troubling—an object of desire. As Laird notes, Marlatt and Warland "evoke a lesbian 'utopia'"[48]—a dream, like that of Namjoshi and Hanscombe, of a new space to call home. In their poem "Double Negative," however, an anxious traversal of national boundaries and cultural spaces highlights the problems attached to this desire for a space that must and yet cannot be a "new" nation. On one level Marlatt and Warland are explicitly constructing an anti-imperialistic poetic sequence. As Laird argues, they "interrogate colonialism as a global political condition, a state of mental subjection, and a language."[49] For example, the poets punctuate the poetic narrative of their journey through Australia with references (often in titles) to the names of places they are passing on the train, English place names that reflect explicit traces of imperialism—"anglo overlays" on the map (*Two Women*, 86). Aboriginal languages, on the other hand, tend to be romanticized as holding a privileged connection to a land that ultimately refuses its mapping:

> Yunta, Paratoo, Ucolta, Yongala
> words we head for down this birthing canal
> "the oldest living language" shaping our tongues lips
> to speak it out (though we do not know the meanings)
> (*Two Women*, 82)

The poets like to imagine their own anti-imperialistic lips being shaped by the informing presence of the aboriginal, but they apply the brakes just in time, attempting to stop short of a highly problematic cultural ventriloquism. The appended parenthetical exclusion clause, "though we do not know the meanings," discloses their anxiety of appropriation. For all of their awareness of the dangers of ventriloquism, the romancing of the aboriginal remains a force in the poem as a whole. The repeated deconstruction of the word itself—"(ab)original," "ab/original" (*Two Women*, 86, 81)—in the poem suggests this most strongly. This complicit desire to claim aboriginal space derails Marlatt and Warland's explicit attempts to present themselves as anti-imperialistic poets.

As London makes clear in her analysis of women's literary partnerships, the discourse of exoticism—and, I would add, of indigenousness—has long been a feature of those partnerships. Drawing on Somerville and Ross's gentrified fascination with the Irishisms of the local peasantry, among other examples, she observes that "going back at least as far as the Brontës, partnership writing would appear to have made its name by trading on the exotic." She theorizes that the familiar nineteenth-century collaborative claim that two (or more) collaborators have managed to write "as one" is also implicitly a claim for oneness with the imperial center. No wonder, she notes, that nineteenth-century collaborations tended to "flourish at the outer reaches of British society—in Scotland, Ireland, and Australia."[50] Marlatt and Warland, two Canadian Caucasian lesbian poets crossing Australian space, participate in collaboration's history of appropriated exoticism no matter how determinedly anti-imperialistic their project.

There is a similar attraction to an exoticized indigenousness briefly expressed in *Flesh and Paper* when the two women, speaking wistfully, look forward to "Observers" saying of the two women (themselves?) they are watching, "Look how they have changed. They have become indigenous" (10). In their eagerness to transgress—literally to cross over—boundaries, regulations, and maps in search of an/other desert space, these contemporary collaborators have problematically crossed *over* (in the other sense of "erased") an always already written text.

Flesh and Paper, framed as it is by two nations, Australia and India, engages in much discussion of "my country" and "your country" (28, 63, 46, 56ff.). The option of inventing a country of their own to disrupt this stultifying binary is briefly considered and, as we've seen, deferred—though still desired. Marlatt and Warland envision a similar project when they repeatedly deconstruct the term "imagination" to yield "imagina-nation" (*Two Women*, 92, 124, 126), and yet their desire imagines a nation that is not entirely theirs to possess. The point of my own musings about the anxieties that hover over twentieth-century collaborators' dreams is not to shake a prim finger at their desires and imaginations. Rather, I want to signal just how public the very act of imagining a collaborative space has become since the day, one hundred years ago, that Edith Somerville and Violet Martin posed together, two women in a garret, reading a page of print. Did their imaginations dream of a singular space—a territory, a nation? The impossible question makes me survey that peaceful-seeming portrait of "two women in a birth" once more and marvel at the energies and desires it may both secrete and release.

Notes

A revised version of sections of this essay appears in my book *Rethinking Women's Collaborative Writing*, which failed to take into account two illuminating treatments of women's collaborative writing that were in press at the time: Bette London's *Writing Double: Women's Literary Partnerships* and Holly Laird's *Women Coauthors*.

1. Burke, introduction to *Authorship from Plato to the Postmodern: A Reader*, xviii.
2. Woodmansee and Jaszi, "On the Author Effect: Recovering Collectivity," 15.
3. Pease, "Author," 266.
4. Burke, *Authorship from Plato to the Postmodern*, 146.
5. Foucault, "What Is an Author?," 121.
6. Sturge Moore, ed., *Works and Days: From the Journal of Michael Field*, xvi. Subsequent references appear parenthetically as *WD* in the text.
7. Field, British Library MSS, Add. 45851.
8. Field, British Library MSS, Add. 45853.
9. Quoted in Faderman, *Surpassing the Love of Men: Romantic Friendship and Love Between Women from the Renaissance to the Present*, 210.
10. Chadwick and de Courtivron, *Significant Others: Creativity and Intimate Partnership*, 9.
11. Jaszi, "On the Author Effect," 52.
12. Kaplan and Rose, "Strange Bedfellows: Feminist Collaboration," 549.
13. Field, British Library MSS, Add. 45853.
14. Ibid., Add. 46777.
15. Ibid., Add. 46779.
16. Masten, "Beaumont and/or Fletcher: Collaboration and the Interpretation of Renaissance Drama," 361–81; 363.

17. Field, British Library MSS, Add. 45852.

18. Quoted in Cronin, *Somerville and Ross*, 21.

19. Ibid., 20.

20. G. Lewis, ed., *The Selected Letters of Somerville and Ross*, 143. Subsequently cited parenthetically as *Letters* in the text.

21. G. Lewis, *Somerville and Ross: The World of the Irish R.M.*, 32.

22. Robinson, *Somerville and Ross: A Critical Appreciation*, 86.

23. Collis, *Somerville and Ross: A Biography*, 45.

24. Ede and Lunsford, *Singular Texts / Plural Authors: Perspectives on Collaborative Writing*, 143.

25. Kaplan and Rose, "Strange Bedfellows," 549.

26. Robinson, *Somerville and Ross*, 42–43.

27. Quoted in Collis, *Somerville and Ross*, 45.

28. Quoted in Robinson, *Somerville and Ross*, 47.

29. Laird, *Women Coauthors*, 5.

30. G. Lewis, *Somerville and Ross*, 70, 72.

31. Keane, introduction to *The Real Charlotte*, by Somerville and Ross, ix.

32. Collis, *Somerville and Ross*, 182.

33. Cronin, *Somerville and Ross*, 22, 100.

34. Robinson, *Somerville and Ross*, 39.

35. Powell, *The Irish Cousins*, 17, 84.

36. Quoted in Collis, *Somerville and Ross*, 181.

37. Foucault, "What Is an Author?," 138.

38. Powell, *The Irish Cousins*, 142.

39. Robinson, *Somerville and Ross*, 19.

40. Lewis, *Somerville and Ross*, 12, 201.

41. Namjoshi and Hanscombe, *Flesh and Paper*, 22. Subsequently cited parenthetically in the text.

42. Marlatt and Warland, *Two Women in a Birth: Poems*, 143. Subsequently cited parenthetically in the text.

43. Michelut, *Linked Alive*, 65.

44. Laird, *Women Coauthors*, 219.

45. Field, British Library MSS, Add. 46781.

46. London, *Writing Double*, 27.

47. Bhabha, "Introduction: Narrating the Nation," 1.

48. Laird, *Women Coauthors*, 220.

49. Ibid., 201.

50. London, *Writing Double*, 120, 119.

Taking Joint Stock

A Critical Survey of Scholarship on
Literary Couples and Collaboration

MARJORIE STONE & JUDITH THOMPSON

As our introductory section and the essays in this book indicate, research on literary couples, collaborative writing, and the construction of
authorship has grown rapidly across a number of fields during the last
two decades. For the most part, however, academics tend to approach
these subjects within the contexts of particular scholarly specializations
or historical periods. The paths of investigation are parallel, not con-
verging or intersecting. In this concluding essay we will survey the
aims, scope, and claims of some influential or representative studies of
coupled and/or collaborative authorship. Our goal is not to provide a
comprehensive critical bibliography. Instead, we offer a selective guide
that integrates research on literary collaboration with the studies of literary couples that precede or intersect with it, paying particular attention to work that theorizes coupled authorship in innovative ways. This
selective survey is designed to indicate how approaches to collaboration
might be altered or amplified if critical conversations took place more
frequently across the barriers formed by disciplinary formations, period
boundaries, generic divisions, and cultural traditions. A series of articles
on collaboration in the 2001 issues of *PMLA*, which appeared just as we

were completing work on this book, suggests that these conversations are now beginning to occur with greater frequency.[1] Yet much research on collaboration continues to take place within specialized contexts, leading to conclusions about coupled and/or collaborative writing that consideration of another scholarly field or historical period might question.

Many scholars turn first to the seminal effects of poststructuralist theories advanced by influential critics such as Michel Foucault and Roland Barthes to explain the transformations in conceptions of textuality and authorship that underlie new approaches to literary collaboration. For reasons addressed more fully in our introductory essay, we adopt a differing approach here. We do so, in part, because identifying certain master theorists as the founders of new paradigms ironically creates a narrative of origins predicated on the idea of the solitary creator. We have also found literary theory in itself less effective than historical and empirical research in challenging our habitual assumptions about how writers in working relationships produce coupled or collaborative texts. The far-reaching impact of poststructuralist theory on approaches to collaboration and constructions of authorship is also well summarized elsewhere.[2] Preferring to begin with studies of literary couples that helped to stimulate our own interest in collaboration, we next consider several broadly constructed (and occasionally overlapping) fields in which coupled or collaborative authorship has been a focus of attention. These fields include: feminist and queer scholarship; pedagogical research on compositional practices; editing and textual studies; investigations of modernism and avant-garde movements; research on the history of authorship and copyright; studies of early modern and Romantic authorship; and postcolonial readings of cross-cultural collaborations.

While studies of literary couples and their writing relationships have contributed to recent interest in literary collaboration, influential work in this area has generally adopted a biographical and/or psychological approach that paradoxically reinforces the paradigm of the solitary writer. Phyllis Rose's widely read *Parallel Lives: Five Victorian Marriages* (1984) is a case in point. As her title suggests, Rose treats marital or partnered "lives" that are "parallel" rather than merged or intersecting in the case of Victorian couples like the Carlyles and the Ruskins. Although she does address the critical reception of Harriet Taylor's collaborations with John Stuart Mill, these collaborations themselves are not her primary concern. Nor, in considering George Eliot and Henry Lewes, does she investigate their attentive engagement with each other's writing. Other studies of literary couples have similarly emphasized a particular theme (marriage, mentorship, the relationship with the muse, the sister bond, homoerotic desire), usually, like Rose, within the context of a single historical period and/or gender or genre. For example, John Tyttell's *Passionate Lives: D. H. Lawrence, F. Scott Fitzgerald, Henry Miller, Dylan Thomas, Sylvia Plath . . . in Love* (1995) adapts Rose's successful format to a treatment of five modernist writers "in love." Within the same period, Thomas Simmons's *Erotic Reckonings: Mastery and Apprenticeship in the Works of Poets and Lovers* (1994) explores the master-apprentice relationships of authors such as Ezra Pound, Louise Bogan, H. D., and Theodore Roethke. Another thematic focus is the author-muse relationship, the subject of Mary K. DeShazer's *Inspiring Women: Reimagining the Muse* (1986), on the muse figures of twentieth-century women poets.

Ruth Perry and Martine Watson Brownley's *Mothering the Mind: Twelve Studies of Writers and Their Silent Partners* (1984) is one of the only studies of writing couples before 1990 to go beyond this focus on a particular theme or type of relationship within a single historical context. Featuring essays on literary couples across three centuries and in different cultural traditions, Perry and Brownley turn to the psychological theories of D. W. Winnicott to demonstrate the role of "necessary others" in nurturing or "mothering" the creativity of writers such as the Shelleys, the Brownings, and Gertrude Stein and Alice B. Toklas. They also treat diverse types of partnerships, including three essays on "Mothers Real and Imagined" and three on other types of familial relationships. Fortunately, the nuanced analyses collected in *Mothering the Mind* complicate the opposition between "writers and their silent partners" implied by the subtitle, which seems oddly inappropriate in cases where both partners were established authors (like the Brownings or the Lewes). This subtitle speaks tellingly to prevailing images of authorship in its evocation of the "scene of writing." While the presence of a supportive partner is acknowledged, the writer is nevertheless pictured as creating individual works in a space of silence. The good "mother" of another's mind, the metaphor implies, is the silent mother.

A similar paradigm of "the writer" and "the other" combined with an emphasis on the biographical is evident in Whitney Chadwick and Isabelle de Courtivron's *Significant Others: Creativity and Intimate Partnership* (1993), an engaging collection focusing on "the realities of living creative lives in partnership." Treating thirteen British, American, and French artistic or literary couples, it pays particular attention to "familial and

companionate structures" and to "the real social and material conditions which enable, or inhibit, the creative life." However, unlike *Mothering the Mind*, this study is limited to "partnerships and collaborations" in
cases where "both partners were either visual artists or writers," as well
as to "couples who have shared a sexual as well as a creative partnership."[3] In examining the reciprocal give-and-take between partners
who are both working artists, Chadwick and de Courtivron's collection
comes closer to charting the territory our own contributors explore. Yet
despite the emphasis in *Significant Others* on the profound ways in which
intimate relationships shape artistic production, the model of authors
and artists as solitary (though linked) creators remains predominant.

Whereas *Significant Others* treats partnerships and collaborations
chiefly within the twentieth century and primarily among heterosexual
couples, Wayne Koestenbaum's *Double Talk: The Erotics of Male Literary
Collaboration* (1989) presents a gay "theory of male collaboration" as
"metaphorical sexual intercourse." Beginning with Wordsworth and
Coleridge but largely concentrating on heterosexual and homosexual
male partners active between 1885 and 1922, Koestenbaum applies the
"same paradigm" to all of the writers he treats, arguing that collaboration's "double voice" both expresses homoeroticism and strives to
conceal it."[4] He also assumes that in all such relationships one partner is
dominant and the other submissive. Expressed in his terms, if "double
writing" is an act of metaphoric anal intercourse, it is also "a scene of
analysis, in which the active collaborator hypnotizes his passive mate"
(7). In other words, Koestenbaum stretches all of the couples he treats in
the same Procrustean bed (albeit a sub rosa and flamboyantly gay one).
Our reservations concerning his binary model of dominant and submissive partners and his treatment of women as passive mediators have already been expressed in our introductory essay. That said, *Double Talk*
remains a groundbreaking study of works written under a "double signature," even though Koestenbaum subsequently reveals a "reverence"
for Romantic individuality (5) that counteracts his more radical observations. Anticipating the theories of literary collaboration that emerged
in the 1990s, Koestenbaum emphasizes that "collaborative works are in-
trinsically *different* than books written by one author," in revealing writing to be a "quality of motion and exchange" (2). He thus opens up conceptions of the text to the play of a dialogical textuality that resists
attribution.

Unlike the studies cited thus far, Lisa Ede and Andrea Lunsford's *Singular Texts / Plural Authors: Perspectives on Collaborative Writing* (1990) does not primarily concern literary collaboration. Nevertheless, like Koestenbaum's book, it has substantially shaped ideas about the collaborative process over the last decade. (As our introductory essay indicated, it was an important early influence on our own thinking and methodology.) Bringing together research in a variety of disciplines and across specializations—collaborative writing in professional, business, and academic contexts; analysis of the citation conventions that mask its prevalence; studies of composition pedagogy; gender theory; early research on electronic modes of collaborative textual production; and a succinct overview of theoretical and historical research on the history of authorship—*Singular Texts / Plural Authors* has stimulated new work on the construction of authorship as well as an increase in collaborative writing practices among critics themselves. Its pragmatic approach provides a welcome counterbalance to the psychobiographical readings of coupled authorship that prevailed in literary criticism up to 1990, while its diverting "intertexts" capture the transitions underway in conceptions and practices of authorship. More than any other work, it underscores the impact of research in composition studies on approaches to literary collaboration (which is also evident in Linda Brodkey's work). In her introduction to *New Visions of Collaborative Writing* (1992), Janis Forman traces this interest in theories of compositional collaboration back to scholarly investigations of collaborative pedagogy in the 1970s.

The importance of research in this field is also apparent in *Author-ity and Textuality: Current Views of Collaborative Writing* (1994), which similarly takes a "broad-spectrum approach," including work by "rhetoric and composition specialists, a business and technical writing specialist, a journalist, literary critics, and a political science researcher."[5] The contributors address a wide range of literary and quasi-literary forms, "from film to comic strips, to animated cartoons, to modernist poetry, to impressionist painting, to the nineteenth- and twentieth-century novel," in which there has been "an often-acknowledged substratum of collaborative textual production" (xiv). They also consider theories of authorship and textuality, diverse models of collaborative writing, definitions of collaboration, the ethics of collaboration, and factors contributing to its success. Among the most interesting contributions are those that put into practice the collaboration they investigate, like Linda K. Hughes and Michael Lund's "Union and Reunion," reflecting upon the process that led to their jointly authored book *The Victorian Serial*. "The real answer to the question, 'Did I write that, or did you?,'" they observe, "is '*We* wrote that,' a 'we' not strictly identified with either one of us, yet not a simple aggregate of two identities either" (49).

As Carey Kaplan and Ellen Cronan Rose point out in "Strange Bedfellows: Feminist Collaboration" (1993), feminist critics have long found "collaboration particularly congenial," a point borne out by collections such as *Feminist Scholarship: Kindling in the Groves of Academe* (1985) and *Common Ground* (1998).[6] Kaplan and Rose turn to lesbian metaphors to theorize their own collaborative practice not because it grew out of a sexual relationship but because of their experience of a "sexual/emotional continuum" and of a reciprocity they did not find either in the "customary hierarchy and competitiveness of heterosexual interaction" or in Koestenbaum's "(male) homosexual model of anxious collaboration" (550–51). They represent their collaboration not as a dance, in which one partner takes the lead, but as a "jazz ensemble": "'She' and 'I' metamorphose into 'we,' hypothetical, invisible, yet nonetheless articulate. 'We' emerges from the space between our individual different voices, its meaning elusive, dispersed, always deferred, never unitary'" (549–50). Rose and Kaplan do not entirely elide the conflicts and contestations of collaboration. As an apt figure for their writing relationship, they describe a postcard picturing a tiger and an alligator "improbably entangled," with a caption on the back reading, "'Strange bedfellows: people were concerned that no matter *what* their offspring looked like, they'd be mean as hell'" (554). That said, they convey the idealistic enthusiasm typical of the period in which they first presented their essay, specifically a paper read at a 1991 MLA session on feminist collaboration in a room overflowing "with women eager to listen to accounts of successful collaborations" (557).

Kaplan and Rose, Lunsford and Ede, and Koestenbaum all figure prominently in the "Preface" to the two-part "Forum on Collaborations" edited by Holly Laird for the fall 1994 and spring 1995 issues of *Tulsa Studies in Women's Literature*, one of the most important studies of writing couples and collaborators to appear in the 1990s. Continuing the project identified by Kaplan and Rose, namely, constructing an adequate "theory of feminist collaboration" (557), the *Tulsa* forum addresses many different kinds of collaboration women writers have participated in: from the contemporary co-novelists Joyce Elbrecht and

Lydia Fakundiny and their jointly produced meta-author Jael B. Juba, to cross-cultural collaborations between members of colonial and colonized cultures, to the interdisciplinary marital collaborations of Linda and Michael Hutcheon (to mention only a few). In one of the most engaging *Tulsa* essays, "Screaming Divas: Collaboration as Feminist Practice," Susan J. Leonardi and Rebecca A. Pope range with exuberant wit over both the delights and discontents of collaboration, analyzing the metaphors that best describe it (cooking, quilting, sexual exchange, mosaic work, part-singing, and conversations — with or without the "screams" of "serious disagreement"). They come down unabashedly in favor of sexual metaphors in their own case, while at the same time acknowledging the dangers of imposing these on the diversity of women's collaborations. As Laird notes, "No one theoretical model or diagrammatic map" is adequate to describe this diversity. "Discrete, plural, personal stories and anecdotalism take the place of a grand metanarrative or overarching theory."[7]

The need for multiple theoretical models is also evident in three full-length studies that further explore the rich vein (and the lost or erased history) of women's collaborations opened up by the *Tulsa* "Forum." In Bette London's *Writing Double: Women's Literary Partnerships* (1999), the spirit-writing of William Butler and George Yeats and collaborations by female mediums in the same period constitute a principal and fascinating strand of investigation, although London also considers the Brontë juvenilia, as well as homophobic responses to coupled women writers in the late nineteenth and early twentieth centuries (including two pairs of writing sisters: Mary and Jane Findlater and Emily and Dorothy Gerard). Laird's own *Women Coauthors* (2000) includes analyses of nineteenth-century collaborators in both England and America (Michael Field, Harriet Taylor and John Stuart Mill, Harriet Jacobs and Lydia Maria Child), as well as the twentieth-century partnerships of Gertrude Stein and Alice B. Toklas, Daphne Marlatt and Betsy Warland, and Louise Erdrich and Michael Dorris, among others. Marlatt and Warland are also among the authors discussed by Lorraine York (one of our own contributors) in *Rethinking Women's Collaborative Writing* (2002), a book that brings much-needed attention to Canadian and postcolonial collaborations in three genres — fiction, poetry, and theater — as well as providing an illuminating analysis of the collaborative criticism of French feminists such as Hélène Cixous and Catherine Clément and the Milan Women's Bookstore Collective. While our own book was substantially completed before these studies appeared, the points of convergence and divergence are striking. Like many of the essays we include, all three studies are much concerned with constructions of authorship and the erasure or invisibility of collaborative writing relationships, particularly those of an intimate or informal kind involving women writers.[8] However, unlike *Literary Couplings*, these studies principally concentrate on full or "overt" coauthorship, although they do recognize that collaboration can occur in many degrees and forms. As our introductory essay indicated, London, Laird, and York also place very different emphases on the potential harmonies versus the conflicts of coauthorship.

Jack Stillinger's *Multiple Authorship and the Myth of Solitary Genius* (1991) points to another important field that has stimulated new approaches to literary couples and collaborators in the 1990s, namely, editing and textual theory. Written by one of the most experienced editors of the last three decades, Stillinger's book counters the idea of the "solitary genius" not primarily through theory but rather through attending to the material processes of literary production within the changing cultural frameworks created by poststructuralist, feminist, and new historicist criticism. Stillinger's close textual studies of works by a range of British and American authors leads him to articulate a new understanding of *"the joint, or composite, or collaborative production of literary works we usually think of as written by a singular author."* The more radical implications of this view emerge in his argument that Mill and Harriet Taylor are "joint authors" of "Mill's" *Autobiography,* and that *On Liberty* and other works by "Mill" may indeed be (as Mill himself claimed) "joint productions."[9] To appreciate how Stillinger's own career embodies transformations in conceptions of authorship, one has only to contrast his 1991 view with that reflected in his earlier coediting with John M. Robson of John Stuart Mill. In the 1960s Stillinger shared Robson's view that despite Mill's own assertions to the contrary, Taylor was "not, in any meaningful sense, the 'joint author'" of *On Liberty* or of other works Mill identified her as a contributor to. Indeed, he points out that in editing Mill's *Autobiography* for the *Collected Works of John Stuart Mill,* neither he nor Robson noticed "that our photographer, in making a facsimile of folio R24r . . . virtually eliminated Harriet's revisions from the picture by purposely using a high-contrast film to block out what he considered superfluous pencilings!" In her 1970 analysis of the debate over the Taylor-Mill intellectual collaboration, Alice Rossi demonstrated how the dismissive or negative views of Taylor's role reflect "cultural expectations about the role of women"—ironically, expectations that Mill and Taylor themselves directly challenged. "The world does not take kindly to a successful collaboration between a married couple," as Phyllis Rose wryly observed, pointing to the twentieth-century example of John Lennon and Yoko Ono."[10]

Paul Eggert cogently critiques Stillinger's claim regarding "collaborative production," suggesting that "much of his argument depends on his narrowing the definition of authorship to mean the contribution of any textual material, however modest in scope, written by people other than the nominal author." Specifically, he suggests that Stillinger has not really "broken the nexus of the single-author/single-ideal text but only reinscribed it in a multiple form." Yet in certain respects Eggert seems less radical than Stillinger in resisting the claim of "joint production" in the case of Mill and Taylor, in reconstituting the "principal author" as the primary "textual agency," and in assuming that the "initiating textual agencies" are recorded at the "documentary level." One is reminded of Robson's reliance on the fact that Mill "held the pen" even though the philosopher described many of his works as the "'fusion of two'" minds.[11] When a woman in a literary partnership wields the pen, the conclusions may be quite different since she is more likely to be constructed as an amanuensis than a man is. In either case, handwriting alone is not necessarily an unequivocal sign of monovocal authorship. As Laird observes, "[W]hat precedes and surrounds a collaborative act of writing is the ever elusive, irrecoverable, and deeply interwoven process of two voices in conversation."[12] In this respect, Mill and Taylor's accounts of their writing process—involving intensive conversation and marking up multiple drafts—anticipates Dorris and Erdrich's descriptions of theirs (see Snapshot 3 in our "Prologue").

Stillinger relates his theory of "multiple authorship" to the work of another influential editor and critic, Jerome McGann, when he quotes McGann's view that "literary production is not an autonomous and self-reflexive activity; it is a social and institutional event." For this reason both resist editorial theories shaped by W. W. Gregg and Fredson Bowers "based on the concept of a single authorship and the ideal of 'realizing'—approximating, recovering (re)constructing—the author's intentions in a critical edition."[13] McGann points out that such attempts to reconstruct an "ideal" text are profoundly ahistorical both because "author's intentions rarely control the state of the transmission of the text" and "literary texts and their meanings are collaborative events."[14] In other words, literary texts are polyvocal: "[L]ike Tennyson's sea," they "'moan round'" with "'many voices'" (76). McGann places ahistorical, formalist editing practices within a tradition of "romantic hermeneutics" in which "texts are largely imagined as scenes of reading rather than scenes of writing," and where the reader is imagined as engaged in a solitary interpretive quest for meaning or a textual *aporia* (4, 12). Although he does not explicitly make the connection, the figure of the "solitary reader" that McGann critiques is the counterpart to the figure of the "solitary genius" that Stillinger places in the company of "multiple" collaborators. Both figures, according to Stillinger and McGann, are a legacy of the Romantic ideology that McGann, in particular, has sought to deconstruct throughout his career. McGann suggests that "one breaks the spell of romantic hermeneutics by socializing the study of texts at the most radical levels" (12). We believe that studies of literary couples and collaborators have proven so fruitful as sites for the deconstruction of traditional ideologies of authorship partly because they "socialize" textual study in precisely the way McGann recommends. Moreover, the effects of this study seem to be intensified when these studies are themselves collaborative, that is, when the text is interpreted not by a "solitary" reader in a silent space but rather by two or more readers interacting with each other in a socialized space.

While McGann claims that texts are "largely imagined as scenes of reading," Linda Brodkey reminds us how compelling the traditional image of the "scene of writing" can be. Drawing on modernist literature and composition research, Brodkey considers how college students invariably picture both the literary author and the student writer as working alone, isolated from time and history. This "familiar icon" or "freezeframe" of the isolated writer "places social life on the other side of writing," privileging "the moment when the writer is an amanuensis, making transcription a synechoche of writing."[15] Brodkey's work precedes and complements Stillinger's in important ways by suggesting how the Romantic image of the "solitary genius" was mediated by the altered cultural contexts of literary modernism. In fact, according to her, "the picture of the solitary scribbler is taken from the album of modernism, where the metaphor of solitude is reiterated as the themes of alienation in modern art and atomism in modern science" (398). In literary modernism the writer is more likely to be pictured in a prison cell than wandering among daffodils or on mountain peaks, and he is "irrevocably male. . . . The women referred to by the picture are not women who write. Rather, they are women who support the men who write: a muse or a mistress, a doting mother, wife or sister" (400). As for those women, like Virginia Woolf, who claim "a room of their own," Brodkey suggests that in doing so they subtly alter the paradigmatic scene of writing by connecting the rooms they claim to the world, society, and material pressures. "[T]he room is your own," citing Woolf, "but it is still bare. It has to be furnished . . . it has to be shared" (406). While our own collection of essays shows that modernist writing often took place in rooms that were "shared"—indeed, sometimes in texts that were shared—critics are only beginning to "socialize" the compositional histories of modernist texts in ways that go beyond the iconic scene of the solitary scribbler.

David Herd's "Collaboration and the Avant-Garde" (1995) reflects the mix of new and residual paradigms of authorship that continues to inflect not only the thinking of contemporary writers like Tony Kushner (see Snapshot 1 in our "Prologue") but also current studies of what might be termed the "scene of collaboration." Investigating the connections between literary partnerships and avant-garde movements, Herd turns to three examples: Wordsworth and Coleridge, Pound and Eliot, and the New York school of poets (John Ashberry, Frank O'Hara, Kenneth Koch, Henry Matthews, and James Schuyler). The latter group collectively produced a special issue of the little magazine *Locus Solus* on "Collaborations." Although he treats some of the same figures as Koestenbaum, Herd explicitly rejects the ahistorical tendency to "homogenize" collaboration that he finds in *Double Talk*, arguing instead that literary collaborations "must be approached historically" because "collaboration emerges from a "marginal" position to become "central and instrumental at strategic junctures in literary and particularly poetic history"—generally during periods involving "disruptive conditions."[16] As a result, the writing such partnerships produces is "saturated" by its historical contexts and is "peculiarly *alive* to its setting" and to literary forms, in part because the collaborating authors inscribe shared speech acts and negotiate conventions that their coalescence may lead them to recognize for the first time (42, 47–49). Herd's thesis leads to a telling critique of Harold Bloom's "aggressively individualistic" approach to authors in such circumstances (44). He suggests that such collaborations should be seen not as agonistic acts but as "forms of social exchange" in a ritual resembling "gift exchange" (52), utilizing a metaphor that also figures prominently in our own essay collection (for example, in Lisa Harper's essay on Yeats and Dorothy Wellesley).

There is interesting support for Herd's often-persuasive argument in a study he does not refer to, namely, Thomas Hines's *Collaborative Form: Studies in the Relations of the Arts* (1991), which analyzes experiments in combining the verbal, visual, and musical arts.[17] Nevertheless, as a historical theory of collaboration, Herd's thesis suffers from several limitations that we emphasize here because these tend to appear in other studies as well. Most notably, he constructs an overarching historical theory from a small number of examples limited by genre, gender, race, and historical context. Assuming that collaboration is an "avant-garde" practice, he considers (as Koestenbaum does) Wordsworth and Coleridge. But otherwise his focus, like that of many recent studies of collaboration or coupled authorship, is principally on late-nineteenth- and twentieth-century writers. Without reference to pre-Romantic textual production or to genres other than poetry (for example, to drama, a form that often provides more collaborative opportunities), he argues that collaboration is "not the setting in which literary works are usually produced," emphasizing what Kenneth Koch calls its *"strangeness"* (38–39; emphasis in original). He counters Stillinger's argument for the historical frequency of collaboration much as Eggert does, objecting to Stillinger's excessively "broad" definition of the term and proposing in its place a "taxonomy of collaborations" that reconstitutes traditional conceptual categories. Thus, he argues that "cases of collaboration, regarding the writer's partner, might equally, if not more appropriately, be taken as an instance of influence," while alterations in a text effected by a partner or editor might be classified as "revision" (39). Not surprisingly, given his assumption that a writing partner like Harriet Taylor can be classed as an "influence" or an "editor," Herd's argument not only leaves the assumption of the solitary author intact as a normative category but also replicates the traditional focus on canonized male authors. While he mentions female collaborators in raising the question of "whether the avant-garde is in an important sense structured by gender" (45), he does not investigate this possibility. His construction of the critical discourse on collaboration mirrors this pattern of exclusion. Thus, he considers the work of Koestenbaum and Stillinger but not the theories of Kaplan and Rose, Ede and Lunsford, or Jewel Spears Brooker's interesting earlier argument (that anticipates his own), namely, that texts such as *The Waste Land* develop in periods of "epistemological crisis," when the "common ground" of shared cultural traditions is lost and the opportunities they provide for collaboration must be gained "entirely through form."[18]

Three emerging (and intersecting) bodies of research underscore the problems with studies that assume collaboration to be a modern, avant-garde, or anomalous phenomenon: interdisciplinary studies of the history of copyright and authorship, like Martha Woodmansee and Peter Jaszi's book *The Construction of Authorship: Textual Appropriation in Law and Literature* (1994); historicist explorations of early modern, eighteenth-century, and Romantic collaborative literary production by scholars such as Jeffrey Masten and Alison Hickey; and investigations of cross-cultural writing partnerships past and present (when one might easily argue that postcolonial literatures have become important sites for avant-garde cultural practices). Even though he defines "collaboration" in restricted terms, Dustin Griffin observes that "literary collaboration is surprisingly common in Restoration and eighteenth century England," adding that "with surprising frequency, the Augustan writer did not appear before the public as a single author, but in the company of fellow writers."[19] However, as Woodmansee has shown, eighteenth-century collaborations are not, in fact, "surprising." She observes that "as we move backward in time, the collective, corporate, or collaborative element in writing . . . becomes even more pronounced." Woodmansee shows that Samuel Johnson—often cast as the "arch-author" responsible for shaping Romantic myths of the solitary genius—participated in many forms of "corporate" textual production. Mark Rose's *Authors and Owners: The Invention of Copyright* (1993) similarly reminds us of the strangeness of the modern assumptions of authorship that Herd takes for granted by delineating the ways in which the "regime of property," codified in the copyright of the individual creative author, differs from the early modern "regime of regulation" from which it developed.[20]

In studies of the early modern period, as Heather Hirschfield demonstrates, a particularly large and transformative body of research on authorship, copyright, and collaboration has been amassed in the last two decades. Jeffrey Masten's representative study in this area, *Textual Intercourse: Collaboration, Authorship, and Sexualities in Renaissance Drama* (1997), has proved influential across a number of fields, in part because Masten so skillfully analyzes not the "death" of the author but "the implications of absence of the author" in a period when neither "*author*" nor its "twin" "*anonymous*" had developed their later meanings.[21] Focusing on the "texts associated with early modern theatres," Masten argues that early modern plays are "polyvocal." They typically began "with a collaborative manuscript, which was then revised, cut, rearranged by bookholders, copyists, and other writers, elaborated and improvised by actors in performance," produced by a company of "sharers," and often further modified through "liminal speeches" to the audience cast in the form of "collaborative commerce." Such texts, Masten points out, "strikingly denaturalize the author-text-reader continuum assumed in later methodologies of interpretation," involving "a dispersal of author/ity, rather than a doubling" or multiplying of it (4, 13–14, 18). In attending not only to play production but to the apparatuses of the first quarto and folio publications of Shakespeare's, Ben Jonson's, and Beaumont and Fletcher's plays, Masten reveals the shortcomings of ahistorical editing practices predicated on the "universality of an individuated style" and a "sovereign authorial consciousness" (17, 20). Paul Werstine's investigation of Philip Henslowe's diaries and papers leads to parallel conclusions about the limitations of Greg's author-centered theory of copy-editing.[22] According to Masten, editors who accept Greg's principles tend to identify texts associated with collaboration as "doubtful," "corrupt," or manifesting a "contagion of style," (15–17), attempting to bring them under a regime of authorial univocality. For similar reasons, as Werstine notes, they also seek to demarcate authorial "foul papers," and theatrical prompt books (115). By attending to the material traces of collaboration embedded in early modern playtexts, however, scholars like Masten and Werstine show how, in the words of Masten, "the production of texts is a social process" (20). Thus, they reach similar conclusions to McGann and Stillinger, though from different historical grounds.

Masten's analysis of the "collaborative homoerotics" of early modern drama (37) is enriched thanks to his attention to the "intersection of the textual and the sexual" (5), as he demonstrates how "the idea of the author . . . emerges in conjunction with" seventeenth-century transformations in this discourse of "patriarchal absolutism" (73). At the same time, author-centered conceptions remained tentative, even in the folios that seem to enshrine the magisterial figures of individual playwrights, given the surviving older senses of the term "author" as authorizing figure, father, begetter, and not writer (120). Paradoxically, Masten finds in Margaret Cavendish's two folio publications of plays in 1662 and 1668 the clearest manifestations of the emerging "paradigm of singular authorship" (159). Noting that Cavendish is excluded from a "textual economy" of "theatrical discourse perceived as a conversation between men," Masten analyzes her deployment of an ideology of "originality" against the masculine authors whom he describes (in a revealing lapse) as "the very sites of authorship's initial construction" (159–60). The lapse is revealing, for despite Masten's claim that his study "will centrally include a consideration of women" (8), he considers only Cavendish among women writers in a closing supplemental chapter. While he does show how she displaces a discourse of homosocial "patriarchal reproduction" not only with a discourse of originality but also with "the newly emergent discourse of companionate marriage" (157), he does not investigate how the ideology of self-inspiration may have provided an opening for women writers generally, given their exclusion from homosocial collaborative networks, classical education, and patriarchal textual lineages. In other words, to an extent not acknowledged in Masten's study, writings by women other than Cavendish (like the Countess of Pembroke, as Demers shows in our essay collection) may also have been significant "sites" of changing conceptions of authorship in the sixteenth and seventeenth centuries.

Like many other scholars, Masten assumes that Romanticism unequivocally established the ideology of the "solitary genius" and the "regime of the author." In an important challenge to this critical commonplace, in a 1996 article Alison Hickey argued that "collaborative relations are an indisputable fact of the Romantic period."[23] Noting the tendency to treat Wordsworth and Coleridge as the only significant Romantic literary partners, Hickey argued that there are many Romantic texts, including those published under single signatures, that "represent their own collaborative origins" (735). Taking the work of Charles and Mary Lamb as exemplary, she shows how the "rival male-male collaborations" embodied in Charles's "triangulated literary relations with Coleridge and [Charles] Lloyd" modulate into the "double singleness" of his partnership with Mary, a sibling partnership modeled in part on a marriage—"rather like an old literary Darby and Joan, " in Mary's terms (745–46). Hickey emphasizes that early modern literary models significantly shape the ways in which Romantic writers like the Lambs represent their collaborations, thereby underscoring a historical continuity that is generally overlooked. "While Charles is drawn to a male-male image of collaboration" in Beaumont and Fletcher (and to homoerotic intimacies and rivalries with Coleridge and Lloyd remarkably like those Masten describes among circles of male Renaissance writers),

"Mary gravitates toward [the] female-female image" of Hermia and Helena sitting on the same cushion in *A Midsummer Night's Dream* to describe her joint labor with her brother on *Tales from Shakespeare* (753). Mary's Shakespeare allusion is fitting because for the Lambs, as for other Romantic writers like the Coleridges (whose collaborations Hickey explores in our own essay collection), "'myriad-minded Shakespeare" was "a site of collaboration in himself'" (751). Nor did such collaborative modes of literary production, self-consciously modeled on precursor couples, cease as the century progressed. As Ann Thompson and Sasha Roberts reveal in their illuminating analysis of another harmoniously productive Shakespearean partnership, Mary and Charles Cowden Clarke explicitly modeled their "loving, living consociation" as Shakespearean critics on the example of the Lambs.[24]

Hickey also draws attention to the political dimensions of Romantic collaboration in exploring its intersections with ideological and social developments. Although "collaborate" did not develop its explicit political meaning (to cooperate with or assist an enemy of one's country) until the mid twentieth century, it may have carried some of these connotations from the moment it first entered the English language in 1802 by way of the French, at a highly charged political moment when the act of collaboration was regarded as revolutionary and potentially treasonous. As Hickey points out, Romantic "ideals of revolutionary fraternity" led contemporary periodicals to construct literary collaborators, "schools," and "sects" in ways that reflect Jacobin versus Anti-Jacobin divisions, class sympathies, and other alliances that were viewed as political collusions. Indeed, "such groupings precede and underlie subsequent notions of Romanticism as a 'movement' and suggest the extent to which the perception of collaboration may have helped to determine the classifications on which literary histories have been based." In a subsequent article Hickey further explored the politically revolutionary nature of Romantic-era collaborations, noting how these arouse anxiety precisely because they reveal that authority is "not organic and inalienable. Rather, it is constructed with reference to other people and forces, it is always partial, it is never fully controllable by any one party, and it is vulnerable to deconstruction."[25]

The question of authority, linked to the question of agency, emerges with particular intensity in cross-cultural collaborations, both in our own period and in earlier centuries. The common and contradictory assumptions that literary collaboration is a relatively modern and/or avant-garde practice—or, alternatively, that it ceased in the Romantic period—not only overlook the ways in which the corporate writing practices of the sixteenth, seventeenth, and eighteenth centuries continued in the nineteenth century but also do not take into account the role of collaboration in the production of works marginalized until relatively recently, namely, "slave narratives" and autobiographies of indigenous peoples. While the essays in our own collection collectively demonstrate that gender ideologies have crucially shaped the formation, structure, and reception of coupled and collaborative writing relationships, postcolonial rereadings of these marginalized genres show that ideologies of race and nation have had equally pervasive effects. Many slave and indigenous subjects' autobiographies are inflected by racist ideologies both in their original production and in their subsequent reception, for it is only the collaboration with an "authorizing" member of the dominant culture that permits the enslaved or native subject's entry into literary discourse. These very conditions of entry then become the grounds for their exclusion from literary histories when, in a species of diachronic doublethink, the collaborations that author/ized them are interpreted as manifestations of their lack of agency and authenticity.

The reception of Harriet Jacobs's *Incidents in the Life of a Slave Girl* (1861), along with the partnership between Jacobs and the white abolitionist Lydia Maria Child that led to its publication, is a key example of this "catch-22" of cross-cultural collaboration. Rafia Zafir points out that "one hundred and twelve years" elapsed between the "anonymous" publication of Jacobs's *Incidents* and "the first modern reprint," in part because "a sceptical readership" assumed Jacobs's work was not genuine until Jean Fagan Yellin's pioneering research demonstrated its authenticity. Its "double" authorship contributed to this assumption since critics assumed that Child had played a much larger part in writing *Incidents* than the evidence, in fact, suggests. However, the same evidence indicates that Child was more than a mere stylistic editor in her interventions. The questions arising from this cross-racial collaboration lead Deborah Garfield to term the Jacobs-Child partnership a "vexed alliance." Other "vexed" collaborations led to the long neglect of *The Narrative of Sojourner Truth* and other African American "oral historical life stories, facilitated by white women."[26]

Cross-cultural collaborations also underlie many black and aboriginal autobiographies produced in the twentieth century, including *Black Elk Speaks* (1931)—the product of a partnership between the Oglala

Sioux elder and John G. Neihardt, a young white poet-historian—
and *The Autobiography of Malcolm X* (1965), involving a partnership between Malcolm X and Alec Haley. Albert E. Stone observes that in
these collaborative autobiographies, where the "self is never alone,"
critics need to consider the "actual interplay of personality and outlook
between the two collaborators," the nature of the audiences openly or
covertly addressed, and the possibility that "discoveries of the subject's
past" may be "*facilitated* but not *invented* by another"—as, according to
Stone, occurs in Haley's collaboration with Malcolm X.[27] Ironically,
these double-voiced autobiographies often cultivate a fiction of what
might be termed the "solitary speaker." Although Stone notes that
many "simulate an oral performance" (234), he largely passes over the
"issues of exploitation" that may open up along the fault lines of racial
difference, particularly when the collaboration is "between a literate
and an illiterate person" (234).

Critics writing from postcolonial perspectives place greater emphasis on these "issues of exploitation," both in past historical periods and
in the present. For instance, Susan K. Bernardin shows how the partnership between Mourning Dove, an Okanogan woman, and her "editor," Lucullus V. McWhorter, on *Cogewea, the Half-Blood: A Depiction of the
Great Montana Cattle Range* (1927) produced a text that in its very title page
reflects "mixed messages" about authorship and authority. Presented as
"by" Mourning Dove, it is "given through" Sho-pow-tan (an Indian
name assumed by McWhorter), with "Notes and Biographical Sketch
by Lucullus Virgil McWhorter." As Bernardin notes, "McWhorter bi-
furcates his editorial role into authentic Indian translator and an authoritative European-American annotator." Furthermore, she "undercuts Mourning Dove's authorial status by suggesting oral transmission."
One of his friends assumed that McWhorter was "'really the father of
this manuscript'" when, in fact, he was the editor—though one who
made so many "finishing touches" that Mourning Dove said "it felt like
it was someone elses [*sic*] book and not mine at all."[28] Elsewhere, however, she said, "We both worked hard on it and we sometimes went on
the warpath but we always patched up a peace and continued friends"
(quoted by Bernardin, 492). Just as Jacobs may not have been able to
publish her narrative without Child's assistance, so without McWhorter
Mourning Dove's novel "probably never would have found a publisher" (493). However, as in the case of Jacobs's *Incidents,* publication
did not ensure critical recognition. *Cogewea* was likewise "critically neglected because of its problematic authorship" (495).

The cultural inequities marking Mourning Dove's relationship with McWhorter appear in magnified form in the intensely conflicted collaboration between the Canadian Metis author Maria Campbell and the white actor Linda Griffiths, as recorded in *The Book of Jessica* (see the final "Snapshot" of our "Prologue"). According to Helen Hoy, "Arguments between Campbell and Griffiths, the (literal) give-and-take of their collaboration, rehearse systematically the sites and tropes of European/Native contestation: land, treaties, ownership, concepts of time, religion, cultural copyright." Like several other critics who have discussed *The Book of Jessica*, Hoy stresses Griffiths's appropriations in this "contestation." Alluding to Griffiths's technique of "sibyling"—that is, acting as a "medium" for Campbell in the collaborative dramatic improvisation that transformed Campbell's autobiography *Halfbreed* (1970) into the play *Jessica*—Hoy asks, "Are sibyls supposed to end up with copyright, with right of first refusal, with editorial *carte blanche*"? Lorraine York, who has analyzed more recent critical treatments of the Campbell-Griffiths partnership (including Hoy's), rightly reminds us that this was "a collaboration in which both authors participated, to some degree," and not a simple act of white "theft" of property. As such, it shares features of other "face-to-face" collaborations, which can be particularly daunting.[29] At the same time, the cultural differences between Campbell and Griffiths (as our "Snapshot" suggests) clearly create formidable barriers to communication and consensus. These differences suggest how important the common class backgrounds and mixed-blood identities of Michael Dorris and Louise Erdrich may have been to their initially more harmonious collaborations.[30]

Cross-cultural collaborations and the critical treatments these generate point to the need for increased dialogue between scholars in postcolonial studies and scholars focusing on collaboration and the construction of authorship. On the one hand, whether cross-cultural collaborations take place in the past, as in Jacobs's *Incidents* or in *Cogowea*, or in the present, as in *The Book of Jessica*, they serve as a healthy check to the tendency to valorize collaboration in several recent studies focusing on contemporary women writers or on "corporate" writing practices of the past. This valorization may obscure complex issues of power: issues of agency, accountability, acknowledgement, attribution and authority (the "five A's"). Not surprisingly, these are some of the same issues that postmodern theoretical celebrations of the "death of the Author" tend to elide, as feminist and postcolonial critics have often noted.[31] However, if postcolonial studies of cross-cultural texts can usefully complicate theoretical and historical work on collaboration, the opposite is also true. Too often critics working in postcolonial contexts accept without question the paradigm of the solitary, inspired author, frequently endorsing notions of authenticity that verge on racial or ethnic essentialism. The collaboratively produced cross-cultural text (whether it be a slave narrative or an indigenous autobiography) becomes more "inauthentic" the more it betrays signs of joint authorship: it is, so to speak, interpreted as a form of collaboration with the enemy. Ironically, such readings reveal a kind of reverse imperialism at work, for postcolonial critics deploy the very same models of proprietary authorship that ideologies of empire helped to consolidate. These models not only ignore the different models of communal production that indigenous oral traditions often provide but also overlook the extent to which—even within European traditions themselves—the "solitary author" has been more a prescriptive fiction than a historical reality.

We hope that this brief, necessarily selective survey will encourage increased cross-fertilization among existing approaches within various specialized fields involving collaboration, coupled writing relationships, and the construction of authorship. It is more difficult to discern significant absences in current discourses or scholarship, or transformations whose effects have not yet been registered. This remains true despite the very helpful syntheses provided by the 2001 *PMLA* "Theories and Methodologies" series on collaboration and authorship that appeared as we were completing work on our own essay collection. To take just one notable example of "absences," when we first began to work on this book, we expected to find a virtual explosion of new research on collaboratively produced electronic hypertexts—manifestations of the "collaborative web" prophesied by Tim Berners-Lee, the man ironically designated as the solitary "inventor" or "father" of the World Wide Web.[32] Surprisingly, however, our bibliographical searches up to 2000 yielded few studies along these lines. Humanities computing technologies may currently be generating new forms of collaborative textual production within the academy. Clearly, electronic chat rooms and listserves are providing fertile spaces for innovative kinds of collaborative exchange. Nevertheless, in their contribution to the *PMLA* series—a survey of developments since the publication of *Singular Texts/Plural Authors* (1991)—Lisa Ede and Andrea Lunsford find relatively little that has changed in almost a decade. They note, in particular, the absence of substantial transformation in the material practices of authorship, in the treatment of authorship in the academy, and in the "commonsense" assumptions naturalizing these. Despite the stimulus of new electronic technologies and signs of change like the "Forum" on "Creative Collaboration" organized by MLA president Linda Hutcheon, ideologies of the proprietary author persist in multifaceted manifestations. Ede and Lunsford conclude, "Far from being dead, the author is now working in the academy in ways that early framers of copyright and authorial autonomy could scarcely have imagined," alluding to the rapidly expanding applications of "intellectual property" outside the academy as well as within it, as charted by researchers like Rosemary Coombe.[33]

As Berners-Lee himself implied at a 1999 conference, the reasons why the "collaborative web" has failed to develop as a collaborative medium of creation on a large scale may have much to do with the colonization of the Web by commercial and corporate bodies using these "IP" protocols to consolidate their economic control. In fact, the "creeping enclosure of the informational 'commons'" that Woodmansee and Jaszi described in 1994 continues apace, as international corporations employ the "ideology of individual creativity" to profit from informational and cultural commodities. One lamentable consequence of corporate uses of the originary author construct is a form of neocolonialism, in which "the traditional, folkloric, and collaborative productions" of developing countries are "subject to appropriation by the culture industries of the developed world," while they go "for the most part unprotected by both national laws in their country of origin and the international copyright system."[34] In other words, in the global informational "commons," as in the history of coupled and collaborative authorship, some creators continue to benefit much more from ideologies of proprietary genius than others.

Like the subject of cross-cultural collaborations in the past and the present, the impact of electronic technologies on authorial assumptions and writing practices involves many subjects calling for extended study. Will the opportunities for multiple virtual partners in Web interactions result in a movement away from the dyadic relationship of the writing couple as the dominant mode of literary collaboration? Or will new technologies merely displace various forms of coupled authorship into modes of serial collaboration that do not greatly differ from the examples of serial and deferred collaboration that several essays in this book have examined? The future of scholarship in this area is likely to remain vexed and variable for some time as institutional conventions and agendas (whether academic, legal, bibliographic, or corporate) continue to promote proprietary definitions of authorship, while new technologies and global networks facilitate more fluid, flexible authorial options and frameworks. Under such circumstances, there may be much we can learn from grounded, historical investigations of writing practices and conceptions of authorship. By reassessing the past we not only make visible the origins and development of our ideologies and preoccupations but also find the means to interrogate and escape from them. The history of literary coupling and collaboration may yet offer up a more dynamic and heteromorphic prospect than we might initially have assumed.

Notes

1. This series appeared under the rubric "Theories and Methodologies" in successive issues of *PMLA* during 2001. A related series on collaborative scholarly practices appeared in the MLA's *Profession* (2001) as a "Presidential Forum" organized by MLA President Linda Hutcheon. For articles on literary collaboration and constructions of authorship in the *PMLA* series, see the entries in this volume's bibliography under the following names: Carringer, Ede and Lunsford, Hirschfield, Hutcheon, Inge, Laird, and Leonardi and Pope. We regret that, due to delays in press, this survey appears a considerable time after it was completed.

2. See, in particular: Ede and Lunsford, *Singular Texts/Plural Authors: Perspectives on Collaborative Writing;* Burke, ed., *Authorship from Plato to the Postmodern: A Reader;* and Leonard and Wharton, Breaking the Silence," in *Author-ity and Textuality.*

3. Chadwick and de Courtivron, *Significant Others: Creativity and Intimate Partnership,* 10, 7, 9.

4. Koestenbaum, *Double Talk: The Erotics of Male Literary Collaboration,* 2–3, 7. Other writing couples treated include Sigmund Freud and Josef Breuer, John Addington Symonds and Havelock Ellis, T. S. Eliot and Ezra Pound, and Joseph Conrad and Ford Madox Ford. Koestenbaum acknowledges that he is not interested in "acts of literary collaboration in general, but a particular sort of writing relationship that existed between men who were Freud's contemporaries" (4). "One angle I stint," he notes, is "historical and Marxist" (9)—a comment that underscores the neglect he concedes by merging two quite different approaches. Subsequent references appear parenthetically in the text.

5. Leonard et al., eds., *Author-ity and Textuality: Current Views of Collaborative Writing,* xiii. Subsequent references appear parenthetically in the text.

6. Kaplan and Rose, "Strange Bedfellows," 557. Subsequent references appear parenthetically in the text. See also Dubois; Peck.

7. Laird, "Preface," "Forum on Collaborations": Part I, 267; Part II, 12.

8. London underscores the "trivializations" that familial "configurations" in literary partnerships tend to produce, particularly for women; thus, to study collaboration is often "to study the conditions of its erasure" (5, 9). Laird notes that women collaborators have been rendered doubly invisible because they "have not supported a great male writer in collaboration" (3), while York observes that, "until the last few years, women's collaborative authorship has been as 'vast' and 'unlit chamber' as Virginia Woolf imagined for her Chloe and Olivia" (15).

9. Stillinger, *Multiple Authorship and the Myth of Solitary Genius*, v (emphasis in original), 50, 68. In *Women Coauthors* Laird is more critical of Stillinger's treatment of the controversy over Taylor's role in the *Autobiography*, arguing that even in 1991 "he portrays her as an editor not an author," characterizing her through stereotypically female roles, including those of "Copyeditor," "Mother-Protector," "Victorian Prude," and "Wicked Sister- and Daughter-in-Law" (46–47). However, Laird herself subsequently argues that Taylor was not a "full collaborator" in "Mill's" *Autobiography;* instead, she was a "contributor to an *Autobiography* not her own," the "coauthor of herself as nonauthor" (48–49).

10. Robson, *The Improvement of Mankind: The Social and Political Thought of John Stuart Mill*, 68; Stillinger, *Multiple Authorship*, 65; Rossi, *John Stuart Mill and Harriet Taylor Mill: Essays on Sex Equality*, 36; P. Rose, *Parallel Lives: Five Victorian Marriages*, 132.

11. Eggert, "Making Sense of Multiple Authorship," 313, 315–16, 318, 322; Robson, *The Improvement of Mankind*, 58, 60.

12. Laird, "Preface," "Forum on Collaborations": Part II, 13.

13. Stillinger, *Multiple Authorship*, 199, 195.

14. McGann, *The Textual Condition*, 22, 60. Subsequent references appear parenthetically in the text.

15. Brodkey, "Modernism and the Scene(s) of Writing, 396–99. Subsequent references appear parenthetically in the text.

16. Herd, "Collaboration and the Avant-Garde," 45, 37, 42. Subsequent references appear parenthetically in the text.

17. Hines's subtitle reflects his focus on works that involve collaborations in different media and not on collaborators themselves. As his study suggests, however, in their reception of collaborative artistic forms, audiences tend to focus on a single medium, much as do in their reception of coauthored works by emphasizing a single author.

18. Brooker, "Common Ground and Collaboration in T. S. Eliot," 236.

19. Griffin, "Critical Opinion: Augustan Collaboration," 1, 7. See the fourth

section of our introductory essay for a critique of the ways in which Griffin's definition of collaboration filters out informal and intimate partnerships.

20. Woodmansee, "On the Author Effect: Recovering Collectivity," 17; M. Rose, *Authors and Owners: The Invention of Copyright*, 23.

21. Hirschfield's survey, "Early Modern Collaboration and Theories of Authorship," which appeared after our own study was completed, treats scholarship on "extraliterary texts," manuscript and print culture, women's writing, and drama (611); Masten, *Textual Intercourse: Collaboration, Authorship, and Sexualities in Renaissance Drama*, 9, 12. Subsequent references appear parenthetically in the text.

22. Werstine, "Post-Theory Problems in Shakespeare Editing." Subsequent references appear parenthetically in the text. We would like to than Paul Werstine for sharing some of his research with us before it appeared in print.

23. Hickey, "Double Bonds: Charles Lamb's Romantic Collaborations," 735–36. Subsequent references appear parenthetically in the text.

24. "Marriage, Gender and the Victorian Woman Critic of Shakespeare: The Works of Charles and Mary Cowden Clarke," forthcoming.

25. Hickey, "Double Bonds: Charles Lamb's Romantic Collaborations," 737; Hickey, "Coleridge, Southey, 'and Co.,'" 307.

26. Garfield and Zafir, introduction to *Harriet Jacobs and "Incidents in the Life of a Slave Girl: New Critical Essays,"* 4; conclusion to *Harriet Jacobs*, 275; Humez, "Reading the Narrative of Sojourner Truth as Collaborative Text," 29.

27. A. Stone, *Autobiographical Occasions and Original Acts: Versions of American Identity from Henry Adams to Nate Shaw*, 233, 261–62. Subsequent references appear parenthetically in the text.

28. Bernardin, "Mixed Messages: Authority and Authorship in Mourning Dove's *Cogewea, the Half-Blood: A Depiction of the Great Montana Cattle Range*, 487, 494. Subsequent references appear parenthetically in the text.

29. Hoy, "'When You Admit You're a Thief, Then You Can Be Honorable': Native/Non-Native Collaborations in 'The Book of Jessica,'" 29, 27–28; York, *Rethinking Women's Collaborative Writing*, 174–76.

30. The less conflicted partnership of Erdrich and Dorris may also reflect their acceptance of a postmodern subjectivity. Jamil Khadar finds in their co-written novel *The Crown of Columbus* a "postcolonial Nativeness" that celebrates "difference, multiplicity, contingent identities, and the subject's constant and complex negotiations of belonging to various, even antagonistic, collectivities." "Postcolonial Nativeness: Nomadism, Cultural Mermory, and the Politics of Identity in Louise Erdrich's and Michael Dorris's *The Crown of Columbus*," 82–83. In the context of such a conception of identity, the self itself becomes a hybridized, serial collaboration. However, the costs of such a dispersal of identity may be apparent in the tragic conclusion to the Erdrich-Dorris partnership noted in the second section of our introductory essay.

31. See, for example, Nancy K. Miller, cited in Burke, ed., *Authorship from Plato to the Postmodern: A Reader*, 196–97, and Barbara Christian, cited in Ede and Lunsford, "Collaboration and Concepts of Authorship," 355. It is not surprising that the fairly recent full-length study of collaboration that is most skeptical of valorizing tendencies is York's book, which is also the study that pays the most attention to cross-cultural partnerships; see the first chapter (esp. 7–10) for York's expression of this skepticism.

32. Campbell, "Wither the Web? Inventor Wonders," J8.

33. Ede and Lunsford, "Collaboration and Concepts of Authorship," 355, 359; Hutcheon, "Creative Collaboration: Introduction"; Coombe, *The Cultural Life of Intellectual Properties: Authorship, Appropriation and the Law*.

34. Jaszi and Woodsmansee, introduction to *The Construction of Authorship*, 10–13.

Bibliography

Ahmed, Leila. *Edward W. Lane: A Study of His Life and Works and of British Ideas of the Middle East in the Nineteenth Century.* London: Longman, 1978.

———. "Western Ethnocentrism and Perceptions of the Harem." *Feminist Studies* 8 (1982): 521–34.

Alaya, Flavia. "The Ring, the Rescue, and the Risorgimento: Reunifying the Brownings' Italy." *Browning Institute Studies* 6 (1978): 1–41.

Alter, Robert. "The Psalms." In *The Literary Guide to the Bible,* edited by Robert Alter and Frank Kermode, 244–62. Cambridge, Mass.: Harvard University Press, Belknap Press, 1987.

Alvarez, A. "Your Story, My Story." *The New Yorker,* February 2, 1998, 58–65.

Anderson, Michael. *Family Structure in Nineteenth Century Lancashire.* Cambridge: Cambridge University Press, 1971.

Andrews, Jennifer. "Framing *The Book of Jessica:* Transformation and the Collaborative Process in Canadian Theatre." *English Studies in Canada* 22 (1996): 297–313.

Armstrong, Nancy. *Desire and Domestic Fiction.* Oxford: Oxford University Press, 1987.

Armstrong, Nancy, and Leonard Tennenhouse. *The Imaginary Puritan: Literature, Intellectual Labor, and the Origins of Personal Life.* Berkeley: University of California Press, 1992.

Armstrong, Tim. "Giving Birth to Oneself: Yeats's Late Sexuality." *Yeats Annual* 8 (1991): 39–58.

Assad, Thomas J. *Three Victorian Travellers.* London: Routledge, 1964.

Auerbach, Nina. "Robert Browning's Last Word." *Victorian Poetry* 22 (1984): 161–73.

Bailey, Ian. "Literary Ex-Lovers Heading to Court." *Halifax Mail Star,* July 1, 1998, B8.

Bakhtin, Mikhail. *The Dialogic Imagination.* Edited by Michael Holquist and

translated by Caryl Emerson and Michael Holquist. Austin: University of
Texas Press, 1981.

Barthes, Roland. "The Death of the Author." In *Image-Music-Text*, 142–48.
New York: Hill, 1982.

———. *The Pleasure of the Text*. Translated by Richard Miller. London: Jonathan
Cape, 1976.

———. "Theory of the Text." In *Untying the Text: A Post-Structuralist Reader*,
edited by Robert Young, 31–47. London: Routledge & Kegan Paul, 1981.

Bartlett, Neil. *Who Was That Man? A Present for Oscar Wilde*. London: Serpent's
Tail, 1988.

Bate, W. Jackson. *Samuel Johnson*. New York: Harcourt Brace Jovanovich, 1977.

Bateson, F. W. *Wordsworth: A Reinterpretation*. Rev. ed. New York and London:
Longmans, Green, 1956.

Battersby, Christine. *Gender and Genius: Towards a Feminist Aesthetics*. Bloomington: Indiana University Press, 1989.

Beauchamp, Virginia Walcott. "Sidney's Sister as Translator of Garnier."
Renaissance News 10 (1957): 8–13.

Beckson, Karl, ed. *Oscar Wilde: The Critical Heritage*. London: Routledge &
Kegan Paul, 1970.

Bednarz, James P. "The Collaborator as Thief: Raleigh's (Re)vision of *The
Faerie Queene*." *ELH* 63 (1996): 279–307.

Berkner, Lutz K. "The Stem Family and the Developmental Cycle of the
Peasant Household: An Eighteenth-Century Austrian Example." *American
Historical Review* 77 (1972): 398–418.

Berlau, Ruth. *Living for Brecht: The Memoirs of Ruth Berlau*. Edited by Hans Bunge
and translated by Geoffrey Skelton. New York: Fromm, 1987.

Bernardin, Susan K. "Mixed Messages: Authority and Authorship in Mourning Dove's *Cogowea, the Half-Blood: A Depiction of the Great Montana Cattle
Range*." *American Literature* 67 (1995): 487–509.

Bèze, Théodore de. *The Psalmes of David, truly opened and explaned by paraphrasis,
according to the right sense of euerie Psalme*. Translated by Anthony Gilby. London: Henry Denham, 1581.

Bhabha, Homi K. "Introduction: Narrating the Nation." In *Nation and Narration*, edited by Homi Bhabha, 1–7. London: Routledge, 1990.

Blanch, Lesley. *The Wilder Shores of Love*. London: John Murray, 1954.

Bleibtreu-Ehrenberg, Gisela. "*Teleny:* Zu einem apokryphen Roman Oscar
Wildes." *Forum Homosexualität und Literatur* 6 (1989): 5–39.

Bloom, Harold. *Yeats*. London: Oxford University Press, 1970.

Bohls, Elizabeth. *Women Travel Writers and the Language of Aesthetics, 1716–1818*.
Cambridge: Cambridge University Press, 1995.

Boswell, James. *Boswell's London Journal, 1762–63*. Edited by Frederick A. Pottle.
New York: McGraw-Hill, 1950.

———. *Boswell on the Grand Tour: Germany and Switzerland, 1764.* Edited by Frederick A. Pottle. New York: McGraw-Hill, 1953.

———. *Boswell in Search of a Wife, 1766–69.* Edited by Frank Brady and Frederick A. Pottle. New York: McGraw-Hill, 1956.

———. *Boswell for the Defence, 1769–1774.* Edited by William K. Wimsatt Jr. and Frederick A. Pottle. New York: McGraw-Hill, 1969.

———. *Boswell's Journal of a Tour to the Hebrides with Samuel Johnson, LL.D.* Edited by Frederick A. Pottle and Charles H. Bennett. New York: McGraw-Hill, 1961.

———. *Boswell: The Ominous Years, 1774–76.* Edited by Charles Ryskamp and Frederick A. Pottle. New York: McGraw-Hill, 1963.

———. *Boswell in Extremes, 1776–78.* Edited by Charles McC. Weis and Frederick A. Pottle. New York: McGraw-Hill, 1970.

———. *Boswell: The Applause of the Jury, 1782–1785.* Edited by Irma S. Lustig and Frederick A. Pottle. New York: McGraw-Hill, 1981.

———. *The Life of Samuel Johnson, LL.D. Together with Boswell's Journal of a Tour to the Hebrides.* Edited by G. B. Hill and revised by L. F. Powell. 6 vols. Oxford: Clarendon Press, 1934–64.

Brady, Frank. *James Boswell: The Later Years, 1769–95.* New York: McGraw-Hill, 1984.

Brain, Tracy. *The Other Sylvia Plath.* London: Longman, 2001.

Brennan, Michael. "The Date of the Countess of Pembroke's Translation of the Psalms." *RES* 33 (1982): 434–36.

———. "'First rais'de by thy blest hand, and what is mine / inspired by thee'": The 'Sidney Psalter' and the Countess of Pembroke's Completion of the Sidneian Psalms." *Sidney Newsletter and Journal* 14 (1996): 37–44.

Britzolakis, Christina. *Sylvia Plath and the Theatre of Mourning.* Oxford: Clarendon Press, 1999.

Brodie, Fawn, M. *The Devil Drives: A Life of Sir Richard Burton.* New York: Norton, 1967.

Brodkey, Linda. "Modernism and the Scene(s) of Writing." *College English* 49 (1987): 396–418.

Brooker, Jewel Spears. "Common Ground and Collaboration in T. S. Eliot." *Centennial Review* 25 (1981): 225–38.

Browning, Elizabeth Barrett. *Aurora Leigh.* Edited by Margaret Reynolds. New York: Norton, 1995.

———. *The Letters of Elizabeth Barrett Browning to Her Sister Arabella.* Edited by Scott Lewis. 2 vols. Waco, Tex.: Wedgestone Press, 2002.

———. "Maude Clarence." In "Poems and Sonnets Notebook." Beinecke Rare Book Room, Yale University.

———. *The Poetical Works.* Edited by Ruth M. Adams. Boston: Houghton Mifflin, 1974.

————. "The Sonnets Notebook." Armstrong Browning Library, Baylor University, Texas.

————. Fair copy of "The Runaway Slave at Pilgrim's Point," with Robert Browning's annotations. Stanzas 27–36. Armstrong Browning Library, Baylor University, Waco, Texas.

Browning, Elizabeth Barrett, and Robert Browning. *The Brownings' Correspondence.* Edited by Philip Kelley, Ronald Hudson, and Scott Lewis. 14 vols. to date. Winfield, Kan.: Wedgestone Press, 1984–.

Browning, Robert. *The Poems.* Edited by John Pettigrew and T. J. Collins. 2 vols. Harmondsworth, Eng.: Penguin, 1981.

Browning, Robert. *The Ring and the Book.* Edited by Richard D. Altick. New Haven, Conn.: Yale University Press, 1971.

Browning, Robert, and Elizabeth Barrett Browning. *The Letters of Robert Browning and Elizabeth Barrett Browning, 1845–1846.* Edited by Elvan Kintner. 2 vols. Cambridge, Mass.: Harvard University Press, 1969.

Brueggemann, Walter. *The Message of the Psalms.* Minneapolis, Minn.: Augsburg, 1984.

Buchanan, George. *Paraphrasis Psalmorum Davidis Poetica, multo quam ante hac castigatior: Auctore Georgio Buchanano.* London: Thomas Vautrollier, 1580.

Bundtzen, Lynda. *The Other Ariel.* Amherst: University of Massachusetts Press, 2001.

Burke, Sean, ed. *Authorship from Plato to the Postmodern: A Reader.* Edinburgh: Edinburgh University Press, 1995.

Burton, Isabel. *The Inner Life of Syria, Palestine, and the Holy Land.* 2 vols. London: Henry King, 1875.

————. *Lady Burton's Edition of Her Husband's Arabian Nights. Translated Literally From the Arabic and Prepared for Household Reading by Justin Huntly McCarthy, M.P.* 6 vols. London: Waterlow, 1886.

————. *The Life of Captain Sir Richard Francis Burton.* 2 vols. London: Chapman, 1893.

Burton, Jean. *Sir Richard Burton's Wife.* New York: Knopf, 1941.

Burton, Richard. *The Book of the Thousand Nights and a Night: A Plain and Literal Translation of the Arabian Nights' Entertainments, with Introduction and Explanatory Notes on the Customs of Moslem Men and a Terminal Essay upon the History of the Nights.* 6 vols. Benares, India: Kama Shastra Society, 1885–86.

————. *Supplemental Nights to The Book of the Thousand and One Nights, with Notes, Anthropological and Explanatory.* 10 vols. Benares, India: Kama Shastra, 1886–88.

Busia, Abena. "Silencing Sycorax: On African Colonial Discourse and the Unvoiced Female." *Cultural Critique* 14 (Winter 1989–90): 81–104.

Byatt, A. S. *Possession: A Romance.* New York: Vintage, 1991.

Byrd, Deborah. "Combatting an Alien Tyranny: Elizabeth Barrett Browning's

Evolution as a Feminist Poet." In *Critical Essays on Elizabeth Barrett Browning*, edited by Sandra Donaldson, 202–17. New York: G. K. Hall, 1999.

Campbell, K. K. "Whither the Web? Inventor Wonders." *Toronto Star*, May 27, 1999, J8.

Carey, John. "Fatal Attraction." *Sunday Times Books* (London), January 25, 1998: 1–2.

Carringer, Robert L. "Collaboration and Concepts of Authorship." *PMLA* 116 (2001): 370–79.

Castle, Terry. "Lab'ring Bards: Birth *Topoi* and English Poetics, 1660–1820." *Journal of English and Germanic Philology* 78 (1979): 193–208.

Cavanagh, Catherine. *Love and Forgiveness in Yeats's Poetry*. Ann Arbor, Mich.: UMI Research Press, 1986.

Caxton, John, trans. *Legenda Aurea*. Westminster, 1483.

Chadwick, Whitney, and Isabelle de Courtivron, eds., *Significant Others: Creativity and Intimate Partnership*. London: Thames & Hudson, 1993.

Chambers, Sir Robert. *A Course of Lectures on the English Law*. Edited by Thomas M. Curley. 2 vols. Madison: University of Wisconsin Press, 1986.

Chartier, Roger. "Figures of the Author." In *Of Authors and Origins*, edited by Brad Sherman and Alain Strowel and translated by L. G. Cochrane, 7–22. Oxford: Clarendon Press, 1994.

Chavkin, Allan, and Nancy Feyl Chavkin, eds. *Conversations with Louise Erdrich and Michael Dorris*. Jackson: University of Mississippi Press, 1994.

Cheng, Vincent J. *Joyce, Race, and Empire*. Cultural Margins 3. Cambridge: Cambridge University Press, 1995.

Churchwell, Sarah. "Secrets and Lies: Plath, Privacy, Publication and Ted Hughes's Birthday Letters." *Contemporary Literature* 42 (2001): 102–48.

Cohen, Ed. *Talk on the Wilde Side: Toward a Genealogy of a Discourse on Male Sexualities*. New York: Routledge, 1993.

———. "Writing Gone Wilde: Homoerotic Desire in the Closet of Representation." *PMLA* 102 (1987): 801–13.

Coleridge, Hartley. *Letters of Hartley Coleridge*. Edited by Grace Evelyn Griggs and Earl Leslie Griggs. London: Oxford University Press, 1936.

———. *New Poems, Including a Selection from His Published Poetry*. Edited by Earl Leslie Griggs. Westport, Conn.: Greenwood, 1972.

Coleridge, Samuel Taylor. *Biographia Literaria*. Edited by James Engell and W. Jackson Bate. 2 vols. Princeton, N.J.: Princeton University Press, 1983.

———. *Biographia Literaria*. Prepared by H. N. Coleridge and completed by Sara Coleridge. Reprint of vol. 3 of *The Complete Works of Samuel Taylor Coleridge*. Edited by W. G. T. Shedd. New York: Harper, 1884.

———. *Collected Letters of Samuel Taylor Coleridge*. Edited by Earl Leslie Griggs. 6 vols. Oxford: Clarendon, 1956–71.

————. *The Complete Poetical Works of Samuel Taylor Coleridge.* Vol. 1. Edited by Ernest Hartley Coleridge. Oxford: Clarendon, 1912.

————. *Essays on His Own Times, Forming a Second Series of The Friend.* Vol. 1. Edited by Sara Coleridge. London: Pickering, 1850.

————. *Notes and Lectures upon Shakespeare, and Some of the Old Poets and Dramatists, with Other Literary Remains of S. T. Coleridge.* Vol. 1. Edited by Sara Coleridge. London: Pickering, 1849.

————. *The Notebooks of Samuel Taylor Coleridge.* Edited by Kathleen Coburn. Princeton, N.J.: Princeton University Press, 1973.

————. *The Poems of Samuel Taylor Coleridge.* Edited by Derwent and Sara Coleridge. London: Moxon, 1852.

Coleridge, Sara. *Memoir and Letters of Sara Coleridge.* Edited by Edith Coleridge. New York: Harper, 1874.

Collis, Maurice. *Somerville and Ross: A Biography.* London: Faber and Faber, 1968.

Coombe, Rosemary J. "Author/izing the Celebrity: Publicity Rights, Post-modern Politics, and Unauthorized Genders." In *The Construction of Authorship: Textual Appropriation in Law and Literature,* edited by Martha Woodmansee and Peter Jaszi, 101–32. Durham, N.C.: Duke University Press, 1994.

————. *The Cultural Life of Intellectual Properties: Authorship, Appropriation and the Law.* Durham, N.C.: Duke University Press, 1998.

Craft, Christopher. *Another Kind of Love: Male Homosexual Desire in English Discourse, 1850–1920.* Berkeley: University of California Press, 1994.

Crawford, Thomas, ed. *The Correspondence of James Boswell and William Johnson Temple, 1756–1795.* Vol. 1, *1756–1777.* New Haven, Conn.: Yale University Press, 1997.

Crewe, Jonathan. *Hidden Designs; The Critical Profession and Renaissance Literature.* New York: Methuen, 1986.

Croft-Cooke, Rupert. *The Unrecorded Life of Oscar Wilde.* London: W. H. Allen, 1972.

Cronin, John. *Somerville and Ross.* Lewisburg: Bucknell University Press, 1972.

Crozier, Dorothy. "Kinship and Occupational Succession." *Sociological Review* 13 (1965): 15–43.

Cullingford, Elizabeth Butler. *Gender and History in Yeats's Love Poetry.* Cambridge: Cambridge University Press, 1993.

Curley, Thomas M., ed. *A Course of Lectures on the English Law Delivered at the University of Oxford 1767–1773 by Sir Robert Chambers, Second Vinerian Professor of English Law, and Composed in Association with Samuel Johnson, Volume II.* Madison: University of Wisconsin Press, 1987.

Dafoe, Chris. "Singer Surfaces from Trial Victorious." *Globe and Mail,* December 13, 1999, A2.

Darlington, Beth. *Home at Grasmere: Part First, Book First of The Recluse*. Ithaca, N.Y.: Cornell University Press, 1977.

Davidoff, Leonore. "Where the Stranger Begins: The Question of Siblings in Historical Analysis." In *Worlds Between: Historical Perspectives on Gender and Class*. New York: Routledge, 1995.

Davidoff, Leonore, and Catherine Hall. *Family Fortunes: Men and Women of the English Middle Class, 1780–1850*. Chicago: University of Chicago Press, 1987.

Davison, Peter. "Dear Sylvia." *Boston Globe*, February 8, 1998, G1.

Day, Douglas. *Swifter Than Reason: The Poetry and Criticism of Robert Graves*. Chapel Hill: University of North Carolina Press, 1963.

Derrida, Jacques. "Living On: Border Lines." In *Deconstruction and Criticism*, edited by Harold Bloom, 75–176. New York: Seabury, 1979.

De Quincey, Thomas. *The Collected Writings of Thomas De Quincey*. Rev. ed. Vol. 2. Edited by David Masson. Edinburgh: Black, 1889.

De Selincourt, Ernest. *Dorothy Wordsworth: A Biography*. Oxford: Clarendon Press, 1933.

DeShazer, Mary K. *Inspiring Women: Reimagining the Muse*. New York: Pergamon, 1986.

DeVane, William C. *A Browning Handbook*. 2nd ed. New York: Appleton-Century-Crofts, 1955.

Devi, Maitreyi. *It Does Not Die*. Chicago: University of Chicago Press, 1994.

Donne, John. *Poetical Works*. Edited by Herbert Grierson. London: Oxford University Press, 1933.

Dubois, Ellen Carol, et al. *Feminist Scholarship: Kindling in the Groves of Academe*. Urbana: University of Illinois Press, 1987.

Dyson, Richard. "On Sylvia Plath." *Sylvia Plath: A Symposium*, edited by Charles Newman, London: Faber and Faber, 1970.

Ede, Lisa, and Andrea Lunsford. "Collaboration and Concepts of Authorship." *PMLA* 116 (2001): 354–69.

———. *Singular Texts/Plural Authors: Perspectives on Collaborative Writing*. Carbondale: Southern Illinois University Press, 1990.

Eggert, Paul. "Making Sense of Multiple Authorship." *TEXT: Transactions of the Society for Textual Scholarship* 8 (1995): 305–23.

Eliade, Mircea. *Bengal Nights*. Chicago: University of Chicago Press, 1994.

Eliot, T. S. "Apology for the Countess of Pembroke." In *The Use of Poetry and the Use of Criticism*, 37–52. London: Faber and Faber, 1933.

Erickson, Lee. *Robert Browning: His Poetry and His Audiences*. Ithaca, N.Y.: Cornell University Press, 1984.

Faderman, Lillian. *Surpassing the Love of Men: Romantic Friendship and Love Between Women from the Renaissance to the Present*. 2nd ed. London: The Women's Press, 1985.

Fallon, Brian. "The Magna Mater's High Priest." Review of *The White Goddess*,

by Robert Graves. http://www.ireland.com/newspaper/weekend/1997/
1129/archive.9711290021g.html. *The Irish Times on the Web,* Nov. 29, 1997.

Favret, Mary. *Romantic Correspondence: Women, Politics and the Fiction of Letters.*
Cambridge: Cambridge University Press, 1993.

Fay, Elizabeth A. *Becoming Wordsworthian: A Performative Aesthetic.* Amherst: University of Massachusetts Press, 1995.

Fenton, James. "A Family Romance." *New York Review of Books,* March 5, 1998,
7–9.

Field, Michael. British Library MSS Add. 45851–45853, 46777, 46779, 46781.

———. *A Selection from the Poems of Michael Field.* London: The Poetry Bookshop,
1923.

Finney, Brian. "Boswell's Hebridean Journal and the Ordeal of Dr. Johnson."
Biography 5 (1982): 319–34.

Fisken, Beth Wynne. "'The Art of Sacred Parody' in Mary Sidney's Psalmes."
Tulsa Studies in Women's Literature 8 (1989): 223–39.

———. "Mary Sidney's Psalmes: Education and Wisdom." In *Silent But for
the Word: Tudor Women as Patrons, Translators and Writers of Religious Works,*
edited by M. P. Hannay, 166–83. Kent, Ohio: Kent State University Press,
1985.

———. "'To the Angell spirit . . .': Mary Sidney's Entry into the 'World of
Words.'" In *The Renaissance Englishwoman in Print: Counterbalancing the Canon,*
edited by Anne M. Haselkorn and Betty S. Travitsky, 263–75. Amherst:
University of Massachusetts Press, 1990.

Fleeman, J. D. Introduction and notes to Samuel Johnson's *A Journey to the Western Islands of Scotland.* Oxford: Clarendon Press, 1985.

Forman, Janis, ed. *New Visions of Collaborative Writing.* Portsmouth, N. H.:
Heinemann, 1992.

Foster, Shirley. *Across New Worlds: Nineteenth-Century Women Travellers and Their
Writings.* New York: Harvester Wheatsheaf, 1986.

Foucault, Michel. *The History of Sexuality: Volume One: An Introduction.* Translated
by Robert Hurley. New York: Vintage, 1980.

———. "What Is an Author?" In *Language, Counter-Memory, Practice,* edited by
Donald F. Bouchard and translated by Donald F. Bouchard and Sherry
Simon, 124–27. Ithaca, N.Y.: Cornell University Press, 1977.

Freer, Coburn. "The Countess of Pembroke in a World of Words." *Style* 5
(1971): 37–56.

Friedman, Susan Stanford. "Creativity and the Childbirth Metaphor: Gender
Difference in Literary Discourse." *Feminist Studies* 13 (1987): 49–82.

Garab, Arra M. "Fabulous Artifice: Yeats's 'Three Bushes' Sequence." *Criticism* 7, no. 3 (1965): 235–49.

Garber, Marjorie. *Vested Interests: Cross-Dressing and Cultural Anxiety.* New York:
Harper Perennial, 1992.

Garfield, Deborah, and Rafia Zafar, eds. *Harriet Jacobs and "Incidents in the Life of a Slave Girl": New Critical Essays*. Cambridge: Cambridge University Press, 1996.

Geier, Thom. "The End of a Controversial Silence." *U.S. News & World Report*, February 9, 1998, 8.

The Geneva Bible. Facsimile of 1560 ed. Introduction by L. E. Berry. Madison: University of Wisconsin Press, 1969.

Gentleman, Amelia. "Accolade for Hughes's Poems of Love and Loss." *The Guardian*, October 8, 1998, 4.

Gere, Anne Ruggles. "Common Properties of Pleasure: Texts in Nineteenth Century Women's Clubs." In *The Construction of Authorship: Textual Appropriation in Law and Literature*, edited by Martha Woodmansee and Peter Jaszi, 383–400. Durham, N.C.: Duke University Press, 1994.

Gibson, Mary Ellis. "One Word More on Browning's 'One Word More.'" *Studies in Browning and His Circle* 12 (1984): 76–86.

Gilbert, Sandra, and Susan Gubar. *The Madwoman in the Attic: The The Woman Writer and the Nineteenth-Century Literary Imagination*. New Haven, Conn.: Yale University Press, 1979.

———. *No Man's Land*. Vol. 1, *The War of the Words*. New Haven, Conn.: Yale University Press, 1988.

———. *No Man's Land*. Vol. 2, *The War of the Words*. New Haven, Conn.: Yale University Press, 1988.

Gill, Stephen. *William Wordsworth: A Life*. Oxford: Clarendon Press, 1989.

Gittings, Robert, and Jo Manton. *Dorothy Wordsworth*. Oxford: Clarendon Press, 1985.

Glendinning, Victoria. *Vita: The Life of V. Sackville-West*. London: Weidenfeld and Nicolson, 1983.

Godwin, William. *An Enquiry Concerning Political Justice and Its Influence on General Virtue and Happiness. Political and Philosophical Writings of William Godwin*. Vols. 3 and 4. London: William Pickering, 1993.

———. *Memoirs of the Author of a Vindication of The Rights of Woman*. Vol. 1 of *Collected Novels and Memoirs of William Godwin*, edited by Mark Philp, 85–142. London: William Pickering, 1992.

Godwin, William, and Mary Wollstonecraft. *Godwin & Mary: Letters of William Godwin and Mary Wollstonecraft*. Edited by Ralph M. Wardle. Lawrence, Kan.: University of Kansas Press, 1966.

Goldberg, Jonathan. *Voice Terminal Echo: Postmodernism and English Renaissance Texts*. New York: Methuen, 1986.

———. "Hamlet's Hand." *Shakespeare Quarterly* 39 (1988): 307–27.

———. *Sodometries: Renaissance Texts, Modern Sexualities*. Stanford, Calif.: Stanford University Press, 1992.

———. "The Countess of Pembroke's Literal Translation." In *Subject and Object in Renaissance Culture,* edited by Margreta de Grazia et al., 321–36. Cambridge: Cambridge University Press, 1996.

Gordon, Robert. "Wordsworth and the Domestic Roots of Power." *Bulletin of Research in the Humanities* 81 (1978): 90–102.

Graves, Robert. *5 Pens in Hand.* New York: Doubleday, 1958.

———. *On Poetry: Collected Talks and Essays.* New York: Doubleday, 1969.

———. *The White Goddess.* 1948. Reprint, New York: Vintage, 1961.

Gray, Paul. "Poet's License." *Time,* February 16, 1998.

Greer, David, ed. *The English Lute Songs; Songs from Manuscript Sources I.* London: Stainer & Bell, 1979.

Grewal, Inderpal. *Home and Harem: Nation, Gender, Empire and the Cultures of Travel.* Durham, N.C.: Duke University Press, 1996.

Griffin, Dustin. "Critical Opinion: Augustan Collaboration." *Essays in Criticism* 37 (1987): 1–10.

Griffiths, Linda, and Maria Campbell. *The Book of Jessica: A Theatrical Transformation.* Toronto: Coach House Press, 1989.

Griggs, Earl Leslie. *Coleridge Fille: A Biography of Sara Coleridge.* London: Oxford University Press, 1940.

———. "Robert Southey's Estimate of Samuel Taylor Coleridge: A Study in Human Relations." *Huntington Library Quarterly* 9 (1945): 61–94.

Haigwood, Laura. "Gender-to-Gender Anxiety and Influence in Robert Browning's *Men and Women.*" *Browning Institute Studies* 14 (1986): 97–118.

Hamilton, A. C. *Sir Philip Sidney: A Study of His Life and Works.* Cambridge: Cambridge University Press, 1977.

Hannay, Margaret P. "'Princes you as men must dy': Genevan Advice to Monarchs in the Psalmes of Mary Sidney." *ELR* 19 (1989): 22–41.

———. *Philip's Phoenix: Mary Sidney, Countess of Pembroke.* New York: Oxford University Press, 1990.

———. "'Unlock my lipps': The Miserere mei Deus of Anne Vaughan Lok and Mary Sidney Herbert, Countess of Pembroke." In *Privileging Gender in Early Modern England,* edited by Jean R. Brink, 19–36. Kirksville, Miss.: Sixteenth Century Journal Publishers, 1993.

———, ed. *Silent But for the Word: Tudor Women as Patrons, Translators, and Writers of Religious Works.* Kent, Ohio: Kent State University Press, 1985.

Harington, John. *Nugae Antiquae.* Edited by Henry Harington. London: Vernon and Hood, 1804.

Heinzelman, Kurt. "The Cult of Domesticity: Dorothy and William Wordsworth at Grasmere." In *Romanticism and Feminism,* edited by Anne K. Mellor. Bloomington, Ind.: Indiana University Press, 1988.

Hemphill McCormick, Anita. "'I shall be beloved—I want no more': Dorothy Wordsworth's Rhetoric and the Appeal to Feeling in *The Grasmere Journals.*" *Philological Quarterly* 69 (1990): 471–93.

Henn, T. R. *The Lonely Tower: Studies in the Poetry of W. B. Yeats.* London: Methuen, 1965.

Herbert, Mary Sidney. *The Collected Works of Mary Sidney Herbert, Countess of Pembroke.* Edited by Margaret Hannay, Noel Kinnamon, and Michael Brennan. 2 vols. Oxford: Clarendon Press, 1998.

Herd, David. "Collaboration and the Avant-Garde." *Critical Review* 35 (1995): 36–63.

Heywood, Thomas. *Gynaikeion or Nine Bookes of Various History Concerning Women; Inscribed by ye names of ye nine Muses.* London: Adam Islip, 1624.

Hickey, Alison. "Coleridge, Southey, 'and Co.'" *Studies in Romanticism* 37 (1998): 305–49.

———. "Double Bonds: Charles Lamb's Romantic Collaborations." *ELH* 63 (1996): 735–71.

Hines, Thomas Jensen. *Collaborative Form: Studies in the Relations of the Arts.* Kent, Ohio: Kent State University Press, 1991.

Hirschfield, Heather. "Early Modern Collaboration and Theories of Authorship." *PMLA* 116 (2001): 609–22.

Holcombe, Lee. *Wives and Property: Reform of the Married Women's Property Law in Nineteenth-Century England.* Toronto: University of Toronto Press, 1983.

Homans, Margaret. *Bearing the Word: Language and Female Experience in Nineteenth-Century Women's Writing.* Chicago: University of Chicago Press, 1986.

Howell, Peter. "The Hottest Guy in Tights." *Toronto Star,* March 21, 1999, D16–17.

Hoy, Helen. "'When You Admit You're a Thief, Then You Can Be Honorable': Native/Non-Native Collaboration in 'The Book of Jessica.'" *Canadian Literature* 136 (1993): 24–39.

Hughes, Linda K., and Michael Lund. "Union and Reunion: Collaborative Authorship." In *Author-ity and Textuality: Current Views of Collaborative Writing,* edited by James S. Leonard et al., 41–60. West Cornwall, Conn.: Locust Hill Press, 1994.

Hughes, Olwyn. Letter. *New York Review of Books,* September 30, 1976, 42–43.

———. Letter. *Times Literary Supplement,* June 17–23, 1988, 677.

Hughes, Ted. "Ted Hughes: The Art of Poetry." Interview with Drue Heinz. *The Paris Review* 37 (1995): 54–94.

———. *Birthday Letters.* New York: Farrar, Straus, & Giroux, 1998.

———. Foreword to *The Journals of Sylvia Plath,* edited by Ted Hughes and Frances McCullough. New York: Dial, 1982.

———. Introduction to *The Collected Poems,* by Sylvia Plath, edited by Ted Hughes, 13–17. London: Faber and Faber, 1981.

———. "Notes on the Chronological Order of Sylvia Plath's Poems." In *The Art of Sylvia Plath,* edited by Charles Newman, 187–95. Bloomington: Indiana University Press, 1970.

——. "The Place Where Sylvia Plath Should Rest in Peace." *The Guardian*, April 20, 1989, 22.

——. "Sylvia Plath and Her Journals." In *Ariel Ascending: Writings about Sylvia Plath*, edited by Paul Alexander. New York: Harper & Row, 1985.

——. "Sylvia Plath: The Facts of Her Life and the Desecration of Her Grave." *The Guardian*, April 22, 1989.

——. "Where Research Becomes Intrusion." *The Observer*, October 29, 1989, 47.

——. *Winter Pollen: Occasional Prose*. Edited by William Scammell. New York: St. Martin's, 1995.

Humez, Jean M. "Reading the Narrative of Sojourner Truth as Collaborative Text." *Frontiers: A Journal of Women's Studies* 16 (1996): 29–52.

Hutcheon, Linda. "Creative Collaboration: Introduction." Presidential Forum. "Creative Collaboration: Alternatives to the Adversarial Academy." *Profession 2001* (2001): 4–6.

Hutcheon, Linda, and Michael Hutcheon. "A Convenience of Marriage: Collaboration and Interdisciplinarity." *PMLA* 116 (2001): 1364–76.

——. "'All Concord's Born of Contraries': Marital Methodologies." "Forum on Collaborations: Part II." *Tulsa Studies in Women's Literature* 14 (spring 1995): 59–64.

Hyde, H. Montgomery. *Oscar Wilde: A Biography*. London: Methuen, 1982.

——. *The Love That Dared Not Speak Its Name*. Boston: Little, Brown, 1970.

Inge, M. Thomas. "Collaboration and Concepts of Authorship." *PMLA* 116 (2001): 623–30.

Irvine, William, and Park Honan. *The Book, the Ring, and the Poet: A Biography of Robert Browning*. New York: McGraw-Hill, 1974.

Jan Mohamed, Abdul R. "The Economy of Michean Allegory: The Function of Racial Difference in Colonialist Literature." In *"Race," Writing and Difference*, edited by Henry Louis Gates Jr., 78–106. Chicago: University of Chicago Press, 1986.

Jardine, Lisa. *Reading Shakespeare Historically*. London: Routledge, 1996.

Jarrell, Randall. "Graves and the White Goddess," in his *Third Book of Criticism*. New York: Farrar, Straus and Giroux, 1969.

Jaszi, Peter. "On the Author Effect: Contemporary Copyright and Collective Creativity." In *The Construction of Authorship: Textual Appropriation in Law and Literature*, edited by Martha Woodmansee and Peter Jaszi, 29–56. Durham, N.C.: Duke University Press, 1994.

Johnson, Claudia L. *Equivocal Beings: Politics, Gender, and Sentimentality in the 1790s. Wollstonecraft, Radcliffe, Burney, Austen*. Chicago: University of Chicago Press, 1995.

Johnson, Samuel. *Diaries, Prayers, and Annals*. Edited by E. L. McAdam Jr. with Donald and Mary Hyde. New Haven, Conn.: Yale University Press, 1958.

———. *The Idler and the Adventurer*. Edited by W. J. Bate, J. M. Bullitt, and L. F. Powell. Vol. II of the Yale Edition of the Works of Samuel Johnson. New Haven, Conn.: Yale University Press, 1963.

———. *A Journey to the Western Islands of Scotland*. Edited by Mary Lascelles. New Haven, Conn.: Yale University Press, 1971.

———. *The Letters of Samuel Johnson*. 5 vols. Edited by Bruce Redford. Princeton, N.J.: Princeton University Press, 1992–94.

Johnston, Kenneth. *Wordsworth and The Recluse*. New Haven, Conn.: Yale University Press, 1984.

Jump, Harriet Devine. *Mary Wollstonecraft: Writer*. London: Harvester Wheatsheaf, 1994.

Kakutani, Michiko. "A Portrait of Plath in Poetry for Its Own Sake." *New York Times*, February 13, 1998.

Kamani, Ginu. "A Terrible Hurt: The Untold Story Behind the Publishing of Maitreyi Devi." http://www.press.uchicago.edu/misc/Chicago/143651 .html (Jan 15, 1998).

Kaplan, Carey, and Ellen Cronan Rose. "Strange Bedfellows: Feminist Collaboration." *Signs* 18 (1993): 547–61.

Karlin, Daniel. "The Brownings' Marriage: Contemporary Representations." *Studies in Browning and His Circle* 21 (1997): 33–52.

———. The Courtship of Elizabeth Barrett and Robert Browning. Oxford: Oxford University Press, 1985.

Keane, Molly. "Introduction." In *The Real Charlotte*, by Edith Somerville and Martin Ross. 1894. Reprint, London: Hogarth Press, 1988.

Keating, Peter. The Haunted Study: A Social History of the Novel, 1875–1914. London: Fontana, 1991.

Kenner, Hugh. "Sincerity Kills." In *Sylvia Plath: New Views on the Poetry*, edited by Gary Lane, 33–44. Baltimore, Md.: Johns Hopkins University Press, 1979.

Khadar, Jamil. "Postcolonial Nativeness: Nomadism, Cultural Memory, and the Politics of Identity in Louise Erdrich's and Michael Dorris's *The Crown of Columbus*." *Ariel* 28 (1997): 81–101.

King, John N. *Tudor Royal Iconography: Literature and Art in an Age of Religious Crisis*. Princeton, N.J.: Princeton University Press, 1989.

Kinnamon, Noel. "The Sidney Psalms: The Penshurst and Tixall Manuscripts." *English Manuscript Studies* 2 (1990): 139–61.

Knoepfelmacher, U. C. "Projection and the Female Other: Romanticism, Browning and the Victorian Dramatic Monologue." 1984. In *Critical Essays on Robert Browning*, edited by Mary Ellis Gibson, 100–19. Reprint, New York: G. K. Hall, 1992.

Knott, John R. *Discourses of Martyrdom in English Literature, 1563–1694*. Cambridge: Cambridge University Press, 1993.

Koch, Vivienne. *W. B. Yeats—The Tragic Phase: A Study of the Last Poems*. London: Routledge & Kegan Paul, 1969.

Koestenbaum, Wayne. *Double Talk: The Erotics of Male Literary Collaboration.* New York: Routledge, 1989.

Kohlenberger, John R., III, ed. *The NIV Interlinear Hebrew-English Old Testament.* Grand Rapids, Mich.: Zondervan, 1982.

Kroll, Jack. "Answering Ariel." *Newsweek,* February 2, 1998, 58–59.

Laird, Holly. "'A Hand Spills from the Book's Threshold': Coauthorship's Readers." *PMLA* 116 (2001): 344–53.

———. "Contradictory Legacies: Michael Field and Feminist Restoration." *Victorian Poetry* 33 (1995): 111–28.

———. "Preface." "Forum on Collaborations: Part I." *Tulsa Studies in Women's Literature* 13 (1994): 235–40.

———. "Preface." "Forum on Collaborations: Part II." *Tulsa Studies in Women's Writing* 14 (1995): 11–18.

———. *Women Coauthors.* Chicago: University of Illinois Press, 2000.

Lamb, Mary Ellen. "The Countess of Pembroke's Patronage." *ELR* 12 (1982): 162–79.

———. *Gender and Authorship in the Sidney Circle.* Madison: University of Wisconsin Press, 1990.

Lane, Edward W. *An Account of the Manners and Customs of the Modern Egyptians.* 1836. Reprint, London: Dent, 1908.

Langland, Elizabeth. *Nobody's Angels: Middle-Class Women and Domestic Ideology in Victorian Culture.* Ithaca, N.Y.: Cornell University Press, 1995.

Lanham, Richard. *The Old Arcadia.* New Haven, Conn.: Yale University Press, 1965.

Lascelles, Mary. "Johnson and Boswell on Their Travels." In *Facts and Notions: Collected Criticism and Research.* Oxford: Clarendon Press, 1972.

Leonard, James. S., et al., eds. *Author-ity and Textuality: Current Views of Collaborative Writing.* West Cornwall, Conn.: Locust Hill Press, 1994.

Leonard, James S. and Christine E. Wharton. "Breaking the Silence." In *Author-ity and Textuality: Current Views of Collaborative Writing.* West Cornwall, Conn.: Locust Hill Press, 1994.

Leonardi, Susan J., and Rebecca A. Pope. "(Co)Labored Li(v)es; or, Love's Labors Queered." *PMLA* 116 (2001): 631–37.

———. "Screaming Divas: Collaboration as Feminist Practice." "Forum on Collaborations: Part I." *Tulsa Studies in Women's Literature* 13 (1994): 259–70.

Levin, Susan. *Dorothy Wordsworth and Romanticism.* New Brunswick, N.J.: Rutgers University Press, 1987.

Levinson, Marjorie. "Spiritual Economics: A Reading of 'Michael.'" In *Wordsworth's Great Period Poems: Four Essays,* 58–79. Cambridge: Cambridge University Press, 1986.

Lewis, Gifford. *Somerville and Ross: The World of the Irish R.M.* Harmondsworth, Eng.: Viking, 1985.

————, ed. *The Selected Letters of Somerville and Ross*. With a foreword by Molly Keane. London: Faber and Faber, 1989.

Lewis, Reina. *Gendering Orientalism: Race, Femininity and Representation*. London: Routledge, 1996.

Leyland, Winston. Introduction to *Teleny* [attrib. Oscar Wilde], edited by Winston Leyland. San Francisco: Gay Sunshine Press, 1984.

Lloyd Jones, G. *The Discovery of Hebrew in Tudor England: A Third Language*. Manchester, Eng.: Manchester University Press, 1983.

Logan, William. "Soiled Desire." *New Criterion* 16 (June 1998): 61–69.

Lok, Anne. "A Meditation of a Penitent Sinner: Written in Maner of a Paraphrase upon the 51. Psalme of Dauid." In *Sermons of John Calvin, upon the Songe that Ezechias made after he had bene sicke and afflicted by the hand of God*. London: John Day, 1560.

London, Bette. *Writing Double: Women's Literary Partnerships*. Ithaca, N.Y.: Cornell University Press, 1999.

Lovell, Mary S. *The Rage to Live: A Biography of Richard and Isabel Burton*. New York: Norton, 1998.

Lund, Elizabeth. "Breaking the Long Silence: Ted Hughes on Sylvia Plath." *The Christian Science Monitor*, March 11, 1998, 14.

Lyall, Sarah. "A Divided Response to Hughes Poems." *New York Times*, January 27, 1998, 1.

————. "In Poetry, Ted Hughes Breaks His Silence on Sylvia Plath." *New York Times*, January 17, 1998, A1.

Malcolm, Janet. *The Silent Woman: Sylvia Plath and Ted Hughes*. New York: Knopf, 1993.

Mani, Lata. "Contentious Traditions: The Debate on *Sati* in Colonial India." In *Recasting Women: Essays in Indian Colonial History*, edited by Kumkum Sangari and Sudesh Vaid, 88–126. New Brunswick, N.J.: Rutgers University Press, 1990.

Markus, Julia. *Dared and Done: The Marriage of Elizabeth Barrett and Robert Browning*. New York: Knopf, 1995.

Marlatt, Daphne, and Betsy Warland. *Two Women in a Birth: Poems*. Toronto: Guernica, 1994.

Marot, Clément, and Théodore Bèze. *Les Psaumes en vers français avec leurs mélodies. Fac-simile de l'édition genevoise de Michel Blanchier, 1562*. Edited by Pierre Pidoux. Geneva: Droz, 1986.

Masten, Jeffrey. "Beaumont and/or Fletcher: Collaboration and the Interpretation of Renaissance Drama." In *The Construction of Authorship: Textual Appropriation in Law and Literature*, edited by Martha Woodmansee and Peter Jaszi, 361–81 Durham, N.C.: Duke University Press, 1994.

————. *Textual Intercourse: Collaboration, Authorship, and Sexualities in Renaissance Drama*. Cambridge, Mass.: Harvard University Press, 1997.

Matthews, T. S. *Jacks or Better: A Narrative.* New York: Harper & Row, 1977.

Matus, Jill. "The 'Eastern-Woman Question': Martineau and Nightingale Visit the Harem." *Nineteenth-Century Contexts* 21 (1998): 49–66.

Mauss, Marcel. *The Gift: The Form and Reason for Exchange in Archaic Societies,* translated by W. D. Halls. London: Routledge, 1990.

May, Steven W. *The Elizabethan Courtier Poets; The Poems and Their Contexts.* Columbia: University of Missouri Press, 1991.

McCalman, Iain. "Introduction: A Romantic Age *Companion.*" In *An Oxford Companion to the Romantic Age: British Culture, 1776–1832,* edited by Iain McCalman, 1–14. Oxford: Oxford University Press, 1999.

McClatchy, J. D. "Old Myths in New Versions." *Poetry* (June 1998): 154–65.

McClintock, Anne. *Imperial Leather: Race, Gender and Sexuality in the Colonial Context.* New York: Routledge, 1995.

McCormick, Anita Hemphill. "'I shall be beloved—I want no more': Dorothy Wordsworth's Rhetoric and the Appeal to Feeling in *The Grasmere Journals.*" *Philological Quarterly* 69 (1990): 471–93.

McFarlane, Ian D. *Buchanan.* London: Duckworth, 1981.

McGann, Jerome J. *The Romantic Ideology: A Critical Investigation.* Chicago: University of Chicago Press, 1983.

———. *The Textual Condition.* Princeton, N.J.: Princeton University Press, 1991.

McLynn. Frank. *Burton: Snow Upon the Desert.* London: John Murray, 1990.

McNally, James. "Touches of *Aurora Leigh* in *The Ring and The Book.*" *Studies in Browning and His Circle* 14 (1986): 85–90.

Mellor, Anne K., ed. *Romanticism and Feminism.* Bloomington: Indiana University Press, 1987.

———. *Romanticism and Gender.* New York: Routledge, 1993.

Melman, Billie. *Women's Orients: English Women and the Middle East, 1718–1918.* London: Macmillan, 1992.

Mermin, Dorothy. "The Domestic Economy of Art: Elizabeth Barrett and Robert Browning." In *Mothering the Mind: Twelve Studies of Writers and Their Silent Partners,* edited by Ruth Perry and Martine Watson Brownley, 82–101. New York: Holmes & Meier, 1984.

———. *Elizabeth Barrett Browning: The Origins of New Poetry.* Chicago: University of Chicago Press, 1989.

Michelut, Dore, et al. *Linked Alive.* Laval, Can.: Editions Trois, 1990.

Middlebrook, Diane Wood. "Poetic Justice for Sylvia Plath." *New York Times,* January 27, 1998, A19.

Miller, Betty. *Robert Browning: A Portrait.* London: John Murray, 1952.

Miller, D. A. "Secret Subjects, Open Secrets." In *The Novel and the Police.* Berkeley: University of California Press, 1988.

Mills, Sara. *Discourses of Difference: An Analysis of Women's Travel Writing and Colonialism.* London: Routledge, 1991.

Milton, John. *Complete Prose Works*. 8 vols. Edited by Don M. Wolfe. New Haven, Conn.: Yale University Press, 1953–82.

Moers, Ellen. *Literary Women*. New York: Doubleday, 1976.

Moffet, Thomas. *The Silkewormes and their Flies, Liuely described in verse*. 1599. Edited by Victor Houliston. Reprint, Binghamton, N.Y.: Renaissance English Text Society, 1989.

Morrell, Lady Ottoline. *Dear Lady Ginger: An Exchange of Letters Between Lady Ottoline Morrell and D'Arcy Cresswell*. Edited by Helen Shaw. Auckland, N.Z.: Auckland University Press, 1983.

Moseley, Ray. "Sylvia Plath's Former Husband Ends 35 Years of Silence." *Chicago Tribune*, January 28, 1998, A1.

Motion, Andrew. "A Thunderbolt from the Blue." *Times* (London) January 17, 1998, 22.

Mudge, Bradford Keyes. *Sara Coleridge, A Victorian Daughter: Her Life and Essays*. New Haven, Conn.: Yale University Press, 1989.

Munich, Adrienne. "Robert Browning's Poetics of Appropriation," *Browning Institute Studies* 15 (1987): 69–77.

Myers, Mitzi. "Unfinished Business: Wollstonecraft's *Maria*." *Wordsworth Circle* 11 (1980): 107–14.

Namjoshi, Suniti, and Gillian Hanscombe. *Flesh and Paper*. Charlottetown, P.E.I.: Ragweed, 1986.

Nandy, Ashis. *The Intimate Enemy: Loss and Recovery of Self Under Colonialism*. Delhi, India: Oxford University Press, 1983.

Newman, Charles, ed. *The Art of Sylvia Plath*. Bloomington: Indiana University Press, 1970.

Oakley, Ann. *Woman's Work: The Housewife, Past and Present*. New York: Pantheon Books, 1974.

O'Quinn, Daniel. "Trembling: Wollstonecraft, Godwin and the Resistance to Literature." *English Literary History* 64 (1997): 761–88.

Orgel, Stephen. "What Is an Editor?" *Shakespeare Studies* 24 (1996): 23–29.

Partridge, Edward B. "Yeats's 'The Three Bushes'—Genesis and Structure." *Accent* 17 (1957): 67–80.

Pastan, Linda. "Scenes from a Marriage." *Washington Post Book World*, March 8, 1998, 5.

Pearsall, Ronald. *The Worm in the Bud: The World of Victorian Sexuality*. London: Pimlico, 1993.

Pease, Donald. "Author." In *Authorship from Plato to the Postmoderns: A Reader*, edited by Sean Burke. Edinburgh: Edinburgh University Press, 1995.

Peck, Elizabeth G. and Joanna Stephens Mink. *Common Ground: Feminist Collaboration in the Academy*. Albany, N.Y.: State University of New York Press, 1998.

Perloff, Marjorie G. "On the Road to *Ariel:* The 'Transitional' Poetry of Sylvia Plath." *Iowa Review* 4 (1973): 94–110.

———. "The Two Ariels: The (Re)Making of the Sylvia Plath Canon." *American Poetry Review* (November 1984): 10–18.

Perry, Ruth, and Martine Watson Brownley, eds. *Mothering the Mind: Twelve Studies of Writers and Their Silent Partners*. New York: Holmes and Meier, 1984.

Piozzi, Hester Thrale. *Thraliana: The Diary of Mrs. Hester Lynch Thrale (Later Mrs. Piozzi)*. Edited by K. C. Balderston. 2 vols. Oxford: Clarendon Press, 1942.

Plath, Sylvia. *The Collected Poems*. Edited by Ted Hughes. London: Faber and Faber, 1981.

———. *The Journals of Sylvia Plath*. Edited by Ted Hughes and Frances McCullough. New York: Dial, 1982.

———. *Letters Home: Correspondence, 1950–1963*. Edited by Aurelia Schober Plath. New York: Harper & Row, 1975.

———. *The Unabridged Journals of Sylvia Plath*. Edited by Karen V. Kukil. London: Faber and Faber, 2000.

———. *Winter Trees*. Edited by Ted Hughes. London: Faber and Faber, 1975.

Polhemus, Robert. *Erotic Faith: Being in Love from Jane Austen to D. H. Lawrence*. Chicago: University of Chicago Press, 1990.

Pollitt, Katha. "Peering into the Bell Jar." *New York Times Book Review*, March 1, 1998, 7.

Poole, Sophia. *The Englishwoman in Egypt: Letters from Cairo, Written During a Residence there in 1842, 1843, and 1844*. 2 vols. London: Charles Knight, 1844.

Poovey, Mary. *The Proper Lady and the Woman Writer: Ideology as Style in the Works of Mary Wollstonecraft, Mary Shelley, and Jane Austen*. Chicago: University of Chicago Press, 1984.

———. *Uneven Developments: The Ideological Work of Gender in Mid-Victorian England*. Chicago: University of Chicago Press, 1988.

Powell, Violet. *The Irish Cousins: The Books and Background of Somerville and Ross*. London: Heinemann, 1970.

Prescott, Anne Lake. "Evil Tongues at the Court of Saul: The Renaissance David as a Slandered Courtier." *Journal of Medieval and Renaissance Studies* 21 (1991): 163–86.

Prins, Yopie. "A Metaphorical Field: Katherine Bradley and Edith Cooper." *Victorian Poetry* 33 (1995): 129–48.

———. "Elizabeth Barrett, Robert Browning, and the *Différance* of Translation." *Victorian Poetry* 29 (1991): 435–51.

Puttenham, George. *The Arte of English Poesie*. Edited by Gladys Doidge Willcock and Alice Walker. Cambridge: Cambridge University Press, 1936.

Radner, John. "Boswell's and Johnson's Sexual Rivalry." *The Age of Johnson* 5 (1992), 201–46.

———. "From Paralysis to Power: Boswell with Johnson in 1775–1778." In *James Boswell: Psychological Interpretations*, edited by Donald J. Newman, 127–48. New York: St. Martin's, 1995.

———. "Pilgrimage and Autonomy: The Visit to Ashbourne." In *Boswell:*

Citizen of the World, Man of Letters, edited by Irma S. Lustig, 203–27. Lexington: University of Kentucky Press, 1995.

———. "'A Very Exact Picture of His Life': Johnson's Role in Writing the *Life of Johnson.*" *The Age of Johnson* 7 (1996): 299–342.

Rajan, Tilottama. "Framing the Corpus: Godwin's Editing of Wollstonecraft in 1798." *Studies in Romanticism* 39 (2000): 511–31.

———. *The Supplement of Reading: Figures of Understanding in Romantic Theory and Practice.* Ithaca, N.Y.: Cornell University Press, 1990.

Read, Katy. "Interview: Louise Erdrich on Native Grounds." *The Globe and Mail,* April 21, 2001: D3.

Reid, Alastair. "Remembering Robert Graves." *The New Yorker,* September 4, 1995: 70–81.

Reiman, Donald H. "Poetry of Familiarity: Wordsworth, Dorothy, and Mary Hutchinson." In *The Evidence of the Imagination: Studies of Interactions Between Life and Art in English Romantic Literature,* edited by Donald H. Reiman et al., 142–77. New York: New York University Press, 1978.

Review of *Birthday Letters,* by Ted Hughes. *Publishers Weekly,* February 2, 1998, 75.

Reynolds, Margaret, and Barbara Rosenbaum. "'Aeschylus' Soliloquy' by Elizabeth Barrett Browning." *Victorian Poetry* 35 (1997): 329–49.

Rice, Edward. *Captain Sir Richard Francis Burton.* New York: Scribner, 1990.

Richardson, Alan. *Literature, Education and Romanticism.* Cambridge: Cambridge University Press, 1994.

Ridenour, George. "Robert Browning and *Aurora Leigh.*" *Victorian Newsletter* 67 (1985): 26–31.

(Riding) Jackson, Laura. "About the Fugitives and Myself." *Carolina Quarterly* 47 (1995): 73–87.

———. "Engaging in the Impossible." *Sulfur* 10–11 (1984): 4–35.

———. Letter to Jay Ansill, June 29, 1985.

———. Letter to Jay Ansill, December 29, 1985.

———. Letter to the *Times Literary Supplement,* November 19, 1990. Laura (Riding) Jackson Papers, Louis Wilson Round Library, University of North Carolina at Chapel Hill.

———. Letters to William Harmon, May 7, 1984, and April 27, 1985. Laura (Riding) Jackson Papers, Louis Wilson Round Library, University of North Carolina at Chapel Hill.

———. "Robert Graves's *The White Goddess.*" In *The Word "Woman" and Other Related Writings,* by Laura (Riding) Jackson, edited by Elizabeth Friedmann and Alan J. Clark, 205–11. New York: Persea Books, 1993.

———. "Some Autobiographical Corrections of Literary History." *Denver Quarterly* 8 (1974): 1–33.

———. "The Word 'Woman.'" In *The Word "Woman" and Other Related Writings,* edited by Elizabeth Friedmann and Alan J. Clark. New York: Persea Books, 1993.

Rigby, Elizabeth. "Lady Travellers." *Quarterly Review* (1845): 98–137.

Robinson, Hilary. *Somerville and Ross: A Critical Appreciation.* New York: St. Martin's, 1980.

Robinson, Jane. *Wayward Women: A Guide to Women Travellers.* New York: Oxford University Press, 1991.

Robson, John M. *The Improvement of Mankind: The Social and Political Thought of John Stuart Mill.* Toronto/London: University of Toronto Press/Routledge & Kegan Paul, 1968.

Rose, Jacqueline. *The Haunting of Sylvia Plath.* Cambridge, Mass.: Harvard University Press, 1991.

Rose, Mark. *Authors and Owners: The Invention of Copyright.* Cambridge, Mass.: Harvard University Press, 1993.

Rose, Phyllis. *Parallel Lives: Five Victorian Marriages.* New York: Vintage Books, 1984.

Rossi, Alice S., ed. *John Stuart Mill and Harriet Taylor Mill: Essays on Sex Equality.* Chicago: University of Chicago Press, 1970.

Rousseau, Jean-Jacques. *Émile.* 1762. Translated by Barbara Foxley. Everyman Series. Toronto: Dent, 1974.

Sabean, David. "Aspects of Kinship Behaviour and Property in Rural Western Europe Before 1800." In *Family and Inheritance: Rural Society in Western Europe, 1200–1800,* edited by Jack Goody et al., 96–111. Cambridge: Cambridge University Press, 1976.

Sackville-West, Vita. *The Letters of Vita Sackville West to Virginia Woolf.* Edited by Louise DeSalvo and Mitchell A. Leaska. New York: William Morrow, 1985.

Said, Edward W. *Orientalism.* New York: Random House, 1979.

St. Clair, William. *The Godwins and the Shelleys: The Biography of a Family.* London: Faber and Faber, 1989.

St. John, J. A. *Egypt and Nubia, Their Scenery and Their People: Being Incidents of History and Travel, From the Best and most Recent Authorities.* London: Chapman, 1845.

Sandstrom, Glen. "'James Lee's Wife'—and Browning's." *Victorian Poetry* 4 (1966): 259–34.

Schelling, Felix E. "'Sidney's Sister, Pembroke's Mother.'" In *Shakespeare and "Demi-Science": Papers on Elizabethan Topics,* 100–25. Philadelphia: University of Pennsylvania Press, 1927.

Schlau, Stacey, and Electa Arenal. "Escribiendo yo, escribiendo ella, escribiendo nosotras: On Co-Laboring." *Tulsa Studies in Women's Literature* 14 (1995): 39–49.

Schleiner, Louise. *Tudor and Stuart Women Writers.* Bloomington: Indiana University Press, 1994.

Scott, Joan W., and Louise A. Tilly. "Women's Work and the Family in Nineteenth-Century Europe." *Comparative Studies in Society and History* 17 (1975): 36–64.

Setz, Wolfram. "Zur Textgestalt des *Teleny.*" *Forum Homosexualität und Literatur* 5 (1988): 69–76.

Seymour-Smith, Martin. *Robert Graves: His Life and Work.* London: Hutchinson, 1982.

Shakespeare, William. *The Tempest.* The Riverside Shakespeare. Edited by G. Blakemore Evans et al. Boston: Houghton Mifflin, 1974.

Sharpe, Jenny. *Allegories of Empire: The Figure of Woman in the Colonial Text.* Minneapolis: University of Minnesota Press, 1993.

Sherman, Stuart. *Telling Time: Clocks, Diaries, and English Diurnal Form, 1660–1785.* Chicago: University of Chicago Press, 1996.

Showalter, Elaine. *A Literature of Their Own: British Women Novelists from Brontë to Lessing.* Princeton, N.J.: Princeton University Press, 1977.

———. *Sexual Anarchy: Gender and Culture at the Fin de Siècle.* London: Penguin, 1990.

Sidney, Philip. *The Poems of Sir Philip Sidney.* Edited by William Ringler Jr. Oxford: Clarendon Press, 1962.

Sidney, Philip. *A Defence of Poetry.* Edited by Jan A. Van Dorsten. London: Oxford University Press, 1966.

———. *The Countess of Pembroke's Arcadia (The Old Arcadia).* Edited by Jean Robertson. Oxford: Clarendon Press, 1973.

———. *The Countess of Pembroke's Arcadia (The New Arcadia).* Edited by Victor Skretkowicz. Oxford: Clarendon Press, 1987.

Silverman, Kaja. *Male Subjectivity at the Margins.* London: Routledge, 1992.

Simmons, Thomas. *Erotic Reckonings: Mastery and Apprenticeship in the Works of Poets and Lovers.* Chicago: University of Illinois Press, 1994.

Smith, Hallett. "English Metrical Psalms in the Sixteenth Century and Their Literary Significance." *Huntington Library Quarterly* 9 (1946): 249–71.

Smith, Iris. "Authors in America: Tony Kushner, Arthur Miller, and Anna Deavere Smith." *Centennial Review* 40 (1996): 125–42.

Somerville, Edith, and Martin Ross. *The Real Charlotte.* 1894. With an introduction by Molly Keane. Reprint, London: Hogarth Press, 1988.

———. *"Some Experiences of an Irish R.M." and "Further Experiences of an Irish R.M."* 1944. With an introduction by Edith Somerville. Reprint, London: Dent, 1982.

Spacks, Patricia Meyer. *Gossip.* Chicago: University of Chicago Press, 1985.

Spender, Stephen. "Warnings from the Grave." In *Sylvia Plath: A Symposium,* edited by Charles Newman, 199–203. London: Faber and Faber, 1970.

Spenser, Edmund. *The Complete Poetical Works of Spenser.* Edited by. R. E. Neil Dodge. Cambridge, Mass.: Riverside, 1908.

Stallworthy, Jon. *Vision and Revision in Yeats's Last Poems.* Oxford: Clarendon Press, 1969.

Steinberg, Theodore L. "The Sidneys and the Psalms." *Studies in Philology* 92 (1995): 1–17.

Steiner, George. "Dying Is an Art." In *Sylvia Plath: A Symposium,* edited by Charles Newman, 211–18. London: Faber and Faber, 1970.

Sternhold, Thomas, et al. *The Whole Booke of Psalmes. Collected into English Meeter.* London: Company of Stationers, 1633.

Stevens, Anthony. *On Jung.* Harmondsworth, Eng.: Penguin, 1991.

Stillinger, Jack. *Multiple Authorship and the Myth of Solitary Genius.* New York: Oxford University Press, 1991.

Stone, Albert E. *Autobiographical Occasions and Original Acts: Versions of American Identity from Henry Adams to Nate Shaw.* Philadelphia: University of Pennsylvania Press, 1982.

Stone, Marjorie. "Bile and the Brownings: A New Poem by RB, EBB's "My Heart and I," and New Questions About the Brownings' Marriage." In *Robert Browning in Context,* edited by John Woolford, 213–32. Winfield, Kan.: Wedgestone Press, 1998.

Stothard, Peter. "Revealed: The Most Tragic Literary Love Story of Our Time." *Times* (London) January 17, 1998, A1.

Sturge Moore, T., and D. C. Sturge Moore, eds. *Works and Days: From the Journal of Michael Field.* London: John Murray, 1933.

Sullivan, Mary Rose, "Elizabeth Barrett Browning and the Art of Collaboration." *Studies in Browning and His Circle* 19 (1991): 47–55.

———. "'Some Interchange of Grace': 'Saul' and *Sonnets from the Portuguese.*" *Browning Institute Studies* 15 (1987): 55–69.

Sunstein, Emily W. *A Different Face: The Life of Mary Wollstonecraft.* New York: Harper & Row, 1975.

Taplin, Gardner B. *The Life of Elizabeth Barrett Browning.* New Haven, Conn.: Yale University Press, 1957.

Taylor, Anya. "'A Father's Tale': Coleridge Foretells the Life of Hartley." *Studies in Romanticism* 30 (1991): 37–56.

Taylor, John. *The Needles Excellency: A New Booke wherin are diuers Admirable Workes wrought with the Needle.* London: James Baler, 1631.

Thomas, Joan. "Searching for Mr. Sugar Daddy." *The Globe and Mail,* March 20, 1999, D15.

Thomas, Max W. "Reading and Writing the Renaissance Commonplace Book: A Question of Authorship?" In *The Construction of Authorship: Textual Appropriation in Law and Literature,* edited by Martha Woodmansee and Peter Jaszi, 401–15. Durham, N.C.: Duke University Press, 1994.

Thompson, Ann, and Sasha Roberts. "Marriage, Gender and the Victorian Woman Critic of Shakespeare: The Work of Charles and Mary Cowden Clarke." In *Victorian Shakespeare: Literature and Culture,* edited by Adrian Poole and Gail Marshall. Houndmills: Palgrave MacMillan, 2003.

Thompson, F. M. L. *The Rise of Respectable Society: A Social History of Victorian Britain, 1830–1900.* Cambridge, Mass.: Harvard University Press, 1988.

Thomson, Ian. "Under the Bell Jar." *The Independent,* March 12, 1988, 21.

Todd, Janet. *The Sign of Angellica: Women, Writing and Fiction, 1660–1800*. London: Virago, 1989.

Tomalin, Claire. *The Life and Death of Mary Wollstonecraft*. London: Weidenfeld and Nicholson, 1974.

Trumbach, Randolph. *The Rise of the Egalitarian Family: Aristocratic Kinship and Domestic Relations in Eighteenth-Century England*. New York: Academic Press, 1978.

Tytell, John. *Passionate Lives: D. H. Lawrence, F. Scott Fitzgerald, Henry Miller, Dylan Thomas, Sylvia Plath . . . in Love*. New York: St. Martin's, 1995.

Vogel, Amber. "Authorized Undertaking: Commentary on Graves and Frost in the Unpublished Correspondence of Laura (Riding) Jackson." *Carolina Quarterly* 49, no. 2 (1997): 27–39.

Vasconcelas, Erika de. "Joined at the Nib." *Globe and Mail*, April 28, 2001, D 20–21.

Vorlicky, Robert, and Susan Jonas, eds. *Tony Kushner in Conversation*. Ann Arbor: University of Michigan Press, 1998.

Wagner, Erica. "Poet Laureate Breaks Decades of Silence." *Times* (London), January 17, 1998, 18.

Walker, Eric C. "Dorothy Wordsworth, William Wordsworth, and the Kirkstone Pass." *Wordsworth Circle* 19 (1988): 116–21.

Wallace, Anne D. "'Inhabited Solitudes': Dorothy Wordsworth's Domesticating Walkers." Proceedings of the "Writing and a Sense of Place" Symposium, *Nordlit* 1 (1997): 99–126.

———. "'Nor in Fading Silks Compose': Sewing, Walking, and Poetic Labor in *Aurora Leigh*." *ELH* 64 (1997): 228–33.

———. *Walking, Literature, and English Culture: The Origins and Uses of Peripatetic in the Nineteenth Century*. Oxford: Clarendon Press, 1993.

Waller, Gary. "'This Matching of Contraries:' The Influence of Calvin and Bruno on the Sidney Circle." *Neophilologus* 56 (1972): 331–43.

———. "'This Matching of Contraries': Calvinism and Courtly Philosophy in the Sidney Psalms." *English Studies* 55 (1974): 22–31.

———. "The Text and Manuscript Variants of the Countess of Pembroke's Psalms." *RES* 26 (1975): 1–18.

———. *Mary Sidney, Countess of Pembroke: A Critical Study of Her Writings and Literary Milieu*. Salzburg: Institut für Anglistik und Amerikanistik, 1979.

———. *The Sidney Family Romance: Mary Wroth, William Herbert, and the Early Modern Construction of Gender*. Detroit, Mich.: Wayne State University Press, 1993.

———. ed. *The Triumph of Death and Other Unpublished and Uncollected Poems by Mary Sidney, Countess of Pembroke (1561–1621)*. Salzburg: Universität Salzburg, Institut für Englische Sprache und Literatur, 1977.

Weeks, Jeffrey. *Coming Out: Homosexual Politics in Britain, from the Nineteenth Century to the Present*. London: Quartet, 1977.

Wellesley, Dorothy. *Selections from the Poems of Dorothy Wellesley.* Edited by W. B. Yeats. London: MacMillan, 1936.

Werstine, Paul. "Post-Theory Problems in Shakespeare Editing." *Yearbook of English Studies* 29 (1999): 103–17.

West, Paul. "Crossing the Water." In *Sylvia Plath: The Critical Heritage,* edited by Linda Wagner, 157–61. London: Routledge, 1988.

[Wilde, Oscar?]. *Teleny.* Edited by Winston Leyland. San Francisco: Gay Sunshine Press, 1984.

Wilkins, W. H. *The Romance of Isabel Lady Burton: The Story of Her Life.* New York: Dodd, Mead, 1897.

Williams, Raymond. *Keywords.* New York: Oxford University Press, 1976.

———. *Problems in Materialism and Culture.* London: Verso, 1980.

Wolfson, Susan J. " 'Domestic Affections': and 'The Spear of Minerva': Felicia Hemans and the Dilemma of Gender." In *Re-Visioning Romanticism: British Women Writers, 1776–1837,* edited by Carol Shiner Wilson and Joel Haefner, 128–66. Philadelphia: University of Pennsylvania Press, 1994.

Wollstonecraft, Mary. *Collected Letters.* Edited by Ralph Wardle. Ithaca, N.Y.: Cornell University Press, 1979.

———. *A Vindication of the Rights of Woman.* Vol 5 of *The Works of Mary Wollstonecraft.* Edited by Janet Todd and Marilyn Butler. London: William Pickering, 1989.

———. *The Wrongs of Woman: or, Maria.* Vol. 1 of *The Works of Mary Wollstonecraft.* Edited by Janet Todd and Marilyn Butler. London William Pickering, 1989.

Woodmansee, Martha. "On the Author Effect: Recovering Collectivity." In *The Construction of Authorship: Textual Appropriation in Law and Literature,* edited by Martha Woodmansee and Peter Jaszi, 15–28. Durham, N.C.: Duke University Press, 1994.

Woodmansee, Martha, and Peter Jaszi, eds. *The Construction of Authorship: Textual Appropriation in Law and Literature.* Durham, N.C.: Duke University Press, 1994.

Woodring, Carl. "Sara fille: Fairy Child." In *Reading Coleridge: Approaches and Applications,* edited by Walter B. Crawford. Ithaca: Cornell University Press, 1979.

Woods, Susanne. "The Body Penitent: A 1560 Calvinist Sonnet Sequence." *ANQ: A Quarterly Journal* 5 (1992): 137–40.

Woof, Pamela. Introduction to *The Grasmere Journals,* by Dorothy Wordsworth. Edited by Pamela Woof. Oxford: Oxford University Press, 1993.

Woolf, Virginia. *Letters of Virginia Woolf.* Edited by Nigel Nicolson and Joanne Trautmann. Vol. 6. New York: Harcourt Brace Jovanovich, 1980.

Wordsworth, Dorothy. *The Journals of Dorothy Wordsworth.* Edited by Mary Moorman. Oxford: Oxford University Press, 1971.

————. *The Grasmere Journals*. Edited by Pamela Woof. Oxford: Oxford University Press, 1993.

Wordsworth, William. *Home at Grasmere: Part First, Book First of The Recluse.* Edited by Beth Darlington. Ithaca, N.Y.: Cornell University Press, 1977.

————. *Lyrical Ballads and Other Poems, 1797–1800.* Edited by James Butler and Karen Green. Ithaca, N.Y.: Cornell University Press, 1992.

————. *The Poetical Works of William Wordsworth.* 2nd ed. Edited by Ernest de Selincourt. Vol. 2. Oxford: Clarendon Press, 1952.

————. "Preface." *Lyrical Ballads,* by William Wordsworth and Samuel Taylor Coleridge. Edited by R. L. Brett and A. R. Jones. Rev. ed. London: Methuen, 1965.

————. *The Prelude, 1799, 1805, 1850.* Edited by Jonathan Wordsworth et al. New York: Norton, 1979.

Wordsworth, William, and Dorothy Wordsworth. *The Letters of William and Dorothy Wordsworth.* Edited by Alan Hill. Vol. 7. Oxford: Clarendon Press, 1988.

Woudhuysen, H. R. *Sir Philip Sidney and the Circulation of Manuscripts, 1558–1640.* Oxford: Clarendon Press, 1996.

Wright, William Aldis, ed. *The Hexaplar Psalter Being the Book of Psalms in Six English Versions.* Cambridge: Cambridge University Press, 1911.

Wroth, Mary. *The Countesse of Mountgomeries URANIA.* London: John Marriott and John Grismand, 1621.

Yaeger, Patricia. *Honey-Mad Women: Emancipatory Strategies in Women's Writing.* New York: Columbia University Press, 1988.

Yeats, William Butler. *The Poems.* Vol. 1 of *The Collected Works of W. B. Yeats.* Edited by Richard Finneran and George Mills Harper. New York: MacMillan, 1989.

————. *The Plays.* Vol. 2 of *The Collected Works of W. B. Yeats.* Edited by Richard Finneran and George Mills Harper. New York: Scribner, 2001.

————. *Later Essays.* Vol. 5 of *The Collected Works of W. B. Yeats.* Edited by Richard Finneran and George Mills Harper. New York: Scribner, 1994.

————. *Letters on Poetry from W. B. Yeats to Dorothy Wellesley.* London: Oxford University Press, 1964.

————, ed. *The Oxford Book of Modern Verse, 1892–1935.* Oxford: Clarendon Press, 1936.

Yeats, William Butler, and Dorothy Wellesley, eds. *Broadsides: A Collection of New Irish and English Songs.* Dublin: Cuala, 1937.

York, Lorraine. *Rethinking Women's Collaborative Writing.* Toronto: University of Toronto Press, 2002.

Young, Frances Berkeley. *Mary Sidney, Countess of Pembroke.* London: David Nutt, 1912.

Zim, Rivkah. *English Metrical Psalms: Poetry as Praise and Prayer, 1535–1601.* Cambridge: Cambridge University Press, 1987.

Contributors

Co-Editors

MARJORIE STONE is professor of English and women's studies at Dalhousie University, Halifax, Canada. She is the author of *Elizabeth Barrett Browning* (1995). She has contributed essays to *Jeremy Bentham: Critical Assessments* (1995); *Robert Browning in Contexts* (1998); *The Culture of Christina Rossetti* (1999); *Critical Essays on Elizabeth Barrett Browning* (2000); *Between Ethics and Aesthetics: Crossing the Boundaries* (2001); and *Feminist Literary History Re(Dis)Covered* (2003). She has also published articles in various journals on the Brownings, Tennyson, Christina Rossetti, Gaskell, Dickens, the body, and feminist theory. She served as 1996–98 president of the Association of Canadian College and University Teachers of English and is currently working on a project tentatively titled "The Black Dove's Mark: Nineteenth-Century Literary History and the Elizabeth Barrett Browning Archives."

JUDITH THOMPSON is associate professor of English at Dalhousie University. She has edited John Thelwall's *The Peripatetic* (2000) and published articles on John Thelwall and Romantic radical culture in *Studies in Romanticism* and in the collection *Romanticism, History and the Possibilities of Genre* (1998). She is currently at work on a full-length study on the poetics of speech and politics of literary relationship in the Romantic period tentatively titled "The Silenced Partner: John Thelwall in the Wordsworth Circle." She acted as coordinator and program chair of the 1999 North American Society for the Study of Romanticism Conference.

Authors

REBECCA CARPENTER is assistant professor of English at Western Maryland College. She has published articles in *Conradia*, *The D. H. Lawrence Review*, and *Etudes lawrenciennes*. She is also a contributor to the MLA volume *Approaches to Teaching D. H. Lawrence* (2001).

SARAH CHURCHWELL received her doctorate from Princeton University and is currently a lecturer in American literature at the University of East Anglia, Norwich, England. She is completing a book-length study tentatively titled *Dead Metaphors: Writing Marilyn Monroe, Janis Joplin, and Sylvia Plath*. In addition to submitting chapters to forthcoming volumes, she has published in *The Antioch Review, Contemporary Literature, Criticism*, and *a/b: Auto/Biography Studies*. She also reviews regularly for the *TLS* and for *The Observer*.

CORINNE BIEMAN DAVIES is associate professor of English at Huron University College, an affiliate of the University of Western Ontario, London, Canada. She has published on the Brownings in *Browning Institute Studies* and *Studies in Browning and His Circle*, as well as on Margaret Atwood and W. D. Valgardson. Her present research on literary collaboration has taken her to India to interview Bhalchandra Nemade and Sudhakar Marathe on their collaborative production of *Cocoon*, an English translation of Nemade's Marathi novel *Kosla*. She is currently working on a book on the Brownings' literary relationship.

PATRICIA DEMERS is professor of English and has served as chair of the English Department at the University of Alberta, and as vice-president of the Social Sciences and Humanities Research Council of Canada. She is the author or editor of eight books on Renaissance literature, children's literature, and women's writing, including *The World of Hannah More* (1996). She has recently published *Women's Writing in English: Early Modern England* (2005) and is preparing a second edition of *From Instruction to Delight: Children's Literature to 1850* (2003).

ROBERT W. GRAY is a doctoral candidate at the University of Alberta. He has published in *Queering Absinthe, Open Letter*, and *ARC*. He served as the editor of *Prairie Fire* magazine's special queer issue "Flaming Prairies," and he and Terry Goldie coedited "Postcolonial and Queer Theory and Praxis," a special issue of *ARIEL*. He is head instructor of Writing for Film & Television at the Vancouver Film School and is the author of the popular Vancouver newspaper series *Tide Pool Sketches*. His other creative work has appeared in journals such as *Dandelion, Event, Other Voices*, and *ARC*.

GERARD GOGGIN is a postdoctoral research fellow at the Centre for Critical and Cultural Studies, University of Queensland, Australia. He holds a doctorate from the University of Sydney, where he wrote a dissertation on masculinity, mentoring, and maternity in the works of Mary Wollstonecraft, William Godwin, and Percy Bysshe Shelley. Gerard is currently writing a cultural history of the Internet and researching new media cultures.

LISA HARPER is a lecturer in the Master of Fine Arts in Writing program at the University of San Francisco. She completed her dissertation in the English Department at the University of California, Davis, where she has specialized in American literature and literature by women. Her dissertation "Embodying Gender: The Politics of Form in American Literature, 1850–1900" examines the relationship between artistic innovation and the representation of gender and sexuality.

ALISON HICKEY is Barbara Morris Caspersen Associate Professor of English at Wellesley College. She is editor of the forthcoming *Modern Library Coleridge*, and she is writing a book tentatively titled "Romantic Collaboration: Coleridge 'and Co.'" Hickey's essays on literary collaboration involving Coleridge and other writers have appeared in *ELH* and *Studies in Romanticism*. She has also published *Impure Conceits: Rhetoric and Ideology in Wordsworth's "Excursion"* (1997).

CHRISTOPHER KEEP is assistant professor of English at the University of Western Ontario. He has published articles in a variety of journals, including *Victorian Studies, Novel,* and *Nineteenth-Century Contexts,* as well as in several collections of essays, including *Blackwell's Companion to the Victorian Novel.* He is currently working on a book-length study of literature and the emergent information economy of the nineteenth century.

JILL MATUS is associate professor of English at the University of Toronto. She is the author of *Unstable Bodies: Victorian Representations of Sexuality and Maternity* (1995) and *Toni Morrison* (1998). She has also published articles on George Eliot, Charlotte Brontë, Mary Elizabeth Braddon, Florence Nightingale, Harriet Martineau, Angela Carter, and Gloria Naylor in *Nineteenth-Century Contexts, English Studies in Canada, Victorian Literature and Culture, University of Toronto Quarterly, Journal of the History of Sexuality,* as well as other journals.

JOHN B. RADNER is associate professor of English at George Mason University, Virginia. He has published articles on Johnson, Boswell, and Swift in *Eighteenth-Century Life, Studies in Eighteenth-Century Culture, Studies in English Literature, The Unknown Samuel Johnson, Utopian Studies,* and *Age of Johnson.* He has contributed essays to *Boswell: Citizen of the World* (1995) and *Boswell: Psychological Interpretations* (1995), and is currently working on a book-length study of the Johnson-Boswell relationship.

AMBER VOGEL has a doctorate in English literature from the University of North Carolina at Chapel Hill, where she now coordinates an interdisciplinary-education initiative. She is currently editing *Getting Across the Intervening Space: Selected Letters of Laura (Riding) Jackson,* and is coediting the second edition of *Southern Writers: A Biographical Dictionary.*

ANNE D. WALLACE is professor of English at the University of Southern Mississippi. Her publications in nineteenth-century British literature and culture include articles on George Eliot, Elizabeth Barrett Browning, William Wordsworth, Dorothy Wordsworth, John Clare, and Charlotte Smith. She has also contributed to the 1993 Oxford book *Walking, Literature, and English Culture*. She is currently completing a book-length study tentatively titled "Sibling Anxieties: Family and Literary Authority in Nineteenth-Century England."

LORRAINE YORK is professor of English at McMaster University, Hamilton, Canada. She is the author of *The Other Side of Dailiness* (1988), a book on photography and contemporary Canadian fiction, and *Front Lines: The Fiction of Timothy Findley* (1990). She has edited *Various Atwoods: Essays on the Later Poems, Short Fiction and Novels* (1995), and is the managing editor of *Essays in Canadian Writing*. In 2002 she published *Rethinking Women's Collaborative Writing: Power, Difference, Property* and is currently writing a book on Canadian literary celebrity.

Index